ALASKA
BEST PLACES®

ALASKA
BEST PLACES®

Restaurants, Lodgings, and Adventure

Edited by Nan Elliot

SASQUATCH BOOKS
SEATTLE

To all those who love the wilderness.
May we all have the courage to protect it.

Copyright © 1997 Sasquatch Books
All rights reserved. No portion of this book may be reproduced or utilized in any form, or by any electronic, mechanical, or other means, without the prior written permission of the publisher.

Printed in the United States of America.
Distributed in Canada by Raincoast Books Ltd.

First Edition

Library of Congress Cataloging in Publication Data
Alaska best places: restaurants, lodgings, and adventure/edited by Nan Elliot.—1st ed.
          p. cm—(Best places destination guides)
             Includes index.
             ISBN 1-57061-057-6
             1. Alaska—Guidebooks. I. Elliot, Nan. II. Series.
          F902.3.A598 1997
          917.9804'51—dc21   96-38109

Cover Design: Karen Schober
Interior Design: Lynne Faulk
Maps: Michael Rohani
Copy editor: Nicky Leach
Composition: Kate Basart
Factchecker: Crystal McSwain

The *Best Places* guidebooks have been published continuously since 1975. The reviews in this edition are based on information available at press time and are subject to change. The editor welcomes information conveyed by users of this book, as long as they have no financial connection with the establishment concerned. A report form is provided at the end of the book.

All *Best Places* guides are available at bulk discounts for corporate gifts, conventions, and fund-raising sales for clubs and organizations.

Sasquatch Books
615 Second Avenue
Seattle, Washington 98104
(206)467-4300
http://www.sasquatchbooks.com

CONTENTS

Introduction

Alaska. The word alone is magic.

One of my many jobs (Alaskans tend to wear lots of different hats) is working as a naturalist on cruise ships sailing the Inside Passage in the summer. As such, I have had the good fortune to watch others first glimpse a little of the magic of this extraordinary land and its unusual people.

One night on board ship, I met a Catholic priest. Harking from somewhere in the Midwest, this fellow was one of the most enthusiastic travelers I'd ever met. He had never been to Alaska, although he had always wanted to come. He was full of questions.

The next day, I found him in the lounge, nose to windowpane, watching the fjords and fishing boats of British Columbia pass by. (For those who are slim on their geography, it takes about a day and a half of sailing north from Vancouver through British Columbia before a ship crosses international boundary waters into Alaska.)

"Father, how do you like the trip so far?" I asked.

"Nan, it's . . . it's overwhelming. Look! There's nothing out there," he said breathlessly as he swept his arm over the panorama of forests and mountains and ocean.

"I know, isn't it grand?" I responded.

"No . . . no . . . " He spoke slowly and shook his head, obviously troubled. "It's too overwhelming for me. If I could go back home today, I would."

I was stunned. "But Father, we haven't even gotten to Alaska yet."

"Yes, I know that, Nan," he said reluctantly.

I couldn't resist. "Father," I said solemnly, "Alaska is God's country."

He looked at me very seriously and with some emotion. Then, slowly, he nodded. "That's what I'm afraid of, Nan. That's what I'm afraid of."

It is said that Alaska is for the young and hearty. But there are others who eloquently disagree. As one old-timer advises, and there is much truth in what he says, "You should go to Alaska when you are very old and you have seen every other beautiful place in the world, because you will never see a place more beautiful in all your life. Wherever you go, nothing in the rest of the world will ever compare again."

There are three reasons why you should come to Alaska at any age: the country—this grand, magnificent, stunning land filled with wonderful wild creatures; the people—there are more characters per square mile in Alaska than anywhere else in the world, I'd wager, and a friendlier bunch of folks you'd be hard-pressed to find; and, finally, adventure, the stuff that can get your blood racing at any age. Up here, you are never too old, if the body is a little willing and the spirit is young.

We are often asked by friends from Outside where they should go and what they should do in Alaska. One dear friend of mine came from New York City and she wanted "to see *everything*." In four days!

If you try to do and see everything, you will find that Alaska is big, really big. The state has 365 million acres. As the former director of Alaska State Parks, Chip Dennerlein, says, "People have a hard time comprehending a million acres. So, try 1,000 acres. If you came to see Alaska and you explored 1,000 acres every day, 365 days of the year, it would take you 1,000 years to cover all of Alaska. That's what 365 million acres means."

Of course, that's what keeps most of us here. In 20 years, with unbelievable opportunities for travel, I've still yet to explore it all. Most Alaskans don't leave home in the summer. Many wait all winter, which is long, to enjoy the summer here, which is short. Alaskans are fierce about their love for this place. If you stay long enough, you, too, will fall in love.

We have written this book for the adventurous, for those who have a little money or a lot of time. Our best advice is this: Pick one place in Alaska and explore it in depth. Kayak for three weeks on Glacier Bay. Ride the ferries through Southeast. Hike for a month in the Wrangells. Float a river in the Arctic. In these experiences, you will find a microcosm of Alaska. Whether you are 30 years old or 80 plus, pack with you a plucky spirit, flexibility (the weather will dictate your every move up here), and a wee bit of appreciation for the absurd. And you will have a marvelous time.

For those of you who really only have a week to see "everything," this book is your road map. It is tailored for the independent traveler—to give you special highlights, take you off the beaten path, and give you the best of local color and the inside scoop. In Alaska, the distances are huge and the experiences unlimited. Thus, it is our hope in these pages to give you better access to quality experiences—experiences that long after you have returned home will shine like a jewel in your memory.

—Nan Elliot
Editor
Anchorage, 1997

Contributors and Acknowledgments

Twenty of Alaska's best writers (including chefs, guides, and wilderness adventurers), plus one Scotsman, have joined forces to bring you the land they love. It is a wild and wonderful team. Some are sober-minded, philosophical, and poetic. Others are hilarious, outrageous, and high-spirited. All have a great zest for life and together have won dozens of awards for their work. They have paddled, filmed, climbed, mushed, fished, and swilled their way across and over Alaska. Two have stood on the summit of the highest mountain in North America, Mount McKinley (also known as Denali). One has rowed nearly the entire coastline of Alaska. The youngest is 25; the oldest is 80.

Southeast Alaska: Marilee Enge, a member of one of the oldest Norwegian immigrant families in Petersburg, wrote about her hometown. A professional journalist, she was part of the *Anchorage Daily News* Pulitzer Prize-winning team who wrote the series "People in Peril." In 1996, she was honored with a journalism fellowship at the University of Michigan. **Susan "Meadow" Brook**, co-author of *The Fiddlehead Cookbook*, illuminates Gustavus, her adopted home for the last 17 years. She moved there, as she says, "in the old days before telephones, television, and tourists." Like most Alaskans, she is inimitably resourceful. She's worked as a forester, agronomist, fish cutter, homesteader, cook, and has owned her own business marketing wild berry preserves.

The Roads North: John Kooistra is no stranger to life on the move. He first hitchhiked to Alaska in 1965 with two fishing rods—and got hooked on the place. A commercial fisherman for 25 years and currently a professor of philosophy at the University of Alaska Fairbanks, John is also a connoisseur of fine wines and a charming essayist. Our bold Scotsman, **David Elliot**, one of the last living members of the old British Raj in India, wrote about the "circular route" and Kennicott-McCarthy. After meting out justice under the banyan tree, he came to California as a professor of history at Caltech. Now emeritus, he got hoodwinked into yet another Alaska project by his ever-loving daughter.

Anchorage: Kim Severson, the lively editor of *8*, a weekly entertainment magazine for the *Anchorage Daily News*, wrote about the town she has sampled so well from taco wagons to the top of skyscrapers. She is funny and quick and probably our team's most devoted urbanite. **Peter Porco**, copy editor and writer at the *Anchorage Daily News*, was the perfect person to write about the city's spectacular backyard, Chugach State Park. Peter has traipsed all over the Chugach Mountains and has served as base camp manager on Mount McKinley (and even climbed to its summit).

Prince William Sound: Natalie Phillips is one of our "fast women," a formidable backcountry racer and marathoner. She's also a feature reporter for the *Anchorage Daily News* and has spent considerable time in the Sound, covering the 1989 *Exxon Valdez* oil spill, paddling a kayak, and fishing out of Cordova. Writing on kayaking, **Jill Fredston** is actually an ocean-going rower who disappears every summer on three- to five-month trips. For a "not-so-old salt," she has rowed about 17,000 miles of wild seas, including much of the coast of Alaska. In winter she works as an avalanche expert.

The Kenai Peninsula: Liz Ruskin, with her crisp, upbeat style, covered Homer and Kachemak Bay for the Kenai Peninsula chapter. On most other days she covers the often wild scene at the Alaska state courts for the *Anchorage Daily News* and formerly wrote for the *Homer News*. Born in Alaska, she is, like Natalie, one of our fast women in running shoes. **Joan Daniels** is a saucy wit and a wilderness woman. She's equally adept at shooting a grizzly as serving him up for tasty hors d'oeuvres. She's cooked and catered everywhere in Alaska, from ski training camps high up on glaciers to dog mushing expeditions along the Iditarod Trail. Who else could serve Oysters Rockefeller and German honey cakes outdoors with panache on the banks of the frozen Yukon River at thirty below zero, and still keep everyone laughing? "Well, you can't just go crashing through life eating sardines out of a can!" she'd say.

Kodiak: One of our most entertaining young writers, **Mark Gillespie**, was born in the Blue Ridge Mountains of Virginia, but moved to Alaska because, as he says, "the mountains are bigger, the outhouses are nicer, and sled dogs are smarter than hound dogs." He's first of all a radio man—a former director of public radio on Kodiak who then founded Alaska Fish Radio, which is heard all over the state. He wrote about the island for us shortly before he left life on "The Rock" to test out life in the wilds of the Interior.

Denali and The Parks Highway: Kris Capps, now a freelance journalist, lives in a little cabin near Denali National Park. She came to Alaska 16 years ago, worked as editor of the *Kodiak Daily Mirror* and the *Valdez Vanguard*, and was a reporter for nearly ten years at the *Fairbanks Daily News-Miner*. In her "other life" she's a wilderness river guide in the Brooks Range, teaches whitewater kayaking, and is the founder of several whitewater races. She was the perfect choice to write about her home, the most popular national park in Alaska.

Fairbanks and the Interior and Nome: Debra McKinney just recently retired after ten years as one of the star reporters for the *Anchorage Daily News* to live in her dream cabin in the hills west of Fairbanks. The Interior is full of characters and that's just what gets McKinney's creative juices flowing; she wrote a wonderfully funny piece (powering her computer off solar batteries). In the winter she lives in Teller on the Bering Sea where her husband teaches school, so she also wrote on the infamous gold-rush town of Nome, and threw in fun information about Prince William Sound.

The Arctic: Photographer **Tom Walker** has spent 30 years in Alaska, and his photographs of this country are stunning. He is the author/photographer of 10 books. He lives in a beautiful log cabin he built himself near Denali National Park. Only recently did he hook into commercial electricity which he says is a great boon, since in the dark of winter he can now see "which boot goes on which foot." Tom wrote about the Arctic, a land he has photographed, wandered, and loved for many years. **David Harding**, another humorous radio man, wrote about Alaska's most northern town on the edge of the Arctic Ocean, Barrow. For 20 years, David has bounced around the state—from Juneau to Bethel to Barrow—working in all forms of media. He is a delightful, knowledgeable character who is proud to say that, throughout his successful mixed–media career, he has never owned a suit.

Southwest Alaska and the Aleutians: Bill Sherwonit, freelance journalist and author, wrote the main of these two chapters. Bill has spent his career writing about nature and the outdoors, and he teaches wilderness writing at the University of Alaska. He not only wrote a book entitled *To The Top Of Denali: Climbing Adventures on North America's Highest Peak*, he also climbed to the top himself. **Sean Stitham**, an itinerant Bush doctor, wrote about Bethel, where he practiced medicine for many years with the Indian Health Service. He has doctored all over Alaska and the world, from Sri Lanka to Africa. With his Irish heritage, red hair, offbeat sense of humor, and fast repartee, he quickly slips into the heartbeat of any community. Born and raised in Alaska, **Henry "Te" Tiffany** built his first log cabin at the age of 16 and has hunted since he was a little boy. He is the youngest licensed big game guide in the state, currently operating three separate expedition camps. At age 25, he is also the youngest writer in this book, but his piece on bear hunting displays a wisdom beyond his years. He was taught to hunt and to love writing by his grandfather, our senior member in this book, **Edward J. Fortier**, also known as "Fast Eddie," who, as the last living spy from World War II in Alaska, is the perfect image of a sourdough Alaskan. No matter how turbulent life has gotten in his 80 years, he has never lost his sense of humor or his passion for Alaska. A small sign outside his cabin door reads: "Come on in. Everything else has gone wrong." Don't let it fool you—he lives the frontier code. He's the first to give encouragement, lend a hand, and help you out of any jam. A reporter for the *National Observer* and editor of *Alaska Magazine* for many years, Ed revisits his old wartime stomping grounds in the Aleutians with a new take on the future. He's planning a hoopla there to welcome in the second millennium, and he's planning on inviting his favorite movie star Meryl Streep—so pack your bags for one of the last great adventures.

Finally, as editor, I (**Nan Elliot**) couldn't resist writing several sections of the book myself—mainly the chapters on Southeast, the Kenai, parts of Denali, chunks of Southwest, etc. As they say, if no one else on the team avows knowledge, it's *mea culpa*. I've had the good fortune through my work as an author, journalist, filmmaker, radio producer, and educator to travel all over Alaska and the world. I first came to Alaska more than 20 years ago to teach Eskimos how to swim. And I fell in love with this country.

So here is my wish for all of you. No matter how long or short your stay, may it be as magical for you as it has been for all of us.

And a final word of thanks from me to those who gave generously of their time, knowledge, and opinions: Marla Berg, Kevin Cassity, John Connolly, Brian and Sharon Davies, Chip Dennerlein, Doug Fesler, Max Hall, Mary Kemppel, Rick Kool, LuluBelle, Bill Luria, Peter McKay, Barb Maier, Debe Marshall, Kim Metcalfe-Helmar, Marge Mullen, Peggy Mullen, Mary Nault, Sarina Ochoa, Laurie Otto, Mara Parker, Cathy Rasmuson, Graham Sunderland, Harry Turner, and "Dr. Vacation," alias Jim Thompson. Lastly, the warmest of thanks to "me dear faither" who, with his wise and sharp eye, edited our enormous first draft.

—N.E.

About *Best Places* Guidebooks

The *Best Places* series is unique in the sense that the guidebooks are written by and for locals, and are therefore coveted by travelers. *Alaska Best Places* is written for people who live in Alaska and who enjoy exploring its bounty. It's written for those who like out-of-the-way places of high character and individualism—qualities that define this state—and who take the time to seek out such places. Those very characteristics make *Alaska Best Places* ideal for tourists, too. The best places in the region are the ones that denizens favor: independently owned establishments of good value, touched with local history, run by lively individuals, and graced with natural beauty.

The *Best Places* guides are completely independent: no advertisers, no sponsors, no favors. Our reviewers know the territory, work incognito, and seek out the very best that Alaska has to offer. We both re-evaluate old favorites and seek out new discoveries. Because we accept no free meals, accommodations, or other complimentary services, we are free to provide tough, candid reports about places that have rested too long on their laurels and to delight in new places whose efforts have paid off. We describe the true strengths, foibles, and unique characteristics of each establishment listed. With this first edition of *Alaska Best Places*, travelers will find the information they need: where to go and when, what to do, and where to eat and stay. We're so sure you'll be satisfied with our guide, we guarantee it.

How to Use This Book

This book is arranged by regions within Alaska. All evaluations are based on numerous reports from local and traveling inspectors. *Best Places* reporters do not identify themselves when they review an establishment, and they accept no free meals, accommodations, or any other services. Final judgments are made by the editor. Every place featured in this book is recommended.

★ **Stars** Restaurants and hotels are rated on a scale of zero to four stars, based on uniqueness, loyalty of local clientele, performance measured against goals, excellence of cooking, value, and professionalism of service. Reviews are listed alphabetically within each star rating. Please see the box, **Alaska Star Ratings,** for additional information.

★★★★	The very best in the region
★★★	Distinguished, with many outstanding features
★★	Excellent; some wonderful qualities
★	A good place
(no stars)	Worth knowing about, if nearby
(unrated)	New or undergoing major changes

Price Range As with most things in Alaska, prices can be flexible and are subject to change. Whenever possible, reviewers have included accurate dollar amounts or ballpark rates based on the range listed here. But as a general rule, contact the establishment directly.

$$$	Expensive (more than $80 for dinner for two; more than $90 for lodgings for two)
$$	Moderate (between expensive and inexpensive)
$	Inexpensive (less than $30 for dinner for two; less than $60 for lodgings for two)

Checks and Credit Cards Many establishments that accept checks only accept local or Alaska checks. Credit cards are abbreviated in this book as follows: American Express (AE); Diners Club (DC); Discover (DIS); MasterCard (MC); Visa (V). Two more cards which are often used: Enroute (E) and a Japanese credit card (JCB).

Maps and Directions Each section in this book begins with a regional map that shows towns and major landmarks being covered. Basic directions are provided with each entry. Whenever possible, contact each business to confirm hours and location.

Minimum Stays Many B&Bs and Wilderness Lodges have a minimum-stay requirement during the peak season, and several do not welcome children. Ask about an establishment's policies before you make your reservation.

Pets Assume that no pets are allowed, unless otherwise specified in the review.

Index All restaurants, lodgings, town names, parks and preserves, and major tourist attractions are listed alphabetically at the back of the book.

Reader Reports At the end of the book is a report form. We receive hundreds of reports from readers suggesting new places or agreeing or disagreeing with our assessments. They greatly help in our evaluations. We encourage you to respond.

Money Back Guarantee Please see the back page.

ALASKA STAR RATINGS
(A Disclaimer)

First of all, if you equate four stars to the best that Paris has to offer, be aware that our stars relate to nobody else's stars in the world! Our rating system is strictly "Alaska Bush Style." Character rates highly. In many places in this far northern state, assigning stars is like trying to compare Belgian chocolates and tropical mangos. Sometimes, the best place is the only place—and you're darn happy to be there, particularly if the rain is blowing horizontally in your face or the temperature has dropped to fifty below zero.

While we do have some wonderful places to eat and sleep—places which rival the best in the world—if you are on a serious four-star gastronomic mission and your toes cannot possibly be pampered outside a world-class hotel, we suggest you keep flying north over the pole to Paris. A singular quest for the finest food and lodging should not be the sole reason you come to Alaska.

While in most major cities you could learn a dozen different languages just by studying the menus, in Alaska, outside of a few towns, the only foreign word you'll see on a menu is deluxe—and it usually follows "cheeseburger." Ah, but do not dismay. There are also hundreds of places all over Alaska to eat (and sleep) which are so extraordinary and so outrageously magical that you will remember them all the days of your life. You cannot make a reservation. They have no maitre d' or concierge. They have no walls. As one of our writers so eloquently says, "The most exquisite meal is the country itself."

—The Editor

SOUTHEAST ALASKA

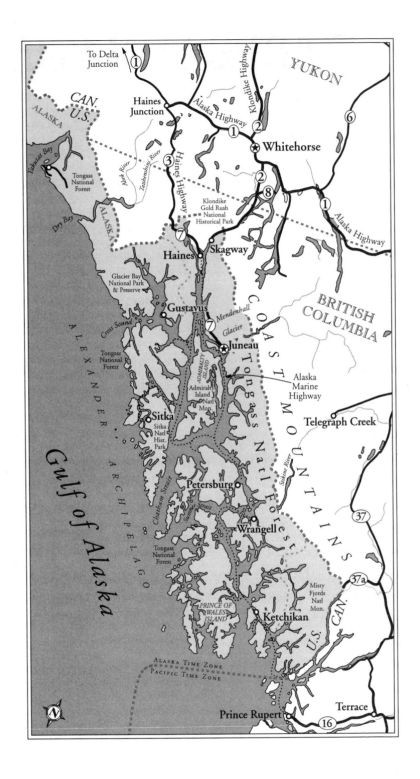

Southeast Alaska

Including Ketchikan, Misty Fjords National
Monument, Sitka, Wrangell, Petersburg, Juneau,
Glacier Bay, Gustavus, Haines, and Skagway

Named in 1867 for Alexander II, czar of Russia, the Alexander Archipelago is a series of islands and waterways that today define Southeast Alaska. Once, it was part of Russian America, when the double-headed eagle flew over this vast northern territory in the New World. For 126 years, Alaska was under the imperial Russian flag until Czar Alexander II sold his far-flung colony to the United States in 1867.

A narrow strip of coastline, bounded on the east by steep, icy mountains and on the west by the North Pacific Ocean, Southeast Alaska more recently was called "The Panhandle." You can see why if you look at a map of the rest of Alaska, which, if we carry the simile forward, looks like the frying pan itself. But that nickname, too, has gone the way of the czars.

Today, the region is spoken of and written about simply as "Southeast." (Note that you spell it with a capital "S.") If you were to fly over it, you would see islands, mountains, fjords, icefields, glaciers, more islands, and more ice-covered mountains, rising like a crescendo to some of the highest summits on the North American continent.

Southeast is rich in culture. The original peoples to inhabit the land were predominantly Tlingit. Today, three major Native groups live in Southeast—Tlingit, Haida, and Tsimshian. Because the weather here was mild and the sea and forest rich with food, the peoples of Southeast Alaska had more time than the Eskimos and Indians of the north to create great art—carved totem poles, clan houses, wooden suits of armor, priceless blankets, great headdresses, masks, and silverwork. Many Native artists today are producing stunning works, blending both the contemporary and the traditional.

Although early inhabitants of Southeast Alaska considered the climate so mild that they did not have tailored clothing, this is not a wise custom to practice today. Southeast weather, even at the best of times, is usually cool. At its worst, it's downright bone-chilling. The sunniest months, although not necessarily the warmest, tend to be April, May, and June. Be forewarned: There is still plenty of snow then, at least in the mountains. But whenever you come, if you get 2 days of sun in a week, consider yourself fortunate. After all, there's a reason why all this country looks so green in the summer. You are traveling in a rain forest.

The Tongass National Forest, a temperate rain forest, covers most of Southeast Alaska. It is the largest national forest in the United States. There are nearly 1,000 islands under its banner. This is one of the country's last old-growth forests. The trees are primarily Sitka spruce and western hemlock interspersed with red and yellow cedar. The water between the islands and the mainland is known as the "Inside Passage"—summer home for cruise ships, fishing boats, ferries, skiffs, kayaks, and rowboats of all sorts.

Water is an extension of everyone's life in Southeast. There are few roads and rarely do they link one community to another. So water serves not only as the transportation corridor, but also as the place of livelihood and recreation. Indeed, the official name of the ferry system is the Alaska Marine Highway. The only other way to get around is by air—bush plane, jet, or helicopter.

The land is dramatic. Carved by glaciers, the valleys have that tell-tale, U-shaped contour. Where the ice retreated, the sea rushed in to create deep, spectacular fjords. Still today, those grand rivers of ice tumble down to the ocean. Warmed by the Japanese current, the sea itself does not freeze, even in winter, but glaciers are constantly kicking out icebergs which you can see floating in the water or tossed up on a sandbar.

Magnificent whales, chubby harbor seals, swooping eagles, wild salmon, and the great Alaska brown bears are just a few of the alluring creatures that call Southeast home.

Towns and villages along the coast have their own special characters, founded on fishing, fur, gold, timber, or tourism. Native peoples have lived here for untold centuries. White folks arrived within the past 300 years—Russian fur traders, Yankee whalers, European explorers, navigators, sailors, fishermen, and gold prospectors have all made their way here. Names on the map hint at the rich stories of a few of those early travelers who came before you.

KETCHIKAN

In the old days, long before the white man came, Tlingit people camped on the banks of Ketchikan Creek and fished for salmon, "the great swimmer." Southeast is home to many thousands of eagles, and spawned-out salmon is the bald eagle's favorite meal. "Ketchikan" comes from the Tlingit word meaning "thundering wings of the eagle." In the 1800s, settlers built a saltry at the mouth of Ketchikan Creek, and by 1930 Ketchikan was one of the world's largest exporters of salmon, with more than a dozen canneries in the area. Money and fish flowed fast and thick. Timber in the forests provided packing boxes for the canneries and, later, raw lumber for Japan and fodder for the local pulp mills.

Today, Ketchikan is the fourth largest city in Alaska, with a population of about 14,000. Fishing and tourism continue to keep the summer economy well greased. Folks in Ketchikan have always been inventive in promoting their town. In the heyday of salmon, it was the "Salmon Capital of the World." Then, when ferry service began in the 1960s, it was billed as "Alaska's First City," as it was the first stop on the ferry route from Seattle to Alaska. For a while, residents tried attracting curious travelers by calling the town the "Rain Capital of Alaska," since Ketchikan gets about 13 feet of rain a year.

Not so long ago, Alaska's First City was a rowdy, rough-and-tumble town of fishermen, loggers, and the occasional miner. But today Ketchikan has received a face lift. Like the famous madams of yesteryear who waited for the return of the fishing fleet, the town has been getting all dolled up for the fleet of cruise ships sailing into port every summer. In the last few years, old weathered buildings have been spruced up and gaily painted with new names reminiscent of a saucier era.

"Sausalito of the North" may be stretching it a bit (particularly if the rain is blowing horizontally), but on a sunny day on the old boardwalk of Creek Street, while eating a fresh halibut sandwich and watching salmon jumping up the falls, one could easily slip into that feel-good, savory, pastoral feeling of old California. One look at the untamed, dramatic landscape all around you in the north country makes up in spades for what Ketchikan lacks in gourmet eateries and constant sun.

Access

Ketchikan has daily jet service year-round via **Alaska Airlines.** The best locally based air service for scheduled or charter operations is **Tacquan Air.** Ketchikan is, of course, still Alaska's First City for the ferries. The cruise ships dock or anchor close to downtown. The ferries of the **Alaska Marine Highway** system dock at the ferry terminal 2 miles north of town. Just north of that terminal is the car ferry to the airport.

Once you get to Ketchikan, there are about 36 miles of road running north to south along the western edge of the island. There are no public buses, so it's best to rent a car. You can drive to scenic overlooks, fishing spots, hiking trails, a lake, wilderness fishing lodges, or your bed and breakfast, if that's where you end up staying.

Information

Be sure to stop first at **Southeast Alaska Visitors Information Center (SEAVIC).** Newly opened in the summer of 1995, the center is a stone's throw from the cruise ship dock. Once inside the door, you are met by 3 totem poles, carved to honor the Tlingit, Haida, and Tsimshian peoples of Southeast Alaska. Look up, not only to see the crests on top of the totems but to see salmon, the lifeblood of these ocean peoples, swimming in a silver stream overhead through an architectural web of massive wooden beams. Like salmon swimming upstream, exhibits wind up the stairs and through various galleries and include "Native Traditions" and a re-creation of a temperate rain forest. There's a library, a trip-planning room, and a place to make reservations for public-use cabins. Located at the southern end of the cruise ship dock, about a minute's walk, at 50 Main Street; (907) 225-8131. Open daily, May–Sept; Tues–Sat, Oct–April.

Tips on the Town

Remember: Ketchikan is on an island called Revillagigedo (pronounced Ruh-villa-hey-hey-do) or "Revilla" for short. (It was named by Spanish explorers for the viceroy of Mexico in the 1800s.) The airport is on another island called Gravina. There are no bridges or roads to Ketchikan from the airport, or from anywhere else, for that matter.

The only way to get from Ketchikan to the airport (outside of hiring a helicopter or swimming) is by boat. A little ferry that runs every 15 minutes or so in the summer will take you and your rental car to the island. The trip across the water is only about 5 minutes, but allow an extra half-hour and some extra cash, as there's a toll.

THINGS TO DO

Walking Tour Towns in Southeast are not very big and are best explored on foot. (If you can walk, walk.) "Streets" are often staircases up the hillsides, trails through the woods, or boardwalks over creeks and sloughs. Walking gives you a feel for the color, flavor, and people. Plus, if you're into flowers, Alaska gardens are a knock-out, and peering over the fence into someone's garden is free. (You might get lucky and be invited to a barbecue.) Don't be intimidated by the weather or you'll never get going. If you start your tour on the dock, there is a giant barometer there called the "Liquid Sunshine Gauge," which burst in 1949, they say, after nearly 18 feet of rain. Pick up a free copy of *Ketchikan Walking Tour Map* from the visitors center, and begin at the **cruise ship dock,** a fun place to watch ships and boats. A walk from the docks up to the **Front Street Overlook** will get your heart pumping and give you a great bird's-eye view of Tongass Narrows. At the north end of Front Street, the street turns into stairs—about 130 of them. Go up, then stroll down to the end of the boardwalk. In order to build roadways along some of these steep mountainsides in the early days, residents used a braced framework of timbers called a trestle. The **Grant Street Trestle** is the only one still in existence in Ketchikan. Walk along **Ketchikan Creek** to the sweet little **City Park,** which has ponds and big trees. The creek is the heart of Ketchikan. Without this creek, there would be no town. Historically, its waters and creeksides have drawn in fish, fishermen, and flamboyant women. As you head

down Bawden Street and turn left along Park Avenue, you'll
cross a bridge over the creek. In the right season, you can often see salmon jumping up the falls or taking the easier route
up the fish ladder to the left of the falls. On the right-hand side,
after the bridge, the **"Married Man's Trail"** is one way to return through the woods to **Creek Street** (more about these 2
locales under "Places to Visit"). **Deer Mountain Hatchery**
was built in 1954 to help rehabilitate the severely depleted runs
of chinook and coho salmon. Hatcheries are designed not to replace Mother Nature, but rather to enhance her efforts. About
300,000 salmon smolts are released every year into the wild.
Only 2 percent will survive the hazards at sea to return here as
adults after their journey through the ocean. The **Totem Heritage Center** (601 Deermount Street; (907) 225-5900) houses
an extraordinary collection of old totem poles. They were
carved by the Tlingit and Haida people who lived in villages
around Ketchikan. (There is a short guided tour. Open daily in
summer, and Tues to Fri in winter.) After a visit to Creek
Street, en route back to the docks, stop in at the library, across
the creek from Creek Street. The windows offer stunning views
of the tumbling rapids of the creek.

Fishing Charters Dozens of charter fishing operators take
customers out of Ketchikan for half-day or day-long excursions.
This is some of the best fishing in all of Southeast Alaska.
Check the visitors center for a list of charter fishing businesses. The most popular saltwater and freshwater fish available in the Ketchikan area are king (chinook) salmon, silver
(coho) salmon, pink (humpback) salmon, red (sockeye) salmon,
chum (dog) salmon, rockfish, halibut, Dolly Varden, cutthroat
trout, rainbow trout, grayling, and steelhead trout. Fishing for
Dolly Varden and trout starts in April. April and May are excellent for steelhead. You can fish throughout the summer for
lingcod, rockfish, red snapper, and halibut. King salmon season is mid-May through early July, followed by runs of sockeye, coho, chums, and pinks well into August.

Deer Mountain Hike On a clear day, Deer Mountain dominates the skyline behind the city of Ketchikan. At 3,001 feet tall,
it is also known as "Ketchikan's barometer." As the old saying
around town goes, "If you can't see the top of Deer Mountain,
it's raining. And if you can see the top of Deer Mountain, it's
about to rain." Rain or shine, this is a popular hike. It gets you
quickly into the rain forest experience. Listen particularly for
the call of ravens. Ravens and eagles are plentiful. The first
overlook can be reached in 50 minutes at a steady walk. It is
only a small break in the forest, but on a clear day, it's a nice
aerobic workout rewarded with a spectacular view of the ocean
and islands below, leading to Dixon Entrance. You come out

above treeline in another mile for even more spectacular views. Then it's on up to the top. The trailhead is a 30-minute walk from downtown, or you can take a taxi to it.

Touring the Roads by Car Ketchikan has 36 miles of road, extending 13 miles to the south of downtown and 23 miles to the north—a mere drop in the bucket for those of you used to driving freeways back home. On a beautiful day, be Buddhist: take it slowly, and you will find a lovely view around each corner as you hug the edge of the sea. Within minutes, you'll even feel worlds apart from downtown Ketchikan. On the **South Tongass Highway,** which is the road heading south from downtown, you can visit totem poles and a Tlingit cultural center, wet a fishing line, catch a salmon, barbecue it while sitting at the ocean's edge watching whales, and at the end of the road hike a trail into the mountains. If you travel north on the highway, traffic is busier. **Totem Bight State Historical Park,** at mile 10, is a must. Plan the day so you end up at **Salmon Falls Resort** for dinner near the end of the road.

Touring by Bike If you have only a few hours, rent a bike and head south toward **Saxman Totem Park.** The South Tongass Highway is more peaceful than the road to the north, except for the tour buses going to Saxman. The road runs right along the edge of the water. If you want to avoid the buses, go in the late afternoon or evening.

Paddling Rent a kayak from **Southeast Exposure,** (907) 225-8829. Before you head out, they give you a lesson in staying safe on the water.

WINTERTIME ACTIVITIES

Don't come. That's advice from the locals. Unless, of course, you love 80 mph winds and sheets of freezing rain blowing in your face. Most of the tourist businesses shut down and locals leave town (for part of the winter anyway). However, if you are into crocheting or are desperate to finish, uninterrupted, all four volumes of Winston Churchill's *History of the English-speaking Peoples,* this is your ace-in-the-hole.

PLACES TO VISIT

Creek Street Creek Street is not really a "street" at all. When a revitalization of the area began in the early 1970s, it was, by some, discreetly billed (perhaps for funding purposes) as "Ketchikan's Historic District." But in 1925, its notoriety stretched all the way to the nation's capital, where Judge James Wickersham had another way of describing it: "The Barbary Coast of the North" or "Alaska's Tenderloin." This was, quite simply put, the red-light district of Ketchikan. Built on pilings, the former houses of the "Ladies of the Line" are linked by boardwalks over the rushing waters of the creek as it spills out into the ocean. In its heyday, Creek Street was called "the only place in the world where both fish and fisherman went up the creek to spawn." Today you can visit Dolly's House, a former bordello that has been turned into a museum. Most of the remaining houses are now little shops. A nice way to finish off your tour of town is to stop at in at **Number Five.** It houses the **Five Star Cafe,** where you can get a jolt of the local coffee, roasted in Ketchikan under the name of Raven's Brew. You can drink Czar's Blend ("fit for royalty") or Deadman's Reach ("special high caffeine with a bite"), eat one of their brimming-with-health sandwiches, or indulge in homemade desserts. Don't miss a trip upstairs into **Parnassus,** an eclectic little bookstore. Right next door is **Soho Coho,** the studio and shop of Ketchikan's infamous fish artist Ray Troll, where you can buy local wearable art with humor from The Deep, such as T-shirts emblazoned with "Ain't No Nookie Like Chinookie," "Salmon Enchanted Evening," and "Spawn 'Til You Die."

Married Man's Trail There are several ways to get to Creek Street. For the sake of history, particularly if you are of the male persuasion, take the "Married Man's Trail" to the right of the bridge over Ketchikan Creek on Park Avenue. In the old days, when a man wanted to visit one of the ladies on Creek Street but didn't want to be seen (for obvious reasons), he took this trail through the woods and approached the houses on Creek Street from the forest side rather than from the more public waterfront side. The trail in those days was just a muddy path through the forest, so even though he was trying to sneak into the bordellos incognito, the girls could tell which of the fellows waiting in the parlor were married by the mud on their trouser legs. This trail will take you right down to Creek Street, or if you veer off to the left you can walk up to the Cape Fox Hotel and take the short tram ride down to Creek Street.

Dolly's House: A Little Place of Business The pale green house with the red trim, Number 24 Creek Street, belonged to "Big Dolly" Arthur, Ketchikan's most famous madam. "I realized I could make a lot more money from the attentions of men than I could waiting tables," said Dolly, who plied her trade here for more than 30 years earlier this century. The government closed down the bawdy houses on Creek Street in 1953, but Dolly lived on there until shortly before her death in 1975. The house is now a museum. Be sure to read the old "Employment Application" posted in the window. How many job interviews have you been to where they asked you: "Are you currently in love?" "What is your unmentionable size?" and, when inquiring about the kind of men the gal preferred, "How small is ok? Tiny?" Open daily in summer; closed winter (Oct to April) when, as the sign says on the door, "Dolly is at the Policeman's Ball." For information, call (907) 225-6329.

Saxman Totem Park Saxman is a Tlingit village 3 miles south of downtown Ketchikan. In the center of the village is the clan house and a very grand avenue of totem poles leading up the hill to the park. They say the totem poles here, which were moved from Pennock, Tongass, and Village Islands and from old Cape Fox Village at Kirk Point, represent the world's largest collection. The U.S. Forest Service directed a restoration project of the old totems beginning in 1939. For more on Saxman, see Viola Garfield's book, published by University of Washington Press: *The Wolf and the Raven*. A guided tour of the park, clan house, and artists' carving shed is available; call (907) 225-9038 for times. The park lies 3 miles south of downtown on the South Tongass Highway.

Totem Bight State Historical Park Ten miles north of town, Totem Bight is a lovely spot with a clan house and totem poles facing out to the sea. It is not an original village site, but rather a re-creation of one in a beautiful natural setting. A short walk through the forest with the smell of cedar and sea breezes brings you to the steps of the Raven Tribal House. Totem poles, carved from soft and durable cedar, were never meant to last forever. Their lifespan after being exposed to the wet and windy elements of Southeastern weather is about 60 years. When people, for whatever reasons, left their villages, and moved to another, the poles were left to topple and rot. Totem Bight State Historical Park was founded in the 1930s, as part of a major restoration effort by the federal government to save, collect, and preserve some of these old poles. Tours are self-guided. Park is open year-round.

FESTIVALS/EVENTS

King Salmon Derby This is the queen, or shall we say king, of salmon derbies in Southeast Alaska, held the last weekend of May and the first 3 weekends of June. In 1995, the winning salmon weighed in at 50 pounds, for a grand prize of $10,000. For more information, call the Ketchikan Chamber of Commerce at (907) 225-3184.

BEST RESTAURANTS

Heen Kahidi Restaurant, Westmark Cape Fox Hotel ★★★
The name means "tree house on the creek." Nestled into the green branches of the spruce, cedar, and western hemlock trees with lovely views out to the Tongass Narrows, you'll feel as if you're eating outdoors with all the comforts of indoors. This is where local folks go for a special night out or to celebrate anniversaries. The service is warm and friendly. The menu is varied enough for any discerning palate: Belgian waffles, cheese blintzes, pan-fried oysters, raspberry kiwi chicken, seafood quesadillas, and the Cape Fox classics of Shrimp in Love, Halibut Olympia, or the favorite, Alaska king crab legs.

■ *In the Cape Fox Hotel; 800 Venetia Way, Ketchikan; (907)
225-8001; $$$; full bar; AE, DC, DIS, MC, V; checks OK;
breakfast, lunch, dinner, daily.* &

Salmon Falls Resort ★★★

In a lovely wooded setting over-
looking the water, Salmon Falls Resort is really a fishing lodge,
but many locals go out here just for dinner. Eighteen miles out
of town, along the North Tongass Highway, the resort has a
rustic charm, with flower boxes and log cabins—just what
you'd expect Alaska to look like. From the windows of its huge
octagonal restaurant, you can see water in all directions—to
the east, a spectacular roaring waterfall, and to the west,
Clarence Strait. Not surprising, the fare here is fish and more
fish. And they do a very nice job with it. You can have halibut,
cod, prawns, scallops, and salmon. Be aware that they have
started catering to busloads of cruise ship passengers at
lunchtime some days of the week. So if you are interested in
lunch with no buses, call ahead and ask. ■ *Look for the sign
on the left, 18 miles out along the North Tongass Hwy; 16707
North Tongass Hwy; toll-free (800) 247-9059 or (907) 225-
2752; $$$; full bar; DC, MC, V; local checks OK; open May
15–Sept 15.* &

Annabelle's Famous Keg and Chowder House ★★

At this fa-
vorite of both locals and tourists, you can eat in The Bar, the
casual side, or in The Parlor, the more elegant side of the
restaurant. Both feature "New York style dining circa 1927,"
the year Annabelle's opened. With its floral-patterned carpet,
heavy, dark-wood decor, and white tablecloths, the Parlor is
reminiscent of those old 1920s mobster movies where the guys
in pin-striped suits are drinking champagne, talking in low
tones, and, as our mothers would say, "up to no good." Seafood,
pasta, salads, and creamy thick pies are all favorites here. For
dinner on the spicier side of life, try Tequila Prawns with
Firecracker Rice or the rich and creamy tortellini with crab and
Gorgonzola cheese. For dessert, the peanut butter pie is as
good as its reputation. ■ *Across from the cruise ship dock, in
the Gilmore Hotel; 326 Front St, Ketchikan; (907) 225-9423;
$$; full bar; all major credit cards; local checks OK; breakfast,
lunch, and dinner daily in summer; no breakfast served in
winter.* &

Five Star Cafe ★★

Many residents wax rhapsodic about this
quaint little cafe on the creek. It has a kind of Berkeley-esque
feeling to it. In the San Francisco Bay area, this cafe might
seem like one of many, but in Ketchikan it is one-of-a-kind. Cus-
tomers are a range of artists, writers, young hippies, old hip-
pies, bookworms, coffee addicts, fishermen, and tourists. The
menu runs from "pseudo caesar" salad and homemade soups
to vegetarian or meat sandwiches and the unusual but popular
P.B.T.H.B. sandwich (peanut butter, tahini, honey, and ba-

nana). ■ *5 Creek St, Ketchikan; (907) 247-STAR; $$; no al-
cohol; no credit cards; local checks OK; summer hours are
7:30am to 5:30pm Mon–Sat, 9am–5pm Sun; shorter hours in
winter and closed Sun and Mon.*

BEST LODGINGS

Westmark Cape Fox Hotel ★★★★ This is the best hotel in
all of Southeast Alaska—maybe in all of Alaska—for its
warmth, views, and peaceful charm. Sitting on the hill, it gazes
down on the town of Ketchikan, the harbor, the islands, the
floatplanes, and the boats sailing up and down the Tongass
Narrows. Up above the tree tops, where the eagles fly, the ho-
tel is out of the noise and huggermugger of the busy little port,
but one can still have the fun of watching all the action. Out
back, there are views into the forest and up Deer Mountain.
Visitors always want rooms facing the water; the locals, com-
ing for a weekend getaway, more often choose the mountain
views. Whatever your preference, trees or water, all the rooms
are spacious and cozy. Designed as a ski lodge, the hotel has
a stone fireplace, lots of pine wood, and large windows.
Blended into this theme are exquisite Southeastern cultural
motifs, from the totem poles in the front garden to a stunning
carved screen on the second floor landing by the distinguished
Tlingit carver Nathan Jackson. To top it off, the staff is so
friendly, it feels just like home. ■ *On the hill, overlooking
downtown Ketchikan. Take a courtesy car from the airport or
ferry terminal, or ride the tram up from Creek St; 800 Vene-
tia Way, Ketchikan; toll-free (800) 544-0970 for reservations,
or (907) 225-8001; $$$; AE, DC, DIS, MC, V; checks OK;
breakfast, lunch, and dinner, daily;* & *two rooms.*

Great Alaska Cedar Works Bed and Breakfast ★★★ A
forested setting right on the beach, this spot is another lovely,
more rustic choice. Next to the owners' log home on the waterfront are two private wood cottages. They are cozy and col-
orfully appointed with fun antiques and real feather beds. Come
here for peace and quiet and old-style warmth and hospitality.
No smoking, inside or out, is allowed. You'll need a car. ■ *Mile
11 on the North Tongass Hwy; 1527 Pond Reef Rd, Ketchikan,
AK 99901; (907) 247-8287; $$; no credit cards; personal or
traveler's checks OK.*

New York Hotel and Cafe ★★ This small hotel has a charm
and simplicity all its own. It is right downtown, across from the
small boat harbor at Thomas Basin. In the old days, there was
a baseball diamond on the tidal flats there. Action was often in-
terrupted by the incoming tides. Undaunted, players used
skiffs to catch fly balls in the outfield. The hotel once had 18
rooms with one bath available on Saturday nights. Now there
are 8 rooms, each with full baths (most have an old claw-foot

bathtub). The hotel is full most of the summer, so you'll need to call for reservations. For the price, location, and sense of history, it's a good deal. A note to the extra-boisterous: The proprietor's mother says, "We run a quiet hotel: business people and sightseers who want to get their sleep at night. Champagne in your room is okay, but raucous partying we don't allow." Ask for the front rooms overlooking Thomas Basin. ■ *Go through town on Front St, turn left on Mill St, then left on Stedman; 207 Stedman St, Ketchikan, AK 99901; (907) 225-0246; $$ (summer), $ (winter); AE, MC, V; local checks OK.*

Captain's Quarters Bed and Breakfast ★★ Within walking distance of downtown, the Captain's Quarters is a cheerful, airy home-away-from-home, with picture-postcard views of the water from the large windows in the upstairs rooms. It is all newly, tastefully furnished with a fun nautical theme. Great views of the Tongass Narrows and the ships, boats, and floatplanes along the busy waterfront. For best views, request the upstairs rooms. No smoking allowed. ■ *Near downtown Ketchikan (a long walk or a short drive); 325 Lund St, Ketchikan, AK 99901; (907) 225-4912; $$; AE, MC, V; checks OK.*

The Oakes House Bed and Breakfast ★★ This luxurious log home offers a more upscale experience. Opened in 1995, it is managed by owner Christine Oakes and her husband Blair, both newly retired from the U.S. Navy. He was Ronald Reagan's personal guard. She was on the bomb squad. Now, they enjoy a different kind of ocean view and also have a sod-roofed sauna at water's edge. ■ *10 miles out of town; 10409 Point Susan Rd, Ketchikan, AK 99901; toll-free (800) 318-7586 or (907) 225-1705; $$$; AE, DC, DIS, MC, V; local checks OK.* &

Ketchikan

*Wilderness
Lodges*

OTHER BED AND BREAKFASTS

Ketchikan Reservation Service In Alaska, bed and breakfasts (or B&Bs) are usually rooms in people's houses. If you are a people person and curious about the local folks, this is definitely the way to go. You'll get a more personal glimpse into Alaska lifestyles. Some are very basic; some are quite special. Wanda Vandergriff at the reservation service can help you make a good choice. Room rates run about $50–$75 for a single and $65–$80 for a double. For more information, contact Ketchikan Reservation Service, 412 D-1 Loop Rd, Ketchikan, AK 99901; toll-free (800) 987-5337 or (907) 247-5337.

WILDERNESS LODGES

Salmon Falls Resort At the northern end of the road from Ketchikan, Salmon Falls Resort sits in a lovely spot on the edge of Behm Canal, with a spectacular waterfall cascading down the mountain behind it. It is the definition of rustic elegance. While it is expensive, it is not nearly as pricey as other fishing resorts listed here. Three days/3 nights cost $1,650 per person; 6 days/ 6 nights cost $3,300 per person. The non-fishing rate for meals and lodging alone is $200/night per person. For reservations, contact Salmon Falls Resort, PO Box 5700, Ketchikan, AK 99901; toll-free (800) 247-9059 or (907)225-2752.

Waterfall Resort If price is no object, then go where the Fortune 500 go and head to the west coast of Prince of Wales Island. This resort is for serious fishermen, the kind who wouldn't even look up if a humpback whale breached right in front of them. It also caters to squeamish fishermen: if you choose, you are so coddled that you need not handle your fish more than a nanosecond (for the photograph) before it is whisked away, filleted, boxed, and frozen for your departure. The humor of this now-luxurious resort, which caters to your every saltwater desire, is that you get to sleep where the cannery workers once slept. Built in 1912, Waterfall is actually an old salmon packing house that operated for six decades. It reopened in 1981 (following renovation) for a fancier crowd. Accommodations serve 84 guests at a time with a 1-to-1 ratio of staff to guests. In 1912, cannery workers earned a pittance a day; you will pay considerably more than that for the privilege of staying here. The cost for 3 nights/4 days is about $2,600 per person; 5 nights/6 days is $3,800 (not including gratuities, spirits, or fishing licenses). Closed Oct through April. For reservations and more information, contact Waterfall Resort, PO Box 6440, Ketchikan, AK 99901; (907) 225-9461.

Yes Bay/Mink Bay Lodges Of the small, secluded wilderness lodges specializing primarily in fresh and saltwater fishing, Yes Bay and Mink Bay Lodges are considered *la crème de la crème* when it comes to savoring the finest and most intimate of Alaska fishing and wilderness experiences. Both lodges are open May to Sept. Yes Bay is casual elegance, only a 20-minute flight from Ketchikan. At Mink Bay, you fish right alongside the bears in Misty Fjords National Monument. (Catch-and-release is especially encouraged.) Prices vary from $2,000 per person for 3 days to $3,000 per person for 5 days. For reservations or more information, write or call the Hack Family, Yes Bay/Mink Bay Lodges, PO Box 6440, Ketchikan, AK 99901; toll-free (800) 999-0784 or (907) 225-7906.

Alaska's Inside Passage Resorts This is a consortium of fishing resorts and companies offering luxury sailing adventures in the southern part of Southeast Alaska. Represented in the group are Yes Bay Lodge, Mink Bay Lodge, Waterfall Resort, and Boardwalk Wilderness Lodge on Prince of Wales Island. They also offer cruising on a 70-foot yacht called the *Midnight Sun,* which can be chartered for up to 6 passengers at a daily or a weekly rate. Your itinerary is custom designed. The daily rate for the yacht is $3,660 per person, and the weekly rate is $22,000. The fishing/yachting season begins in April or May and runs through mid-September. To obtain more information, a promotional video, and reservations, contact 1170 Coast Village Rd, 2nd floor, Santa Barbara, CA 93108-2717; toll-free (800) 350-3474 or (805) 969-8780 (in Santa Barbara).

MISTY FJORDS NATIONAL MONUMENT

Twenty-two miles west of Ketchikan by air, Misty Fjords National Monument is a lovely jewel set within the Tongass National Forest. In 1978, by presidential decree, it achieved fully protected wilderness status, although it is located within multiple-use national forest land. Carved out by glaciers during the last great period of the ice age more than 10,000 years ago, Misty Fjords is, as its name suggests, a series of deep-water fjords left by receding glaciers, tall granite cliffs, and almost perpetual swirling mist.

In **Punchbowl Cove,** one of the more popular destinations, sheer granite walls rise to a height of more than 3,000 feet. Some have called it the Yosemite of the North. Special to the awe-inspiring beauty of Misty Fjords is its stillness and peace. With more and more visitors coming each year, particularly for quick visits via floatplane, this aspect may change radically—although for the benefit of all of us, let us hope not. There are many ways you can explore the monument—by plane, boat, kayak, and foot.

Misty Fjords National Monument

Several outfitters offer flightseeing or flightseeing/cruising packages for a half-day or day-long visit. Another option is to rent one of the Forest Service cabins, take a floatplane in, and get dropped off for several days. Better yet is to go in under your own power, using a kayak that can be rented in Ketchikan, and then take several days to explore the bays and coves on your own.

Please note: This is a wilderness area. There are no visitor facilities. You must bring with you everything you will need, from maps, nautical charts, and compass to food, tents, warm clothing, and plenty of rain gear. Consult local knowledge on weather, water, boats, safety, itinerary, and necessary skills. A good place to start is the trip-planning room at SEAVIC, (907) 225-8131, the visitors information center.

Alaska Cruises, (907) 225-6044, offers day trips to Misty Fjords with several options such as flying one way and cruising back. **Tacquan Air Alaska,** toll-free (800) 770-8800 or (907) 225-8800, offers a variety of tours, from flightseeing over Misty Fjords and LeConte Glacier to drop-offs for wilderness sportfishing, camping, or kayaking trips. Highly respected for their safety record and local pilot knowledge, Tacquan has been in operation for 18 years. For information on **trails and**

public-use cabins, write U.S. Forest Service, Ketchikan Ranger Station, 3031 Tongass Avenue, Ketchikan, AK 99901.

SITKA

To fully appreciate this lovely town on the western edge of Baranof Island, it is important to know something of its rich history. When Chicago was merely a fort town in the middle of the prairies and San Francisco a small mission, Sitka was hailed as the "Paris of the West." Ships docked here from all over the world. Today only 8,000 people live in Sitka year-round. But that is a large part of her charm.

For many years, Sitka was the capital of Russian America. In the center of town, dominating the low skyline, is the onion-shaped dome of the old wooden church known as St. Michael's Cathedral.

Sitka was home to the Tlingits before the Russians, and today it is the blending and preservation of the history of both cultures that gives Sitka its unique flavor. As the ironies of history often unfold, the fortunes and legacy of an empire here rose and fell on a funny, bewhiskered fellow—the sea otter.

▼
Sitka
▲

Alaska was once a treasure chest of sea otters. To the Russian hunters, this creature's fur was known as "soft gold," and the pelts brought high prices in the courts of China. But as the sea otters began to disappear, hunted to near extinction, Russia's interest in her far-flung colony began to wane. In 1867, the advice given the czar was "Sell! Sell the colony before someone takes it by force." So after 126 years of rule in this wilderness outpost, Russia sold her colony to the Americans under a storm of controversy here at home. But history has proven much the contrary. The purchase price of $7.2 million has been recouped many times over.

Its economy is now founded primarily on fishing and tourism. It has a beautiful setting, with sparkling waters, emerald islands, rocky beaches, and a safe harbor for ships. Even though thousands of tourists from the cruise ships land on her shores every week in the summer, Sitka manages to maintain her individual character and charm.

Access

Sitka lies on the west side of Baranof Island. As with most Southeastern towns, there are no roads to Sitka. Access is by air or sea. **Alaska Airlines,** (800) 426-0333, has scheduled flights daily going both north and south, summer and winter. The **Alaska Marine Highway,** (800) 642-0066, has ferry service to Sitka throughout the year from ports in Alaska, Canada, and Washington. The ferry terminal is located north of town, near the end of the road. From downtown Sitka, the road extends about 7 miles in either direction. Rental cars are available

at the airport. The airport is only 5 minutes or so from downtown Sitka, and there is a limousine service that runs year-
round. Experienced air charters are **Bellair,** (907) 747-8636,
and **Mountain Aviation,** (907) 966-2288.

Information

Stop first at the **Centennial Building Visitors Information**
(330 Harbor Drive; (907) 747-3225). It is located in the heart of
downtown, inside the Centennial Building at the edge of the
harbor. For more information, write to the Sitka Convention
and Visitors Bureau at PO Box 1226, Sitka, AK 99835; (907)
747-5940. **Old Harbor Bookstore** (201 Lincoln St, Sitka, AK
99835; (907) 747-8808) has a wonderful array of books on Sitka,
Southeast, and Alaska, and also sells nautical charts.

Sitka **Ranger District (Tongass National Forest)** has
information about public-use recreational cabins on beaches,
mountain lakes, and remote islands in the national forest. Cost
for cabin rentals is $25/night—the best deal going in all of
Alaska. For descriptions and reservations, contact 201 Katlian,
Suite 109, Sitka, AK 99835; (907) 747-6671. The **Alaska De-**
partment of Fish and Game is a good source of information
on fishing and hunting in the area, regulations, seasons, and licenses. Contact 304 Lake St, Rm 103, Sitka, AK 99835; (907)
747-6688.

The local paper, the *Daily Sitka Sentinel,* is published
five times a week. The famed "Police Blotter" lies within. The
public radio station, **Raven Radio** (KCAW), may be found at
104.7 FM.

THINGS TO DO

"Sitka Walking Tour" (guided) This is not a generic title, so
don't get confused. Of all the guided tours in Sitka, this is the
best. With her love of stories and nature, longtime resident
Jane Eidler gives her walking tours a personable and humorous twist. She worked for both the National Park Service and
the U.S. Forest Service in Alaska as a ranger/naturalist before
settling in Sitka 20 years ago to raise her family. The tour is historical and anecdotal, which, to quote that time-honored news-
man Paul Harvey, tells "the rest of the story." Rain or shine, she
and her business partner Lisa Busch will give you the behind-
the-scenes of Sitka and then point you in the right direction to
explore the Sitka National Historical Park on your own. Tours
start at the Centennial Building. Times vary. For the latest information, call Jane's message phone, (907) 747-5354, or Lisa,
(907) 747-5353.

Sitka Walking Tour (self-guided) If you miss Jane's tour and
are on your own, here are a few of the highlights of any walk
around Sitka. First, look for the unmistakable onion-shaped
dome spires of **St. Michael's Cathedral** in the center of town.

The cathedral burned to the ground in a terrible fire in 1966. Bucket brigades saved precious icons, and 10 years later it was rebuilt to the original design. The Centennial Building, at the edge of the water, offers some wonderful shows throughout the summer including the **Sitka Summer Music Festival**, daily performances by the powerful **Alaska Native Dancers** in full regalia, and the all-women **New Archangel Dancers,** who celebrate the town's Russian past with folk dances from the old country. (Tours of Sitka from "The Alaska Native Perspective" are given by the Sitka Tribe of Alaska, (907) 747-3207.) Next door is the library, haunt of bookworms and brides. With a beautiful view of Sitka Sound through its windows, the library is popular for weddings as well as an attractive place to read or do research. A 5-minute walk along Harbor Drive and up the stairs to **Castle Hill** offers a commanding view of the sea, mountains, and islands. This was the original village site for the Tlingit people before the arrival of the Russian invaders. Old Russian cannons punctuate the circular stone wall where once stood the governors' residence known as "Baranov's Castle," named for the first governor of Russian America. Baranov himself never lived here. But many of the 13 Russian governors who followed him to Alaska did. On October 18, 1867, the flag of the czars was lowered and the Stars and Stripes raised. **The Pioneer Home** was built to honor this northern land's early pioneers. The gardens are brilliant with colorful flowers and visitors are always welcome. The oldtimers here have stories to tell. Up the hill is the **Russian Blockhouse,** built of logs, a replica of the blockhouse that was part of the fort and stockade dividing the Tlingit and Russian sections of old Sitka. Surrounding it is the peaceful **Russian Graveyard.** Look for the old stone Russian crosses. **Governors Walk** is the old name for the promenade along Sitka's main street (Lincoln Street) from Castle Hill along the waterfront to the woods by Indian River. This area is now **Sitka National Historical Park.** The walk is lovely, about 15 minutes. On the way, you will pass **The Bishop's House** and **Sheldon Jackson Museum** before you arrive at the historical park with its scenic paths through woods and totem poles.

Hikes Whether you go on a short hike or long one, plan for wet, cool weather. And remember: this is bear country. Don't let that keep you from enjoying the woods, but be alert. The buddy system always makes good sense. If you do go alone, sing, recite poetry, whistle, or make noise occasionally, particularly in deep grass, thick brush, bends in the trail, or when you can see the streams are filled with salmon and the hills covered with berries. Bears love both. Unless you surprise them, mistakenly get in between a mother and her cubs, or have the great misfortune to encounter a bear with a toothache, for the most part, any bear will be more frightened of you than you are of it. With that in mind, here are some popular hikes in the Sitka area. The ranger station has a full listing of hikes and directions. For information, call (907) 747-6671.

Gavan Hill Trail. This is a lovely hike, that will get you up high. It takes about 3 hours to make the steep climb to the summit, at elevation 2,505 feet. A plank trail, mainly wooden stairs, has been built all the way up, and the kids in town are now calling it "The Stairmaster." The trail begins at the edge of downtown. The marked trailhead is just past the house at 508 Baranof Street.

Harbor Mountain Ridge Trail. This is the hike to do on a clear day. The views are spectacular. Drive 4 miles north of town along Halibut Point Road, turn right, and go 5 miles up Harbor Mountain Rd, which was built during World War II as an access to a military lookout. The trail begins where the road ends and wanders 2 miles along ridges and alpine meadows. It'll take 2 hours one way. The end of the trail intersects with the Gavan Hill Trail. Here's where the fun can begin. If you really want to make it a day, you can continue down Gavan Hill and end up back in Sitka. If you have buddies who want to start from the opposite direction, you can pass car keys and meet back in town for a beer.

Indian River Trail. If it's a cloudy day, this is the perfect hike. You can walk to the trailhead from downtown. The trail is flat, wandering through typical rain forest and alongside muskeg meadows. Much of the time you are walking by the river. The falls are about 5 miles in. Walk softly and you may see deer or sometimes bear. Head east along Sawmill Creek Road to Indian River Road. This is the next road east of the Troopers Academy driveway. The trail begins just west of the pumphouse, about half a mile along the road.

Mount Edgecumbe Trail. This trail leads to the top of Mount Edgecumbe, the volcano that is one of Sitka's most stunning landmarks. This hike is good on a sunny day. You need a skiff to get to the trailhead as the mountain is on Kruzof Island, about 10 miles west of Sitka. Ask at the visitors center in Sitka about rentals. The trail begins behind Fred's Creek Cabin and is wet and muddy in places and steep for the last 3 miles. It's about 7 miles one way and will take you about 5 hours to get to the summit. Reserve the cabin through the U.S. Forest Service, (907) 747-6671, for a few nights, so you won't have such a long journey back.

To the Ends of the Road From downtown Sitka, the road runs about 7 miles to the north and 7 miles to the east. If you have access to wheels, it's great for biking or a scenic drive. To the north, follow Halibut Point Road. Near the end of the road is the site of the Russians' first fort on the island. Nature and bird lovers won't want to miss the **Starrigavan Bird Viewing Platform,** on the right side of the road, just past Old Sitka. There is a beautifully designed boardwalk and interpretive trail about the life of the estuary at Starrigavan Bay. To the east of downtown Sitka, follow Sawmill Creek Road, which extends about 5 miles out to Herring Cove. Near the end of the road, there is a dirt road to **Blue Lake,** then, at the very end, another dirt road that continues to **Green Lake.** It's a beautiful mountain bike ride. **Whale Park,** 3 miles out, sits on the edge of the cliff and is an excellent spot for peaceful picnicking and whale watching. Frolicking whale sculptures welcome you to a series of artful wooden gazebos, boardwalks, and stairways to the beach.

Kayak Rentals Get out on the water. Go anywhere. With all the islands in Sitka Sound and the proximity to Olga and Neva Straits, the paddling around Sitka is more protected than many other places in Southeast. Rent a kayak from Larry Edwards at **Bidarka Boats,** (907) 747-8996. He has reasonable rates and gives an orientation on paddling and safety skills. **Sitka Sea Kayaking Adventure,** (907) 789-0052, has a 3-hour guided kayak tour for $65/person.

Bicycle and Scuba Gear Rentals The waters surrounding Southeast can be very colorful in spring, when the plankton are blooming. The water is cold, but **Southeast Diving and Sports** (203 Lincoln Street; (907) 747-8279) can outfit and advise you. They also rent mountain bikes. The shop is near St. Michael's Cathedral.

WINTERTIME ACTIVITIES

Whales and Herring From mid-September to mid-January, Sitka is a seaside cafe for dozens and dozens of humpback whales. These huge creatures make winter migrations to the warmer climates of Hawaii and Mexico, but they hang around the rich marine waters of Sitka Sound, bulking up for the journey by feeding on herring. The first wave of humpback whales returns to Alaska in March from the whales' winter breeding grounds. By the third week or so of March, there is another marine-life extravaganza when the herring return—millions and millions of herring. The Department of Fish and Game sometimes opens this fishery to fishermen for a matter of minutes. Dozens of boats congregate in anticipation in the Sound, like runners waiting for the starter's pistol to go off in the 100-yard dash. The opening is calculated to occur at the moment before the female is ready to release her eggs, and fortunes are made and lost with one set of the net. The Japanese particularly prize the eggs as a delicacy that is salted and eaten on New Year's Day. You can view the fishery from Halibut Point Road or charter a boat into the Sound to watch the action.

Sitka National Historical Park   Do not miss this gem of a national park. A museum houses beautifully displayed cultural treasures, but the real treasure is found along the 2-mile trail through the totem pole park, which weaves through the forest and along the beach. The carved cedar totem poles blend so well into the woods that the faces of frogs, ravens, whales, and other creatures appearing out of the mist seem almost magical. The visitors center is also home to master artists from Southeast Indian clans. You can watch them working—making mountain goat wool, spruce tree roots, abalone shells, and cedar bark into masks, ceremonial regalia, robes, jewelry, and other traditional art works. The park and visitors center are open year-round.

One of the few surviving examples of Russian colonial architecture in North America, the Russian **Bishop's House** is also part of Sitka National Historical Park. It stands near the heart of downtown on Lincoln Street. Built in the 1840s by Finnish shipwrights, the house was elaborately restored in the 1980s at a cost of $5 million, all from private donations. The first resident of the house was Ivan Veniaminov, known as Bishop Innocent, and later canonized as St. Innocent. The bishop was an impressive man. Wherever he was, he learned the local dialects, paddled hundreds of miles by kayak to the farthest islands of his parish, and built chapels; later he built St. Michael's Cathedral. One visitor to Sitka described him as "quite Herculean and very clever." Among the many rooms, you will see the small Chapel of the Annunciation and the bishop's personal chambers. Note the clock he invented and built, which keeps accurate time with the dripping of water. From May to October, the Bishop's House is open daily; in winter, it is open by appointment.

For more information, contact the National Park Service, Sitka National Historical Park, 106 Metlakatla Street, Sitka, AK 99835; (907) 747-6281.

Sheldon Jackson Museum   On the campus at Sheldon Jackson College, 5 minutes from Sitka National Historical Park, the Sheldon Jackson Museum is an octagonal treasure box crammed full of beautiful Native tools, art, boats, and clothing, the likes of which you may not see in such artistry anywhere else in Alaska. This little museum is the perfect size—a visual cornucopia in a postage stamp–sized building so you never get "museum feet." The college and museum are named for the 5-foot-tall, fiesty Presbyterian missionary Sheldon Jackson, who came to Alaska in 1877. He lobbied vigorously in Congress for funds to educate Native peoples; he was responsible for the "school ma'am schooner," which transported teachers into ru-

Sitka
_____
*Places
to Visit*

ral Alaska; and he helped import the first reindeer herds to what was then the Territory of Alaska to fend off widespread starvation in the villages. Many of the treasures in this museum come from early journeys to Native villages.

Alaska Raptor Rehabilitation Center Although Buddy, the center's most famous resident, is flying free with the angels now, there are others who still need your help. Volta collided with a powerline. Contact hit an airplane. Elder got trapped in barbed wire while trying to steal ducks. Beauty is from Kodiak and Midi can't fly. While these 5 unfortunates are all bald eagles, many other raptors live here. "Help Us Help the Birds!" is the slogan used by the center, which receives no state or federal funding. Your contributions support the work here and help these "patients" return to the wild. About 80 percent of the injuries these birds have suffered are human-caused by such things as bullets, traps, oil slicks, and the like. Presentations and tours at the center usually coincide with cruise ship schedules. The center is located off Sawmill Creek Road, a 10-minute walk from the historical park. For more information, call (907) 747-8662.

Pies Hands down, the **Nugget Restaurant** at the Sitka Airport has the best pies in town. They are famous all over Alaska. You will often see folks boarding planes with the tell-tale bakery boxes tucked under their arms for pie lovers back home. The pies are baked in town but sold only at the Nugget. The list is long, but here's a sampling of the most popular, available in season: strawberry, banana-coconut, blackberry-rhubarb, chocolate "moose," and cherry crisp. Airport food can be notoriously bad, but the Nugget offers pretty tasty fare—a relief, since bad weather year-round often grounds travelers in Sitka. Open daily, 5:30am to 7:30pm.

Bald Eagle Sightings Okay, get ready. We're about to—gasp!—give **McDonald's** "Golden Arches" its first four-star rating ever (at least in this guidebook series). It's not, however, for its Big Mac, but for its parking lot, which is the best place in town to see bald eagles. The tree and beach at low tide are often jammed with 30 or more eagles. Head north from town (about 1.5 miles) on Halibut Point Road.

Watching the Sunset While we're on the subject of extraordinary parking lots, amble up Halibut Point Road from McDonald's a few hundred yards to **SeaMart,** the local grocery store. The parking lot drops off into Sitka Sound. People laugh when they tell you (but they swear they're not kidding) that unless you are up in the mountains, this is the best place in Sitka to watch the sunset. They're right.

Crimes Gotham City has nothing on Sitka. This is a town that thrives on the "Police Blotter." Printed 5 days a week in the

Sitka Sentinel, the column is sometimes so quaint that the *Anchorage Daily News* reprints selections for its readers statewide. Consider these top-of-the-list, heinous crimes: "June 12—Two boys apprehended playing hackysack in the middle of Lincoln Street. They promised never to do it again." "June 21—Police were unable to locate the vehicle which drove over the traffic cones at Sheldon Jackson College. An officer put the cones back in their upright position." "July 3—A woman reported finding a 50-pound box of frozen fish in the middle of the highway. She put it in her freezer until the owner can claim it."

The Pioneer Bar Also known as "The P-Bar," this is an old-time establishment, famous, as one local says, for "all-around characters and fishermen." Windows overlook the harbor, and the walls are plastered with photos of boats and fish, with this maxim overhead: "There is nothing, absolutely nothing, half so much worth doing as simply messing about in boats." It can get smoky, but it's a friendly, down-home meeting place. For live action, go Friday night. Located at 212 Katlian Street; (907) 747-3456.

Famous Ghost They say she was never happy when she returned to Russia; she loved Sitka. Her bones are in the old country, and her ghost has been seen at St. Michael's Cathedral and several times at the Bishop's House. She is **Princess Maksoutov,** second wife of the last governor of Russian America. One story has it that during the restoration of the Bishop's House in the 1980s, an historian was late for the escorted tour of the house, an event on the agenda of the Second International Conference on Russian America. As he entered, a woman in period costume silently indicated with a sweep of her arm that he should follow her upstairs. She led the way to the chapel where the other conferees were assembled. He turned to thank her, but she had disappeared. He later remarked to his colleagues that the guide in costume was a nice touch. They looked baffled. It was not until he was looking through the archives at historical portraits that he came across the portrait of the second Princess Maksoutov. There she was—his guide at the Bishop's House.

SHOPPING

Sitka Rose Gallery Named for the Sitka rose bush that blooms out front, this lovely little gallery is situated in a quaint Victorian house on Lincoln Street, across from the harbor. The little turreted building is 100 years old and a piece of art in itself. The gallery features sculpture, painting, and Native art, representing more than 80 artists around Alaska. Teri Rofkar, one of the owners and an internationally renowned weaver, is full of stories and good advice on what's best to do in Sitka. ("If

I were you, I wouldn't be shopping; I'd be fishing," she tells one customer with a warm-hearted laugh.) Go in and chat. It's a delightful experience.

The Russian American Company With its rich assortment of Russian and Alaskan handicrafts, this store is upstairs at the **MacDonald Bayview Trading Company** (407 Lincoln Street; (907) 747-6228) in downtown Sitka. A tribute to one part of Sitka's heritage, it has some gorgeous and colorful things, from hand-painted lacquer boxes and religious icons to nesting dolls and Russian candy. Right next door, overlooking the water, is the pleasant **Bayview Restaurant,** (907) 747-5440, where you can keep in the Russian theme. Besides good soup-and-sandwich fare, it has samplings from the old country like borscht and piroshki. Open daily in the summer.

DESTINATIONS OUT

Sea Otter & Wildlife Quest This tour, offered by **Allen Marine Tours,** cruises down Olga and Neva Straits toward Salisbury Sound. On the way, you'll see bald eagles, sometimes eaglets in the nest, Sitka deer, maybe a bear, very often a humpback whale, and almost always those "little old men of the sea," the sea otters. In fact, if you don't see an otter, a whale, or a bear, these guys will give you half your money back. Even in rainy or foggy weather, it's one of the best wildlife tours, and it's all in protected waters. Trips depart from Crescent Harbor in downtown Sitka. Fare is $85/adults; $40/children 12 and under. Operates May to Oct. Contact Allen Marine Tours, PO Box 1049, Sitka, AK 99835-1049; (907) 747-8100.

Stellar Wildlife and Exploring A favorite tour of these local naturalists is a late-evening sunset cruise to St. Lazaria Island to watch the petrels return from the sea. The beautiful island wildlife refuge with its steep, sharp cliffs is black with birds such as the little clown-faced puffins and common murres. (Be advised this trip is over open water if you are prone to seasickness.) The 30-foot vessel, equipped with underwater hydrophone for listening to whales, can take 4 people fishing or 6 people touring. Contact Stellar Wildlife and Exploring, 2810 Sawmill Creek Boulevard, Sitka, AK 99835; (907) 747-6157.

FESTIVALS/EVENTS

Sitka Summer Music Festival If you love music and beauty and beautiful music, come to Sitka in June. In 1996, the Sitka Summer Music Festival celebrated its 25th birthday. Internationally renowned musicians come back year after year and consider it an honor to be asked to play here. The people of Sitka love "their" musicians and they treat them like visiting royalty with down-home style. It's all very contagious. The grandeur of the stage at the Centennial Building frames the concerts to perfection. The backdrop is all windows out to ice-streaked mountains and Sitka Sound. Look particularly for the performances of a lively, bearded, energetic, elf-like violinist who answers to the name of Paul Rosenthal. A former student of Jascha Heifetz, Paul is the genius behind the festival and a delightful character to boot. For tickets and information, contact PO Box 3333, Sitka, AK 99835; (907) 747-6774.

Sitka Writers' Symposium This popular writers' gathering coincides with the music festival in the middle of June. You do not have to be a writer to participate. You just have to love ideas, the written word, and the discussion of the values and forces that influence our global village. Every year, the Island Institute in Sitka pulls together a small faculty—usually writers, poets, and always one leader who is an Alaska Native—and organizes the week-long forum around a current topic of interest. Writers are welcome to bring their manuscripts for critique. For more information, contact the Island Institute, Box 2420, Sitka, AK 99835; (907) 747-3794.

BEST RESTAURANTS

Editor's note: Many locals, when asked to name the best restaurant in town, say "The Fiddlehead in Juneau." When pressed, they start grinning and inevitably answer, "Tell people to make friends really quickly so they'll get invited over for dinner." Never fear: there are a few pleasurable gastronomic experiences in Sitka; but if you do get invited over for dinner, don't refuse.

The Channel Club ★ Seven miles from downtown, the Channel Club is for serious carnivores. Bill and Dotty Aragón have owned it for more than 22 years. They serve "corn-fed Nebraska beef, which is fresh cut on the premises and has never been frozen." They also serve plenty of fresh seafood and boast a salad bar with 35 different kinds of salads. The windows look out to Sitka Sound and the interior is "Alaska bush," complete with moose antlers, crab shells, and glass fish balls hanging from the walls. Limited seating for nonsmokers. ■ *7 miles out along Halibut Point Rd (call a taxi or the Channel Club's courtesy van); 2906 Halibut Point Rd, Sitka; (907) 747-9916; $$ (steak: $16–$20, salmon: $16); full bar; AE, DC, MC, V; local checks OK; dinner daily, summer and winter (closed 3 weeks in Jan for maintenance).*

The Raven Room ★ If you want a white-tablecloth, candlelit dinner, the Raven Room is your best choice. In the heart of town, the restaurant has a nice view of the harbor and reflects Sitka's friendly, small-town atmosphere. The staff is welcoming, the service prompt, and, considering the lack of real competition in town, the menu is quite inventive. Seafood dishes include spotted prawn sauté with crisp snow peas, seafood fettuccine, broiled tropical halibut topped with pineapple salsa and a splash of tequila, the local favorite of beer-batter halibut, and Dungeness crab. ■ *First floor of Hotel Westmark Shee Atika, in the center of town; 330 Seward St, Sitka; (907) 747-6465; $$$; full bar; AE, DC, DIS, MC, V; local checks only; breakfast, lunch, and dinner, daily.* ⟁

The Backdoor Cafe This is the place for the best coffee and gossip in town. At the back door of the Old Harbor Bookstore, the little cafe is somewhat like a cave, but anybody who's anybody in Sitka comes in here. ■ *Walk through the Old Harbor Bookstore or come around the alley to the back door; 104 Barracks St, Sitka; (907) 747-8856; $; no credit cards; checks OK.*

Marina Restaurant Although the menu is part Mexican and part Italian, go Italian. Even the waiters will give you a wink and an aside to steer clear of the south-of-the-border section. The pasta and pizza are delicious and the views of Sitka Sound are nice. It is the only restaurant in town open late for dinner. During the music festival, you can hobnob here with musicians after their evening concerts. ■ *A 5-minute walk west along Harbor Dr from the Centennial Building; 205 Harbor Dr, Sitka; (907) 747-8840; $$; full bar; AE, DC, MC, V; local checks OK; lunch and dinner, daily; closed Sun, Jan and Feb.* ⟁

Van Winkle and Daigler Frontier Cuisine The names of the owners—Van Winkle and Daigler—and the location of this cheerful restaurant have inspired the local tongue-in-cheek nickname "VD by the Sea." Our best tip: Go mid-afternoon to eat mud pie. Why? When the restaurant is full, it's far too smoky. The second reason is that the scene is classic Alaska bush. The sea view is terrific, but at busy times you'd never know it, because pick-ups park right in front of the windows. This is the kind of set-up that makes half of Alaska shake their heads, roll their eyes, and mutter, "Only in Alaska!" The other half, of course, are those who own the pick-ups and the restaurant, and who are too busy eating to care two hoots about the view. ■ *A 5-minute walk from the Centennial Building; 228 Harbor Dr, Sitka; (907) 747-3396; $$; full bar; AE, MC, V; local checks OK; lunch and dinner, daily, and breakfast on Sun.*

BEST LODGINGS

Westmark Shee Atika Lodge ★★ "Shee Atika" is an old name for Sitka. It is the name the Tlingit people gave to their home here, long before the arrival of the Russians. "Shee" is Baranof Island. "Shee Atika" means roughly "the settlement on the outside of Shee." Some translate it as "the village behind the islands." Today, this downtown hotel is owned by the Tlingit people of the region, under the aegis of the Shee Atika Corporation, and managed by Holland-America/Westours. Recently renovated, the hotel is decorated with Tlingit motifs and artworks. For the best views, reserve a room on the fourth or fifth floors, east wing, overlooking the water. The third floor, west wing, can be noisy late at night when the bar streetside lets out. ■ *Located in the center of town; 330 Seward St, Sitka, AK 99835; (907) 747-6241; $$$; AE, DC, DIS, MC, V; checks OK; breakfast, lunch, and dinner, daily.* ♿

Crescent Harbor Hideaway ★

A stone's throw from the water, this charming historic home, recently renovated, overlooks Crescent Harbor. It has 2 guest units equipped with private bath and entrances. Devotees of Stellar sea lions or pelagic birds should opt to stay here and join their B&B hosts on an ocean adventure. Walt Cunningham and Susan Stanford are experienced commercial fishermen, biologists, and marine mammal researchers. They offer custom-designed, small boat charters for their guests. No smoking. ■ *Directly across from Crescent Harbor, downtown; 709 Lincoln St, Sitka, AK 99835; (907) 747-4900 (phone and fax); $$ ($65–105/double); MC, V; checks OK; continental breakfast; open year-round.*

Karras Bed and Breakfast ★

The Karras' home reflects a delightful mixture of Greek and Tlingit cultures, homey atmosphere, unique foods, and some great views. It's like having Santa Claus and Earth Mother running a B&B. Bertha is Tlingit and gathers traditional food from the woods and sea coast to bring to her table. Pete is Greek, and at Christmas he actually moonlights as Jolly Old Saint Nick. In summer, he wields a fishing rod and a spatula. He's a great breakfast cook. (No smoking or alcohol allowed.) ■ *Up the hill from the Pioneer Bar; 230 Kogwanton St, Sitka, AK 99835; (907) 747-3978; $$; MC, V; checks, traveler's checks OK; breakfast daily.*

WILDERNESS LODGES/CABINS

Baranof Wilderness Lodge at Baranof Warm Springs Bay

★★★★ This lodge is located 20 air miles over the mountains from Sitka, on the east side of Baranof Island, and the flight alone will stop your heart from beating. Jagged peaks, glaciers, and mountain passes sail past the cockpit windows until you descend, swooping over a roaring river and a spectacular waterfall, to land on floats at the head of Warm Springs Bay. You'll fall in love with this bay and the lodge, originally built in the 1980s by the grandson of Alaska's most beloved territorial governor, Ernest "Pop" Gruening. Cabins sit close to the water, meals are family style and delicious, and the fishing is great. ■ *20 air miles from Sitka, on the east side of Baranof Island; PO Box 2187, Sitka, AK 99835 (June–Sept), (907) 752-0154; PO Box 42, Norden, CA 95724 (Oct–April), (916) 582-8132.*

Tongass National Forest Cabins

The best deal in all of Southeast Alaska are the 23 U.S. Forest Service cabins located on Baranof and Chichagof Islands, which can be rented for $25/night. They are situated in some of the loveliest spots in

Southeast, and several have the best fishing for miles. A few are exquisitely built log cabins, but most others are simple A-frames. They are minimally equipped and you will need to bring everything with you—sleeping bags, pads, matches, food, gear. Access is by hiking, kayaking, fly-in, or skiffing. ■ *U.S. Forest Service Sitka Ranger District, 201 Katlian St, Ste 109, Sitka, AK 99835; (907) 747-6671.*

WRANGELL

A visit to Wrangell and Petersburg offers a fascinating "Tale of Two Cities" perspective upon the divided economy and culture of Southeast Alaska. In Southeast, there are loggers and there are fishermen, and they don't always get along. Wrangell, the lumber town, is much older than Petersburg, the fishing town, with a history that weaves together threads of the ancient Tlingit culture and the cultures of three world powers—Russia, Britain, and the United States—who have occupied the region in more recent times. Today, Wrangell's mill is closed, and it's trying hard to develop a tourist industry, but it retains its gritty mill-town character.

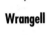

Wrangell

Although the town was founded by Russian traders in the early 1800s, the Tlingits long dominated the region. Perhaps the greatest carver in the history of the Tlingit nation lived here 200 years ago. The museum holds four of his totem poles, thought to be the oldest Tlingit house posts in existence. A replica of a clan house on Shakes Island, in the city harbor, contains copies of the old posts, crafted by modern master carvers.

Aside from the museum and Shakes House, Wrangell does not offer much sense of its rich history. It's an unpretentious little town that, until recently, relied on the timber industry for its livelihood. When political and economic tides conspired to shut down the local sawmill, Wrangell was set adrift. That's bound to change, though. Wrangell is the gateway to the Stikine River, a wild and spectacular waterway with headwaters in Canada. Nearby, there is also Anan Creek Black Bear Observatory, which is becoming so popular with visitors the Forest Service is currently pondering a lottery system to limit the number of people per day.

Access

Wrangell has daily jet service year-round via Alaska Airlines. The state ferry also makes frequent stops here.

Information

Pick up information at the **Wrangell Chamber of Commerce,** PO Box 49, Wrangell, AK 99929; (907) 874-3901.

PLACES TO VISIT

Chief Shakes House Chief Shakes House, situated on Shakes Island in the city boat harbor, is a wonderful replica of an original clan house built by a Civilian Conservation Corps crew in the 1930s. There were eight chiefs named "Shakes." Shakes House is open when cruise ships are in port, or by appointment. To visit, call Nora Rinchart at (907) 874-2023 or Margaret Sturtevant at (907) 874-3747.

Wrangell Museum The museum is in temporary quarters until the new cultural center is completed. It's still worth a visit to see the original Shakes totem poles and artifacts from the early days of white settlement. Located at Second and Bevier Streets; (907) 874-3770.

Petroglyph Beach About a 10-minute walk north of the dock is a beach where ancient artists—for reasons unknown today—carved symbols, faces, fish, and seashell spirals into the rocks. Several thousand years old, these carved rocks perhaps served as territorial markers or pointed the way to good fishing on the Stikine River. Perhaps they were ritual carvings to invoke the spirit helpers of the animals killed in the hunt. Many shapes are geometric; others are recognizable as fish or whales. Along the way, you may meet local children peddling garnets from Garnet Ledge near the mouth of the Stikine River.

DESTINATIONS OUT

Anan Black Bear Observatory/Cabin Thirty miles south of Wrangell, large runs of salmon returning to Anan Lake attract a bevy of black bears. The Forest Service maintains a popular rental cabin here. There is also a day observatory, a mile upstream from the cabin. For more information, contact U.S. Forest Service, Wrangell Ranger District, 525 Bennett St, PO Box 51, Wrangell, AK 99929; (907) 874-2323.

Wrangell

Destinations Out

Stikine River From its headwaters in British Columbia, the Stikine River flows for 400 miles, entering salt water about 5 miles north of Wrangell. It is a popular destination for birders, fishermen, and river runners. Depending on the time of year, you can see hooligan running, sea lions feeding, and thousands of bald eagles perched on trees and stumps. The river served as a transportation route into Canada during the Stikine, Cassiar, and Klondike Gold Rushes that took place here between 1861 and 1898. Sixteen miles upriver, the Forest Service maintains Chief Shakes Hot Springs, where you can soak in the hot tubs. Near the mouth of the river is Garnet Ledge, where the children of Wrangell mine the garnets they sell you in town. The Stikine is fast flowing, averaging 8 knots per hour. River runners who venture onto the Stikine usually start at Telegraph Creek (pop. 300), in British Columbia. It is the only town along the river and about 130 miles from Alaska tidewater. Above Telegraph Creek is the Stikine's spectacular Grand Canyon, where cliff walls jut straight up from the river edge, reaching up to 1,000 feet in elevation. The canyon is about 55 miles long and considered dangerous and unnavigable.

Stikine Recreational Cabins   The U.S. Forest Service, Wrangell Ranger District, maintains 13 primitive cabins along the lower Stikine River. These can be reserved for $25/day. The Forest Service also sells maps showing Stikine River canoe and kayak trails for $3 each. For information and reservations, contact U.S. Forest Service, PO Box 51, Wrangell, AK 99929; (907) 874-2323.

GUIDES/OUTFITTERS

Alaska Water Inc.   This company offers custom-designed jet-boat adventures on the Stikine River. They provide a flotation suit, beverages, guided history, and as much excitement or relaxation as you want. Call (800) 347-4462 or (907) 874-2378.

PETERSBURG

Compared with Wrangell, the fishing town of Petersburg is more prosperous, capitalizing on its abundant salmon, natural beauty, and Scandinavian charm. While both communities welcome visitors, neither is on the Love Boat circuit.

Petersburg was founded just before the turn of the century by sturdy Norwegian immigrants who were drawn here by plentiful salmon and halibut and an inexhaustible supply of natural ice from the nearby LeConte Glacier, in which they packed their catch. Many of them were fishermen from the fjord country of western Norway who found a landscape of tall mountains and deep waters remarkably like their homeland. A century later, Petersburg is still dominated by a Scandinavian esthetic and work ethic. The homes are square, wooden, and solid. Descendants of the early immigrants are raising their families here, and some of the boats you see in the harbor are operated by fourth- and fifth-generation Petersburg fishermen.

Above all, Petersburg is an authentic fishing community, untouched by the big-business tourism that has radically changed such places as Juneau and Sitka. You won't find mega-cruise ships, shops filled with trinkets, T-shirts, or gourmet ice cream. Instead, you'll experience a bustling seaport going about the business of catching, processing, and selling seafood. For that reason, Petersburg has never worked very hard at attracting tourists, and services are a bit thin.

If you are comfortable in rain jacket and rubber boots, you're sure to enjoy Petersburg. More than 100 inches of rain falls every year, moisture that nurtures salmon streams and gives the rain forest a thousand shades of green. Consider yourself blessed when the sun breaks through and reveals the stunning coastal mountain range with its jutting pinnacle, Devil's Thumb.

Access

Petersburg is served by Alaska Airlines daily jet service. It's possible to leave San Francisco in the morning and arrive in Petersburg in the afternoon. The Alaska Marine Highway vessels also make frequent stops here.

Information

Stop in at **Petersburg Visitors Center,** (907) 772-4636, 1 block above Main Street, to pick up information. **Viking Travel,** (800) 327-2571 or (907) 772-3818, also books charters.

THINGS TO DO

Whales, Icebergs, and Mountains Classic Petersburg excursions are whale watching in Frederick Sound; a visit to LeConte Glacier, the southernmost tidewater glacier in North America; and flightseeing around Devil's Thumb. The best local charters are **Sights Southeast** for whale watching, (907) 772-4503; **Real Alaska Adventures** for boat trips of all kinds, (907) 772-4121; and **Pacific Wing** for flightseeing, (907) 772-9258.

Walking Everywhere Stroll the boardwalks that cross Mitkof Island's muskeg meadows. Wander along the harbor. Get up early, buy a caffe latte at Helse, and park yourself on a bench overlooking the "Old Boat Harbor," a block off Main Street. During salmon season, you'll see cannery laborers hurrying to jobs, fishing crews readying their gear, and boats of all kinds coming and going. All this activity may inspire the more adventurous to rent a skiff and motor down Wrangell Narrows—really the best way to get a feel for how people live here.

Hiking There are several good hiking trails. **Three Lakes Trail** is a delightful hike, mostly on boardwalk, which connects three lakes named Sand, Hill, and Crane. Go to Mile 21 on Mitkof Highway, then turn on Three Lakes Road. The trail begins at the sign for Crane Lake. The **Ohmer Creek Trail** starts a couple of miles beyond the Three Lakes turnoff on Mitkof Highway. You walk 2 miles through a deep, green, old-growth forest, across a floating bridge over a series of pools, and into a wildflower meadow. The **Raven's Roost Trail** is more challenging. It's 8 miles round-trip to a rustic cabin, and views of Frederick Sound are great. The trail begins 2 miles from downtown, near the airport. The cabin may be reserved at the U.S. Forest Service visitors center for $25/night.

Kayaking Rent a boat or take a guided trip through **Tongass Kayak Adventures**. Trips range from afternoon paddles to Petersburg Creek ($45/person) to multi-day trips to LeConte Glacier. Week-long tours are $1,295/person. For information, contact Tongass Kayak Adventures, PO Box 787, Petersburg, AK 99833; (907) 772-4600.

Mountain Biking Pedal remote roads with **Terry's Unforgettable Charters and Expeditions,** 901 Sandy Beach Rd, (907) 772-2200.

FESTIVALS/EVENTS

Little Norway Festival This festival takes place the third weekend of May and commemorates Syttende Mai (May 17), the day in 1814 when Norway declared its independence from Sweden. The celebration includes smorgasbords for sampling Scandinavian delicacies, displays of traditional crafts, and a community-wide pageant that's a kitschy mix of old-country dancing and corny Norwegian humor.

Petersburg's Salmon Derby This fishing derby takes place Memorial Day weekend. What sets it apart from all the other derbies in Southeast is the level of competition. Casual sports fishers will find themselves competing with the most competitive and successful commercial fishermen anywhere. But that doesn't mean the skipper of a 78-foot seiner has a leg up. It's still a matter of luck.

BEST RESTAURANTS

Helse ★★ This cozy little cafe on Sing Lee Alley, in the heart of Petersburg's historic district, is the best place to eat in town, bar none. Unfortunately, it offers only coffee and lunch. Deli sandwiches are huge, and specials run from grain salads to enchiladas. A bowl of soup and fresh, homemade bread is always a good choice here. ■ *Downtown, at the corner of Nordic Dr and Sing Lee Alley; 3 Sing Lee Alley, Petersburg; (907) 772-3444; $; no alcohol; no credit cards; checks OK; open 7am–6pm.*

Homestead Cafe ★ The local fishermen are in their element in this little cafe. The Homestead serves good, standard American breakfast fare: eggs, bacon, blueberry pancakes, and omelets. You can't go wrong with burgers the rest of the day. Fish is always available but mostly comes fried. Coffee refills are endless, and that's what keeps the oldtimers on their breaks coming back day after day at 10am and 3pm on the nose. Note that the stools nearest the door are unofficially reserved for the town elders. You'll have to endure uncomfortable stares if you happen to be sitting there when coffee time rolls around. ■ *Center of downtown; 206 Nordic Dr, Petersburg; (907) 772-3900; $$; AE, DC, DIS, MC, V; checks OK; open 24 hours, Mon–Sat.*

Pellerito's Pizza ★ Pellerito's is conveniently located across from the ferry terminal, half a mile from downtown. The pizza is good but service is very slow. If possible, call ahead with your order. A large "crab bait" pizza (aka "the works") is $25.

■ *Across from ferry terminal; 1105 S Nordic Dr, Petersburg; (907) 772-3727; $$; full bar; MC, V; local checks OK; open 4pm–10pm, year-round.*

BEST LODGINGS

Broom Hus ★ Sylvia Nilsen's house is one of the solid old Norwegian places that make Petersburg distinctive. The location is terrific—midway between the ferry terminal and downtown—making it a short walk in either direction. You get the basement suite with a pretty garden entrance. From the boat harbor across the street, you can walk to town entirely on the floats. Rate is $80/double. ■ *Midway between the ferry terminal and downtown Petersburg; (907) 772-3459.*

Water's Edge Bed and Breakfast ★ Barry and Kathy Bracken's bed and breakfast is on the bottom level of their split-level seaside home on Sandy Beach Road about 1.5 miles from downtown. They have two rooms—one on the water side and one tucked in the woods with a partial view of the beach. They're located on the edge of the water and have a spectacular view of Frederick Sound and the mountains on the mainland. Barry is a former biologist who offers naturalist excursions and fishing charters on his 28-foot cruiser. Rate is $80–$90/double. ■ *About 1.5 miles from downtown Petersburg, on Sandy Beach Rd (call for directions); (907) 772-3736.*

Petersburg

Lodgings

Scandia House When the Scandia House burned down in 1994, Petersburg lost its oldest, funkiest hotel. But the new Scandia House is clean, quiet, and comfortable and retains the central downtown location. There are rooms of every configuration. All have baths; many have kitchenettes. Rates are $80 to $120 for a double. ■ *Center of downtown Petersburg; (800) 772-5006 or (907) 772-4281.*

WILDERNESS LODGES

Rocky Point Resort ★★★ Only 12 miles from town, this lodge still feels remote. It caters to serious sports fishers. From June to September, guests fish for the region's best: salmon, ling cod, halibut, and trout. The price includes three hearty homecooked meals a day, guided fishing, gear, and use of skiffs: $265/person/day. ■ *12 miles from Petersburg; PO Box 1251, Petersburg, AK 99833; (907) 772-4405; open June–Sept.*

JUNEAU

Flying into Juneau over islands and the Coast Mountains, dipping between mountain peaks to make a landing on Juneau's runway, in full view of the Mendenhall Glacier on a spectacular, bluebird day, you'll look below at sparkling waters, fishing boats, and the occasional multimillion-dollar yacht, and you'll wonder, "Why doesn't everyone in the world live here?"

Not to give away too many family secrets, but an average 90 inches of rain per year and Taku winds that can blow bricks off buildings in the wintertime are a few small clues. As in the rest of Alaska, the cold and dark seem to chase away the snow-birds. But that's what makes it a grand place for those of us on the far edges of sanity and for visitors from saner climates who want to see how the other half lives.

Still, there are a million other reasons that make Juneau a wonderful place to live, work, and play. With the ocean at their front door step and mountains rising steeply out the back-bed-room window, Juneauites love to play—and they play hard. They paddle, hang-glide, sail, parasail, ice climb, kayak, and row in all kinds of wild weather. The sun comes out, and they're off to hike the ridges. They helicopter pianos to the top of Mount Roberts, while the party folks scramble up through the mud with tuxedos and ball gowns in their knapsacks, and then dance till dawn.

This is the capital city of Alaska. It was gold in "them thar hills" that lured a couple of unsteady old prospectors here more than 100 years ago, and it was oil that sucked in a lot of the present-day generation in their younger years. Not the raw stuff, but what it could buy. That whole, heady, high-adrenaline environment came from having, as one young lawyer described it, "all that raw meat on the table." Alaska was rolling in dough from the late 1960s to the early 1980s. Oil was discovered at Prudhoe Bay on the North Slope in 1968, then in the 1980s the price of oil took a nose dive and the oil reserves began tapering off. However, 90 percent of the state's budget is still run on oil, and the seat of state government is in Juneau. Only 30,000 people live in Juneau today. A few thousand less were here in the 1970s, but that kind of money put Juneau on the world map.

True to the city's frontier character, many of the high-flying deals were cut in the old Bubble Room in the Baranof Hotel, under the capricious eye of the Bubble Lady, a painted portrait of a saucy gal dressed in strategically placed bubbles. (Alas, although the new bar there is still called the Bubble Room, the fair lady went up in flames during a fire several years ago.)

The Bubble Lady's place of honor is not surprising given the town's founding fathers. Joe Juneau and Dick Harris, two down-on-their-luck-and-much-in-their-cups prospectors, tottered off the boat in Sitka in the fall of 1880 and were grubstaked by an old mining engineer there named George Pilz. But they did not impress their employer with their high moral character. "Sinful was the way they spent their days," Pilz complained. Between hooch and women, they squandered nearly everything he gave them. They dragged back to Sitka empty-handed.

Pilz knew there was gold up north. The Indians had told him so. But winter was coming. And there was no one else but these two ne'er-do-wells to send out. If not for their guide, Chief Cowee of the Auk Indian tribe, Juneau's history might have been quite different. The chief led them to a small tributary flowing into Gastineau Channel, soon to be known as the legendary Gold Creek. The rush was on!

"I broke some rock with a hammer," wrote Harris later. "Juneau and I could hardly believe our eyes. We knew it was gold, but . . . so much!" News of the fabulously rich strike spread like wildfire. Prospectors poured in from all over the Territory of Alaska. Harris named the region Silver Bow. The miners, in turn, named the town Harrisburg. But then, one day, they got mad at Harris and renamed the town after his partner, Joe Juneau. Both founders died penniless—Harris in a sanitorium in Oregon and Juneau in Dawson City, where he went following the Klondike Gold Rush. Both are home now, buried in Juneau in Evergreen Cemetery. Alaskans have a special fondness for their homegrown characters.

While some made fortunes panning in Juneau's rivers and creeks, the big money was in hard-rock mining. Three big companies had large-scale mining operations going full-tilt here at one time. The mountains behind Juneau are a honeycomb of old mining tunnels. The first and most profitable mine, though, was on Douglas Island, just across Gastineau Channel from downtown Juneau. Over the course of 35 years, $66 million was taken out. At its zenith, there were four mines, 2,000 workers, and diggings 2,000 feet beneath the surface of the earth. Safety standards were not high priority. The first big gold came out of the Glory Hole, which was not named because of "hallelujah-there's-gold-here!" but because it sent so many men on that one-way road to glory.

Juneau

While Juneau was booming as the first really big gold strike in the Territory of Alaska, Sitka's star was waning with the declining fortunes of the fur industry. So, in 1906, the capital of the territory moved from Sitka to Juneau. There it has stayed—despite several attempts in recent years by many vociferous parties to move it northwards to the whistlestop of Willow.

For such a small town in a fairly remote location, Juneau has a highly educated, well-traveled, articulate, and artistic populace. With wilderness only moments away, in town there's professional theater and music, a strong sense of community, a university, and the best high school drill team in the whole world—no fooling.

Somewhat like the weather here, Juneau has two distinct seasons: the political season or the convening of the state legislature, called "the session," which runs from January to May, and the tourist season, which starts with the arrival of the first cruise ships toward the end of May and lasts until the beginning of October, when the last ship sails out of Gastineau Channel. The average high temperature in July is 65°F and the average low temperature in January is 20°F.

Access

You can get to Juneau only by air or sea. There are no roads to the state's capital. However, Juneau has regularly scheduled, daily air service on **Alaska Airlines,** (800) 426-0333, and **Delta Airlines,** (800) 221-1212 (winter only). Juneau is also a regular stop on the ferry system. For a booklet with times, schedules, rates, and reservations, contact the **Alaska Marine Highway System,** PO Box 25535, Juneau, AK 99802-5535; toll-free (800) 642-0066. The ferry links up with Alaska's road system about a 7- to 9-hour ferry ride north from Juneau to Haines or Skagway. Juneau is also on the regular itinerary of Alaska ports of call for more than 20 cruise ships.

Information

You can pick up information in two places. **Davis Log Cabin Visitors Information Center** is housed in a replica of an old log cabin built in the late 1800s, which once served as a church, an office for the city brewery, and a soda works. It's a 5- to 10-minute walk up the hill to 134 Third Street, Juneau; (907) 586-2284, fax (907) 586-6304. The 24-hour "events hotline" is (907) 586-JUNO. In the summer, there are visitor information booths and a kiosk down at the cruise ship docks.

Tucked into a corner of Centennial Hall, on Egan Drive, the **U.S. Forest Service and National Park Service Information Center** has films, displays, notebooks about backcountry travel, trails, and public-use cabins in the Tongass National Forest, and information on all of Alaska's national parks system, including nearby Glacier Bay National Park. This is also where you obtain a permit for bear viewing at Pack Creek on Admiralty Island. The information center is open daily in summer. Call (907) 586-8751.

Tips on the Town

As one notable bush pilot once said, "Alaska has some of the worst weather that God inflicts upon this earth." Take note. Winter or summer, you can get weathered in (or out of) all Southeastern communities. Even in the height of tourist season, fog can keep you grounded or stranded. So make your plans accordingly. It is not uncommon, given winter storms, to board the plane in Seattle, overfly Juneau, land in Anchorage, fly back to Juneau, overfly Juneau, and end up where you started from. If you think it's funny, just wait; this routine can sometimes go on for days. In that vein, note rule number one for flying in small planes: if the pilot says, "We don't go," do not insist on going if you value your life, no matter what your high-powered schedule says.

Walking Tour of Town In all Southeastern towns, you will learn the most by walking. In Juneau, that takes particular stamina, because streets and stairways (which serve as streets) go straight uphill and up the sides of mountains. Pick up a free walking tour map at the visitors center. The following are a few highlights of any self-guided tour of Alaska's capital city. Starting from the waterfront, note the **Juneau City Library,** 292 Marine Way, (907) 586-5324, which has a commanding view of Gastineau Channel. It is built on top of a parking garage and has windows facing in almost all directions. Up the hill, on Main Street and Fourth Avenue, stands the **State Capitol Building,** (907) 465-2479, with its marble pillars. The Governor's Office is on the third floor and, when the legislature is in session on the second floor, you can sit in and watch the show. Tours of the capitol are available. Across the street is the State Office Building (referred to in Juneau as **"The S.O.B."**). The **State of Alaska Historical Library,** 333 Willoughby Avenue, 8th Floor, (907) 465-2925, yet another Southeastern library with a great view, resides in the S.O.B., off a large airy atrium where free organ recitals happen at noon on Fridays. The **Governor's Mansion,** white-columned with the Mosquito totem pole in front, is a few blocks around the corner, on Calhoun Avenue. It is not open to visitors. However, if you happen to be in Juneau in early December, you may be in time for the governor's holiday open house. All are welcome. Make your way back to Seventh Avenue, above the capitol, to the **Wickersham House,** (907) 586-9001, former home of one of Alaska's important early-day figures, Judge James Wickersham. It is now a museum. If you're up for more exercise, a lovely walk up Basin Road from Seventh Avenue takes you along famous Gold Creek and into the historic Silver Bow mining area between Mount Juneau and Mount Roberts. **Perseverance Trail** continues up from here to **Ebner Falls,** about a 45-minute walk one-way from the Wickersham House.

Juneau

Things to Do

Mount Roberts' Tram A tram starts from the cruise ship dock and travels up the steep slope of Mount Roberts. This is the easy, nonaerobic way to climb the mountain. On a clear day, the view from this alpine lookout is spectacular. If you want a more vigorous workout, you can climb to the same spot in about an hour through lovely steep woods. The trail starts at the top of Star Hill.

Helicopter/Flightseeing Tours At least once during your trip to Alaska you should get up in the air, if only to experience the vastness of this land. **Temsco Helicopters,** (907) 789-9501, offers the Mendenhall Glacier Tour. During this air tour, you actually land on the glacier and glimpse the enormous reservoir of ice in the Juneau Icefield that feeds so many of Southeast's rivers of ice. **Era Helicopters,** (907) 586-2030, which has been dubbed the Indiana Jones of the two helicopter services, takes you up Taku Inlet. One pilot-passenger described it as "more of a rollercoaster ride, very exciting, where you actually fly down inside a glacier." **Wings of Alaska,** (907) 789-0790, flies fixed-wing aircraft for flightseeing adventures over the Juneau icefield or to Taku Glacier Lodge.

Mendenhall Float Trip No self-respecting Alaskan would call this a wilderness trip, when you float through several subdivisions and underneath the highway bridge, but tourists love it, and a lot of cruise ship passengers choose to take this trip. It's not wild water, but there are a few thrills and chills, and it's still beautiful country, as you start off in Mendenhall Lake at the foot of Mendenhall Glacier.

Hiking Juneau has wonderful hiking. Trails and ridges abound. Here are some favorites. The trailheads to **Perseverance-Ebner Falls, Mount Juneau, Granite Creek Basin,** and **Mount Roberts** are all within easy walking distance of downtown. The mellow route takes you to Ebner Falls; a more energetic hike takes you farther, past the falls, to Granite Creek basin. Mount Juneau is the steep mountain rising behind the city. Steep is the watchword here, so be careful. Mount Roberts rises to the west of downtown and is not as steep an ascent as Mount Juneau. **Mount Jumbo** is also a popular climb. This is the highest peak on Douglas Island, which can be seen by looking across Gastineau Channel from city center. (Hiking guides are listed in "Suggested Viewing/Reading" at the end of the chapter.)

Juneau

*Things
to Do*

Biking Located downtown, the folks at **Mountain Gears** (210 N Franklin St, Juneau, AK 99801; (907) 586-4327) can take you on guided bike trips around town or by road to the Mendenhall Glacier. You can also rent your own bike, complete with lock, helmet, and map.

WINTERTIME ACTIVITIES

Eaglecrest Ski Area Juneau is the home and training ground of Olympic downhill skier Hillary Lindh. She grew up skiing the slopes of Eaglecrest, high up on Douglas Island—a ski resort with 30 alpine trails, 8 kilometers of Nordic ski trails, and a vertical drop of 1,400 feet. Skiing here is geared to the intermediate and advanced skier. For information, contact Eaglecrest Ski Area, 155 S Seward Street, Juneau, AK 99801; (907) 790-2000. For ski conditions, call (907) 586-5330.

Juneau-Douglas High School Drill Team From little Juneau, Alaska, they've dazzled the world. In 1995, going toe to toe with the best on the planet, they swept the competition in Nagoya, Japan, to steal three world championships in the International Dance Drill Competition. There's even a proud subsidiary known as "Drill Team Dads." If you're in Juneau during the school year or on the Fourth of July, check them out. The team performs throughout the winter at all Juneau-Douglas High School basketball games and at special events around the state. For a schedule of performances, call the high school at (907) 463-1923.

GUIDES/OUTFITTERS

Alaska Discovery Wilderness Adventures This is one of the oldest and most respected wilderness expedition guiding companies in the state, with quality trips led by knowledgeable and enthusiastic guides. The company emphasizes "leave no trace" camping and donates 10 percent of its profits to environmental organizations working toward the preservation of Alaska's special places. Southeast is home, and the company offers 1- to 12-day canoeing, sea kayaking, and rafting trips to see glaciers, wild rivers, bears, and other wildlife. Canoe Admiralty Island, kayak through Glacier Bay, and raft the Tatshenshini and Alsek Rivers. For a brochure, contact Alaska Discovery Wilderness Adventures, 5449 Shaune Dr, Juneau, AK 99802-0669; (800) 586-1911 or (907) 780-6226; fax (907) 780-4220.

Alaska Rainforest Tours This outfitter offers trip-planning services for the independent, environmentally conscious traveler—a one-stop shopping guide for wilderness travel, whale watching, remote lodges, bed and breakfasts, charter fishing boats, supreme kayaking trips, and much more. The philosophy of the company is to encourage small-scale, grassroots, participatory experiences. They steer travelers into well-run, locally owned small businesses offering high-quality experiences. To receive their *Alaska: The Catalog for Independent Travelers,* mail a check for $5 to Alaska Rainforest Tours, 369 S Franklin Street, Suite 200, Juneau, AK 99801; call (907) 463-3466; fax toll-free from U.S. (800) 493-4453; or from overseas and Canada, fax (local access code + 1) 907-463-4453.

Juneau

*Guides/
Outfitters*

Marine Adventure Sailing Tours (MAST) "If there are whales doing back somersaults with full twists, I'm not going to sail over to the beach and dig clams," says Captain Andy Spear, with his warm, trademark grin, as he describes the custom-tailored trips he puts together for clients from all over the world. The very rich, the very fun, the very talented, and the very smart have sailed with Captain Spear on the *Adventuress,* a 50-foot Down East cutter. This is one of the great deals in Southeast. For under $1,500/day, you can charter the entire boat for four people with full service—that means captain, crew, and gourmet meals. Some of the most popular custom-designed, week-long voyages are to Glacier Bay and Tracy Arm–Ford's Terror. But beware: the captain also plays Cupid. On one such trip to Glacier Bay, Andy, in cahoots with an until-then-luckless

Australian suitor, dressed him and his girlfriend in survival suits so that they could swim in the frigid water with the seals. Then Andy floated a bottle of the finest champagne over on an iceberg. The fellow's girlfriend, who had resisted marriage proposals for 10 years, finally succumbed to the magic of the moment. You will too. For a video of adventure sailing trips, send a returnable $10 deposit to MAST, 945 Fritz Cove Road, Juneau, AK 99801; or call (907) 789-0919. You can also find MAST on the World Wide Web: http://www.alaska.net/~mast.

Wilderness Swift Charters Takes visitors on 3-day voyages to the best of Southeast Alaska via "The Mothership." The *Wilderness Swift* and *Merlin* transport passengers to view glaciers, bears, whales, and bald eagles, and for camping and hiking. It is a unique, small, intimate, participatory experience. You bring food, camping gear, and kayaks on board (kayaks can be rented in town), and the "mothership" carries you off to special places where you can paddle, camp, and hike on shore. This is the best of both worlds, land and sea. Note the company policy: "Wilderness Swift Charters serves only nonconsumptive, low-impact users. In keeping with local, small business efforts to honor the wilderness, we cannot offer hunting and fishing charters." For more information, contact Wilderness Swift Charters, PO Box 22026, Juneau, AK 99802; (907) 463-4942.

Alaska Wilderness Recreation and Tourism Association A group of more than 200 outdoor-oriented businesses. A directory is available by mailing $5 to AWRTA, PO Box 22827, Juneau, AK 99802; (907) 463-3038; or visit their Web site, http://www.alaska.net/~awrta.

PLACES TO VISIT

Alaska State Museum Permanent exhibits take you on a journey through the history of Russian America, the stories of the diverse Native peoples here, and the rich natural history of Alaska. Open daily in summer. Around the corner from Centennial Hall, at 395 Whittier Street; (907) 465-2901.

Mendenhall Glacier A stunning view as you fly in on a clear day, the Mendenhall Glacier, along with the surrounding mountains, is the jewel in Juneau's crown. While it may not be the most spectacular glacier in Alaska—a vast land covered with thousands of glaciers—at only 15 miles from downtown Juneau, it is one of the most dramatic so close to civilization. Hiking trails wind up the rocks on either side of the glacier. Never walk on the ice; glaciers are defined as "rivers of moving ice," and they are riddled with deep, hidden crevasses. There is a U.S. Forest Service Visitors Center at the glacier, located at Mendenhall Loop Road; (907) 789-0097.

Gastineau Salmon Hatchery Visitors Center This hatchery is also known as Douglas Island Pink and Chum (DIPAC), which locals pronounce "die-pack," and that is how it is popularly known. To learn about the lifecycle of the salmon, stop here, on the edge of Gastineau Channel, at 2697 Channel Drive, Juneau; (907) 463-4810.

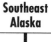

SHOPPING

Annie Kaill's Fine Craft Gallery Friendly, fun, and affordable gifts from Alaska. Open daily, year-round. Located downtown, at 244 Front Street, Juneau; (907) 586-2880.

Foggy Mountain Shop Rugged outdoor clothing and gear. Located across the street from the Baranof Hotel, at 134 N Franklin Street, Juneau; (907) 586-6780.

Portfolio Arts One of the few galleries in Alaska where you can see not only beautiful Native art from Southeast but also intriguing Inupiat and Yup'ik Eskimo art from the north. Everything is one of a kind. Located downtown, at 210 Ferry Way, Suite 101, Juneau; (907) 586-8111.

Decker Gallery Rie Munoz, a popular, longtime Juneau artist, is featured here. Her bright and cheerful artwork, depicting village people and everyday life in Alaska, can be seen in homes throughout the state. Located downtown, at 233 S Franklin Street, Juneau; (907) 463-5536.

Nightlife

William Spear Design A visit here is a hilarious experience, from the art itself down to the folks running the shop, who include Bill (the wacky artist), his classy wife Susan, and Deanne, a Tlingit comedienne of inexhaustible good humor. Bill's a pin designer. But these are no ordinary pins. Some are exquisite colorful jewelry (birds and fish); some are renegade (the death-and-sex series); and some are autobiographical ("The night my goddamn drink caught on fire"). And they're sold everywhere from Chamonix, France, to Barrow, Alaska. Located at 165 S Franklin Street. Write to 227 Seventh Avenue, Juneau, AK 99801; (907) 586-4132. Also check out their Web site: Http://www.carmel-net.com/spearpins.

NIGHTLIFE

Naa Kahidi Theater This is a unique, professional Native theater company, supported by the clans of Southeastern Alaska. Dressed in traditional regalia, from stunning masks to the famous Chilkat dancing robes, performers engage in a dramatic re-creation of the legends and stories of their people. One cannot help but be moved by the spirit and beauty of the performances. The group has toured extensively throughout Alaska and the United States. There are performances all summer at the Sealaska Cultural Arts Park on South Franklin Street. For information, contact Naa Kahidi Theater, One Sealaska Plaza, Suite 201, Juneau, AK 99801; (907) 463-4844.

Perseverance Theatre   This is community, regional, professional, and multicultural theater at its best. From its first Juneau production, *Pure Gold,* with local old-timers re-telling gold-rush stories and grizzly bear encounters, to the staging of *Yup'ik Antigone,* a Yup'ik Eskimo rendition of the famous Greek tragedy, which toured New York and Paris, Perseverance Theatre has vaulted into the hearts of Juneau, and all of Alaska. Call for performance schedules. The theater is located on Douglas Island. For more information, contact Perseverance Theatre, 914 Third St, Douglas, AK 99824; (907) 364-2421.

Bar Scene   Tourists go to the Red Dog Saloon; locals go to the Alaskan Hotel; old-time Juneau (young and old) goes to the Triangle; and the politicians schmooze in the Bubble Room of the Baranof Hotel (but the story is they loosen up later at the Triangle). The Red Dog, the Alaskan, and the Triangle are all within shooting distance of each other on Franklin Street. You can't miss 'em. Ask any local. The Baranof Hotel is a couple of blocks up the hill on Franklin Street. Slide into any one of these scenes with an Alaskan Amber or Alaska Pale Ale, brewed right here in the capital city.

DESTINATIONS OUT

Tracy Arm Adventure Cruise   While cruise ships and large passenger boats also cruise out to the enchanting glaciers in Tracy Arm, if you want the premier experience, our advice is to go small by signing up for a day trip with **Wilderness Swift Charters'** cruise, narrated by Alaska naturalists. Space is limited to 10 passengers. Book early with **Alaska Rainforest Tours,** (907) 463-3466 or (907) 586-2959. A day trip out of Juneau, Tracy Arm will take you thousands of years back into the Ice Age. Be out on deck when you "cross the bar," the terminal moraine of the glacier, which now lies at the head of this 2,000-year-old jewel-like fjord. From here, it is 25 miles of steep canyon walls, intense blue-green water, and intricate maneuvering through icebergs to get to the north and south faces of the Sawyer Glacier.

Taku Glacier Lodge   Picturesque **Taku Glacier Lodge** lies at the end of a spectacular flight over the mountains and up Taku Inlet, a deep-water fjord south of Juneau. **Wings of Alaska,** (907) 789-0790, flies seaplanes from Juneau's downtown waterfront for a 3-hour tour that includes a salmon barbecue at the lodge (1 hour of flightseeing, 2 hours at the lodge). Built in 1923, 30 miles from Juneau, Taku Lodge was once used as a hunting and fishing camp. Today, the lodge entertains folks for lunch and dinner all through the summer, from mid-May to October. The historic log cabin sits across from the Hole-in-the-Wall Glacier, and even has a resident black bear named Scarface, whom you can often see nosing about the premises. For more information, contact Wings of Alaska, PO Box 33597, Juneau, AK 99803; phone and fax (907) 586-8258.

Pack Creek Bear Viewing

The **Stan Price Brown Bear Sanctuary** at Pack Creek on Admiralty Island recently has become a popular destination. Named for a marvelous old homesteader who lived here among the bears until his death in 1989, the sanctuary is only 28 miles from Juneau. To protect Pack Creek from its own popularity, the Forest Service has now initiated a permit system, designating two places for watching bears: a gravel bar near the mouth of the creek and an observation tower deeper into the woods that offers wonderful opportunities to observe bears in their natural habitat. You will see the crumbling remains of Stan's cabin, floathouse, and gardens. No camping is allowed near Pack Creek, only on nearby islands. Permits are required from June 1 to Sept 10. For more details, and lists of guides and charter services to Pack Creek, contact U.S. Forest Service Information Center, 101 Egan Dr, Juneau, AK 99801; (907) 586-8751; or Admiralty Island National Monument, (907) 586-8790.

Tenakee, Pelican, and Elfin Cove

Cruise the Inside Passage of Alaska in "The Big Blue Canoes," aka the Alaska state ferries, and visit some of Alaska's picturesque fishing hamlets and hot springs. Everyone travels by ferry in Southeast. It's fun, colorful, local, and a cheap way to get out on the water to see fjords, whales, and fishing boats, and catch up on the regional gossip—a cruise ship experience at bargain rates. Even the visiting circus travels by ferry, including the elephants.

FESTIVALS/EVENTS

Fourth of July

In the early days of Juneau's history, the Fourth of July was the highlight of summer. There were canoe races, rock-drilling contests, and firemen battling each other with firehoses. The firemen today are still dousing each other (and the crowd) with firehoses, to the beat of local bands, in an all-day street dance on Douglas Island. That's after the parade and the sand sculpture contest, a race against the tides. This is the height of old-fashioned, rip-roaring good fun found everywhere in Southeast on the Fourth. But it is the spectacular fireworks over the harbor at midnight on July 3 that set Juneau apart.

Alaska Folk Festival

A springtime, cabin-fever, musical jamboree that goes on for 10 days in April, this event attracts talented musicians and bands from all over Alaska. Alaskans know how to make music, and they know how to party. This is a good time. Call the visitors center for details; (907) 586-2284.

The Fiddlehead Restaurant and Bakery ★★★★

Homey and folksy, the original Fiddlehead Restaurant and Bakery has been a welcome oasis for Southeasterners for more than 20 years. This former natural foods hippie collective now has another dimension, with elegant, candlelit dining upstairs in the Fireweed Room. The Fireweed Room features a piano-bar with live jazz and folk music. The menu varies from homemade soups and pastas (served with the unique "fiddlehead pesto," made from the tender tips of ferns for which the restaurant is named) to the freshest of seafoods, homebaked breads, and rich desserts. *The Fiddlehead Cookbook* (St. Martin's Press, 1991) shares some of the restaurant's secrets. ■ *Around the corner from the Alaska State Museum; 429 W Willoughby Ave, Juneau; (907) 586-3150; $$–$$$; full bar; AE, MC, V; local checks OK; breakfast, lunch, and dinner daily, year-round; ⅙ downstairs only.*

Channel Bowl Cafe ★★★

Tucked into a spare corner of the old bowling alley, this little cafe has been tickling the funny bone of Juneau for years. Master humorist and owner Laurie Berg runs a "full-service cafe," a throw-back to the old diners of the 1940s. Almost everyone in Juneau has flipped burgers here—including the governor of Alaska. This is the ultimate breakfast spot, and local gossip is free. Note the off-beat humor on the walls. Order the Mount Jumbo plate, "Breakfast to Match our Mountains," or another hometown favorite, Blueberry-Pecan Fancy Pancakes. If you love chocolate-chunk cookies, the hands-down, melt-in-your-mouth best, anywhere in the world, are here. Pray that Laurie has baked some that day. ■ *A stone's throw from the Fiddlehead Restaurant and Bakery; 608 W Willoughby Ave, Juneau; (907) 586-6139; $; no credit cards; checks OK; breakfast and lunch.*

Georgio's at the Pier ★★★

When it first opened in 1995, Georgio's knocked the socks off Juneauites with its stunning Alaska/European-style desserts (that translates as big and artful!). This comfortable Italian trattoria features almost exclusively pizza, pasta, and fresh seafood. An outdoor deck allows you to eat right by the water on sunny days. ■ *At the cruise ship dock; 544 S Franklin St, Juneau; (907) 586-4700; $$$; full bar; AE, DC, DIS, MC, V; checks OK; in summer, lunch and dinner daily; in winter, lunch Mon–Sat and dinner Mon–Fri. ⅙*

Silverbow Inn and Restaurant ★★★

At the turn of the century, this was "The San Francisco Bakery." Today, the wonderful old brick ovens are still in use, turning out more than 100 loaves of bread and dozens of bagels a day for the capital city. Served with delicious bread, seafood dishes here are elegant—a fine meal in a country-kitchen atmosphere. Excellent wine selection. ■ *Downtown, close to the State Capitol; 120 Second St, Juneau; (907) 586-4146; $$$; beer and wine; all major credit cards; local checks OK; dinners, daily; closed Sun, Oct–May.* ♿

Valentine's Coffee House and Bakery ★★ A bright, savory

aroma–filled gathering place, this little coffee house has a cheerful ambience. Everything is baked from scratch. There are good coffee drinks, exceptional coffee cakes, and interesting and tasty sandwiches (their Italian Summer Garden Sandwich on focaccia is a favorite). Tempting desserts include great "snaps" (as in ginger snaps and ginger crinkles). ■ *Downtown Juneau; 111 Seward St, Juneau; (907) 463-5144; $; no credit cards; local checks OK; open weekdays, 6:30am–7pm; weekends 8am to 6pm; closed Sun in winter.* ♿

Armadillo Tex Mex Cafe ★ "Armadillo's" (interchangeably

known as "The Tex Mex") is a bigtime favorite in Juneau. Why? It's cheap, and you get a lot of food. It's basic, but that's the charm of the place—friendly people, easy banter, and casual dining. The food ranges from nachos, *chalupas*, barbecued ribs, and tacos to Armadillo specialties such as enchiladas Azteca, fajitas, and huevos rancheros. ■ *Across from the cruise ship dock; 431 S Franklin St, Juneau; (907) 586-1880; $–$$ (2 tacos, $10; fajitas, $13, for example); beer and wine; MC, V; local checks OK; lunch and dinner daily, year-round (no lunch on Sun).*

Heritage Coffee Co. ★ Close to the cruise ship dock, Heritage

is one of the most popular and well-known coffee haunts in Juneau. In summer, it is populated more by tourists than by locals. The front windows are good for people-watching, and the cafe features a wide selection of pastries, soups, salads, and sandwiches. ■ *Midway between the cruise ship docks and the State Capitol; 174 S Franklin St, Juneau; (907) 586-1752; $; AE, DIS, MC, V; local checks OK; open weekdays, 6:30am–6:30pm; weekends, 7am–5pm (slightly later in summer).*

Olivia's de Mexico ★ Take a tip from Olivia's countrymen.

The Mexican crews off the cruise ships all eat at Olivia's. During the legislative session, there are standing lines at lunchtime. Even though it's in the basement, it's colorful and festive. Here, diners get the genuine article—the distinctive taste from south of the border—because that's the way Olivia cooked it at home. Chile verde and chiles rellenos are popular, and Olivia makes daily specials such as *posole*, a meat and hominy stew. ■ *Downtown; 222 Seward St, Juneau; (907) 586-6870; $; MC, V; local checks OK; open year-round; lunch served weekdays, dinner served Mon–Sat; closed Sun.*

Juneau

Restaurants

The Hot Bite "Out the road" at the Auke Bay Marina, the Hot Bite is a good place to know about. After a hard day fishing, or if you're biking roundtrip to Mendenhall Glacier from downtown Juneau, tank up here. It's just a shack in the parking lot, with picnic tables in a screened-in porch, and it's high on the grease quotient; but locals love it. Try the grilled chicken or great halibut burgers, with a side of tart vinegar chips, and wash them down with a thick, creamy milkshake. ■ *On the road to Auke Bay; Auke Bay Boat Harbor, Auke Bay; (907) 790-2483; $; local checks OK; open summer only.*

BEST LODGINGS

Westmark Juneau ★★★ If it's traditional comfort and a lovely view you're looking for, this hotel, which overlooks Gastineau Channel, is just the ticket. The rooms are quite spacious, with a color scheme of peaches and greens. Choose a water view, the higher up the better. There are no-smoking floors and rooms with exercise equipment, so you can jog or climb mountains in the comfort of your own room. But why do that when nature provides the real thing right outside your door? ■ *Downtown, directly across from the wharf; 51 W Egan Dr, Juneau, AK 99801; mail: PO Box 20929, Juneau, AK 99801; toll-free (800) 544-0970; (907) 586-6900; fax (907) 463-3567; $$$; AE, DC, DIS, V; checks OK.* &

Lodgings

▲

The Baranof ★★ For years, the Baranof (built in 1939) was *the* hotel in Juneau, in more ways than one. As its finery began to fade, its character continued to grow. During the legislative sessions of old, this is where a lot of horse-trading went on, and deals were sealed on the back of cocktail napkins. It's still a popular haunt during the legislative session. But in summer, it's all tourists. It's been remodeled in recent years; the rooms are still quite small, though, and the street side can be noisy. We recommend the corner, water-view suites on the sixth and seventh floors. ■ *Near the State Capitol; 127 N Franklin St, Juneau, AK 99801; toll-free (800)544-0970; (907) 586-2660; fax (907) 586-8315; $$$; AE, DC, DIS, MC, V; checks OK.*

BED AND BREAKFASTS

Alaska Bed and Breakfast Association If you enjoy getting to know local people, you can slip into Juneau in a very personal way by opting to stay in someone's home. Karla Hart's association will place you according to your interests and travel desires. You can wake up serenaded by the French horn or charmed by the aroma of sourdough pancakes. You can be by the water, in the mountains, or right downtown. If your passion is birds, they'll place you with the fellow who literally wrote the book on Alaska's birds. For more information, contact Alaska Bed and Breakfast Association, 369 S Franklin St, Suite 200, Juneau, AK 99801; (907) 586-2959 or fax (800) 493-4453.

GUSTAVUS/GLACIER BAY

Gustavus is unique in Southeast, tucked into the forest and spreading out on a flat outwash plain created by glaciers that receded more than 200 years ago. It is also on the edge of Glacier Bay National Park, and a dusty, 10-mile road connects the tiny town and park headquarters at Bartlett Cove. If you are flying into the park, you land in Gustavus.

Tlingit Indians built camps and smokehouses here for centuries. Then, in 1914, the first wave of white homesteaders arrived and called the settlement Strawberry Point because of the abundance of wild strawberries. A second wave of homesteaders arrived in the 1960s and 1970s, armed with *Whole Earth Catalogs* and a desire for back-to-the-land lifestyles. Gustavus (pop. 400) exudes small-town friendliness. People wave at each other, and pickup trucks still outnumber cars.

Bartlett Cove, 10 miles down the road at Glacier Bay National Park, offers a very different experience from Gustavus. Gustavus appeals to independent travelers who want free time along with sightseeing, while visitors who stay at Bartlett Cove generally are on package tours designed to put the maximum amount of wilderness scenery in front of their video camera viewfinders.

Besides park headquarters, Bartlett Cove is home to the only developed campground in the area, as well as **Glacier Bay Lodge,** a handsome cedar, glass, and stone structure with wide porches and a massive stone fireplace. A boardwalk connects the guest rooms to the lodge. All manner of excursions are available as part of package tours sold by the lodge operator, or can be arranged once you get to the lodge. Nature walks, fireside programs, guided and unguided kayaking, sport fishing, whale watching, day and overnight cruises into Glacier Bay, and flightseeing are some of the options.

When Captain James Cook, on his voyages of discovery, sailed up Icy Strait more than 200 years ago, there was no Glacier Bay, only a huge wall of ice stretching across the opening to what we know today as Glacier Bay. In this blink of geologic time, the ice has receded and opened up a treasure of fjords and cascading rivers of ice—one of our most precious national parks. You can now travel 60 miles upbay into the West Arm, which is the most dramatic and glacially active area of the park. This is the route the cruise ships take. But the best way to see the bay is slowly, over 10 days or 2 weeks, by small boat, paddling or under sail. Watch for seals, puffins, and bears.

Access

Air taxis in Juneau, Sitka, Skagway, and Haines offer scenic flights to Gustavus (see Things to Do in Juneau). For those who prefer to do their flightseeing in a Boeing 737, **Alaska Airlines,** (800) 426-0333, has daily jet service in the summer.

Exploring by Bike At the hub of Gustavus is a recreated 1930s-era gas-station-cum-English-cottage-flower-garden, the perfect symbol of Alaskans' two loves—the internal combustion engine and Mother Nature. Most bed and breakfasts have old 3-speed cruisers for biking through town. Pedal about a mile north from the gas station to **Fireweed Gallery,** (907) 697-2325, open afternoons in summer. Bill Locher, a retired engineer turned stone carver, has a small gallery displaying local and Alaska sculpture and paintings. Go a half-mile south from the gas station to **Gusto Building Supply,** where you can pick up a fishing license and lots of gossip; stop in at the **Beartrack Mercantile,** a well-provisioned general store (pick up a visitor's map or the booklet *Trails of Glacier Bay and Gustavus* for a list of off-road hikes); and grab a bite to eat at **Strawberry Point Cafe,** which is open for lunch and dinner and specializes in pizza, soups, and seafood. Pedal another mile to the dock, which juts into Icy Passage and offers a 360-degree panorama of everything Southeast—mountains, islands, forests, dunes, and ocean surf. The Gustavus dock is the best place to watch the sunset and sunrise. The salt air is a good tonic but bracing. At the Salmon River bridge on the main road, turn at the wooden fish sign, and follow the alder-smoke fragrance to **Salmon River Smokehouse,** (907) 697-2330. The cedar-shake building with the Ray Troll mural turns out award-winning smoked salmon and the best smoked halibut in Alaska. Free samples available.

Fishing and Whale Watching The chief attractions in Gustavus, besides relaxing, are fishing and whale watching. The world's record halibut (400-plus pounds), caught on sport gear, was hooked just a few miles from the Gustavus dock. Nearby Point Adolphus is summer home to humpback whales. It's best to book your outdoor trips once you arrive and check the weather; kayaking or sailing in rain or heavy ocean swells can be miserable.

GUIDES/OUTFITTERS

Glacier Bay Sea Kayaks, (907) 697-2257, rents seaworthy kayaks and gear for exploring the waterways around Gustavus. **Alaska Discovery,** (907) 697-2411, offers fully equipped, guided sea kayak tours of Bartlett Cove and the Beardslee Island Archipelago for adventurous, but inexperienced, day trippers, $119/person. Evening paddles ($39) and longer trips are also available. **Spirit Walker Expeditions,** (800) KAYAKER, offers complete 1-day, guided sea kayak excursions to Pleasant Island and longer trips to nearby wilderness areas.

    Woodwind Sail Boat Charters, (907) 697-2282, offers a 1-day bargain trip. Gustavus skipper Fritz Koschmann can take 1 to 4 passengers on his cat-rigged Sharpie sailboat for $140.

Captain Conner, an historic prisoner-transport vessel converted to an excursion boat, can take you to Point Adolphus for a half-day of whale watching; $89/person. This is a comfortable way to go if it's raining. **Gusto Charters,** (907) 697-2561 or (907) 697-2416, whisks passengers to Point Adolphus in its 50-foot motor yacht. Once there, you can paddle in kayaks for up-close whale watching; minimum two people: $180/person per day with kayak usage. **Gustavus Marine Charters,** (907) 697-2233, is highly recommended for tours of Glacier Bay National Park and Icy Strait. If at all possible, set aside a minimum of 3 days to fully absorb the wonder and the subtlety of the park.

Alaska Seair Adventures, (907) 697-2215, is first choice for those who want the ultimate custom trip—picnicking on an alpine lake overlooking Icy Strait, serious fishing for trophy salmon or halibut, gunkholing—you name it. You can do it in complete comfort from plane to motor yacht; the latter is equipped with a skiff for beach-combing excursions.

BEST LODGINGS

Gustavus Inn ★★★★ More than 25 years ago, Jack and Sally Lesh began the transformation of a homestead on the Salmon River into a small, comfortable country inn—no mean feat considering there was no electricity, no telephone, no stores, only sporadic mail and barge service, and eight children to raise. At the time, Gustavus was considered a featureless backwater, but Sal's good cooking and the unpretentious charm of the old homestead earned the inn a loyal following among Alaska cognoscenti. Today, their son Dave and his wife JoAnn continue the tradition of offering the best of country living. Guest rooms look onto the stunning garden or across hay fields to the ocean. They might serve their popular Halibut Caddy Ganty, a concoction of halibut and sour cream, or black cod steamed in sake and topped with morel mushrooms from the woods nearby. Dessert might be homemade ice cream or lemon meringue pie with sweet red raspberries from the garden. This is one of Alaska's very best. ■ *About 1.5 miles from the Gustavus airport, on the Salmon River (call for reservations and directions); May–Sept: PO Box 60, Gustavus, AK 99826; Oct–April: 7920 Outlook, Prairie Village, KS 66208; (800) 649-5220 year-round or (907) 697-2254 May–Sept; $$$ ($130/person/night, double occupancy, which includes all meals; singles: $190/night); beer and wine for guests and friends only; AE, MC, V; checks OK; dinner for nonguests by reservation only; closed mid-Sept–mid-May.* ♿

Good River Bed and Breakfast ★ The homespun guest house is made of timbers salvaged from an old fish trap. Each log has been painstakingly chiseled with a decorative bevel and perfectly dovetail-notched at the ends. Inside, hand-thrown ceramic tiles surround the wood stove, and homemade quilts top the beds. The craftsmanship continues at breakfast: flapjacks are served with spruce-tip syrup, wild berry jams, and smoked salmon. The four guest rooms are not spacious, but the living room (with harpsichord) and deck are cheerful places to relax. For those who desire more privacy, a snug, rustic cabin with cooking facilities is also available. The cabin has no indoor plumbing, but many guests think of the "one-holer" as another addition to their life list of Alaska experiences. ■ *Off Good River Rd, about 4 miles from the Gustavus airport; PO Box 37, Gustavus, AK 99826; (907) 697-2241; $$ ($70/double occupancy, $50/guest cabin); no credit cards; checks OK; closed mid-Sept–end of May.*

HAINES

Haines has what every Southeasterner often pines for—SUN. (On the average, Ketchikan gets 160 inches of rain a year; Juneau gets 90 inches; and Haines gets 60 inches. Skagway gets only 30 inches, but beware of the wind.) Both Haines and Skagway are in the rainshadow of the Fairweather Mountain Range, which catches much of the precipitation blowing off the Gulf of Alaska.

This is one of the most picturesque towns in all of Southeast, sleeping peacefully in unbelievable mountain splendor, where road meets sea. From the 1940s until the 1980s, when Skagway was linked to the Alaska–Canada Highway, Haines had a unique position in Southeast life: it had a road—a road that actually went somewhere. In its commanding position at the head of the Inside Passage, Haines was the beginning (or the end, depending on your perspective) of the road to the Interior. It sits on the edge of the forests and fjords of Southeast Alaska and the wide glacial valleys, mountain kingdoms, and more severe climates of the north. Its population is one of resilient oldtimers who've done it all and young adventurers who are trying to do it all with boundless enthusiasm for all that this mountain–ocean playground offers.

The architectural centerpiece of Haines is striking and one-of-a-kind. Sitting just up the hill from the water, framed by breathtaking snowy mountains, is a grassy parade ground ringed by old Victorian buildings. This is historic Fort William H. Seward, once known as the Chilkoot Barracks, a former Army post built in the early part of the century and deactivated in the 1940s. A group of returning World War II veterans bought the fort years ago. Today the buildings include private homes, a hotel, and an art center. In the old days, the parade ground was the place where new recruits, on skis for the first time, learned to discharge their firearms (preferably without killing anyone). Now, this grassy arena serves as a popular summer location for salmon bakes, dance performances, and informal football.

At 90 miles north of Juneau—the same latitude as Oslo, Norway—Haines lies on a peninsula between the mouths of two rivers, the Chilkat and the Chilkoot. Situated at the edge of a deep fjord called Lynn Canal, the town and surrounding Chilkat Valley have a population of about 2,300. The Tlingit people called it *Dei-shu,* or "End of the Trail." Traders called it "Chilkoot"; the missionaries called it "Haines."

Haines is so picturesque that in recent years the Walt Disney Company, the National Geographic Society, the British Broadcasting Corporation (BBC), and wildlife photographers from around the world have "discovered" it. Jack London's classic story *White Fang,* which was filmed here in 1990, is Haines' latest claim-to-fame in the movie business. Almost everybody in town was an extra and had a jolly good time.

Access

Haines is linked to the Alaska Highway, also known as the Alaska–Canada (Alcan) Highway, by a 160-mile road built in the 1940s called the **Haines Highway**. This means that from Haines, you can drive anywhere the roads go in Alaska or, at Haines Junction, turn right and go back home to America (through Canada, of course). Haines is also linked to the state ferry system, (800) 642-0066. If you want to get to Skagway, there is the **Haines-Skagway Water Taxi,** (907) 766-3395, for $30 roundtrip. Several small flight services also fly in and out of Haines. The best are **Haines Airways,** (907) 766-2646, and **Skagway Air,** (907) 983-2218.

Information

The **Haines Visitors Information Center** is located on Second Avenue, near Willard Street, in downtown Haines, and is open daily in summer. For information year-round, contact the Haines Visitor Bureau, PO Box 530, Haines, AK 99827; (800) 458-3579 or (907) 766-2234. For weather forecasts and marine conditions around the clock, call (907) 766-2727.

Tips on the Town

If you want to see Haines the way it was, put your speed shoes on. This town is fast becoming discovered as an outdoor mecca not only by the young and go-for-the-gusto crowd, but also by seniors aboard the huge cruise ships that started to dock here in 1995. Their arrival doubles or even triples the population of the town in a single day.

THINGS TO DO

Alaska Chilkat Bald Eagle Preserve Located between Mile 10 and Mile 26 on the Haines Highway, this area is known as the Valley of the Eagles. About 200 eagles reside here year-round; but in the fall and early winter, their ranks swell to nearly 4,000, lining the sand bars and filling the cottonwood trees. Warm water, which wells up from the bottom of the Chilkat River, keeps part of the river ice-free all winter, allowing these birds to feast on the carcasses of salmon. It's the largest gathering of eagles in the world. A 5-mile stretch along the Chilkat River between Mile 18 and Mile 22 is the main eagle-viewing area and is called the Eagle Council Grounds. The greatest concentrations of eagles gather in the fall, peak in November, and taper off by February. For more information on the preserve, call (907) 766-2202.

Chilkat Dancers and Salmon Bake Performing in traditional regalia, with narration and a marvelous touch of humor, these Native dancers have been an inspiration to other Southeastern Native communities in reviving their arts through performing for tourists. Sometimes they perform on stage at the Chilkat Center for the Arts on the west side of Fort Seward, and sometimes in the longhouse in the center of the parade grounds. For a schedule of performances, call (907) 766-2160. The dance performance and salmon bake is a fun combo at the parade grounds. Grilled over an alderwood fire, the all-you-can-eat salmon is truly delicious. For times, call Hotel Halsingland at (907) 766-2000.

Kayaking Experienced paddlers can rent kayaks, after a safety check-out, from **Deishu Expeditions** at 12 Portage Street in Fort Seward. It's often hard to catch them at home, but leave a note or phone message, as the folks here are often out instructing and guiding other paddlers. Call (907) 766-2427.

Fishing Charters Just to be out on the water is a treat. Haines and Skagway are not the richest fishing grounds in Southeast Alaska, but they're still good compared to most other places in the world. Several charter companies offer trips for both saltwater and freshwater fishing: **Jim's Jaunts,** (907) 766-2935; and **First Out, Last In Charters,** (907) 766-2854. For more information, call the **Alaska Department of Fish and Game** in Haines, (907) 766-2625.

Biking Haines is so small, and the country around it so grand, that you'll find biking is a nice way to get around from Chilkat Inlet to the west and Chilkoot Lake to the north. You can't lose; both directions provide intense beauty. Rent mountain or road bikes at **Sockeye Cycle** on Portage Street, Fort Seward, (907) 766-2869.

Hiking The mountain that rises directly behind Haines, **Mount Ripinski** (3,610 feet), is a rigorous but wonderful climb on a clear day. Make noise in the forest, as bears abound. A smaller mountain, also with good views, **Mount Riley** (1,760 feet), rises south of town in Chilkat State Park, the highest point on the Chilkat Peninsula. For a forest and beach walk, head to Chilkat State Park and the 6.5-mile **Seduction Point Trail,** which has beautiful views of water, glaciers, and mountains and the chance to see bears, whales, seals, and sea lions. Check tides before setting out on this trail.

Camping Two exquisite campgrounds lie at the ends of the roads running out of town. To the northwest is Chilkoot Lake State Recreation Site at the head of Lutak Inlet. To the south, across the peninsula and along Mud Bay Road, is Chilkat State Park. It sits at the edge of the ocean and has knock-out views across to the water to the Davidson and Rainbow Glaciers.

GUIDES/OUTFITTERS

For those looking for a guide service, climbing school, and custom expedition outfitter, **Alaska Mountain School** is your best bet. Its instructors and guides have worked in mountains all over the world. The school offers 4-day trips into the Chilkat Mountains as an introduction to the basics of safe mountaineering. Activities include crevasse travel and peak climbing. Longer mountaineering and wilderness trips will take you on the Tsirku Icefield Traverse or combine sea kayaking and glacier trekking. For more information, contact Alaska Mountain School, PO Box 1081, Haines, AK 99827; (907) 766-3366. The folks at **Chilkat Guides** specialize in river trips. They offer a half-day float through the Chilkat Bald Eagle Preserve along the Chilkat River. It's scenic, peaceful, and departs daily. (Note: The eagles follow the salmon; therefore, you may not see many eagles during the early part of the summer. The greatest concentrations of the birds are found in the fall and early winter.) Chilkat Guides also offers 2-day adventures, but their *crème de la crème* trips are the 10-day and 13-day expeditions down the Tatshenshini and Alsek Rivers, which flow through two spectacular wilderness areas. For information, contact Chilkat Guides, PO Box 170, Haines, AK 99827; (907) 766-2491; fax (907) 766-2409.

For kayaking adventures to suit all comers, look no further than **Deishu Expeditions.** The company offers a sunrise or sunset paddle or multiple-day trips in search of the great whales. Located on Portage Street, just up from the cruise ship dock; (907) 766-2427. If you prefer jet boat and rafting trips, **River Adventures** will take you on the upper Chilkat River. Trips depart morning and afternoon, daily, in summer; (907) 766-2050.

PLACES TO VISIT

American Bald Eagle Foundation This small museum is truly a labor of love. A tribute to the bald eagle, it's also filled with the wildlife of the Chilkat Valley (once alive, but now stuffed) and resides just around the corner from the Mountain Market, close to the center of town. For information, contact American

Bald Eagle Foundation, PO Box 49, Haines, AK 99827; (907) 766-3094.

Sheldon Museum and Cultural Center

One of 5 accredited museums in the state, this tiny museum will give you a feel for the history of Haines, its Native peoples and their traditional art, shipwrecks along the Inside Passage, early pioneers of the region, and more. Open daily in summer. Located at the corner of Main and Front Streets. For information, contact PO Box 269, Haines, AK 99827; (907) 766-2366.

SHOPPING

Haines has a wealth of artists and a lovely blend of traditional and contemporary art. There are probably 100 artists making a living off their art here in Haines (quite extraordinary in a town of only a few thousand). Spend some time poking around. Here are a few places to start. **Alaskan Indian Arts,** (907) 766-2160, and **Wild Iris,** (907) 766-2300, are both located in the historic building on the west side of the Fort Seward parade ground. **Sea Wolf Gallery,** (907) 766-2540, on the parade ground, and **Whale Rider Gallery,** on Portage Street, feature the work of Tresham Gregg. His signature style can be seen in wonderful masks such as the mythical sea wolf, a tiny mosquito mask, a raven encircled with rabbit fur, or a wolf head mask with fur tails. A block or so from the visitors center, **Chilkat Valley Arts,** (907) 766-2990, owned by artist Sue Folletti, features other outstanding local talent. Next door is **Inside Passage Artisans,** (907) 766-2539. Most of these shops and galleries are open year-round. Locals say, "It's a Haines tradition" (in contrast with Skagway, where artists head south for winter).

HANGOUTS

The **Officer's Club Lounge** is a dignified bar in the Hotel Halsingland and a popular watering hole for locals. After all, this used to be the purview of the Commander, so it feels like drinking in somebody's home with big windows and a nice view. Located down by the water is the **Lighthouse Restaurant** whose claim to fame is its buttermilk pie—Alaska slices at Alaska prices. That translates as big and expensive. On Main and Front Streets; (907) 766-2442. Thirty-three miles "out the road" toward the Interior (otherwise known as the Haines Highway) is the historic **33 Mile Roadhouse,** (907)767-5510. Everybody in Haines goes to milepost 33 for the "best burgers in town." The pies are pretty good, too.

DESTINATIONS OUT

The Golden Circle Route You'll find 360 miles of indescribable beauty, by road, and 15 miles of scenic cruising, over water, along the Golden Circle Route. You can drive a car, or go slow and savor the scenery while riding a bicycle. If you want a guided bike tour, call **Sockeye Cycle,** (907) 766-2869. The company runs a summer expedition along this route, which takes 9 days. By car or bike, follow the Haines Highway to Haines Junction, on the rim of Kluane National Park; turn right on the Alaska Highway, head toward Whitehorse in the Yukon, and then ride back through the mountains to Skagway in Alaska. At this point, just a few miles of water at the head of Lynn Canal separate you from Haines. You can take the ferry or the Haines-Skagway Water Taxi back to Haines.

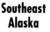

Flightseeing Flights over Glacier Bay National Park, which lies a short distance to the west, are offered by **Haines Airways,** (907) 766-2646. **Mountain Flying Service,** (907) 766-3007, a new little company, will take you on several unusual aerial adventures, such as landings on the beaches of the Gulf Coast or setting down on top of a glacier.

FESTIVALS/EVENTS

Mayfest Mother Nature puts on this show. In May, everything is waking up after a long winter's sleep. It's a great time to be anywhere in Southeast, but particularly in Haines. Long days make for great cross-country skiing in Chilkat Pass. The first 2 weeks of May, hooligan are running upriver, followed by a whole bevy of sea lions; the sky is white with sea gulls. Whales are returning. Native folks dip-net for fish. People from the Yukon come to the coast with moose meat for trading. Hooligan oil is a prized commodity. The Native peoples of the Interior use it for dipping meats and dried fish. (In the old days, it was so valuable that the routes to the Interior were often called "The Grease Trail.") Good places to watch nature's show, particularly the hooligan and sea lions, are at Mile 4 on the Haines Highway, alongside the Chilkat River, and at the bridge over Lutak Inlet, on your way to Chilkoot Lake.

Haines

*Festivals/
Events*

Kluane to Chilkat Bike Relay Race Held on the weekend closest to the summer solstice (June 21), this relatively new bicycling event has taken off like a rocket. In 1995, more than 600 bike relay teams participated. Racers roar off in a mass start from Haines Junction in the Yukon, then follow the road over the pass to Haines, about 150 miles. The terrain is rugged and demanding, but competitors like the nice local flavor and say the race has not yet been invaded by big-time serious racers from Outside (meaning non-Alaskans).

Southeast Alaska State Fair (and Bald Eagle Music Festival)
Around the second week of August, folks from all over Southeast gather in Haines for a good old-fashioned fair, featuring big names in the music world and talented musicians from around the state. There are also the famous pig races, a parade, great food, and dancing, of course. Never mind that it almost

always rains that weekend; everybody loves the fair. For more information, call (907) 766-2476.

Alaska Bald Eagle Festival The gathering of bald eagles on the Council Grounds of the Chilkat River from October to December is the largest concentration of eagles in the world. In their honor, Haines puts on a festival of local artists and musicians, usually the second weekend of November, but the really big-name, flamboyant performance artists here are white-headed, wear more than 7,000 feathers, and weigh in at about 13 pounds each. For more information, contact the Haines Chamber of Commerce, PO Box 1449, Haines, AK 99827; (800) 246-6268 or (907) 766-2202.

BEST RESTAURANTS

Mountain Market ★★ Thoughtful, wholesome food is served in this combination deli–health food store. Except for the sandwiches, the cuisine is largely vegetarian, with great muffins, good soups, daily specials like enchilada bake, Singapore stir-fry, and basil-pesto pasta, and the best coffee drinks in town. Fishermen, kayakers, mountain climbers, cabin dwellers, artists, and alternative-lifestyle folks may be found holding court here on any given day. ■ *Corner of 3rd Ave and Haines Hwy; 151 3rd Ave S, Haines; (907) 766-3340; $; MC, V; local checks OK; breakfast, lunch, and dinner daily, winter and summer.* ❧

Commander's Room ★ The commander of the fort once lived here; today you can eat here. The menu, entitled "Military Dining Portfolio," is a replica of the original writing portfolios used by the Army at Fort Seward. Many of the menu items celebrate past characters like that beer-guzzling bear "Three-Per"; the Great Dane named Gus who flew co-pilot with the commander and wolfed down steak every night; and the commander's wife, Eleanor, who, either through stroke of genius or perverseness, composed the music to Alaska's Flag Song. (Genius? Because only the best voices in the state can actually sing this song. Perverse? Because the rest of us make it painful to your ears.) The restaurant, with windows looking out onto the parade ground, specializes in fresh, locally caught seafood. The fresh Dungeness crab is entertainment unto itself. Make this your first choice. ■ *In the Halsingland Hotel, Fort Seward, Haines: (907) 766-2000; fax (907) 766-2445; $$; full bar in the Officer's Club Lounge; AE, DC, MC, V; local checks OK; open daily for breakfast and dinner; closed Dec–Feb.* ❧

Fort Seward Lodge Restaurant & Saloon ★ The seasonal specialty is all-you-can-eat crab, plucked right from the waters of Lynn Canal. Service is friendly, the atmosphere cozy, and from some tables you have a view of the water. While you're waiting for dinner, make a homemade dart with an autographed dollar bill and fire it at the ceiling. It is wise here to go for the house specialties—prime rib or crab. ■ *Part of historic Fort Seward, Haines; toll-free (800) 478-7772 or (907) 766-2009; $–$$; DIS, MC, V; local checks OK; dinner, nightly in summer; 5 nights in winter (varies); open year-round, except for 2 weeks in Jan for maintenance; ♿ restaurant but not bathrooms.*

BEST LODGINGS

Hotel Halsingland ★★ Overlooking Lynn Canal, with mountains in all directions, the hotel is part of historic Fort Seward. The old Victorian buildings have a kind of faded gentility to them, and so do the rooms. The hotel itself was once home to the commanding officer of the fort. It has 35 rooms with private baths and 4 economy rooms with shared baths. The former owner, an immigrant from Sweden, named the hotel after a province of her native homeland. The complex includes the Officer's Inn Bed and Breakfast, which has 13 guest rooms and is up the hill from the hotel. ■ *Located on the east side of the Fort Seward parade ground in Haines; PO Box 1589, Haines, AK 99827; toll-free (800) 542-6363 or (907) 766-2000; fax (907) 766-2445; $–$$ (economy rooms, single/$40; Officer's Inn B&B, double/$95); full bar in the Officer's Club Lounge; AE, DIS, MC, V; local checks OK; closed Dec–Feb.* ♿

The Riverhouse ★★ A private cottage beside the Chilkat River with a third-floor tower bedroom, solar power, private garden and deck, hot tub, and bicycles, this lovely oasis is a mile from town. No smoking. ■ *A mile from downtown, on the Chilkat River; PO Box 1009, Haines, AK 99827; in Alaska, toll-free (800) 478-1399; (907) 766-2060; $$$ (daily: $115 for two, $18 each additional guest up to four; weekly: $685 for two; $900 for four); MC, V; checks OK; open mid-May–Oct.*

Summer Inn Bed and Breakfast ★★ A 5-bedroom historic house, this charming inn has beautiful views of Lynn Canal from the upstairs front bedrooms. It was built by Tim Vogel, a member of Soapy Smith's notorious gang of hoodlums, who skedaddled out of Skagway when Soapy was gunned down around the turn of the century. Quite a dandy, and known as a ladies' man, Vogel was a colorful character in the history of Haines. In the evening, you can take a bubble bath in the scoundrel's original tub, circa 1912. It's cheerful, homey, and a great location. They serve a hearty breakfast here and, in the afternoon, homemade cookies and tea. ■ *Downtown Haines, 2 blocks off Main St; 117 Second Ave, Haines, AK 99827; mail: PO Box 1198, Haines, AK 99827; (907) 766-2970; $–$$ (summer: single/$60, double/$70, triple/$90; winter rates are lower); MC, V; checks OK; open year-round.*

In the fall of 1896, a prospector named George Washington Carmack was panning for gold on a tributary of the Klondike River in Canada. Something glittered. He brushed away the gravel. And there, lying "like thick slabs of cheese" in a sandwich, was the first taste of the gold that would electrify the world. "I felt," he said later, "like I had just dealt myself a royal flush in the game of life."

The rush was on. Skagway, on the Alaska side of the coastal mountains, provided access to the quickest route into the Canadian Klondike, up and over the Chilkoot Pass. From bank presidents to lowly clerks, oyster pirates to boarding-house matrons, everywhere around the globe, people lured by the gold walked out of their jobs, bound for the Klondike. Most of the gold claims were already staked by the time the masses had clambered and clawed their way over glaciers and peaks to get there. But not a soul forgot the glory days of the gold rush and its grand, unparalleled adventures as immortalized in Robert Service's poem *The Spell of the Yukon.*

For every soul who came to dig gold out of the ground, hundreds more followed to dig gold out of the other guy's pocket. In those wild days, it was written about Skagway that a man could come into town from the Klondike with a fortune in his pockets and the next morning not even have money for a meal. "I have stumbled upon a few rough corners of the globe in my wandering, but I think the most outrageously lawless quarter I ever struck was Skagway," wrote a visitor in 1898.

One of the most lawless fellows could be found in Clancy's Saloon, headquarters for the notorious Soapy Smith gang. As a two-bit con man down south, Soapy picked up his nickname, as well as some extra cash, by using a trick involving soap to swindle the unsuspecting out of their dough. But when he arrived in the north, he hit the big time, and locals were soon calling him the King of Skagway. It was a glorious but brief reign, for Soapy eventually pinched one poke too many. On July 8, 1898, *The Skagway News* headlines read: "Soapy Smith's Last Bluff; Shot Through the Heart by Frank Reid."

Skagway has always been known for throwing a good party. But don't believe all you hear, particularly about winter in Skagway, because most of the people you're bound to meet don't live here, including the shopkeepers. When the last cruise ship sails down Lynn Canal in late September, folks start boarding up their shops and heading for Bali, Boston, Washington, or Tahiti.

That leaves about 700 people when the snow flies. And they love it!

Access

Skagway can be reached year-round by scheduled and chartered air services out of Juneau and Haines. **Skagway Air,** (907) 983-2218, with the dance-hall queen doing the high-step on the tail flaps and the motto "We can can-can," is a good first choice. In summer, there's a water taxi between Skagway and Haines, (907) 766-3395, and the **Alaska state ferry**. From the Alaska Highway, it's 110 miles via the South Klondike Highway.

Information

The best place to start is at the old railroad depot, now home to the **Klondike Gold Rush National Historical Park.** Located in the heart of town, on Second Avenue and Broadway, the park visitors center is open daily in the summer, with scaled-back hours in winter. The visitors center offers films, exhibits, walking tours, ranger talks, and the latest information on conditions on the Chilkoot Trail. **Skagway Visitors Information,** (907) 983-2855, has a great little brochure, *Skagway Walking Tour,* for a do-it-yourself guided trip. Located on Fifth, just off Broadway. The town's newspaper, *The Skagway News,* is published biweekly at 264 Broadway; (907) 983-2354.

THINGS TO DO

Klondike Gold Rush National Historical Park This park is

unique among national parks in that it encompasses both historic downtown Skagway (the beginning—and the end—of the trail of gold) and the routes and mountain passes that thousands of goldseekers flowed over to get to the goldfields of the Canadian Klondike. It was certainly "the last grand adventure" of the 19th century. Over the years, the National Park Service has restored many of the old buildings and is working to renovate others, breathing life into the stories of the characters who once proliferated here. Visit, for instance, the **Mascot Saloon,** a hop and a skip down Broadway, or nearby **Jeff Smith's Parlor,** the gambling dive and hang-out of the nefarious Soapy Smith. Two routes led into the Klondike from Skagway: the 33-mile **Chilkoot Trail,** which you can still walk today, and the **White Pass Trail,** the route followed by the trains of the White Pass & Yukon Railroad. The park is managed through the international cooperation of the national park services of both the United States and Canada.

Hike the Chilkoot Trail For those who love history and moun-

tains, a hike along the Chilkoot Trail is a wonderful adventure. Go prepared, though: The distance (33 miles) may not look intimidating, but the route is rugged and there's plenty of snow, even in July. The park service can give you maps, information, latest trail conditions, and an excellent brochure, *A Hiker's*

Guide to the Chilkoot Trail. For more information, contact Klondike Gold Rush National Historical Park, PO Box 517, Skagway, AK 99840; (907) 983-2921; or, in Canada, contact Yukon
National Historic Sites, Canadian Park Service, 205–300 Main
Street, Whitehorse, Yukon, Canada Y1A 2B5; (403) 667-3910.

Ride the White Pass & Yukon Railroad They said the route
was "too steep for even a billygoat," but they hadn't counted on
Michael J. Heney, a brilliant engineer. The route followed the
old White Pass Trail and took miners into the Klondike. Heney
was known for getting the job done. His famous rallying cry
was "Give me enough snoose and dynamite, and I'll build you
a road to Hell!" From the end of May to the end of September,
the train departs twice daily for White Pass Summit, returning
to Skagway 3 hours later. Round-trip fare is $75/adults and $38
children. For more information, call toll-free in the U.S. (800)
343-7373 or, in Skagway, (907) 983-2217.

Explore Skagway Whether on foot, by buggy, or in a vintage
car, tours abound. The National Park Service offers walking
tours of historic Skagway that depart several times daily from
its visitors center, (907) 983-2921, at the old railroad depot. A
marvelous raconteur and performer, Steve Hites, runs a fleet
of yellow vintage cars, **Skagway Street Car Company,** (907)
983-2908. His drivers are dressed in flamboyant costumes of
the era and entertain you with story after story of yesteryear,
as they toot about town. If you want to get from here to there
in horse and buggy, just flag one down.

Go Hiking or Biking The quickest and easiest trails up into
the mountains are those that go to Lower and Upper Dewey
Lakes. If you have only a few hours, hike to **Lower Dewey
Lake,** a beautiful 2.5-mile jaunt and 600-foot elevation gain. The
trail begins near the Westmark Hotel. Ask for directions. If
time allows, continue to **Upper Dewey Lake,** a round trip of
7 miles. **Klondike Summit to Sea Cruise** is a 2-hour guided
bike trip offered by **Sockeye Cycles,** (907) 983-2851. They'll
drive you up to the pass; then you "coast" back down to the sea.
You won't lack for speed or beauty on this trip.

NIGHTLIFE

Skagway's local character, **"Buckwheat,"** the same guy responsible for the **Buckwheat Ski Classic** held in Skagway the
third weekend of March, has his own one-man show during the
summer, performing *The Cremation of Sam McGee* and other
Robert Service favorites along with a few other rousing tales
of the north. Presented by the Skagway Street Car Company,
it's only $6, nightly, at the Arctic Brotherhood Hall, during
the cruise ship season. The "Longest Running Show in the
North," or so the town claims, is an historic musical comedy
about Skagway and that legendary con man Soapy Smith.

The Days of '98 has matinee and evening shows, with mock gambling in the Eagles Hall on Sixth and Broadway. Join Soapy Smith and Squirrel Tooth Alice for a look at the wild days. For tickets, call (907) 983-2545. Afterwards (or before or any other part of the day), head on down to the **Red Onion Saloon,** on Second Avenue and Broadway, for toe-tapping honky-tonk piano or live music and dancing. This was once a brothel. Look up at the second-story windows and pay homage to the ladies. There's a ghost roaming around up there too. Dance- and music-wise, things really get revved up on a Saturday night. It's a good time.

FESTIVALS/EVENTS

Victorian Yuletide As the dark and wintry days of December roll around, Skagway gets decked out in lights to celebrate an old-fashioned Victorian Christmas. Children set their shoes outside to be filled with treats at night. The tree is lit in the center of town, followed by a parade of lighted boats in the harbor. There are organ recitals, singalongs, teas, tours of restored Victorian homes, and a Yuletide Ball at the Elks Lodge. Festivities occur during the first two weeks of December. For more information, call (907) 983-2885.

Fourth of July Four days after Soapy Smith rode his white stallion down Broadway at the head of the Fourth of July parade in 1898, he lay dead, shot through the heart in a shoot-out with Frank Reid down on the docks. Skagway holds a wonderful small-town Fourth. Soapy, or his reincarnated self, still leads the parade on his white horse; the parade marches a few blocks down Broadway; and, just in case you didn't get a good look, it turns around and marches back.

Skagway

Restaurants

Klondike Trail of '98 International Road Relay This is a wildly popular relay race (on foot), which starts at night and runs up and over the mountains the 110 miles from Skagway to Whitehorse. It's a fun team event for those who love to punish themselves through sleep deprivation and heavy, heart-pumping exercise. To commemorate the Klondike Gold Rush, the race began in 1983 with six teams. In 1995, there were 115 teams from all over the country. Part of the competition seems to be coming up with the most unusual name for your team, such as Midnight Claim Jumpers, Take No Prisoners, Wild Women Do, Out of the Ooze & Born To Cruise, Food Factory Flamethrowers, Vestigial Appendages, or One Knight Stands. The relay usually takes place the first week in September. For more information, call (907) 983-2854.

BEST RESTAURANTS

Lorna's at the Skagway Inn ★★★ Chef/owner Lorna Mc-Dermott is a graduate of Le Cordon Bleu. Oysters are her specialty. Appetizers include calamari and escargot. Entrees feature fresh Alaska seafood, from Sitka rockfish prepared in an almond crust with jalapeño butter to red salmon broiled with dill sauce. For dessert, try the delicious white-chocolate bread pudding with rum sauce. Good wines and imported beers. ■ *5 blocks down Broadway from the old railroad depot in the Skagway Inn; (907) 983-3161; $$$$; MC, V; local checks OK; dinner nightly; open May–Sept.* ♿

Stowaway Cafe ★★ If the sun's shining, sit out on the deck and enjoy waterfront dining. The food is quite tasty, creative, and thoughtful, from Mom's Incredible Spinach Salad and Hilbo's Hot Scallop and Bacon Salad to seafood gumbo, mesquite-grilled halibut, blackened salmon, and Crab Ho-Chi Hilbo (fresh crabs in Creole seasonings flamed with bourbon). For dessert, there's a heavy Southern leaning with pecan pie and bread pudding in bourbon sauce. ■ *Near the small boat harbor; 205 Congress Way, Skagway; (907) 983-3463; $$; no alcohol; MC, V; local checks OK; open for lunch and dinner in summer; closed winter.*

Sweet Tooth Cafe A comfy place for breakfast, this cheerful cafe is a gathering spot for locals. Buttermilk pancakes, homemade bread, donuts, and French toast are the main fare. For lunch, go for the halibut burger. Of course, if you have a sweet tooth, their specialties are sundaes and ice cream floats. ■ *Broadway and 3rd, Skagway; (907) 983-2405; $ (full breakfast up to $6.50); MC, V; local checks OK; open daily, year-round, 6am–2pm in winter; 6am–9pm in summer.*

BEST LODGINGS

Skagway Inn Bed and Breakfast ★★★ In 1897, this now-historic inn was a brothel and stood in the red-light district a few blocks off Broadway. Moved to its present location in 1916, the inn has 12 rooms, each named for a different woman who might have once lived there; it is said that in two of the rooms, ghosts linger on. Innkeepers Sioux and Don Plummer say that men particularly get a bang out of their reservations when they are told, "Oh, you'll be spending the night with Hattie. She's up there waiting." They'll re-emerge for breakfast in the morning with a long sigh, "Lulu never showed up last night." Nor, for that matter, did Alice, Birdie, Cleo, Dottie, Essie, Flo, Grace, Ida, Kitty, or Mimi. But hope springs eternal. And while you're waiting for the spirits of these gentle, tarnished doves, this is as comfortable, friendly, and charming a place to tuck in as you will find anywhere in this part of the country. Bathrooms are shared, and not just by ghosts. Make your reservations well in advance and ask for Alice, Flo, or Lulu. ■ *5 blocks down Broadway from the old railroad depot; PO Box 500, Skagway, AK 99840; toll-free in Alaska (800) 478-2290 or (907) 983-2289; fax (907) 983-2713; Web site http://puffin.ptialaska.net/~sgyinn;*

$–$$ (rates start at $55); DIS, MC, V; checks OK; dinner, May–Sept, breakfast included in price all year; open year-round. ⅃

Golden North Hotel ★★ With its golden dome and over-whelming red interior décor, it's a landmark on Broadway. A step through the door and you'll feel as if you're in an old bor-dello (only they swear it never was one). The hotel lobby is jammed with gold-rush antiques and paraphernalia, from the old player piano, which used to spin out tunes like "The Wed-ding March of the Painted Doll," to the corrugated scrub board on the stairway labeled "Maid of Honor." Floral velveteen wall-paper in loud colors (mainly red) covers the bedroom walls, with antique furniture and pseudo antiques donated by many of the original gold-rush families. The claw-foot bathtubs are so long that, if you're short, you may want to bring a snorkel. Un-less you're superstitious, Number 13, the corner room under the dome, is the loveliest. Watch for ghosts in Number 24. And the double bed in Number 6 is perfect if you and your partner are under five feet tall. ■ *On the corner of 3rd and Broad-way; PO Box 431, Skagway, AK 99840; (907) 983-2451 or (907) 983-2294; fax (907) 983-2755; $–$$ (rooms w/bath start at $60; economy rooms w/shared bath, $40; winter rates lower); MC, V; local checks OK; open year-round.*

Westmark Inn ★★ With touches of the Gay Nineties and a friendly atmosphere, the Westmark—with no original foothold in Skagway—does a good job of fitting in. Be forewarned: This is where the tour buses load and unload. But if you've opted for "character" accommodations in too much of Alaska already and you're looking for standard motel comfort where the bed is long enough to cover your feet and the shower is private, this could be your place. ■ *3rd and Spring St; PO Box 515, Skagway, AK 99840; (800) 544-0970 or (907) 983-2291; fax (907) 983-6100; $$; AE, DC, DIS, MC, V; traveler's checks OK; closed mid-Sept–end of May.*

SUGGESTED VIEWING/READING

Alaska Geographic Society. *The Chilkat River Valley.* An-chorage, 1984. All about the history, wildlife, and eagles of this valley, where the picturesque town of Haines is located.

Berton, Pierre. *The Klondike Fever: The Life and Death of the Last Great Gold Rush.* New York: Alfred A. Knopf, 1958. An exciting, anecdote-filled, and beautifully written story of the Klondike Gold Rush.

Browning, Robert. *Fisheries of the North Pacific.* Anchor-age: Alaska Northwest Publishing Co., 1980. A very informative book on the history, species, boats, gear, and processing of fish, the lifeblood of Southeast Alaska.

Chevigny, Hector. *Russian America: The Great Alaskan Venture 1741–1867.* Portland, Oregon: Binford & Mort, 1965.

City of Gold. National Film Board of Canada, 1958. An excellent film by Pierre Berton. Tells the story of the "Ninety-eighters" and the Klondike Gold Rush. Available in Alaska libraries.

Folly or Fortune. University of Alaska Fairbanks, 1985. Part III of the award-winning video series *Alaska: A History in Five Parts*, available from Alaska libraries and national parks and from the Alaska Natural History Association, 605 W 4th Avenue, Suite 85, Anchorage, AK 99501; (907) 274-8440.

Jonas, Shirley. *Ghosts of the Klondike: They Haunt the Frozen North.* Skagway: Lynn Canal Publishing, 1993.

Juneau Trails. Juneau: Alaska Natural History Association/Tongass National Forest, 1991.

King, Mary Lou. *90 Short Walks Around Juneau.* Juneau: Taku Conservation Society/Juneau Audubon Society, 1987.

O'Clair, Rita. *The Nature of Southeast Alaska.* Seattle: Alaska Northwest Books, 1992. A guide to plants, animals, and habitats.

Service, Robert W. *Best Tales of the Yukon.* Philadelphia: Running Press, 1983. Service immortalized the Klondike Gold Rush and the raw beauty of the frozen North in colorful ballads.

Troll, Ray, and Matsen, Brad. *Shocking Fish Tales.* Seattle: Alaska Northwest Books, 1991. Ray Troll is Ketchikan's irreverent and wacky fish artist, whose gallery is on Creek Street. His "sole brother" in this collaboration—Brad Matsen—is as zany and eloquent with the accompanying words as Ray is with his pen and pastels.

White Fang. Walt Disney Home Video, distributed 1991. There is also a *White Fang II*, out on home video.

Wynne, Kate. *Guide to Marine Mammals of Alaska.* Fairbanks: Alaska Sea Grant Program, University of Alaska Fairbanks, 1992.

THE ROADS NORTH

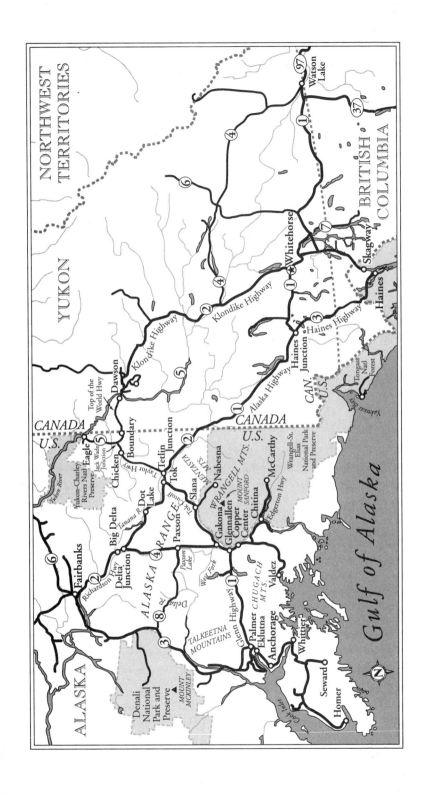

The Roads North

*Including the Alaska Highway (Canadian Border
to Tok, Taylor Highway to Chicken and Eagle, and
Tok Cutoff to Gakona Junction), the Richardson Highway
(Glennallen to Fairbanks), the Alaska Highway
(Tok to Delta Junction), and the Circular Route
(Anchorage-Glennallen-Valdez-Whittier-Anchorage)*

You will surely want to drive. Some people have the time to drive from the Lower 48 all the way to Alaska on the Alaska–Canada Highway (aka The Alcan). If you choose this option, you will be a road warrior by the time you cross the border. Others arrive in Haines or Skagway in Southeast Alaska via the Alaska Marine Highway and drive the 400 miles to Interior Alaska through Canada or the 800 or so miles to Anchorage. If you choose this option, be sure to reserve ferry space well in advance, as it gets booked solid in the summer. You can also fly to Anchorage and rent a car.

Be sure to carry *The Milepost* with you. Billed—correctly—as the Bible of North Country Travel, it takes you mile-marker to mile-marker down all the roads of Alaska. A note about lodging and food along the route: the watchword is "practical." If you need to sleep and shower, there is probably a place to do it. One alternative to be considered for those with energy and equipment is camping. Not only is it cheap, but you can pick your spot and otherwise control your destiny.

As for food, many of the operative words like "best" and "cuisine" become tongue-in-cheek in the Alaska outback. You would do well to substitute "available" for "best" and "chow" for "cuisine." The old adage about the best spice being a good appetite applies here. The real meal is the country itself.

THE ALASKA HIGHWAY

From the Canadian Border to Tok

In the old days, the Alaska Highway nominally began in Dawson Creek, British Columbia, at Mile 0. It really began where the pavement ended in Fort St. John 50 miles later. From there on, the trip hovered between novelty and tedium, with novelty predominating in the beginning and intense tedium at the end. It was like being trapped inside a house that was being dry-walled for 5 days. Dust hung in the air inside the vehicle. Opening windows only sucked it in faster through the trunk or tailgate. There was no way to get fresh air without stopping and getting out of the car. If you followed another car at any distance of less than half a mile, dust was a steady entree. The real knuckle-blancher was seeing a semi truck bearing down, stones sparking out from the wheels as dust in great churning petticoats billowed out behind. These were both IFR (Instrument-Flight-Rating) situations with religious overtones.

The road was tightly wound around the contours of hills, lakes, and rivers, with sharp, steeply banked turns. One developed an empathy for the magnitude of this wartime project of 1942, which punched a road through some of the most unforgiving terrain and climate in the world in less than a year. Typically, the traveler prepared for the arduous journey with extra tires and gas. It was harder to prepare psychologically. You knew that the trip was long and that none of it would be lost. So you tried to settle in behind the wheel and be patient. But after a couple of days, you just wanted to get it over. You drove faster and faster, taking on the turns by using both lanes, hoping no one else would appear there to claim his. This backslide into recklessness was made even more palpable by the white crosses—little wooden obituaries that stood at the places where fatalities had occurred.

Now, the highway is paved. Many of the worst stretches have been eliminated. There are ample gas and amenities, and having a sign on your vehicle that states "Alaska or Bust" says more about you than the trip. Even the crosses are gone, removed after people complained that they gave the drive a macabre tone. Still, it is a long stretch of driving, and some of the same psychology that held in the old days colors your responses today. You become very anxious to arrive at the Alaska border, and it is a relief to see the solitary little customs compound show up in the middle of nowhere (unless either you or your car gets treated to a strip search).

**The Alaska
Highway**

As if to say "Welcome back to the States," the road widens and becomes more a flowing river of blacktop than a dropped rope. Gas drops below two bucks a gallon and looks like a bargain. Tok, your first "real" Alaska town, is just 90 miles down the road. Things are looking up. If you're not immune to the spare beauty of the landscape by this time, there is lots to appreciate.

You are now in Alaska, a huge state that once spanned four time zones, since reduced to two. More precisely, you're in "Interior" Alaska. The destination no longer recedes like a carrot on the horizon, and there is time to take it all in. From the border all the way to Fairbanks, the Alaska Highway follows the Tanana River drainage. The climate is continental, protected from moderating ocean influences by the Wrangell–St. Elias Mountains to the south. Temperatures vary with the amount of daylight, reaching as high as 90°F in the summer and as low as –60°F in winter. Precipitation averages about 12 inches a year, only slightly more than arid. Any that falls as snow from early October on is part of the scenery until spring. In June and July, the sun makes a wide arc around most of the sky, rising in the north and setting there roughly 20 hours later. In winter, it's the other way around: the sun rises in the south and sets there perhaps 4 hours later, little more than an ornament for the cold.

For a relatively new civilization, the country has a strangely historical feel to it. The immensity and barrenness of the northern landscape lend a sense of timelessness that is unrelenting. Since each day lengthens or shortens by up to 6 minutes a day, one does not get absent-minded. The sense of urgency is caught nicely by all the migrating waterfowl, as well as in the miner's reference to the first snow on the mountain tops as "termination dust." This usually comes in late August and used to mean that it was time to head out before the rivers froze and the last boat left for the south.

Speaking of miners, it was mining that opened up the Interior and that was the *raison d'être* for almost every town here. What is a "real" Alaska town? The typical Alaska town was created around one natural resource and defined by it. A "real" Alaska town might, therefore, be a fishing town, a mining town, a trading town, or, more recently, a tourist town. Alternatively, it may have always been here, as in the case of aboriginal villages built around traditional food sources. If the reason for being here disappears, these towns become ghost towns. There are no ghost towns in Ohio, but there are plenty in Alaska. So there is a strong feeling for history in Alaska—for time inexorably moving on.

TOK

The first "real" Alaska town you arrive in, after driving the Alaska Highway, is Tok. Its reason for being there is incorporated in its old name, Tok Junction. No, that reason is not in the "tok" part, as baby boomers might be inclined to surmise, but in the "junction" part. Not a town of obvious grace and beauty, Tok occurs in a floodplain of thousands of acres. The only defining characteristic is that two roads join, making it a logical place to sell needed things to travelers passing through on the way to or from mining districts such as Valdez, Anchorage, and Fairbanks, and from the Lower 48. A town naturally sprang up.

Tok had its beginnings as a construction camp on the Alaska–Canada Highway in 1942, when the road was being pushed through as part of the defense effort against an anticipated Japanese invasion. One story about the origin of Tok's name is that it is an abbreviation of "Tokyo Camp." The population today is 1,250, and the mean monthly temperature in January is truly mean: −19°F; in July, it is 59°F.

Information

First, stop at **Tok Mainstreet Visitors Center,** located at the junction of Alaska Highway and Tok Cutoff (Box 389, Tok, AK 99780; (907) 883-5775 or (907) 883-5887). Open daily, May through September. **Alaska Public Lands Information Center,** (907) 883-5667, is next door to the visitors center and open daily in summer. Managed under the auspices of the U.S. Fish and Wildlife Service is **Tetlin Wildlife Refuge,** (907) 883-5312, which is across the highway from the Public Lands Information Center. Open weekdays, year-round.

BEST RESTAURANTS

Tok Gateway Salmon Bake ★ Like most places in Alaska, it's billed as a salmon bake, but the fish is grilled. No matter. Essentially, this is a barbecue with ribs, buffalo burgers, reindeer sausage, king salmon, and halibut. One advantage of a limited menu is that the establishment can pay attention to the few items it serves. Fresh salmon and halibut, grilled just right, are hard to top. ■ *⅞ mile east of the junction; Alaska Hwy, Mile 1313.1; (907) 883-5555; open Mon–Sat in summer, 6am–9pm, and Sun, 4pm–9pm.*

Fast Eddy's Fast Eddy's is connected with Young's Motel, one of the clean, modern motels in Tok. There's a salad bar, sandwiches, pizza, Alaska seafood, and steaks. No new wrinkles here, but the food is well prepared. The place is busy, always a good sign. ■ *¾ mile east of the junction; Alaska Hwy, Mile 1313.3; (907) 883-4411; dinner entrees run about $15; open year-round, 6am–midnight.*

BEST LODGINGS

Cleft of the Rock Bed and Breakfast ★★ One of the first things you notice as you drive in is a real lawn and an absence of the usual Alaska collection of extra cars and odds and ends that might someday rise again like the old South. The guest rooms in the house are located in the daylight basement and share a bathroom. They are clean and acceptable, but the stars are awarded for the two log cabins you pass on the way in. The smaller one has just been built, complete with running water and bathroom. The larger one sleeps up to five adults and has a kitchen, loft, and bath. Both cabins are nicely situated on the lawn, among scattered trees, and come with lawn chairs begging to be used after a long day's drive. Reserve ahead. Full, hot breakfast served. ■ *Off Alaska Hwy, 3 miles west of Tok. Turn right on Sundog Trail and go ½ mile; Alaska Hwy, Mile 1316.5; PO Box 122, Tok, AK 99780; toll-free in Alaska (800) 478-5646; (907) 883-4219; fax (907) 883-5963; $60–$95 for two; MC, V.*

THE TAYLOR HIGHWAY

To Chicken and Eagle

In Alaska, the road map, like the average menu, is limited to basics, and if you don't like the options, that's tough. Even Anchorage, Alaska's largest city, has just two roads: one going north and one going south. Fairbanks does better, with three, but in deep winter many residents suspect that all three go in and none out. Indeed, when the temperature is minus 40°F or minus 50°F, a long car trip is serious business and one packs basic survival gear.

Alaskans know most of the roads by heart. They still excite us but the prospect of a fresh road is like spring. One road not heavily traveled, even by Alaskans, is the road to Eagle.

Eagle has a mystique about it. Alaskans know it as a checkpoint on the 1,000-mile Yukon Quest Sled Dog Race and as a town that cannot be reached by road in winter. It is a town for real Alaskans, for folks who don't need a bank or the security of an international airport within taxi distance. The name itself inspires. A town named "Finch" or "Dove" wouldn't have the same draw. Chicken, on the same road, catches the ear too, but its mystique is so bound by absurdity it never gets off the ground. So Eagle it is, with a Chicken thrown in. If you venture down this road, your heart will soar like a hawk.

Most people travel to Alaska in summer, when the long, magic days open up possibilities limited only by stamina. If you drive to Eagle in late September with the days getting short,

---

CHICKEN

Chicken, at Mile 66, is an obvious draw. Who could resist such a burlesque name? And why "Chicken"? The story goes that early miners wanted to name the town "Ptarmigan" because of the bird's abundance there, but no one knew how to spell it. So they settled for Chicken. To our eye, a ptarmigan does not much resemble a chicken but then, that's the charm of the story.

The best thing to do in Chicken is to get the Chicken postmark on your letters at the post office, a small log building with flower boxes and a flagpole outside. Mail service to Chicken (pop. 37) is by air twice a week, weather permitting. If there is any more economic belt-tightening, Chicken's tiny post office, which was established in 1903, may be eliminated—a notion that worries the postmistress. So buy your year's stamps in Chicken from someone who cares, and keep Chicken's mail service from getting fried.

— John Kooistra

you get a sky full of stars in place of the same number of mosquitoes. And the Northern Lights! Also, a nearly empty road. Each summer season, more than 20,000 people take the Klondike Loop, leaving the Alaska Highway at Whitehorse, driving to Dawson City, then reconnecting with the Alaska Highway 12 miles east of Tok at Tetlin Junction. Heading west from Dawson, the road is gravel. The road that forms the Klondike Loop is better suited to heavy traffic than the spur road up to Eagle. The Canadian section has been improved, with heavy visitor traffic in mind. Improvements on the Alaska section are in progress and scheduled over the next few years. So be prepared for industrial-strength road construction, pilot cars, and lengthy waits.

The Taylor Highway (Alaska 5) runs from Tetlin Junction to Eagle, 160 miles of unpaved road, with the appropriately named "Top of the World Highway" branching off to Dawson City at Jack Wade Junction, 96 miles into the drive. The road is marked with mileposts. From Jack Wade Junction to Eagle, it's 65 miles of narrow, winding, eminently cursable and memorable road. This stretch takes you back decades to the bad old Alaska Highway days, something to be considered before making the drive. The road is less than two lanes wide in those places where it hugs the mountainside in tight turns as it follows various river valleys. We cannot recall a single guard rail. It would not be a comfortable jaunt for a large motor home towing a getaway car. However, the scenery is terrific, and when the road is not brailling its way through the gorges and valleys, it is up on top of the world overlooking a landscape that goes on like a clear conscience. A sunset looks small up here: it's so far away and takes up so little of the horizon. If you want photos, bring one of those disposable panoramic cameras. The wide-angle bite will still be too narrow, but several overlapping vistas can be put together to catch some sense of that space.

The road to Eagle from Jack Wade Junction was finally punched through in 1953, after 8 years of construction. One Eagle resident said the trip out to Tetlin Junction used to take 7 hours; now it takes 4, with more than half devoted to the Eagle spur. This is 4 hours for someone who has and means business, not someone who's there to savor the sights and the feel of the country. For touring, better stick with the original 7 hours with lots of stops.

The Alaska Highway parallels the Tanana River and drainage, so it stays low. From Tetlin Junction, the road begins to ascend mountains appropriately called "domes." They are old and soft hills when compared to the brash, rugged, snow-covered Wrangell–St. Elias Range to the south, which contains some of the highest mountains in North America. Within 2 or 3 miles, you ascend enough to get a view of the hills, which is exciting after all the valley travel on the Alaska Highway. The

▼

**The Taylor
Highway**

▲

vista is exciting in an ancient way, going out and out in layers of hills and distance. You truly start to feel "on top of the world," especially after about 25 miles, at the point where the road goes above timberline and skirts Mount Fairplay (5,541 feet), the second highest point on the way to Eagle.

Gold was discovered in this area in 1886. This is the "Fortymile Country," named after the old town located where the Fortymile River enters the Yukon, a few miles east of the border. Chicken Creek and Wade Creek were also rich finds. In many places, the Taylor Highway runs right over the top or right beside the old horse and wagon road that was built and used by the miners and freight haulers.

At Mile 34.4, there is a pullout on the left (west) and a mind-altering view. If you go in late September, there are no services until you get to Eagle, though food, gas, and "likker" are available in Chicken during the summer. Blueberries and crowberries are everywhere. Blue teeth, here we come!

Beyond Chicken, rivers are a big part of the scenery. From Mile 76 to Mile 80, the road rises high above Walker Fork, which cuts an average of 800 feet into solid rock. It is one of the most scenic stretches of the highway. Pull over, peer into the canyon, and listen to the river far below. (During summer traffic this would not be a safe practice, so exercise due caution.)

Mile 96 brings a parting of the ways: east into Canada and Dawson City or north to Eagle. In either case, the road stays on top of the hills and you can see it winding around hilltops miles in the distance. After 10 miles on "the roof," the road descends toward the Fortymile River bridge, a place for putting in your raft or canoe for running the river.

For much of the next 30 miles the road hugs O'Brien Creek with lots of tight places and turns in the road. There are no guard rails and some of the drop-offs are precipitous. The views draw a fine line between prudence and curiosity. When the road leaves the valley around Mile 136, things open up and you're on top of the world again, traversing American Pass. A few miles away only one tiny building is visible, making it seem lonelier still. The sign in front announces "American Summit Liquor," surely one of the world's most isolated liquor stores.

The Taylor Highway is not maintained by the state beyond mid-October, the time of the general onset of serious snow. Before then, people from Eagle make their last drives of the year out to the big cities of Anchorage and Fairbanks for winter supplies.

EAGLE

Eagle was named in 1897 for the eagles that nested on the nearby bluff. At the time there were only 28 miners, but by spring of 1898, there were 1,700 people in Eagle—10 times the number who live here today. In 1899, the Army established Fort Egbert, just west of the town, to maintain law and order; to build roads, trails, and the telegraph; and to help unfortunate civilians. Judge James Wickersham presided over the first federal court in the Alaska Interior: the Third Judicial District, which covers 300,000 square miles. Eagle was the commercial, judicial, and military center for the Interior during the Klondike gold rush.

Today, Judge Wickersham's original courthouse serves as a museum, and Fort Egbert's military buildings have been completely restored. And there's the town itself—a cluster of old buildings and cabins, an old school, and a library, as well as the Yukon River. Eagle Village is an Athabascan settlement on the banks of the Yukon, 3 miles upstream.

Eagle has charm. It is a real Alaska town—and one reason why you went to so much trouble and expense to come to Alaska in the first place. The town itself is attractive, squeezed down to the river by the mountains in two levels. Most of the town is on the second level—the sensible level—protected from the vagaries of the river.

Both the town and the residents have personality to spare. The impact of tourism is evident, but this community has not turned itself inside out catering to it. Few places take credit cards, and the nearest bank is in Delta Junction, 275 miles away, so come prepared. Most impressive, though, is the absence of a bar or liquor store, a notoriously profitable business in a state where many folks head for the bar to wait for spring.

If you go out to Eagle Village, you'll pass the town's primary airport, marked by signs displaying the silhouette of a Boeing 747, a droll touch. If a 747 ever lands in Eagle, it won't be a scheduled stop. Eagle Village is less than a mile down the road from the airport. The houses line the river bank, and empty chairs sit waiting along the edge of the bluff. This is the best show in town. All the action is on the river.

Unless you want to winter in, start driving out before termination dust settles for good on Mount Fairplay. At night from your sleeping bag, watch the stars preen. That old ribbon of wonder, the Milky Way, will have you by the hair of your neck.

THINGS TO DO

Historical Tour   Given by Eagle Historical Society, (907) 547-2325. Meets at the courthouse daily, at 9am, Memorial Day through Labor Day. For more information, write PO Box 23, Eagle City, AK 99738.

Float Trips   Float the Fortymile or Yukon River. Canoes can be rented in Dawson City or in Eagle at **Eagle Canoe Rentals,** (907) 547-2203. Float trips can be outfitted and arranged through **Elmore Enterprises,** PO Box 145, Eagle, AK 99738; (907) 547-2355; fax (907) 547-2208. You can float through the

Yukon–Charley Rivers National Preserve to Circle on the road system north of Fairbanks. Get any of your buddies driving north to pick you up.

BEST RESTAURANT

Riverside Cafe The best restaurant in town also happens to be the only restaurant. The log cafe with central wood stove is attractively situated, overlooking the Yukon. It is warm and friendly and supplies the town coffee table. You bring the conversation. Gravy-sogged rolls and canned fruit notwithstanding, the core of the dinners is straightforward and ample. Pies are homemade. ▪ *Front St, by the Yukon River; Box 36, Eagle, AK 99738; (907) 547-2220; fax (907) 547-2202; no credit cards; checks OK.*

THE TOK CUTOFF

To Gakona Junction

Technically, this road is part of the Glenn Highway, running from Tok to Anchorage, but the first 125 miles have always been called the Tok Cutoff. It was built from Tok on the Alaska Highway to Gakona Junction on the Richardson Highway—a shortcut from one highway to another.

Be prepared for a lot of "frost heaves" and cracks on this portion of highway. It's nearly impossible to put a road surface down over permafrost that lasts beyond a couple of seasons. It isn't that Alaska refuses to put money into highways; it just can't keep up with ongoing deterioration.

The Tok Cutoff

The first 10 miles of road south out of Tok are straight, true, and well-surfaced. From there, you can kiss the straight and well-surfaced goodbye and the scenery hello, as you are in the mountains for about the next 50 miles. The road follows the Tok and Little Tok Rivers most of the way to Mentasta Summit. **Eagle Trail State Recreation Site,** 15 miles out of Tok, has 40 campsites in a forest of large spruce. It's on the old trail that ran from Valdez to Eagle, a section of which has signed hiking trails.

The road continues on in quiet grandeur through the mountains. The food and lodging on this route, even though they do not merit stars, can still be part of a great adventure. **Mineral Lakes B&B,** 35 miles south of Tok, has cabins overlooking the lakes, but with no running water or electricity. You do get a memorable view of the Mentasta Mountains and a chance to go fishing. There's a canoe and motor boat for rent. **Mentasta Lodge,** 47 miles south of Tok, has cabins and a bar and cafe. When people live year-round in such extreme climate and geography, a special resonance may occur that also deserves stars. Call it character.

Beyond Mentasta Lodge, the road runs beside the Slana

River. On this side of Mentasta Summit, the rivers flow south into the Copper River and Prince William Sound instead of north into the Tanana River and then finally the Yukon. As you emerge from the Mentasta Mountains, if the weather is clear, you'll get your first glimpse of **Mount Sanford** (16,237 feet). Welcome to the Wrangell Mountains. The country opens up, but the scene is always dominated by Mount Sanford, 35 miles away.

The **Nebesna Road** branches off to the southeast at Slana and allows access into the Wrangell–St. Elias National Park and Preserve (see below). A park ranger station, a quarter-mile down the road, offers information about the park and road conditions. The road is paved for the first 4 miles and gravel thereafter. Twenty-eight miles out, the road becomes rough and fords several streams. The area is open to camping. The road ends after 45 miles at the old mining town of Nebesna, which is pretty much of a ghost town, although various population figures for the area say "less than 25." The last 3 miles are the roughest. Don't expect a chocolate shake at the end.

From Slana to Gakona Junction the road is less than exciting, unless you're looking for the perfect frost heave or road fissure to facilitate signature headprints in the roof of your vehicle. The highway is relatively straight, as there is nothing for it to go around and much of the country is permafrost. You come to **Chistochina,** one of the more beautiful Alaska names to the ear. Besides Mount Sanford and **Mount Drum** (to the right of Sanford), startling scenery is absent, except if you travel at sunrise, sunset, full moon, first snow, first leaves, or first love, in which case the magic will be there with no help needed from terrestial aberrations.

About 3 miles before the Tok Cutoff joins the Richardson Highway at Gakona Junction, the road drops into the shallow canyon created by the Copper River.

BEST RESTAURANT

Gakona Lodge ★ Gakona Lodge is an old roadhouse, built in 1905. It was added to the National Register of Historic Places in 1977 and makes an interesting stop. It is one in a series of roadhouses that once ran up the old Richardson Trail, spaced about a day's travel apart. Most of the roadhouses have burned down now. Gakona Lodge and Rika's Roadhouse at Big Delta are still operating as historic places, while Black Rapids Lodge, at Mile 227.4, is standing but in serious decline. At Gakona, a cluster of mostly log buildings includes the old carriage house, which is now a restaurant, and the main lodge. The historic feel has been maintained. The dining room is dark and comfortable. The log walls come complete with mounted animal heads and old-time Alaska tools. The menu consists of steaks and seafood with salad bar. Bring your poke. ■ *By the bridge, Mile*

2, *Tok Cutoff; PO Box 285, Gakona Junction, AK 99586;*
(907) 822-3482; $$.

THE RICHARDSON HIGHWAY

From Glennallen to Fairbanks

Unless you are agoraphobic, it is hard to imagine not liking driving the roads of Alaska. There is space, something hard to get away from in Alaska. Most of the time, the scenery will knock your eyeballs out. But there are also miles of wet lowlands. The country around Glennallen has stretches of lowland permafrost stuff, marshy bogs with trees like pipecleaners. You've got about 40 miles of this to drive through until you get to more exciting parts. The redeeming features are the distant regal mountains—Sanford (16,237 feet), Wrangell (14,163 feet), and Drum (12,010 feet)—which form a postcard backdrop.

For the first 30 miles, the Richardson Highway north from Glennallen is utilitarian. It's relatively straight with sections of generous frost heaves. The scenic attractions are caribou, if you're lucky, and views of the Gulkana River Gorge on the west side of the highway. The Gulkana River is a good salmon and rafting river. It runs out of Paxson and Summit Lakes. The float from Paxson Lake to Sourdough Campground at Mile 147.6 is popular for experienced river runners.

Your first good look at the Alaska Range comes when you round Hogan Hill, a row of shark's teeth running all the way across the horizon. The range begins near Tok, running west and then southwest through Denali National Park, ultimately becoming the Aleutian Chain. Mount McKinley (20,320 feet) is the highest mountain of this range and the highest in North America.

Here in the foothills of the Alaska Range, you can see the trans-Alaska oil pipeline curving and silver, winding its way across the terrain like a sculpture, sometimes above ground and sometimes under. Paxson Lake appears west of the highway—a long, deep lake, famous for lake trout.

Paxson Lake was named after the owner of Paxson Lodge, at Mile 185.5, one of the early roadhouses. The original lodge burned, but the new lodge goes by the same name. The town of Paxson has a population of 33. Before 1972, the year the George Parks Highway was completed, the only way to drive to Denali National Park, then known as Mount McKinley National Park, was to take the Denali Highway west from Paxson for 135 miles. If you wanted to drive to Fairbanks at that time, you also went through Paxson.

The road continues north from Paxson, climbing right alongside the Gulkana River, by now a sprightly creek that runs between Summit and Paxson Lakes. Summit Lake is at the di-

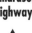

The
Richardson
Highway

▲

vide, where the waters run either north or south. The elevation here is 3,210 feet. Midway along the lake, a blackened hole and standing chimney mark the spot where Summit Lake Lodge stood until 1993, another piece of history turned into firewood.

For the next 40 miles, the road makes its way through the Alaska Range. You'll find serious mountains and scenery here, and the road is some of the best highway in Alaska. A canyon curves alongside the headwaters of the Delta River, with the Alaska pipeline showing up here and there as if it were shadowing you. At Mile 204, there's a pullout where spring water gushes through a pipe out of the side of the mountain. Fill up there and save the freight from France.

At Mile 227.4, you'll see the old Black Rapids Roadhouse on the east side of the road. It was one of the roadhouses on the Valdez Trail, and the part now falling down dates from 1905. It was originally called "The Black Rapids Hunting Lodge." The old roadhouses have been replaced by pump stations for the Alaska pipeline, a sign of the times.

The mountains get bigger. To the west, you see three of the great peaks of the Alaska Range: Deborah (12,339 feet), Hess (11,940 feet), and Hayes (13,832 feet). They don't look that big until you find out they're 40 miles away and dominate the horizon a good portion of the way into Fairbanks.

▼

**The
Richardson
Highway**

▲

The last 20 miles into Delta Junction puts you down on the flats. It might seem like it would be a letdown, but it's not. The scenery now comes as a marvel of straightness.

At the junction of the Richardson Highway and the official end of the Alaska Highway is **Delta Junction**. The Delta River, which you have followed from its source in the mountains down to the floodplains, runs right beside the town. People seem to be on their own time here, as well as having some to share.

The Richardson Highway continues into Fairbanks, 100 miles to the northwest, following first the Delta River and then the Tanana, which it joins at Big Delta, 10 miles down the road. If you have time, take the gravel road that runs along the river to Big Delta. There are good views of the mile-wide river bed and the Alaska Range as the road follows the bluff. Take the first turn to the left after passing the sign for Jack Warren Road, 2 miles out of Delta.

BIG DELTA STATE HISTORICAL PARK

In 1909, the Alaska Road Commission installed a ferry across the Tanana River on the old Valdez-to-Fairbanks trail to accommodate traffic to the gold fields. This was a natural place for a roadhouse, and John Hajdukovich built one that year. In 1917, he hired a Swedish immigrant, Rika Wallen, to run it for him. She bought it in 1923, and it became known as Rika's. She had a large garden and raised animals and poultry to supply the table. Rika operated the roadhouse into the late 1940s and lived there until her death in 1969, at the age of 94. After the ferry was replaced by a bridge, people no longer had to stop as they did in the past. More than 2,000 people crossed the river by ferry in 1925. Now, people don't even slow down.

In 1986, **Rika's Roadhouse** (Big Delta, Mile 275, Richardson Highway; (907) 895-4201) was reopened as a living history homestead, after being restored by the Alaska Division of Parks and Outdoor Recreation. Admission is free. Staff are attired in period costumes. During the tourist season, the restaurant is open daily and features homebaked goods. Just before crossing the Big Delta bridge, you'll see a parking area and interpretive display for the trans-Alaska pipeline, which makes an impressive sight as it crosses the river, especially in winter when it's all lit up. Only 90 miles remain to Fairbanks— Alaska's second largest city with 50,000 people—and the terminus of the Richardson Highway.

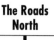
THE ALASKA HIGHWAY

From Tok to Delta Junction

The last chunk of the Alaska Highway runs from Tok to Delta Junction, where it joins the Richardson Highway for the trip into Fairbanks. It covers a scenic 100 miles. The road out of Tok runs for 15 miles, with hardly a bend until the road gets close to the Mentasta Mountains.

A rustic and scenic camping spot, the **Moon Lake State Recreation Site** comes at Mile 1331.9. A lovely spot, a quarter-mile off the highway, it has swimming and a small sandy beach.

Jan Lake Road turns off to the south at Mile 1353.7. **Jan Lake** is a half-mile back, nestled among the mixed birch- and spruce-covered hills. It is a pretty location and a good picnic spot. The lake is small and stocked with small rainbows. In the fall, if you're lucky, you'll see hundreds of sandhill cranes fly over in wavering filaments, sun reflecting off their beating wings as if from waves.

The road crosses the Johnson River bridge at Mile 1380.5. Most of the rivers have access roads that allow for a more intimate look and possible campsites (no amenities). Johnson River is especially nice in this regard. In a few miles, the road leaves the mountains and goes straight over flat land for 40 miles, right into Delta Junction. It is still a beautiful drive, but the beauty now comes with distance. To the south, there's a line of mountains. The closer ones are soft, while those farther back are white and craggy—the beginnings of the Alaska Range. The rivers are glacial and run in braids across broad shallow beds. At Mile 1403.6, Sawmill Creek Road takes off to the north, right through the **Delta Barley Project,** an agricultural project. There's an interpretive sign explaining the

The Alaska Highway

project, and you can decide if you want to face a gravel road to see more.

Although you expect to see signs for moose and caribou crossings, it is a surprise to see a sign warning you to watch out for bison. A herd of bison was transplanted from Montana in the 1920s to see how they'd do. They've done fine, much to the chagrin of the farmers who have been feeding them whether they wanted to or not. The **Bison Range,** 70,000 acres of grassland for fall and winter grazing, was established south of the highway to reduce agricultural losses. The last 25 miles into Delta is all new blacktop and has wide shoulders, a welcome stretch after all the frost heaves one enjoys as part of the Alaska road package.

DELTA JUNCTION

Delta Junction was established as a construction camp on the Richardson Highway in 1919. It is the official end of the Alaska Highway, and from here you have the choice of Alaska 4 south or Alaska 2 on into Fairbanks. Delta Junction's population is listed at 736. If you want to put your finger on the pulse of the town, go to **Shop-Rite Grocery and Deli,** (907) 895-4653. It all happens here. Dog food in 40-pound bags is stacked up beside the plywood deli booths. There's an espresso cart and fresh-made donuts from the bakery. The homemade soups come after the coffee-and-donut rush subsides. No yuppies here, just farmers mumbling about getting the rest of the hay in and other folks in work clothes and quilted jackets. The weather is *the* topic in the fall with all the geese and cranes filtering through in long strings; but it's also the topic the rest of the year because there's always weather.

THE CIRCULAR ROUTE

Anchorage-Glennallen-Valdez-Whittier-Anchorage, with a side trip to Chitina and McCarthy

A journey by land and sea, this route combines a series of scenic dramas. You can start either way. The route we have laid out has Anchorage as its starting point.

In essence, this is a spectacular drive out of Anchorage to Glennallen along the Glenn Highway, turning right onto the Richardson Highway, peeling off shortly (if you have a few extra days for a side trip to historic Kennicott and McCarthy, reached by the Edgerton Highway), then back to the Richardson Highway and heading south to the port town of Valdez. Explore Valdez (see Prince William Sound chapter), then take the ferry, part of the Alaska Marine Highway system, through Prince William Sound to the port town of Whittier. Drive your car off the ferry and onto the train. Go through the tunnel in the mountains and come out on the Seward Highway, just an hour or so south of Anchorage. Allow at least 4 or 5 days for the trip, the longer the better. The mountains and rivers beckon to the hiker, backpacker, fisherman, or rafter. And a side trip to McCarthy always offers a good time.

THE GLENN HIGHWAY

From Anchorage to Glennallen

The route lies east out of Anchorage, a journey of about 200 miles. Half an hour out of town, the Athabascan village of **Eklutna** is on your left and a beautiful mountain lake of the same name is 14 miles up a dirt road, off the highway to the right. Just before the bridge, look to the left and you'll see sofas and chairs lined up on the bluff overlooking the highway, where the locals lounge around watching the traffic flow.

Right before the Knik River bridge is the old road into **Palmer,** a scenic detour through this agricultural valley. After the bridge, you cross the Palmer Hay Flats. Be on the look-out for moose, particularly in the early morning. **Pioneer Peak** rises behind you, dominating the valley. It was named for the midwestern pioneers who came here in the 1930s to start a new life, fleeing the Dust Bowl during the Depression. Some of the most fantastic cold-weather vegetables are grown here—70-pound cabbages and foot-long carrots. If you're in the area during late August and the first of September, stick around for one of the state's most popular events—the **Alaska State Fair.** You'll pass the fairgrounds on the right as you head toward Palmer.

To visit the **Musk Ox Farm,** (907) 745-4151, turn at Mile 50.1, just past Palmer. These marvelous creatures can even be your namesake. For a modest donation of $50, you can have a musk ox named after you or your best friend. Contrary to their name, it's not the musk for which these animals are famous. In fact, they have no musk glands. Furthermore, they're not even oxen. They're really related to the goat and antelope family. But their great treasure is their underhairs, called *qiviut,* which are finer, lighter, and warmer than cashmere. Hats and scarves from qiviut make truly lovely, if expensive, gifts. The farm is open daily, May to September, with tours every half hour.

The next stretch of highway provides scenery of matchless beauty. The road follows the Matanuska River, then climbs the outer fringe of the Talkeetna Mountains, with the Chugach Mountains off to the right across the valley. As is true elsewhere in Alaska, many of the peaks in the Chugach are still unnamed, a reminder that this is still a young country, only recently explored. The stark and rugged mountains are interspersed with glaciers, including the Matanuska Glacier, which appears soon in this journey, off to the west. Meanwhile, you climb through a forest of aspen interspersed with evergreen:

THE DRUNKEN FOREST

At first sight, the trees seem to weave—first to the left, then to the right. No, it's not your eyes playing tricks on you. The trees really are leaning. Most of the land in northern Alaska consists of permanently frozen ground or "permafrost." During the summer, the top few inches of soil above the permafrost thaws out. It is in these few inches of moist soil that plants extend their roots. Trees growing in a permafrost zone can put down only shallow roots. The frozen soil inhibits further growth. Thus, their anchors are shaky and unstable. They will often grow at an angle, listing first this way, then that. Scientists call this "the drunken forest."

a lovely sight at any time, but if you hit it at the height of fall colors, it's a vision of golden beauty. Chickaloon is summer home to **NOVA: The Adventure Company,** (800) 746-5753, whitewater river-rafting guides who will take you on half-day trips down the Matanuska River. They offer everything from peaceful floats to wet and wild rides, depending on your thrills-and-chills quotient. Trips cost $50 to $80 per person.

King Mountain, one of the few named peaks in the area, rises with majesty to the south. Up above the confluence of the Chickaloon and Matanuska Rivers, there is a fine view over the valley. The road follows the shore of Long Lake and brings you to the **Matanuska Glacier.** This glacier comes close enough to the highway to be more or less readily accessible. However, the approach is controlled by a private operation, **Matanuska Glacier Park Resort,** (907) 745-2534, which owns some 540 acres in this area. The resort is a short drive from the highway over a steep, unpaved road. For a fee, you can drive within half a mile of the glacier. If you've never seen a glacier close up, it's a special experience.

Beyond Sheep Mountain, the road climbs to **Eureka Summit** (Eureka Lodge is a possible pie stop), and the scenery changes dramatically. The Chugach Mountains fall away to the south, as **Mount Drum** and the Wrangells appear in the east. A tundra-like plain opens up, studded by several lakes and stunted trees—the "drunken forest" in local parlance. (See box.) The vast **Nelchina Glacier** interrupts the dark range of the Chugach and gives its name to the caribou herd that frequents this area. Keep a look-out for these wild reindeer.

GLENNALLEN

For a taste of local color, tune into the radio message board *Caribou Clatter* on KCAM (790 on your AM dial during the news at 7am, noon, 5pm, and 9pm). In other regions of Alaska, this same radio message program has been called *Ptarmigan Telegraph, Tundra Drums,* and *Cabin Trapline.* The messages you hear are sometimes strange and wondrous, and always full of local color. To send a message on KCAM, call (907) 822-3306.

In Glennallen, at the junction of the Glenn and Richardson Highways, is a charming log cabin **visitors information booth,** dripping with flowers.

BEST LODGINGS

Sheep Mountain Lodge ★★★ As you climb up to Sheep Mountain, the trees thin out and it's possible to catch glimpses of Dall sheep high up on the mountains. The best place to break your trip or, for that matter, to stop for several days of adventure is Sheep Mountain Lodge. The lodge is run by David Cohen and his wife Diane Schneider. It is the best—and the only—place of this superb quality for many, many miles. Rustic and charming, the lodge is right on the highway. The entry is set off by a brilliant bank of lovingly tended flowers, which provides a special touch of class to this wilderness outpost. Individual cabins are sturdy and tastefully designed with comfort in mind. Views are stunning—wide-open country, glaciers, light woods. The hospitality is warm, and the lodge's dining room provides generous Alaska fare with a spicy Southwest touch. There is also a bunkhouse for larger parties or those on the cheap. ▪ *Mile 113.5, Glenn Hwy; HC 03, Box 8490, Palmer, AK 99645; (907) 745-5121; open May–Oct; some years open earlier for spring skiing.*

New Caribou Hotel An attractive place to stay if you get sleepy in Glennallen. It's on the tour-bus circuit, but the rooms are cheerful. ▪ *PO Box 329, Glennallen, AK 99588; toll-free in Alaska, (800) 478-3302; (907) 822-3302.*

THE RICHARDSON HIGHWAY
From Glennallen to Valdez

Turn right from the Glenn onto the Richardson Highway and head south. In a few miles you'll see the signs for the Copper Center Loop, a small road that swings you into the community of **Copper Center** and back out to the main road again. Along the way is the ranger station for **Wrangell–St. Elias National Park,** open daily in the summer, with books, maps, and information. If you are going on to McCarthy and Kennicott, check here for McCarthy Road conditions.

Traveling south on the Richardson Highway, the most intriguing sight—apart from spectacular nature—is a section of the oil pipeline, which transects Alaska, running 800 miles from the Arctic Ocean to the North Pacific, from Prudhoe Bay to Valdez. At various points, the pipeline parallels the road, crosses it, and recrosses it, all the way to Valdez. Shortly before descending into the port town of Valdez, often called Lit-

The Roads North

▼

The Circular Route

The Richardson Highway

▲

tle Switzerland because of the spectacular mountains and ice-fields, you'll pass the site of the World Extreme Skiing Championships, held in March every year at **Thompson Pass.**

BEST LODGINGS

Copper Center Lodge ★★ In Copper Center, there's a very cozy hotel, an old roadhouse brought up to date for comfort and still in operation. The roadhouse, on the banks of the Copper River, opened its door to travelers in 1898 and has been welcoming them ever since. It's a warm, family-run enterprise. ■ *Mile 101, Richardson Hwy, the Loop Rd; Drawer J, Copper Center, AK 99573; (907) 822-3245; fax (907) 822-5035; $$.*

WRANGELL–ST. ELIAS NATIONAL PARK AND PRESERVE

The Wrangell–St. Elias region is a mountain and ice kingdom of extraordinary beauty. It is the largest national park in the United States and has some of the highest peaks and the most extensive sweep of glaciers on the North American continent. It is mind boggling. Thirteen mountains rise more than 14,000 feet; four of them are higher than 16,000 feet. Mount St. Elias (18,008 feet) is the second highest peak in North America, next to Mount McKinley (20,320 feet) in Alaska. There are 75 named glaciers and many more unnamed glaciers. Together with its neighboring park in Canada, Kluane National Park, this region has been designated a World Heritage Site by the United Nations. Signed by 111 member nations, the World Heritage Convention declares such sites to be of such exceptional interest and such universal value that their protection is the responsibility of all mankind.

While several of the high peaks such as Mounts Sanford, Drum, and Blackburn and the still-active volcano of Mount Wrangell, can be viewed from the highways that skirt its borders, this is just a hint of what lies beyond.

This is a park for the wilderness seeker. There are relatively few visitor facilities. Only two unpaved roads penetrate the park at all: the McCarthy Road in the west and the Slana–Nebesna Road in the north. The National Park Service stresses that in this mountainous region where help is often days away, visitors need to be skilled in backcountry travel and carry proper survival gear. You need to be both self-motivated and self-sufficient. Park headquarters is at Mile 105.5 on the Old Richardson Highway, near Copper Center. It is open daily in the summer and weekdays in winter. There is also a ranger station at Nebesna, (907) 822-5238, and in the little town of Chitina, (907) 823-2205.

For more information, contact Superintendent, Wrangell–St. Elias National Park and Preserve, PO Box 439, Copper Center, AK 99573; (907) 822-5235.

EDGERTON HIGHWAY/McCARTHY ROAD
Includes Chitina, McCarthy, and Kennicott

A terrific side trip en route to Valdez begins when you peel off on the Edgerton Highway, which takes you to Chitina. From there, continue along the McCarthy Road to the Kennicott River, park the car, hop on the self-propelled aerial tram, and visit the historic mines and old ghost town of Kennicott and the picturesque town of McCarthy nearby.

At Mile 82.6, Richardson Highway, turn left onto the Edgerton Highway. Here, the scenery changes again. There is a sudden surge of political activism as you cruise through seemingly remote wilderness around **Kenny Lake,** where huge hand-painted signs on old boards scream "Dirty State Government!" and other such individualistic opinions.

CHITINA

Tundra gives way here to meadows and trees of middling size. Liberty Falls, a short distance off the road, is quite lovely, with clear cascading water and a scramble up the hillsides for the more energetic. From here, head on to **Chitina** (pronounced Chitna), which sits at the end of the gravel road under the shadow of Spirit Mountain. The year-round population here is about 50, but on a summer weekend, when the salmon are running in the Copper River and the dip-netters running right behind them, the population can sometimes balloon to 3,000 folks.

PLACES TO VISIT

There are two promising watering holes in Chitina. **Raven Dance** (Mile 32.5 on the Edgerton Highway) offers espresso and healthy stuff at the near end of town, called uptown Chitina. A little sign posted near the entrance gives the "Answers to the Top Ten Questions." Here are a few: "1) 59 miles, 3 hours, bumpy, dusty; 2) 50, counting the kids and dogs; 3) Seldom below minus 30° F; 4) Haul water, chop wood; Bonus Answer: Because the ones that run on weekends have all been fished out." Drive through town and stop at the far end, where the old fisherman stands with his dip net at the front door of the **It'll Do Cafe,** (907) 823-2244, open daily in summer.

Spirit Mountain Artworks (Box 22, Chitina, AK 99566; (907) 823-2222), just across the street from the cafe, is the creation of Art Koeninger. He bought the building for a song, intending to use parts for salvage, then became entranced by it, spent a fortune, renovated it, and now it's on the National Register of Historic Places. It's a fun gallery of fine Alaska art. "Husbands Welcome" says the sign out front. More than 80 Alaska artists are featured here. Art himself is a custom jeweler.

THE MCCARTHY ROAD

Now begins the fun. As you drive through imposing walls of rock, you are entering the McCarthy Road, built along the old railroad bed of the Copper River and Northwestern Railway, 59 miles of dirt washboard and potholes. When you can spare time from the futile effort of trying to avoid these pitfalls, enjoy the lovely forest, but keep your eyes peeled for other drivers careening around the corners and for miscellaneous old railroad spikes. These are not good for your tires. Although it's only 59 miles, it will take you at least 3 hours. In the height of summer, it can be a long, dusty ride.

Above the trees, the Wrangell Mountains rise stark and bare, and you can spot the sharp division between the lighter limestone on top and the darker volcanic rock below. That division is where the metals—copper and gold—are to be found. On the ground, the erratic spruce hen or ptarmigan may scuttle across your path as you bounce along at a comfortable 20 mph. About 15 miles out, the road narrows somewhat just before you get to the **Kuskalana Bridge,** but the change is not dramatic. The bridge is! It is an old railway trestle that has been reinforced. The view into the river gorge is heart-stopping and should be the biggest thrill you get on the way. If you want more thrills, some people bungee-jump here. Think of that!

If you avoid a flat (a minor miracle—so do carry mounted spares) or other mishap, you should reach the end of the road at Copperpoint, a minuscule encampment on the banks of the Kennicott River. Now you are faced with fording whitewater rapids. Do not attempt this in your car unless it is winter and forty below.

The McCarthy Road ends at the whitewater of the Kennicott River, and the next stage of the journey involves pulling yourself and your gear hand-over-hand across an open aerial tramway. At first blush, this might look somewhat intimidating, but plunge ahead. The skills are simple and easily learned; there are always a few extra hands to help pull, and in the end the trip becomes a joy ride, even for one who gets vertigo.

Unfortunately, you may soon be deprived of this experience, as a footbridge is proposed in the near future. If you hurry, you might get to ride the tram before it slips into history.

MCCARTHY/KENNICOTT

Copper was discovered in these hills in the 1860s. Some mining took place in the last part of the century, but with the completion of the Copper River and Northwestern Railway in 1911, which ran from Cordova on the coast 200 miles into the mountains, business really boomed. The story of that railroad, built across the face of two moving glaciers by the brilliant engineer and wild Irishman Michael J. Heney, is a saga of great propor-

THRILL OF THE WATER

On your birthday, heed the Alaska code: "Do something daring you've never done before."

Whitewater river rafting is one of the entertainments provided for eager visitors to Kennicott/McCarthy. A half-day trip goes about 5 miles down the Kennicott River. The full-day show goes farther down through the gorge and joins the Nizina River.

The procedure is simple. Cross the tramway from McCarthy back to Copperpoint, where Howard or one of his guides at **Copper Oar** *will outfit you with rubber boots, waterproof gear, and life jackets, just in case you get splashed or dunked. Then carefully heed the instructions on shore: "Hold on and stay in the raft." You don't want to go overboard; this glacier river—flowing directly out of the ice—is nippy. However, if you should get punted out, be sure to keep your nose above water, point your feet downriver, and grab the rope thrown you. Best yet, stay pinned in the middle and let the young folks get wet.*

Narrowly avoiding several booby traps with one shove of the raft, you are off into the raging water, twirling, plunging, and bouncing along. A deluge descends over the front passengers, and they discover that water has found its way in where it ought not to be. And so it goes until, before you realize it, you have reached the end of the tour and are hauling the boat out of the water (unless you are going the full day). If you've never done this before, no matter what your age it's really quite thrilling. If you're lucky, and it's your birthday that day, you might find your shoes (trucked down to water's edge) tied up with ribbons, and special homebaked ginger cookies inside from the local gourmet chef. Watch for her monthly column—"Cooking With Carly"—in the Wrangell–St. Elias News.

—David C. Elliot
(upon the occasion of his 78th birthday)

**The Circular
Route**

*McCarthy/
Kennicott*

tions. (So you will not be confused or think we are bad spellers, note that the spelling of Kennicott Glacier, named for Robert Kennicott, early explorer and geologist, is spelled with an *i*. The Lodge spells its name the same way, as does the settlement of Kennicott. But you will see that any reference to the Kennecott Mines is spelled with an *e*. This is what is known as a historical mistake, now historical fact. Someone from those yesteryears misspelled Kennicott, and it stuck.)

The ore that came out of the Kennecott Mines high up on the hills here was about 80 percent pure copper in the early days. It was the richest and purest deposit of copper in the world. But the large costs of transportation required that it be further refined on the spot, and as the percentage of copper in the native ore declined in later years, refinement became increasingly important.

This was performed in the multistoried, red building that you can still see framed dramatically against the hillside today. The ore was brought down from the mines and decanted into a vertical process where, level after level, it was crushed, pulverized, shaken, washed, and sifted until it was ready to be tipped into waiting railroad cars. To this mechanical operation, the mine added a chemical separation process in the 1920s. This took place in a separate building across the road.

Both of these buildings, as well as the vast steam plant for generating electricity, can be seen on a guided tour (see Things to Do, below), which takes a couple of hours. As you climb up the 192 steps in the processing plant, you will be astonished at the solidity of this rundown building. Much of the machinery has been ravaged by past salvage operations, but nonetheless this journey into the past is quite special. Kennicott was once a boom town with more than 800 workers, until the price of copper fell and the operation was abandoned. Today it is a ghost town, with the exception of one or two hardy souls who live here in cabins year-round.

▼
The Circular Route

McCarthy/ Kennicott

▲

The little town of McCarthy sprang up at the edge of the Kennicott River, just across the tramway today. It was a place for miners' relaxation in the old days. Only a handful of folks live here now, but it is a popular destination for Alaskans all summer long, particularly for celebrations on the Fourth of July and Labor Day. Five miles up the hill is the ghost town of Kennicott and the Kennicott Lodge.

Access

Drive the roads from Anchorage to McCarthy (see The Circular Route); or take the fast route with regularly scheduled air service from Anchorage through Gulkana to McCarthy on **Ellis Air Taxi,** (800) 478-3368 or (907) 822-3368. Service is year-round, Wednesday and Friday departures and return. A van service, to save driving the McCarthy Road, is available in summer, departing from Chitina, Glennallen, and Valdez. Call **Backcountry Connection,** toll-free in Alaska, (800) 478-5292, or (907) 822-5292.

THINGS TO DO

Flightseeing In this mountain kingdom of castle peaks, glaciers, and stunning valleys, flightseeing is a stunning experience not to be missed. A tempestuous sea of wild and jagged peaks spreads before you (and the pilot carefully misses them all), as you fly up bare rocky passes. The multicolored cliffs are reminiscent of southwestern deserts. Glaciers tumble from the brilliant snowfields down icefalls to black crushed rock below. As your eyes get used to the dimensions of aerial vision, you may spot herds of mountain goats. Two good charter air services fly trips out of McCarthy: **Wrangell Mountain Air** (PO Box MXY #16, McCarthy, AK 99588; (800) 478-1160 or (907) 554-4400) and **McCarthy Air** (Box MXY #16, McCarthy, AK 99588; (800) 245-6909).

River Rafting For whitewater thrills, head back across the tram over the Kennicott River (by now you're an old pro) and sign up with **Copper Oar.** Their office is located in a little cabin at the end of the McCarthy Road. For information, contact Copper Oar, PO Box MXY, McCarthy, AK 99588; phone/fax (907) 554-4453 (May–Sept); voice mail (907) 566-0771.

Tours of the Ghost Town With headquarters in the Mother Lode Powerhouse of the Kennecott Mines, just past the Kennicott Lodge, **St. Elias Alpine Guides** (PO Box 111241, Anchorage, AK 99511; (907) 277-6867) has the only access to the privately owned old mine buildings. This is a fascinating tour if you're into history or mining, so take advantage of it if it's still offered. The future of these old buildings is quite uncertain, and a unique piece of history may slip between our proverbial fingers. Some of the guides live year-round in McCarthy and are as interesting as the buildings. The tour costs $25/person and can be arranged through the Kennicott Lodge.

WILDERNESS GUIDES

Copper Oar If you want to go rafting for a day or 10 days, hop aboard with these experienced guides. They have a variety of trip offerings, from a 2-hour spin down the Kennicott River to 10 days down the Chitina and Copper Rivers (to Cordova on Prince William Sound). In operation since 1985, the company is owned by river guide Howard Mozen. Contact him at Copper Oar, PO Box MXY, McCarthy, AK 99588; phone/fax (907) 554-4453 (May–Sept); voice mail (907) 566-0771.

St. Elias Alpine Guides This highly respected guide service, owned by Bob Jacobs, who resides in Anchorage, will take you on ghost-town tours, climbing on glaciers, rappelling off mountains, or on long backpacking journeys and first ascents in the Wrangells. For a brochure, contact St. Elias Alpine Guides, PO Box 111241, Anchorage, AK 99511; (907) 277-6867.

BEST LODGINGS

Kennicott Glacier Lodge ★★★ This is a fine wilderness resort, dedicated to the pleasure of hikers, river rafters, and all outdoorsmen and women. It does not encourage reading in bed, but you can take lunch on the verandah, which has a breathtaking view that extends from the Chugach Mountains to Mount Blackburn, the highest mountain in the Wrangells, and takes in Kennicott Glacier. Descended from the drafts-

The Roads
North
▬

▼
The Circular
Route
▬
McCarthy/
Kennicott

89

**The Roads
North**

▼

**The Circular
Route**

*McCarthy/
Kennicott*

▲

men's quarters or bunkhouse of the old mining days, it is still painted in the symbolic red and white colors of the day. Bathrooms are shared. Dining is family style with simple but hearty meals. And the staff couldn't be friendlier. The lodge accommodates only 50 guests, so book early. ■ *Across the Kennicott Glacier, 5 miles up the road from McCarthy; Box 103940, Anchorage, AK 99510; toll-free (800) 582-5128; (907) 258-2350; $$$ ($160/night double, with glacier view); beer and wine only; AE, MC, V; local checks OK; open summer only, mid-May–mid-Sept.*

McCarthy Lodge and Ma Johnson Hotel ★★ You can't get much more classic Alaska than this moose-horn–bedecked lodge in the center of town. While up at Kennicott, it's more the polo shirts-and-Courvoisier crowd, down in McCarthy it's t-shirts and beer. Who enjoys themselves more? Go test it out. McCarthy Lodge recently started doing group bookings for winter getaways in the Wrangells. ■ *In McCarthy. Over the river and through the woods, follow the signs; PO Box MXY, via Glennallen, AK 99588; (907) 554-4402; fax (907) 554-4404; $$$; full bar; MC, V; no checks; breakfast and dinner included in room cost; open summers; winter adventure packages available for group reservations.*

THE EDGERTON CUT OFF TO VALDEZ

After a side trip to McCarthy, it's only 83 miles down the Richardson Highway to the port of Valdez. You'll drive alongside the Tonsina River, with the trans-Alaska oil pipeline crossing the highway at several points en route, carrying oil from the North Slope to the terminal on the edge of Prince William Sound. From there, it will be loaded into supertankers and shipped south. Thompson Pass (2,771 feet) is the site of death-defying skiing championships every spring and a winter playground for snow enthusiasts year-round.

Spend an afternoon rafting rivers, exploring Valdez, or hiking a mountain, then hop on the ferry from Valdez to Whittier. (See Prince William Sound chapter for more details.) It's a gorgeous trip through the Sound past Columbia Glacier—about 7 hours. In Whittier, the train schedule usually matches the ferry schedule, so you drive right on the flatcars, roll through the tunnel in the mountains (about a half-hour trip), and come out the other side, where you drive off and onto the Seward Highway. From there, it's only an hour north into Anchorage. And voilà! The circle is complete.

SUGGESTED READING

Janson, Lone. *The Copper Spike.* Anchorage: Alaska Northwest Publishing Co., 1975. The story of the Copper River and Northwestern Railway and early stories of Valdez,

Cordova, and Katalla.

The Milepost. Bellevue, Washington: Vernon Publications Inc., published yearly. Don't drive the roads without it. This is truly, as it touts itself, the "Bible of North Country Travel Since 1949," taking you from milepost to milepost along all Alaska's roads.

McPhee, John. *Coming Into the Country.* New York: Noonday Press, 1991. The story of Alaska and Alaskans, from life in remote bush areas to urban centers. Excellent writing, and one of McPhee's best.

ANCHORAGE AND BEYOND

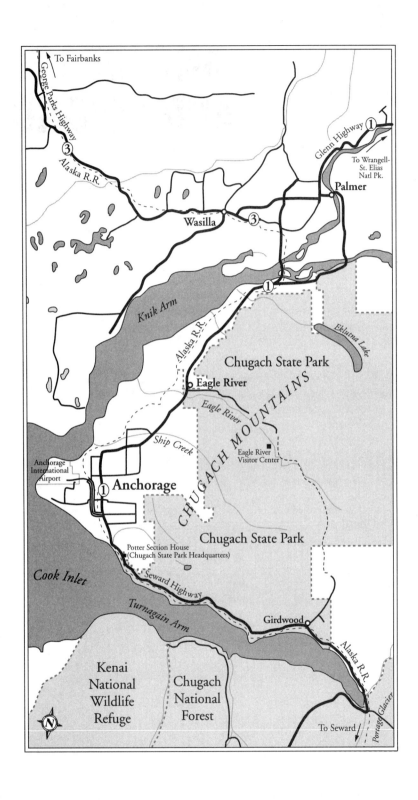

Anchorage and Beyond

Including Palmer, Eagle River, Girdwood, and Chugach State Park

For many people, the greater Anchorage area is where you can get it all: a city with a small, albeit enthusiastic, nightlife, restaurants, and plays, plus access to the half-million–acre Chugach State Park, an area packed with trails, streams, glaciers, bears, and moose. To the north, the wilderness playgrounds of the Susitna and Matanuska Valleys give way to views of the Chugach and Alaska Ranges. If the weather cooperates, Mount McKinley, which locals simply call Denali or "The Mountain," juts above the horizon. And in the right season, salmon run so thick you have to watch your step crossing a stream.

Seasons are alternately fleeting and harsh. Summer is short and intense. By September, the leaves are turning a vibrant gold. By October, frost has arrived and snow (euphemistically called "termination dust") is settling into the mountains. Winter hits hard and stays well into April. Temperatures can drop to below zero for a week or two at a time, but usually stay in the teens and 20s. By mid-May, the land comes alive again. The 6 hours of winter sunlight has nearly tripled. Summer is just a few weeks away. Not that the region has what most people from the Lower 48 would call "summer." Temperatures rarely get above 70°F, and rain is common. The average temperature in Anchorage in July is about 57°F. But on days when the sun shines until midnight and the Chugach Mountains scream with color, this place is spectacular.

PALMER/EAGLE RIVER

Palmer sits at the center of what little agricultural life Southcentral Alaska has. The town's roots were put down during the Great Depression, when the federal government sent Dust Bowl farmers north. To this day, farmers still try to make the best of a short but intense growing season, raising huge cabbages and oversized zucchini. Stop at any number of farmers' stalls along the highway for sweet carrots, lettuce, and a cabbage so big you'll have to buy it a separate plane ticket home.

Eagle River, a town of 26,000, lies midway between Palmer and Anchorage. Sheer mountainsides and a river-scored valley dwarf any hint of suburban sprawl. This is one entrance to Anchorage's marvelous backyard: Chugach State Park. (See below.) **Eagle River Visitors Center,** (907) 694-2108, can provide information about the park and suggest good day hikes.

BEST RESTAURANTS

Bombay House ★★ With the determination of a devoted gardener, Parminder Jassal turned this little hole-in-the-wall into a polished spot for surprisingly good—and occasionally remarkable—Indian food. Ashok Mehra from New Delhi runs the kitchen. As a concession to more timid western palates they have tempered the hot spices. Be sure to ask for more heat when you try the tangy, spicy lamb vindaloo and contrast it with a gentle, buttery tikka masala, a dish of tandoor-cooked meat in a rich sauce of cream and tomato. ▪ *On the east side of the main street through Eagle River; Eagle River Shopping Ctr, Old Glenn Hwy; (907) 696-6055; $$; beer and wine; MC, V, DIS; checks OK; dinner daily.* ♿

Vagabond Blues ★ With its warm wood floors and ambience, this is a delightful harbor for the gentle-hearted in Palmer. Great cinnamon rolls, espresso, pastries, bread, pasta salads, and bagel sandwiches top the menu. Soups such as a creamy broccoli with large florets are homemade and served in a local artist's handmade pottery bowls. The strawberry pie alone is worth the drive. Live music featuring local talent on weekends adds to the panache. ▪ *Koslosky Center in downtown Palmer; 642 S Alaska St, Palmer; (907) 745-2233; $; no alcohol; no credit cards; local checks only; open daily.* ♿

ANCHORAGE

People who live in Anchorage often say the best thing about it is that it's 20 minutes away from the real Alaska. Built on the fortunes of the railroad, war, and oil, it began in 1915 as a tent city on the banks of Ship Creek. Today, half the state's population lives in this metropolis. A center for politics and the arts, it's also a gateway for adventures into Alaska's outback.

The Park Strip was once the very edge of town. In the 1920s, it was a combined airfield and golf course. Today it defines the edge of downtown. There, you can watch sunny, late-night softball games, during which an outfielder is as likely to watch the midnight sunset in awe as watch the play. Though few in number, highly trained chefs prepare the world's best seafood with aplomb. Anglers pull 40-pound king salmon out of **Ship Creek,** a river of wildlife in the shadow of downtown's glass-skinned office buildings. During the right season (early March), a visitor can see the start of the most famous sled-dog race in the world, cross-country ski to lunch, then go to a Broadway musical in the evening.

BEST ESPRESSO

One of our favorite java joints is **Side Street Espresso,**
412 G Street, in the heart of downtown, (907) 258-9055.
*Move over, Seattle. These guys probably serve the best lattes
on the West Coast. The place is tiny and has only five tables.
But the folks here are funny and friendly. Pay attention to
their daily special announcements, delivered with a twist of
artistic humor. The two big roasting companies in town
are* **Cafe Del Mundo** *and* **Kaladi Brothers Coffee Company.** *First to truly launch Anchorage onto the coffee scene
was roastmaster Perry Merkel with Cafe Del Mundo. He runs
several cafes downtown and his main one in midtown at
341 E Benson Boulevard, (907) 274-0026. Kaladi Brothers
Coffee Company has its main operation at 6921 Brayton
Drive, (907) 344-6510, with lots of great food and a warm
atmosphere.*

Access

Most people fly to Anchorage. Some drive the Alaska Highway
through Canada from the Lower 48. Others take cruise ships.
Once here, as with all big cities, you can choose between rental
cars and public transportation. The bus system, called **The
People Mover,** (907) 343-6543, will move you about town. The
Alaska Railroad, (907) 265-2494, a 5-minute walk from downtown, will take you north to Denali National Park or south to
Seward on Resurrection Bay.

Anchorage

Information

Information

The little log cabin with cascades of flowers, located in the
heart of downtown on Fourth Avenue and F Street, is the most
charming and popular of the five tourist centers maintained by
the **Anchorage Convention and Visitors Bureau,** (907) 274-
3531. The first kiosk for a self-guided tour of old Anchorage's
colorful past stands directly outside. Catty-corner, in the old
Federal Building, is the **Alaska Public Lands Information
Center** (605 W Fourth Avenue, Suite 105; (907) 271-2737), with
its marvelous display and information on parks, refuges,
forests, hikes, cabins, wildlife, and more. The *Anchorage Daily
News* publishes an arts/entertainment guide named "8" every Friday, which contains food, music, theater, and special
events around town. For another sprightly look at the local
arts scene, pick up a copy of *Visual Dog,* at Cyrano's Bookstore, downtown at 413 D Street.

ART AND CULTURE

The **Alaska Center for the Performing Arts** in Town Square
is the hub of dance, music, and theater performances in town.

You can't miss it. In summer, the little park in front is ablaze with colorful flowers. In winter, it's lit up with Christmas lights. It covers the ground between E and G Streets and Fifth and Sixth Avenues. The box office has a display showing each season's events and sells you tickets, or you can reserve them through Carrstix ticket outlets, (907) 263-2787.

During the summer, Native dance groups perform daily as part of the **Alaska Native Performance Series** at the Anchorage Museum of History, 121 W 7th Avenue; (907) 263-5170. The AFN Convention (Alaska Federation of Natives) offers a wonderful opportunity to see dancing from villages all over Alaska at *Quyana* ("Thank You"). Quyana performances take place in October at the Egan Convention Center, 555 W 5th Avenue, directly across from the performing arts center.

Anchorage has a symphony orchestra and its own opera company. With the dark winters, community theater, too, has always been important in the far north. Some of the most successful and ambitious in recent years have been **Valley Performing Arts,** headquartered in the Matanuska Valley, (907) 745-2484; **Cyrano's Off-Center Playhouse,** 413 D Street, (907) 274-2599; and the **University of Alaska Anchorage Drama Department,** (907) 786-4721.

The only major venue for sculpture and painting in the area is the **Anchorage Museum of History and Art,** (907) 343-4326. The upper floor is devoted to the history of Alaska. During tourist season, the museum hosts major touring exhibits, such as the Smithsonian's "Crossroads of Continents" or glass art by Seattle artist Dale Chihuly.

For the world's largest selection of books on Alaska and the North, visit **Cook Inlet Book Company,** 415 W 5th Avenue, (907) 258-4544. Conveniently located downtown, it also has a large magazine selection and is open 7 days a week.

THINGS TO DO

Coastal Trail Bike, walk, blade, jog, or ski the Tony Knowles Coastal Trail, which runs for miles along the shores of Cook Inlet. This is one of the great treasures of the city, coursing like a lifeline from neighborhood to airport to wilderness trails. Everybody uses the trail, including porcupines, moose, and bears. Once you get to **Kincaid Park**, the wilderness trails there are a mecca for running in the summer and skiing in the winter, and are the site of world-class cross-country ski races. Bikes can be rented downtown at **Anchorage Coastal Bicycle Rentals** (414 K Street; (907) 279-1999); or **Downtown Bicycle Rental** (145 W Sixth; (907) 279-5293). Skis can be rented at **REI** (1200 W Northern Lights Boulevard; (907) 272-4565), which also has interesting weekly programs covering everything from mountain climbing to ski waxing.

Historic Walking Tour Look for the blue, three-sided kiosks. An award-winning stroll from kiosk to kiosk is filled with gossip, stories, and photographs from yesteryear, which will take you on a self-guided journey through old Anchorage. The first kiosk stands in front of the log cabin visitors center on Fourth Avenue. Meet that beloved rascal Joe Spenard, movie mogul Cap Lathrop, Creampuff Bill, and No-Kill-'Em Gillam. Visit "Silk Stocking Row" and see where the fancy folks lived, or Bootlegger's Cove, once honeycombed with whiskey tunnels. Some thought the Wild West had had its final fling, but this was a new frontier. "The only thing more prevalent than the fine dust which clogs the air is the raw whiskey with which they wash it down," observed one disgusted federal bureaucrat in Anchorage's early days, thoroughly unimpressed by the new railroad town and the moral fiber of its inhabitants.

Chugach State Park Whether you have half a day or a day, head for the mountains. This is as wild as anywhere in Alaska. And it's in Anchorage's own backyard. (See below.)

NIGHTLIFE

Spenard, once the racier part of Anchorage, is home to **Chilkoot Charlie's,** a bar with the infamous motto "We cheat the other guy and pass the savings on to you." Chilkoot's, at 2435 Spenard Road, (907) 272-1010, has a loyal crowd and a lot of one-timers who come to catch live bands, drink beer, and walk around on wood chips in what's billed as a rustic Alaska saloon.

Anchorage

*Festivals/
Events*

Don't miss the **Fly By Night Club,** 3300 Spenard Road, (907) 279-7726, with the *Whale Fat Follies,* billed as "the show the Alaska Chamber of Commerce doesn't want you to see." It'll tell you more about the inside humor of Alaska than you'll learn anywhere else. After the show, a hoppin' little house band plays some rockin' blues. **The Wave,** 3103 Spenard Road, (907) 561-9283, is a mixed but largely gay bar where you'll find the biggest retro and Top 40 dance club in town.

Coffeehouses are a fast-growing part of Anchorage nightlife. **Cyrano's Cafe and Bookstore,** 413 D Street, (907) 274-2599, has coffee and a small theater, and often hosts readings and film nights. **The Java Joint,** 2911 Spenard Road, (907) 562-5555, offers local art, good lattes, and live entertainment ranging from Irish night to punk night.

FESTIVALS/EVENTS

Fur Rondy To see the real Anchorage, visit in mid-February for the winter festival more formally known as the Fur Rendezvous. That's French, Alaska-style, for a fur get-together. Originally, trappers came in from the Bush to sell their pelts and spend some money. The cabin-fever festival today features all that's great and strange about Anchorage. On opening night, a spectacular display of fireworks lights up the winter sky. Anchorage goes all out here because on the Fourth of July the long daylight hours make fireworks nearly invisible. People participate in more than 100 contests ranging from ice bowling to oyster slurping.

Iditarod Trail Sled Dog Race   This race kicks off from Fourth Avenue in downtown Anchorage, the first Saturday of every March. The city is packed with television cameras, howling dogs, racing colors, and fur-clad mushers. For a brief moment, it all feels very glamorous. But in a couple of hours they are out of here and on their way across the wilderness, more than a thousand miles to Nome, and the city quiets down again.

Alaska State Fair   The fair dominates the tiny town of Palmer in the Matanuska Valley during the last week in August and the first weekend in September. The 10-day event is a cornucopia of music, rodeos, horse shows, carnival rides, food booths, and agricultural displays. Yes, they really do have 80-pound cabbages, 23-pound kale, and zucchinis as big as your arm. It's a good time. Everybody goes to the fair.

BEST RESTAURANTS

Jens' Restaurant ★★★★ Jens Hansen, of the restaurant that bears his name, is a wild Dane who is at once enchanting, zany, and incredibly knowledgeable about food. He'll eat caviar by the tablespoonful and dance on his wine bar, but when it comes to serious cooking, he's the man. No one else in the city has such a way with black cod, salmon, or halibut. His menu will always reflect his heritage: cabbage, root vegetables, smoked or cured fish, and light veal and pork meatballs called frikadeller. Mussels in mustard sauce make a nice nosh with a glass of wine, or go all out with a traditional rack of lamb or the pepper steak favored by locals. Inexpensive but tasty wines and crack waiters make for a nice evening. If you're feeling rich and rowdy, stick around after dinner and party with the well-to-do but silly crowd that pools in the wine bar next to the restaurant. ■ *In the strip mall on the corner of 36th Ave and Arctic Blvd; 701 W 36th Ave, Anchorage; (907) 561-5367; $$; beer and wine; V, MC, AE, DIS, DC; local checks only; lunch, Mon–Fri, dinner Tues–Sat.* ⅊

Marx Bros. Cafe ★★★★ Chef Jack Amon likes to claim he was the first in Alaska to start cooking with sun-dried tomatoes. For more than a decade, this little historic house in downtown, built during the early railroad era, has been home to some of the city's most innovative cuisine. In the summer, greens and edible flowers from the garden garnish delicious Alaska seafood such as halibut baked with a macadamia-nut crust or roasted poblano chiles rellenos stuffed with Alaska king crab. In the winter, fixed-price ethnic nights feature cuisine from the likes of Tuscany and Provence. Try a caesar salad whipped up tableside by master artist Van Hale, also co-owner and keeper of the impressive 10,000-bottle cellar, one of the top three cellars in town. Don't miss the crème caramel made with rum and coconut milk. Candlelight and sweet views of Cook Inlet (ask for a view table when you make a reservation) only add to the panache. ■ *On Third Ave, downtown near the Elks Club; 627 W Third Ave, Anchorage; (907) 278-2133; fax (907) 258-6279; $$$; beer and wine; MC, V, AE, DC; checks OK; dinner, daily (closed Sun in winter); dining room but no bathrooms.*

Sacks Cafe ★★★★ Consistently adventurous food built with top-notch ingredients makes Sacks a welcome oasis. Knockout starters include sweet ahi tuna, barely seared on the outside and served over a healthy bed of Napa cabbage slaw with crisp-fried, grated ginger and a pat of hot wasabe. Chef Daniel Wendell dreams up a dish or two every night, centered on fresh Alaska fin fish graced with some exotic combination of favorites like pecans, pine nuts, oriental sauces, black beans, or ginger. The venison is butter-soft and roasted with pepper and red chile with a subtly smoky roasted tomato demiglace. Soups are stand-outs and include a slightly spicy African peanut and a cold cantaloupe soup kissed with cinnamon. Locals love lunch here, returning for spinach salad with marinated Swiss cheese and Thai chicken sandwich with spicy peanut dressing on a baguette. The chocolate gâteau and ginger crème brulée are close to ethereal. ■ *Fifth Ave, across from the Alaska Center for the Performing Arts; 625 W Fifth Ave, Anchorage; (907) 276-3546; $$; wine and beer; V, MC, AE; local checks only; lunch Mon–Sat, dinner daily, Sun brunch.* &

Anchorage

Restaurants

Crow's Nest ★★★ The bird's-eye view, fancy service, and feeling of elegance makes dinner here a pleasure. Chef Simon Newall adds a new zing to some old-fashioned dishes such as escargot (served with a sauce trilogy featuring pesto, wild mushrooms, and garlic butter) or lobster and crab bisque, which he livens up with citrus and cognac. The fresh Kodiak scallops are huge, sweet, and cooked to perfection. The wine list is one of the finest in Anchorage. Feel pampered when they serve your entree from under a dramatic silver dome, and enjoy the best view of the city from downtown. Be sure to specify *which* view you'd like: take the inlet in the summer and the city in winter's darkness. They also have the fanciest brunch in town—the only one with fresh oysters and, sometimes, leg of lamb. ■ *At the top of the Hotel Captain Cook; 939 W Fifth Ave, Anchorage; (907) 276-6000; $$$; full bar; V, MC, DIS, AE, DC; checks with major credit card OK; dinners Mon–Sat (often closed Tues or Wed in winter); Sun brunch.* &

OTHER BESTS

A recent readers' poll conducted by the Anchorage Daily News *highlighted a few other bests that local Anchorage folks rate highly.*

Best Bookstore
Borders Music and Books. Cyrano's Bookstore took second, followed closely by Metro Music and Books.

Best Rooftop View
The big winner is the Crow's Nest in the Captain Cook.

Best Alaska-Style Bar
Chilkoot Charlie's was first. The Fly By Night Club was a distant second.

Best View of the City
A few people voted for "the one in my rear view mirror," but the winner was our beloved Flattop Mountain.

Best Overnight Hike
Crow Pass first, Resurrection Trail second, and Williwaw Lakes third.

Best Day Hike
Flattop Mountain, with McHugh Peak and Wolverine Peak second and third, respectively.

Best Place to Ride a Bike
The Coastal Trail, Kincaid Park, and Eklutna Lake.

Best Unfettered Stretch of Pavement for In-line Skating
Again, the Coastal Trail. The highway-hugging bike path from Muldoon to Eagle River was second. An airport runway ranked third, but we're not sure how safe or legal that is.

Best Local Beer
Alaska Amber from Alaska Brewing Co. in Juneau blew away the competition. Bird Creek's Ol' 55 came in second, and Alaska Pale Ale from Juneau took third.

Best Burger
Arctic Roadrunner.

Best Pizza
Only a handful of votes separated the winner, Pizza Olympia on Spenard Road, from second place, L'Aroma, next to New Sagaya.

F Street Station ★★★ A freewheeling, casual bar with a surprisingly terrific kitchen, F Street has redefined bar food in Alaska. The cheeseburgers, served with crisp, hand-cut fries, are the best in the city. Calamari is tender and the sautéed scallops worthy. Go for the daily special, whether it's a saffron-infused seafood chowder, a piece of swordfish in a light beurre blanc, or a steak sandwich cooked rare and served with wild mushrooms on a baguette. A lot of legal types hang out here. Avoid crowds by heading in for a late lunch or supper. ■ *325 F St, Anchorage; (907) 272-5196; $; full bar; MC, V, AE; local checks only; lunch and dinner daily.* ₷

Simon and Seafort's Saloon and Grill ★★★ Part of a West Coast restaurant chain that has honed its art to a fine edge, Simon's is probably the most popular place in Anchorage for steaks and seafood. The consistency, the opportunity for a beautiful view of Cook Inlet, and the occasional flashes of greatness with fish and shellstock make going here a fun, warm, and pleasurable occasion. Even in the height of tourist season, you can usually get a table if you're willing to wait and munch in the bar. It's light and airy with a bustling and upbeat atmosphere. Wild Alaska salmon is good, with cracked black pepper and honey, served over greens with artichoke tartar sauce. The locals love the prime rib, made-from-scratch margaritas using fresh lime juice, and the largest selection of single malt scotches in Alaska. ■ *Main floor of an office building on L St and Fifth Ave; 420 L St, Anchorage; (907) 274-3502; $$; full bar; MC, V, AE; checks OK; lunch and dinner, Mon–Sat, dinner Sun.* ₷

Anchorage

Restaurants

Tempura Kitchen ★★★ Popular with the small Japanese community in Anchorage, this is a tasty experience. Take all the side-striped shrimp you can when they're in season. (Shrimpers start pulling them from Prince William Sound in mid-April and continue until the end of July. Some are caught during a short fall season, as well.) Order them as sushi, with the heads deep fried on the side, or fried whole and served with a wedge of lemon. Try the sushi made with snapper and served with ponzu sauce, or simply trust the sushi chefs, who always know what's best. ■ *Off Spenard Rd, south of 36th Ave; 3826 Spenard Rd, Anchorage; (907) 277-2741; $$; beer and wine; V, MC, DIS, AE, DC; local checks only; lunch, Mon–Fri; dinner daily.* ₷

Campo Bello ★★ Campo Bello offers a fine menu, from hearty ragouts to delicate pastas and seafood dishes. Although this restaurant is still a newcomer and prone to rough spots, the gentle, candlelit interior offers a wonderful backdrop for fine art and promising food. Appetizers are particularly inventive, and the lively calamari scalloppine with capers and lemon comes to the table fork-tender. Meals are accompanied by a winning caesar salad or cup of homemade soup. ■ *In a strip* *mall near Arctic and 36th; 601 W 36th Ave, Anchorage; (907) 563-2040; $$; MC, V; local checks only; lunch, Mon–Fri; dinner, Mon–Sat.* ᐊ

Corsair ★★ This is dining in the Old World style—a continental cuisine rich with sauces and butter, everything flamed or carved tableside. You slip down wide stairs and enter a dark restaurant where waiters in tuxedos do almost every dish at your table, from tossing salads to flaming after-dinner drinks. Go ahead, splurge on that good bottle of Burgundy; they've got probably the best cellar in town. Hans Kruger and crew also do nice rich things with oysters, such as topping them with pâté and béarnaise sauce. Heck, why not get a chateaubriand (a thick center cut of beef tenderloin for two) and have it carved tableside? On Thursdays, Kruger does three-course German meals that are worth a visit—if only for his spaetzle and homemade sauerkraut. ■ *West end of Fifth Ave, downtown; 944 W Fifth Ave, Anchorage; (907) 278-4502; $$$; full bar; MC, V, AE, DC, DIS; checks OK; dinner, Mon–Sat.* ᐊ

Four Corners Deli and Gesine's at Four Corners ★★ Gesine Marquez creates fantastic lunches and elegant dinners in what started as a soup-and-sandwich joint. The dinner menu includes appetizers such as gnocchi with wild mushroom and chive-garlic sauce, langostino étouffée, and a goat-cheese galette. Dinners feature quail, scallops, salmon, and venison. Alas, the atmosphere is distinctly deli. This matters less at Saturday brunch and lunch, which feature everything from sautéed beef tips over rice to roasted-eggplant sandwiches, warm chèvre, and broccoli pesto. ■ *Corner of Jewell Lake and Raspberry Rds; 6700 Jewell Lake Rd, Anchorage; (907) 243-0507; $$; wine and beer only; AE, MC, V; local checks; continental breakfast, lunch, and dinner Tues–Sat, Sat brunch.* ᐊ

Korea House ★★ Anchorage is blessed with about a half-dozen Korean restaurants, but this is the favorite among Korean Airlines crews and local Korean food fans. It's hard to locate, but it's worth the work. Charbroiled beef, called *bulgogi* (literally meaning "fire meat"), is a good place to start on the 38-item menu. We're mad for *pa jon*, a thin, pan-fried cake filled with green onion and just a touch of oyster. Try *bibim bab*, a large bowl of short-grained, steamed rice with various bits of seasoned vegetables and beef, a fresh fried egg, and a little bowl of red pepper paste. ■ *In a strip mall north of 36th Ave; 3337 Fairbanks St, Anchorage; (907) 276-5188; $$; beer and wine; AE, MC, V; local checks only; lunch and dinner daily.* ᐊ

Siam Cuisine ★★ Siam is in an old family dining place that's been remodeled into a quiet and soothing spot. It offers a few Vietnamese and Laotian dishes, along with fine, near-elegant Thai preparations. They've got the best fresh spring rolls in town. Try also *nam nuong,* a large platter of skewered chicken meatballs, cold vermicelli, and various vegetables and fruits. Take a rice-flour wrapper and form perfect, bite-sized packages of yummy flavors. ∎ *South end of town; 1911 W Dimond Blvd, Anchorage; (907) 344-3663; $; beer and wine; V, MC, AE; local checks only; lunch, Mon–Sat; dinner, daily.* &

Villa Nova ★★ Villa Nova is fun, continental, and homey, with wicker-nested Chianti bottles and braided breads decorating the walls. Chefs tend to favor heavier sauces, cheese, and spices. The rich tournedos gorgonzola or lamb osso buco will melt in your mouth. For lighter fare try the surprising *cacciucco,* an Italian seafood stew, which is literally served in the kitchen pot, or scampi da Jeff, a tasty pasta-and-grilled-prawn dish. The gnocchi and seafood fettuccine are delicious. The wine list is quite diverse. And the elegant homemade desserts are not to be missed: domo, a cake laced with the flavors of oranges, chocolate, and raspberries, or cassata da Grand Marnier, home-made chocolate cups filled with ice cream, marmalade, pistachio nuts, and liqueur. ∎ *In a strip mall near Arctic and International Blvds; 5121 Arctic Blvd, Anchorage; (907) 561-1660; $$; beer and wine; AE, DIS, DC, MC, V; local checks only; dinner, Mon–Sat.* &

Aladdin's ★ Aladdin's brings the warm touch of Middle Eastern flavors to the cold far north. The smoky Casbah salad with fire-roasted bell peppers and eggplant is rich with olive oil. The *kefta* sandwich, with spicy, grilled ground beef, packs a garlic punch. Couscous with lamb and *tajinzitoun* chicken with green olives and spicy tomato are good too. In addition, there's a lovely selection of dips, including baba ghanouj and hummus. ∎ *In a strip mall off Old Seward Hwy, north of Tudor Rd; 4240 Old Seward Hwy, Anchorage; (907) 561-2373; $$; wine and beer; V, MC, AE, DIS, DC; local checks only; lunch, Mon–Fri; dinner, Mon–Sat.* &

Humpy's Great Alaska Ale House ★ Is it the location? The 36 beers on tap? Or the bar food? Who knows? Ever since its birth a few years ago, Humpy's has been a smash hit. Sometimes congenially filled with office workers and bicycle fanatics and at other times packed with frat boys gone to seed, Humpy's draws a crowd. The kitchen is so small, it's a wonder they can handle the 166-seat restaurant (make that 226-seat restaurant with the addition of the summer-only patio). Stick with pub grub, which they do well. ∎ *Across from the Alaska Center for the Performing Arts; 610 W Sixth Ave, Anchorage; (907) 276-2337; $; full bar; AE, DIS, MC, V; local checks only; lunch and dinner, daily.* &

Taqueria Janitzio ★ A strictly take-out joint in a silver, red, and green bus in Spenard, Taqueria Janitzio is a great example of how surprising Alaska can be. Imagine finding beef tongue tacos kissed with cilantro and served with a lemon wedge in this far northern city. Four siblings from Mexico run this little spot. They make everything from scratch, including tortillas and salsas. Try also corn *gorditos* stuffed with spiced chicken or beef or a tostada *tarasca* with Apache beef, consisting of a crisp, fried corn tortilla covered with cold, chopped beef that has been marinated like ceviche. On the weekends, the crew makes authentic *menudo* (a classic Mexican soup with tripe).

■ *On Spenard Rd, just past 36th Ave. Look for the red, green, and silver bus; 3611 Spenard Rd, Anchorage; (907) 563-1909; $; no alcohol; no credit cards; local checks only; lunch and early supper, daily.* &

Bagel Factory This isn't Manhattan. But if you're casting your critical eye around for a little taste of home, get your bagels here. They feature the "31 flavors" approach to bagelmaking (flavoring dough with jalapeños, cheese, pesto, and the like), but they also serve the tried-and-true favorites, such as onion, garlic, or sesame bagels. A nice spot for Sunday breakfast, with thoughtfully prepared frittatas and omelets. You'll see lots of local upwardly mobiles here on weekend mornings, reading the paper and planning the day's adventure. ■ *In a 1-story mall off the corner of 36th Ave and C St; 142 W 34th Ave, Anchorage; (907) 561-8871; $; beer and wine; no credit cards; local checks only; breakfast and lunch, daily.* &

Downtown Deli and Cafe One of the few spots to open early and close late, the comfortable Downtown Deli is often packed with summertime tourists. In the winter, locals stop by in the morning for bowls of good oatmeal, lox and bagels, omelets, and filling cheese blintzes, or schedule working lunches built around bagel sandwiches and matzoh-ball soup. Butcher-block tabletops, lots of room, and quick service are draws, but so is the fact that Alaska Governor Tony Knowles owns the place. He still drops by when he's in town, and the deli stands as a testament to how little space separates the average Alaskan from the pinnacles of power. ■ *On Fourth Ave, near the log cabin visitors center; 525 W Fourth Ave, Anchorage; (907) 276-7116; $; beer and wine; AE, V, MC, DIS; local checks only; breakfast, lunch, and dinner, daily.* &

Middleway Cafe and Coffeehouse This small, cafeteria-style espresso bar and restaurant is very much into macrobiotics, organics, and vegetarian fare. Wraps are a nice choice. These are essentially cold burritos built with *chapati*, East Indian wheat tortillas. The Middleway has winning fillings such as hummus and pistachios, rounded out with red bell pepper-lemon yogurt dressing. The atmosphere is mellow, with a crowd sporting everything from pierced earrings to pinstripes. Right next to REI. A healthy choice. ■ *In the mall, Spenard Rd and Northern*

272-6433; $; no alcohol; no credit cards; local checks only;
lunch, Mon–Sat; dinner, Tues–Sat. ♿

BEST LODGINGS

Hotel Captain Cook ★★★★ This is the hotel that former Governor Walter Hickel built, and it remains the top of the line for Anchorage. When the big oil money was flowing in the 1970s and early 1980s, the Hotel Captain Cook and its elegant bars and restaurants served as a backdrop for deal-making and high-class partying. Towers Two and Three were renovated in the mid-1990s, so request a room in either tower. Ask for a view of Cook Inlet, available on the fifth floor and above, or a southwest corner room for a view of both water and mountains with morning and evening sun. Like all Alaska hotels, prices drop sharply in September. ▪ *Corner of Fifth Ave and K Street, downtown; 939 W Fifth Ave, Anchorage, AK 99501; mail: PO Box 102280, Anchorage, AK 99510; toll-free in Alaska (800) 478-3100; (907) 276-6000; $$$; AE, MC V, DC, DIS; checks OK; Crow's Nest, dinner Mon–Sat, Sun brunch.* ♿

Anchorage Hotel ★★★ A charming, historic lodging, the Anchorage Hotel lays claim to being the city's oldest. Since its birth in 1916, many notables have stayed in its 26 rooms, including painter Sydney Laurence. Guests step from busy E Street into a quiet, almost formal lobby with a fireplace and marble chess set. After 8 years of renovations, the rooms are clean but lack a personality that belies the hotel's history. Some rooms face the street, and traffic noise carries. Rooms 301 and 303 overlook Fourth Avenue and E Street, a terrific viewpoint for watching the start of the Iditarod Sled Dog Race. Daily newspapers and continental breakfast come with each room. ▪ *E St and Fourth Ave; 330 E St, Anchorage, AK 99501; (800) 544-0988, (907) 272-4553; $$$; AE, DC, DIS, MC, V; checks OK.* ♿

Anchorage
Lodgings

Copper Whale Inn ★★★ Something between a bed and breakfast and a country inn, the comfortable, Nantucket-styled Copper Whale is a rarity among Anchorage housing. It is charming and quaint, with a staff who are informal yet reserved. Only five of the eight rooms have private baths, but seven have picture windows with unobstructed views of Cook Inlet to the west. Continental breakfast includes pastries made at a nearby bakery and fresh fruit. Book early. ▪ *Corner of Fifth Ave and L St, downtown; 440 L St, Anchorage, AK 99501; (907) 258-7999; $$; V, MC, AE, DIS; checks OK.* ♿

Anchorage Hilton ★★ In the heart of downtown, the Anchorage Hilton is often packed with tourists and conventioneers. With 597 rooms, it's the biggest hotel downtown, and the lobby always feels more like Grand Central Station than a place

BEST WAYS TO DIE

Alaska is not Disneyland. Those glaciers are real and have taken lives. Ditto that moose and the lovely snow falling outside your lodge window.

Bears, moose, sightseeing flights, cruise ship gangplanks, halibut fishing, calving glaciers, icy rivers—you name it, and someone's died from it in Alaska. Even the most humbly adventurous traveler to Alaska must be aware of the state's natural dangers. While you might have the street savvy to avoid a mugger back home, such skills are useless when a city-bound moose is angry and looking right at you.

To that end, here's a little guide to the best ways to die in Alaska.

Try to get close to the wildlife. *Both bears and moose can cover an amazing amount of real estate in a short time, and they're likely to be on any number of popular trails around Anchorage. In the summer of 1995, two local people out for a day's jog on McHugh Creek Trail, minutes away from downtown Anchorage, were killed by a grizzly. Earlier that winter, a moose trampled a man to death as he tried to enter a building at the University of Alaska Anchorage Sports Center. The rule is simple: don't feed them, don't pet them, don't hang around them, don't harass them, and don't surprise them. If you see a creature in the woods, back away slowly. Wear bells on your pack, clap, or sing to let bears know you're coming. Don't get between a moose and her baby, and don't try to go around a moose.*

Walk on the mudflats that surround Anchorage. *That appealing shoreline is actually mud. And not just any mud. The consistency is more akin to wet cement or quicksand. You get a foot stuck and you'll have a hard time pulling it out. Matters get dicier if the tide is coming in or going out (and it's always doing one or the other four times a day). Anchorage has the second highest tides in the world. Water levels can change several feet in a matter of minutes. People have gotten stuck and drowned while rescue workers tried to beat the tide. Don't go there.*

Don't worry about your gear. *Sure, that peak seems close enough to scramble up in an hour or two. Who needs water, good hiking boots, or emergency rations? You do. What was meant to be a short hike can turn into an overnight ordeal if you get lost or hurt. Remember, most of what surrounds Anchorage is wilderness. There are no park rangers or other hikers just around the bend. In all likelihood, you will be on your own. Basic emergency and survival gear should be tucked into your*

▼

Anchorage

Lodgings

▲

pack, including water, food, matches, firestarter, extra clothing, bug dope, a compass, a knife, a small first-aid kit, and a topographical map.

Don't respect the cold. *Cold can creep into any Alaska day. And if you add cold to the problems outlined above, you can easily lose your life. Hypothermia may set in quickly if you get dunked in one of the many glacial streams, or simply get rained on or caught overnight at the right time of year. Dress for variable weather, and pack a space blanket and waterproof matches.*

Panic, act macho, and don't follow your intuition. *Fear is a warning. It means something is unsafe. Listen to it. It's sort of like the adage about anything that sounds too good to be true. If it seems dangerous, it probably is.*

Don't do your homework. *Even in Alaska, knowledge is power. Check out guidebooks and talk to locals. Learn about how to stay safe in the woods, avoid avalanches, and handle a bear attack. The Alaska Public Lands Information Center, 605 W Fourth Avenue, in downtown Anchorage, (907) 271-2737, has a variety of free brochures covering much of what you'll need to know.*

—Kim Severson

for respite. But it's convenient. In the summer, the vendor-laden Saturday Market or the train to Denali are short strolls away. In the winter, the Iditarod Sled Dog Race starts a block away, and the Fur Rendezvous festival happens all around the hotel block. Locals like the rooftop view from the bar in the Top of the World restaurant. Rooms are nicely appointed but small. Try for a corner room in the Anchorage tower, the original section of the hotel. ■ *Corner of Third Ave and E St, downtown; 500 W Third Ave, Anchorage, AK 99501; (800) 245-2527, (907) 272-7411; $$$; AE, MC, V, DIS; checks OK; Top of the World, dinner, nightly in summer, Tues–Sat in winter; Sun brunch.* &

Regal Alaskan Hotel ★ The Regal is located on Lake Hood, the busiest lake in Anchorage. Locals scramble to get to the deck on sunny days to drink local ale and watch the floatplanes vie for space with the ducks during take-offs and landings. The place is especially Alaskan in the winter, with leather chairs facing the fireplace and glass-enclosed stuffed bears. In March, as dogs and mushers are racing from Anchorage to Nome, the hotel serves as the official Iditarod Race headquarters, and guests can follow the progress of their favorite mushers on a frequently updated board in the lobby or from printouts issued every few hours from the computer room. The rooms are quite spacious, and the hotel has a restaurant, the Flying Machine, open daily. ■ *Near the airport on Spenard Rd; 4800 Spenard Rd, Anchorage, AK 99517; (800) 544-0553, (907) 243-2300; $$$; AE, MC,V, DC; checks OK.* &

BED AND BREAKFASTS

Decide whether you want to be in town, on the hillside near the mountain wilderness, or somewhere in between. The **Aurora Winds,** at 7501 Upper O'Malley Road, (907) 346-2533, is an exceptional and large bed and breakfast tucked into the foothills of the Chugach Mountains. Downtown, try the quiet, exclusive feel of **Two Morrow's Place Bed and Breakfast,** 1325 O Street, (907) 277-9939, or the more congenial **Bed & Breakfast on the Park,** 602 West 10th Avenue, (800) 353-0878 or (907) 277-0878. There, Helen Tucker and Stella Hughton, former owners of the Willow Trading Post, preside over a former log-cabin church, peeling mangos for breakfast and sharing tips on politics and gardening. For more information on the range of bed and breakfasts, try **Alaska Private Lodging,** (907) 258-1717, **Alaska Sourdough Bed and Breakfast Association,** (907) 563-6244, or **Alaskans Who Care Reservation Service,** (907) 562-7626.

WILDERNESS LODGE

Riversong Lodge Gourmets who love to catch their own food and savor it, too, will want to book a small plane for the 70-mile flight north of Anchorage to this little lodge on the Yentna River. Kirsten and Carl Dixon prepare the best Alaska seafood and wild game by night and take guests to favorite red and silver salmon fishing holes by day. Top winemakers from France and California, editors from fancy food magazines, and renowned national chefs have all eaten here. Do not expect luxury. The lodge is rustic—10 cabins, not all with private baths. However, there is a communal sauna and bathhouse so that you can get to know your neighbors and primp for dinner. Day guests are welcome for fishing and lunch (about $200 a person for the day). ■ *On the Yentna River near Lake Creek, accessible only by air; 2463 Cottonwood St, Anchorage, AK 99508; (907) 563-2040 in Anchorage, (907) 274-2710 at the lodge; $$$; beer and wine; AE, MC, V; checks OK; open summer, part of winter.*

GIRDWOOD

This woodsy, ski enthusiasts' oasis south of Anchorage, with funky little cabins tucked into the hollows and expensive condos facing the mountain, has long been a mecca for downhill skiers. Summer brings a wealth of beautiful views, from hanging glaciers to mountains covered with blueberry patches.

High on the ski slopes is one of the more elegant dining experiences in the region.

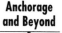

The town was started by a gold miner who staked a claim on Crow Creek. Today, Girdwood is a little village of about 1,200 that swells to some 3,000 when the snow falls. In winter, skiers try their hand at challenging Nordic routes or schuss down breathtaking Mount Alyeska in the abundant company of snowboarders. There are seven lifts and an aerial tram. This is the only ski resort in the country where you plunge down powder-filled slopes while looking at the ocean below.

In summer, Girdwood is a good place for rafting trips, hikes, and live music featuring local performers. The pinnacle of the music scene is the **Girdwood Forest Faire,** a folk music festival held the first weekend in July. It's also a fine time to see the town in its tie-dyed finest. In fall, the hillsides are filled with berry pickers; in spring, the same hills offer rare black morel mushrooms and fiddlehead ferns. But beware: anytime but deep winter, when they're mainly snoozing, you'll find bears also roaming these valleys and hillsides.

Tips on the Drive from Anchorage to Girdwood

Here are a few places of interest along the Seward Highway to Girdwood. For dinner, consider the cozy **Turnagain House,** (907) 653-7500, in Indian, which has delicious seafood (try the silver salmon when it's in season or the Alaska scallop and shrimp in basil-saffron cream sauce). Often crowded in summer, but in winter it's a charming little dining room with a fireplace and view of the inlet. For a more casual nosh, stop by the **Cafe of the Lyon Family,** (907) 653-7302, a little diner in Bird Creek that serves terrific corned-beef hash, scones, and espresso.

BEST RESTAURANTS

Seven Glaciers Restaurant and Lounge ★★★ Opened in 1994, this elegant restaurant—with crack waitstaff and stunning view of the mountains—sits high on Mount Alyeska. To get there, you take a Swiss-built tram to the 2,300-foot level. Fresh, local ingredients such as blueberries, oysters, and boletus mushrooms often grace the menu. Executive chef Michael Flynn emphasizes game (his tart, filled with rabbit pâté and grilled rabbit loin, is a knockout), but seafood and vegetarian dishes also shine. The foie gras and scallop appetizer is sublime. Swordfish with black olive tapenade and porcini mushrooms or shrimp over penne with capers and tomatoes are also good choices. Desserts emphasize the vertical milieu, with tall, fanciful presentations. ▪ *Take the tram from the Alyeska Prince Hotel; 1000 Arlberg Ave, Girdwood; (800) 880-3880, (907) 754-2237; $$; full bar; AE, V, DC, MC, DIS; local checks only; dinner daily, summer; Fri and Sat, winter (closed Oct).* &

HURRAH FOR THE BERRIES!

Heck, they're everywhere. Alaska's native fruit.

When they're ripe, you have to jump to get them. They're fragile and coveted by others. Wind and rain are their natural enemies. Birds and bears are their fans. You cannot argue with these competitors. Berries torture you with their abundance. When you're surrounded by endless acres of them, it's hard to focus on filling your pail. Blinders may be the answer.

Gathering berries is a ritual that pulls you out of your daily routine and into the wild places. Being up high, with a grand view that encompasses countless miles of teeming wilderness, is a fine reward in itself and one that seduces berry pickers and scrambles other priorities. If you miss the berry season completely, you'll miss the berries and the memories of collecting them all year long. Falling into your cabin to escape a wicked blizzard, only to find a bubbling, steaming berry pie with a tender, toasted crust on your winter dining table, is a comfort you don't want to miss.

Berries often appear unexpectedly. To hear some first-rate cussing, be along when I stumble onto berries and have no container. Bad. Once I slipped off my knee socks and picked them both brimful of lowbush cranberries. I've been chewed on by vampire bugs after sacrificing my long-sleeved shirt for picking, tying off the cuff ends with knots. Scarves or kerchiefs work well, if you tie up the corners. A hat will do (line it with leaves if you use Brylcreem).

The cheerfully serious gleaners are the Native people. They pick using buckets and empty into barrels, mixing all the different berries together and lacing them with sugar. After making this great large compote, they leave it outside and scoop out of it all winter long. Sounds good to me.

When picking, my trick is to dangle 1-gallon plastic jars from my waist. They're lightweight, don't spill, and leave both hands free—a super advantage.

Your picking companions are très important. *I'm wary of anyone who is prone to whining of any sort and anyone who tells me they picked one and three-fourths cups last week. They may lack stamina! You'll benefit by being discreet about your hot, secret berry patch. A person with absolutely no friends and a family living in Borneo is the best. And a little secret: test men here. Remember, guys love pies. So start picking, dude. No doubt, dudette will be making the pies. Picking berries takes hours. Sorting takes hours. Making pies takes hours. Eating pies takes seconds.*

Back to the competition. The strongest carnivore left on

earth prefers berries for dessert all day long. His name is B-E-A-R. Don't fail to consider these characters, as they are not always casual about their daily forage. Educate yourself as much as you can about their usual behavior and act according to your philosophy. People who are way too romantic about "vibing" bears have limited experience with them. My favorite companion is an armed guard who also carries the picnic lunch.

A fruit that's a little different is the rose hip. You can pick bushels of these hardy things after the first frost. They're super dried in baskets for tea or puréed and made into catsup or treated like apple butter. They also make excellent wine.

All of the berries enrich your Thanksgiving table. They're great in stuffing, in condiments, as sauces, or in pies. They're super with game meats and they contribute to your glowing satisfaction!

Most of the time, I make a pie, cobbler, or a fruity cake with some of my fresh berries and preserve the rest. Without fail, I honor my mother's lifetime rule: Whatever is jammed, jarred, or frozen cannot be opened until the first snowfall. Works perfect!

— Joan Daniels

Taco's by Dos Amigos Taco's (yes, it's spelled in the possessive) is a great spot for Arizona-style Mexican food based on family recipes. The salsa is first rate, and the fish tacos sell out before dinner. With fresh halibut and a creamy sauce, these babies fly out of the place, so go early. The cheese quesadilla, which kids love, is a dollar, and coffee's a quarter. But most impressive are the 55 bottles of different hot sauces. For a truly spicy ride, order a *carne asada* taco (chunks of steak cooked in salsa and served on a soft corn tortilla) and douse with Capital Punishment hot sauce. ■ *In the strip mall at the turnoff for Girdwood; Girdwood Station Mall, Girdwood; (907) 783-2155; $; no alcohol; no credit cards; checks OK; 11am–9pm daily.*

The Double Musky ★ A favorite among Alaskans, the Double Musky is known for its impeccable pepper steak and gargantuan Cajun portions. (Be advised they don't take reservations, and sometimes the wait is long.) With remnants of Mardi Gras past hanging from the walls, the Musky is casual but expensive. The appetizer menu offers halibut ceviche, coconut salmon, Cajun-spiced shrimp peelers, scallops with mushrooms, and deep-fried zucchini. The dinner menu features steaks, seafood, and spicy Cajun and creole dishes. The rolls are studded with jalapeño peppers, and the pepper steak is covered with a spicy coating of well-crushed peppercorns and Burgundy sauce. The fiery shrimp étouffée is flawless. ■ *Crow Creek Rd (follow signs), Girdwood; (907) 783-2822; $$; full bar; AE, MC, V, DIS, DC; no checks; dinner daily, except Mon (closed Nov).* &

BEST LODGINGS

Alyeska Prince Hotel ★★★★ The Alyeska Prince Hotel is a grand, château-style, resort hotel that rises eight elegant stories at the base of Mount Alyeska. Cherry wood and granite accent rooms and lobby. The hotel was opened in 1994 by the Seibu Corporation of Japan, and many rooms are geared for the Japanese visitor. Most rooms have two double beds only (few kings, no queens), but elegant, small touches—such as towel warmers, bathrobes, and fresh roses on room-service trays in the dead of winter—will win your heart. They'll even give you a wake-up call when the Northern Lights are visible. ■ *At the base of Alyeska ski area in Girdwood at 1000 Arlberg Ave, Girdwood; PO Box 249, Girdwood, AK 99587; (800) 880-3880 or (907) 754-1111; $$$; MC, V, AE, DC; checks OK.* &

CHUGACH STATE PARK

Nowhere else does genuine full-bore wilderness lie so close to a major city. Chugach State Park is as raw as it gets. The peaks loom tall and jagged—up to 8,000 feet high. Valleys and rocks show abundant evidence of relentless scouring by ancient glaciers. Some of the world's last remaining icefields lie only a few dozen miles from downtown Anchorage. In any other state, Chugach State Park, created in 1970, would be a national park not a state park. It is that much of a treasure.

This is one of Alaska's best-kept secrets. The remoter, more rugged regions see so little visitation that, even by Alaska standards, they are relatively empty. Statistically, July and August are Anchorage's rainiest months, while April, May, and June are the driest. Many of the trails are snow-covered or muddy even in April, but not the southernmost slopes facing Turnagain Arm. By June and July, most valleys have opened up, but then it's the height of mosquito season. (In Alaska, there's always a trade-off.) September, although cooler, offers some magnificent fall colors, berry picking, rutting moose, and fewer visitors.

Chugach is also an easy place to get killed. Whether by exposure, hypothermia, falls, avalanches, drownings, disorientation, or mauling by bears, people die here every year. Proximity to Anchorage offers only an illusion of safety. Only those with real outdoor savvy should venture too far beyond the trailheads and campgrounds. Also, be sure you know when and where the hunters are out. When in doubt, wear red. For a handy "cheat sheet" on hunting in the park, contact Alaska Department of Fish and Game, (907) 267-2349.

Access

Despite its rugged character, Chugach is eminently accessible along two sides of its triangular rim. Of 30 access points, however, only 15 offer a parking area and trailhead. But these are more than enough to put visitors in touch with the park's most outstanding features. Although the park has about 100 miles of trails, many valleys have no trails at all. Fording glacier rivers and fighting your way through dense undergrowth without getting lost is a deterrent to many of the less adventurous. This is one reason why the remote regions of the park see few visitors. But the rewards are grand.

To get to the park you need a car, or a bicycle if you have legs of iron. However, be aware that within the park the use of mountain bikes is limited. Ditto for snowmobiles, all-terrain vehicles, and horses. Check with backcountry rangers, (907) 345-5014, or stop by park headquarters in the old Potter section house located south of town, Mile 115, Seward Highway. The **Alaska Backpacker Shuttle,** (800) 266-8625, is another transportation option. It can take you and your gear from the airport or the youth hostel to the Crow Pass trailhead, Eagle River Visitors Center, or other park access points for about $35 one-way, minimum two persons.

VISITOR FACILITIES

Eagle River Visitors Center The visitors center is about 25 miles from downtown Anchorage at Mile 12, Eagle River Road; (907) 694-2108. Open Tuesday through Sunday, June through August. Also open in wintertime. Call for hours.

Chugach State Park Headquarters The Potter Section House at Mile 115, on the Seward Highway, is not only a visitors center but also a small museum for the Alaska Railroad, which skirts the park along Turnagain Arm; (907) 345-5014.

Public-Use Cabins Yuditna Creek cabin, 4 miles or so from Eklutna Lake parking area, is far from luxurious, but it is wheelchair-accessible and can accommodate as many as 8 people snugly. Bring all your own gear and food. Rent is $35/night for a maximum of 3 nights and only one weekend a month. (Reservations must be made in person.) For information on this and other cabins, call Alaska Department of Natural Resources Public Information Center, (907) 269-8400.

Hikers can rent a U.S. Forest Service cabin near **Crow Pass,** an A-frame that can sleep 10. It's bare bones: no bedding, no cooking gear, and no wood stove. Because of avalanche hazard, it is available only in summer for $25/night. Maximum stay of 3 nights. For reservations, call Alaska Public Lands Information Center, (907) 271-2599.

Finally, along the park's 40-mile **Eklutna Traverse** are three A-frame huts that are free and require no reservations. The names of the huts are **Pichler's Perch, Whiteout,** and **Eagle River**. They have no wood stoves or amenities. These backcountry cabins were built and are maintained by the Mountaineering Club for this extreme traverse and are meant to be shared with all travelers.

THINGS TO DO

Chugach State Park is a superb place to backpack, ski tour, or climb mountains. Most visitors come to day hike and gawk at the scenery. They also pick berries, run hills, scramble up mountains, canoe, kayak, study nature, and watch wildlife. The park is home to most mammal species in Alaska. Fishing is limited. Windsurfing is only for the experts. Ice climbers enjoy a number of good frozen waterfalls, though none are high.

One boundary of the park is the **Seward Highway,** one of America's National Scenic Byways. On one side is **Turnagain Arm,** where, in the right season, you may spot beluga or killer whales, windsurfers, or unusual bore tides. On the other side of the highway, look for Dall sheep on the cliffs at Windy Corner. But be careful. When you want to rubber-neck at the beauty along Turnagain Arm, pull off the winding two-lane highway into a turnout, or you may end up as the kind of casualty that makes this one of the most hazardous stretches of roadway in the state.

For quick trips to the park for a view, here are two drives: the parking lot for Flattop Mountain at **Glen Alps** (20 minutes from the airport) and Alpenglow Ski Resort at **Arctic Valley** (40 minutes from the airport). Each destination is located on the front range facing Anchorage. Both are exceptional for getting the visitor above treeline with no legwork. Both provide awesome views.

For those with more time, **Flattop** is the city's most-climbed mountain. Shaped as its name suggests, it rises 3,510 feet above sea level. You start from the Glen Alps parking lot. Again, although it is popular, Flattop is not a cakewalk. It is quite steep, particularly toward the summit, and people have died on its flanks. So wear good shoes and pay attention. From Alpenglow's parking area, **Rendezvous Peak,** which rises 1,500 feet above the trailhead, is easier and more suitable for little children.

Those who want a strenuous climb, but not the bother of a long approach, should trek up **Bird Ridge** along Turnagain Arm on the south (about 4,000 feet elevation gain) or the **Pioneer Ridge–Knik River Trail** on the north of the park, which climbs the back of mile-high Pioneer Peak. Each trail rises right out of the parking lot and quickly puts the hiker/runner in possession of an outstanding vista. **Falls Creek** is another choice Turnagain Arm day hike that starts upward as soon as the car door is shut. Visitors enter a beautiful little alpine valley where, above treeline, they are almost sure to spot Dall sheep on the high escarpments. **Wolverine Peak** facing Anchorage is yet another easy-to-get-to trail that offers moderate hiking through spruce forest and tundra meadows and takes 6 to 9 hours round-trip.

Want to soak in exquisite natural wonders but don't want to walk very far? Try driving northeast of Anchorage to **Eklutna Lake,** the largest lake in the park, which is glacially carved and has saw-toothed mountains rising to 7,000 feet above it.

For river runners, **Eagle River,** northeast of Anchorage, is the only river in the park where there is any regular canoeing, kayaking, or rafting. An 11-mile segment can be managed by most experienced boaters. But unless you are very experienced and have scouted the rapids, do not go past the bridge on the highway. This can be a deathtrap. For those who want a taste of the river but don't have a boat, contact **Midnight Sun River Runners,** (907) 338-7238. Their 4-hour rafting tour costs $55/adult, $28/children (who must be 5 years old). A 30-minute whitewater add-on trip costs an additional $10 (children must be at least 8 years old). They run two tours daily in summer and will pick you up at your hotel.

For those who desire a deeper drink of Chugach splendors, a 28-mile backpacking trek, **Girdwood to Eagle River Traverse,** crosses from Girdwood over Crow Pass and down Raven Creek to the Eagle River Trail, northeast of the city. This cuts through the wilderness heart of the park, covering part of the historic Iditarod Trail that once carried travelers from Seward into the Interior before the advent of the railroad.

If you're nervous going into the Chugach wilderness by yourself, call **Great Alaska Gourmet Adventures,** (907) 346-1087. Guides will custom-design a "soft" adventure with gourmet meals to fit your experience level.

FESTIVALS/EVENTS

Crow Pass Crossing A 28-mile wilderness footrace held every July traverses the mountains from Girdwood to Eagle River. Winners complete the race in about 3 hours. Most backpackers, however, cover the same route in 2 or 3 days, parking a "getaway car" at one end, then driving around in a second car to begin at the other trailhead.

Winter and Summer Solstices Visitors who chance upon Chugach in the third week of June or December may want to join solstice celebrations on Flattop Mountain. In summer and

Chugach State Park

Festivals/ Events

winter, since the 1960s, solstice worshippers camp out all night en masse on the peak's huge summit field. Festivities, which sometimes even include bands playing to the glories of endless sunlight, are sponsored by the Mountaineering Club of Alaska and take place on the Saturday closest to the solstice. Legend maintains that not a single solstice has been missed. In winter, not surprisingly, the numbers are fewer. One December, only one soul proved hardy enough to brave the severe cold and wind so that the record could remain unbroken.

SUGGESTED READING

Nienhueser, Helen, and Wolfe, John Jr. *55 Ways to the Wilderness in Southcentral Alaska.* Seattle: The Mountaineers, 1994. This is by far the best guide to wilderness adventures around Anchorage, with detailed information about numerous hikes in the area, including 19 in Chugach State Park. The book tells you how to get to each trailhead, lets you know what to expect on the trail, and offers good advice on safety.

Rich, Kim. *Johnny's Girl.* New York: Morrow, 1993. For sheer atmosphere and recent history, you can't beat this book by a talented journalist, based on life with her father, Johnny, a small-time hood in Anchorage's blossoming underworld in the 1960s.

Zimmerman, Jenny. *A Naturalist's Guide to Chugach State Park.* Anchorage, 1993. This guide covers a wide range of topics, from natural history and animals to hiking and wilderness safety. For those with no knowledge of the park, this is a good overview.

▼

Chugach State Park

Festivals/ Events

PRINCE WILLIAM SOUND

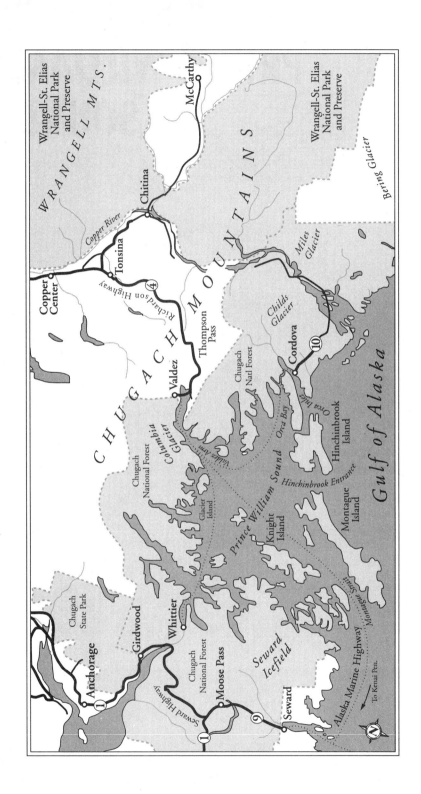

Prince William Sound

Including Whittier, Valdez, and Cordova

In the far northern Gulf of Alaska lies Prince William Sound, a marvelous wilderness of deep fjords, towering snow-capped mountains, rich blue seas teeming with wildlife, and chiseled tidewater glaciers. Only a few remote fishing towns and two tiny Eskimo villages dot the coast of this vast array of forest, islands, and waterways.

When the sun shines, there is nothing quite so exhilarating as paddling a kayak through bobbing icebergs and curious sea otters, watching huge chunks of ice break off the face of glaciers, feeling the crisp breeze, and riding the swell of waves created by falling ice.

Almost all of Prince William Sound—its 3,500 miles of coastline and 150 glaciers—lies within the boundaries of Chugach National Forest, which was established by President Theodore Roosevelt in 1907, and today ranks as the second largest national forest in the United States. (The first is the Tongass National Forest, which encompasses most of Southeast Alaska.)

The weather and seas in the Gulf of Alaska are legendary and tumultuous. But the waters of Prince William Sound are mostly protected from storms in the gulf by a series of islands. Standing guard at the entrance of the Sound are the two largest—Hinchinbrook and Montague. On the east side are Orca Bay and the little fishing town of Cordova. Continuing northeast, you'll find Valdez Arm, a long spectacular fjord, leading through the Valdez Narrows to the head of the bay and the oil-boom town of Valdez. Anchoring the middle of the Sound are three tiny islands named Naked, Peak, and Storey. Just south of them is lovely Knight Island, with its myriad of coves and bays.

On the west side of the Sound is the bunker town of Whittier, gateway to the railroad tracks and the Seward Highway leading to Anchorage. To the northwest, amid rafts of sea otters and seals, lie College and Harriman Fjords with glacier after glacier plunging into their waters. The 1898 Harriman Expedition named a number of glaciers here after the Ivy League and Little Ivy League colleges of the East Coast, such as Williams, Vassar, Harvard, and Yale.

When the great navigator Captain James Cook of the Royal British Navy first ventured into the Sound in 1778, he named it Sandwich Sound for the Earl of Sandwich. But by the time Cook returned to England, the earl had fallen from grace, so the name was changed to Prince William Sound after the king's third son.

Access

The state ferry, **Alaska Marine Highway,** (800) 642-0066, can take you from Whittier to Valdez and Cordova, or from Seward to Valdez and Cordova, or vice versa. You can walk on, or take your car and drive the road system at your destination's end. Not only does the ferry provide transportation, but it's communal, fun, and a great way to view the remoteness of the Sound.

There are only two places from which you can access the Sound by road. **Valdez** on the east is at the beginning of the Richardson Highway, and **Whittier** on the west is about an hour's drive south of Anchorage, with an additional 30-minute train ride through the mountains. Otherwise, you need to take a boat or a plane.

Information

Dotted throughout the Sound are 24 public-use cabins managed by the U.S. Forest Service and available for $25/night. For more information, contact U.S. Forest Service, **Chugach National Forest,** 3301 C Street, Suite 300, Anchorage, AK 99503-3998; (907) 271-2500, and ask for *Public Recreation Cabins: Chugach National Forest Alaska,* a 30-page pamphlet that describes each cabin and how to get there.

WHITTIER

South of Anchorage and through the mountains at the end of the tracks, where the railroad meets the sea, Whittier is the launching point for many Prince William Sound adventures. But Whittier itself is not a place to linger. The same mountains that cut off Whittier from the road system also trap storms over the town, which gets about 15 feet of rain and 20 feet of snow a year. If the sun does happen to shine, you'll find yourself surrounded by mountains dripping with glaciers. But too often it is grey and dreary in Whittier, so the trick is to keep the visit short.

Until World War II, there was no Whittier. This may explain the rather unusual look to the town, which today depends primarily on fishing and tourism. Created as a major logistics center and built to be a self-contained U.S. Army community, the town is housed in a gray, bunker-like skyscraper. The Army pulled out in 1963 and left behind two towers. One is empty, its windows broken; the other contains nearly the whole town. The first couple of floors of the 14-story war relic hold government offices, a library, and local businesses. The upper floors are condominiums where most of the town's 200 residents live.

Access

On the map, Whittier looks awfully close to Anchorage. But a wall of mountains cuts it off from the road system. To get to Whittier, you travel south on the Seward Highway from Anchorage for about an hour. Right before the Portage Glacier turnoff, there is a large parking lot on the left where the train will stop. You can drive your car on or park your car and ride as a passenger. The trip takes 30 minutes through the mountains to the edge of Passage Canal on Prince William Sound. There's talk of turning those tracks into a road someday, but it's still just talk. Make reservations with the **Alaska Railroad,** (907) 265-2607. Ask for the Whittier schedule.

Information

Older Alaskans of Whittier, a group of local, retired volunteers, run the visitors center, which is located in an old railroad car, a stone's throw from where the train stops. Charter operations to get you out of Whittier and into the Sound are listed at the visitors center. For a copy of the list, contact **Greater Whittier Chamber of Commerce,** PO Box 607, Whittier, AK 99693; (907) 344-3340.

GUIDES/OUTFITTERS

From Whittier, you can take a whirlwind **tour of the western Sound** or a more relaxed **glacier trip**. You can go **whale watching** or launch a 1- to 10-day **kayak trip** and paddle to good camping in one of the many sheltered bays. Or you can stay in one of a dozen Forest Service cabins. Whittier is also a good place to **catch a fishing charter** for salmon or halibut.

Adventures & Delight   Offers 1- to 10-day trips out of Whittier into the Sound. Cost is $95 to $2,100. Stop in at their adventure-travel information center in downtown Anchorage at 414 K Street, Anchorage, AK 99501; (800) 288-3134 or (907) 276-8282.

Honey Charters   Offers custom taxi charters and tours from fishing to whale watching to glacier viewing. The water-taxi service also provides drop-off service for kayak trips and overnight stays at remote cabins. The boat can carry up to six people, plus gear. In the summer, their office is in the two-story log cabin in the Harbor Triangle in Whittier. For information, call (907) 472-2493 or (907) 344-3340.

Lazy Otter Charters Inc.   Provides water-taxi service, can carry up to six people plus gear, and is available for sightseeing, photography, and drop-offs for kayaking and camping anywhere in western Prince William Sound. Perry Passage and southern Knight Island are good places for seeing orca and humpback whales. For information, call (907) 345-1175.

Major Marine Tours   Offers a 6 ½-hour round trip out of Whittier to Blackstone Bay. The boat stays in fairly calm waters and

Prince William Sound

Whittier

Guides/ Outfitters

travels past 10 glaciers, some quite dramatic and active. The boat holds about 150 folks and the trip, which includes the railroad fare from the highway, costs $116. They sometimes offer end-of-the-season specials around Labor Day. For information, call (907) 274-7300.

National Outdoor Leadership School (NOLS) Based in Wyoming, but has an outpost in Palmer, Alaska. One of its offerings is kayaking trips in the Sound. Not just paddling experiences, these trips (2 to 4 weeks) are designed to train group leaders and teach outdoor skills. They are set up for different age groups, including a master's course for folks 50 and over. A 2-week trip costs about $1,900. For information, contact (907) 745-4047.

Phillips' Cruises and Tours Offers a 6-hour, whirlwind tour of 26 glaciers. Their 330-passenger *Klondike Express* travels through protected waters to glaciers in Harriman and College Fjords. They've been in business for more than 20 years and have this trip down to a science. The $120 ticket includes lunch, but you have to make your own way to Whittier. For information, call (800) 544-0529 or (907) 276-8023.

Prince William Sound Kayak Center The largest supplier of rental kayaks for Prince William Sound trips. They rent single and double kayaks at daily and weekly rates. Prices run roughly $40/day to $240/week. Make reservations well in advance. Write: PO Box 233008, Anchorage, AK 99523; (907) 472-2452.

BEST RESTAURANTS

Hobo Bay Trading Company ★ Babs has been running this little joint for more than 17 years. She's a local renegade who can usually be found in the thick of local politics. Fishermen resupplying in Whittier will always treat themselves to a Babs Burger or a Buffalo Babs Burger made with real buffalo meat. Her burgers—beef or buffalo—have a bite. They come with a hot pepper on top. She also serves Alaska-made ice cream and pies. ■ *Get off the ferry or the train and head for the harbormaster's steel-blue building; 1 Windy Pl, Whittier; (907) 472-2374; $ (burgers cost $5.75–$7); no credit cards; checks "under protest," Babs said; open 11am–8pm Tues–Sun; closed mid-Sept–mid-May.*

The Tsunami Cafe Unlike a lot of small shops in Alaska, this little cafe stays open all year long. Tsunami's pizza is the showpiece, particularly the shrimp and garlic one. The shrimp comes from the Sound, and the crust is homemade. Breads and hamburger buns are also baked fresh there. Owner Bill Coumbe serves good beer, which will save you from having to visit either of the town's two dark and dingy bars. ■ *The Harbor Triangle, Whittier; (907) 472-2462; $$ (sandwiches run $7–$9, pizza for two is about $20); beer and wine; MC, V; lo-*

cal checks only; open 11am–9pm, sometimes earlier if a break-fast cook can be found. ♿

VALDEZ

This little oil town is known as the Switzerland of Alaska because of its jagged, snow-capped peaks and emerald-green mountain slopes. The name is Spanish. But to pronounce it correctly is to mispronounce it to an Alaskan's ears. Here you say "Val-deez." It's home to 3,500 people. It averages 26 feet of rain a year, and its record snowfall is more than 46 feet.

The town has seen its share of booms and busts. Around the turn of the century, Valdez was one port of entry to the rich gold fields in the Canadian Klondike. The gold route from Valdez to the Klondike was advertised all over the United States and drew about 4,000 hopeful gold seekers. A tent town sprang up and some of the miners stuck around. They later hacked a dogsled trail into the interior of Alaska, followed by a rough wagon route that eventually became the Richardson Highway to the gold-rush town of Fairbanks, some 400 miles away.

By the 1920s, the population was declining. It stayed that way, culminating in the greatest earthquake ever recorded on the North American continent. The epicenter for that quake was in Prince William Sound: late afternoon, the Friday before Easter 1964, a terrifying force let loose. It measured 8.6 on the Richter scale. The ensuing tsunami created waves that swept over the dock and town. Thirty people died. Two more people aboard a steamer tied to the dock were also killed.

Valdez

In the late 1960s, the town's population began to swell again. Oil was discovered on the North Slope and Valdez was chosen to be the terminus for the 800-mile trans-Alaska oil pipeline. Work on the pipeline began in 1974. The town's population skyrocketed to 10,000. When construction ended in 1977, the population plummeted to 3,500. It stayed there until 1989. Then, ironically, on Good Friday, exactly 25 years after the earthquake, disaster struck again. The *Exxon Valdez* oil tanker ran aground at Bligh Reef, spilling 11 million gallons of North Slope crude oil into the pristine waters of Prince William Sound. Alaskans were devastated. And yet, in one of those twists of fate that often occur, the ensuing clean-up effort ushered in another economic boom.

But don't expect to roll into this oil town today and get the latest environmental statistics on Prince William Sound. Oil is king here. So the spill is something most locals are not anxious to talk about. However, if you want to retrace a little history on your own, check out the **Pipeline Club.** It's the bar where Captain Joe Hazelwood of *Exxon Valdez* fame had that scotch-on-the-rocks before his ship ended up on the rocks at Bligh Reef that fateful night.

OCEAN PADDLING TIPS
(FROM A NOT-SO-OLD SALT)

On a sunny day, if you're paddling through icebergs with curious seals bobbing up and down, sea kayaking can be magical. But on a stormy day, bucking 8-foot seas with sheets of rain blowing in your face, it can be perilous if you're not prepared. Here are a few tips to keep you safe and happy.

Design the trip to fit your paddling experience. If you are a relative beginner, choose protected waters, pick routes close to shore, and minimize crossings. Remember, even "inside" waters can get rough. One recipe for trouble is to charter out to your destination with the idea of paddling back, which forces you to cover unfamiliar terrain in changeable weather conditions. An added stress is that you are often racing an end-of-the-trip deadline. It's best to paddle both ways.

Choose experienced partners—ones who are willing to share their knowledge and will not push you beyond your comfort level. Ideally, pick a group of six or less. Big groups are often hard to keep together. They also have a greater impact on the land. Keep boats within easy voice range. Never travel alone. (Remember, for purposes of self-rescue, two people in a double kayak is essentially one boat traveling alone.)

Take good equipment. This includes reliable rain gear, multiple layers of warm clothes, a synthetic sleeping bag (duck or goose down, like cotton, is not warm when wet), and a sturdy, waterproof tent.

Access

You can reach Valdez by driving from Anchorage. It's a long day, but a beautiful drive. **Alaska Airlines** has regularly scheduled flights. Or you can take the train to Whittier and board the ferry to Valdez on the **Alaska Marine Highway,** (907) 272-7116. A 7-hour trip through the Sound, this water route passes right by the Columbia Glacier.

Information

The **Valdez Convention & Visitors Bureau's Visitors Information Center,** (907) 835-2984, is located at the intersection of Chenega and Fairbanks Drives. **One Call Does It All,** (907) 835-4988, is a co-op of bed and breakfasts and boat/plane charters that offers free reservation and information services.

THINGS TO DO

Alyeska Pipeline Tours The Alyeska Pipeline Terminal, which is co-owned by 8 oil companies, changed the face of Valdez when it and the trans-Alaska oil pipeline were constructed in the mid-1970s. The pipeline stretches 800 miles from Prudhoe

Pack your gear into small, waterproof stuff sacks. Line them with garbage bags for extra protection against the wet. Color code them for organization. You'll have an easier time packing your boat with several small bags than with a few large ones.

Always bring extra food and allow yourself extra time to return. Waiting out bad weather is a reality of sea kayaking. People have died trying to get back for work on Monday morning. Make your paddling decisions solely on the basis of wind and waves. Anticipate changes in the weather. Assess how they will affect sea conditions. Look for bailout options as the weather begins to turn, i.e., where you can beach your boats in an emergency. Weather can change very fast in Alaska.

Be familiar with potential hazards: hypothermia, cold-water immersion, rolling icebergs, calving tidewater glaciers, surge waves, rough water, strong currents, and bears. It is also important to learn basic paddle and rescue skills before you set out.

If you have never been in a kayak and have little experience reading the ocean or navigating, take a guided trip. This is probably your safest and most enjoyable alternative. If you are prepared and pay attention, sea kayaking can be wonderful. When you return home, it will be with a sense of peace and a few new muscles.

—Jill Fredston

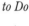
Bay on Alaska's North Slope over several mountain ranges to the Valdez terminal. Construction of the line began in 1974 and was completed in 1977. The pipeline is 48 inches in diameter and has a carrying capacity of 1.16 million barrels of oil a day. About 50 tankers are filled with crude oil monthly. Tours of the terminal cost $15 per person and operate daily from May to mid-October. Tours meet at the Valdez Airport. Call ahead for reservations, (907) 835-2686.

Backcountry Skiing Skiing on Thompson Pass is booming. With miles of untracked powder on the slopes of the pass, local entrepreneurs have figured out ways to get skiers up and down the mountains. Air charters—both helicopter and fixed-wing planes on skis—can give you a lift to the top of a 1,000-foot run. This is steep terrain with tons of windblown snow. You need to be aware of avalanches. Be trained in assessing the dangers, know the precautions, and bring the appropriate gear. Try **Alaska Backcountry Adventures,** (907) 776-5147; **Alaska Extreme Inc.,** (907) 783-2417; or **Chugach Powder Snowcat Skiing,** (907) 835-5105.

Hiking Trails The U.S. Forest Service Visitors Center, (907) 424-7661, is on the edge of town and open only in summer. Two popular hiking trails are the **Soloman Gulch Trail,** which leads up from the fish hatchery to Soloman Lake, and the **Goat Trail,** which follows the original road through Keystone Canyon to Valdez. The Goat trailhead is at Horsetail Falls, about 13.5 miles out of Valdez.

DESTINATIONS OUT

Columbia Glacier This is one of the most active tidewater glaciers in Alaska. Rapidly receding since 1978, it has lost about 6 miles of its once spectacular face. The trip to Columbia takes you through the Valdez Narrows and out into the Sound heading west. On the way, you pass two marine parks popular for camping and fishing. Tours and outfitters that offer trips to the glacier include **Stan Stephens Cruises,** (800) 992-1297; **Alaska Wilderness Sailing and Kayaking**, (907) 835-5175; and **Anadyr Sea Kayak Adventures,** (907) 835-2814.

Whitewater Rafting North of town, go whitewater rafting on the Lowe River through Keystone Canyon. **Keystone Raft and Kayak Adventures,** (907) 835-2606, offer popular day trips.

The Richardson Highway This road leads north out of Valdez toward the Alaska Interior. The road first winds up past Bridal Veil and Horsetail Falls through Keystone Canyon to Thompson Pass. About 30 miles from Valdez, **Thompson Pass** is spectacular and notable for holding most of the state's highest snowfall records. Near the top is the turnoff for the **Worthington Glacier State Recreation Area.** You can drive to the face of the Worthington Glacier. All along the Richardson Highway to Glennallen, you will get glimpses of the trans-Alaska oil pipeline. The road cuts between the mountains of the **Wrangell–St. Elias National Park and Preserve** (see The Roads North chapter). To the east are the impressive Mounts Wrangell, Drum, Stanford, and Blackburn, some of Alaska's most picturesque summits. Just 30 miles shy of Glennallen is the community of Copper Center. The tiny town, which sits on the banks of the Copper River, was founded during the gold-rush era of 1898. An old fishwheel still sits in the river. The **Copper Center Lodge and Trading Post,** (907) 822-3245, was built in the early 1930s. Still in operation today, it houses a small museum containing Athabascan baskets, Russian artifacts, and mining memorabilia.

GUIDES/OUTFITTERS

Alaska Wilderness Sailing and Kayaking Formerly known as Alaska Wilderness Safaris, they offer half-day and full-day kayaking trips from Growler Island across from Columbia Glacier. Owners Jim and Nancy Lethcoe, authors of two guidebooks to Prince William Sound, are very knowledgeable. First, you have to get to the island. Most folks go with **Stan Stephens Cruises.** From Growler Island, there are five different trips the Lethcoes offer paddlers. "It's really great for people who don't want to camp in the rain," Jim Lethcoe said. They also do custom sailing trips early or late in the season. For more information, contact PO Box 1313, Valdez, AK 99686; (907) 835-5175.

Anadyr Sea Kayak Adventures Offers 3-hour guided kayaking trips with instruction and day-long guided trips out of Galena Bay to nearby glaciers. Owner Hedy Sarney will also help you plan a longer, custom-designed trip and will rent kayaks to experienced boaters. For more information, contact PO Box 1821, Valdez, AK 99686; (907) 835-2814.

Keystone Raft and Kayak Adventures They have one of the most popular river trips—a thrilling ride down the Lowe River through Keystone Canyon, with Class III rapids, at $30/person. Two other popular half-day and day trips are down the Tsina River and the Tonsina River. They also offer 10-day trips down the Copper River for $1,900/person. You can go by raft, or they will supply support for experienced kayakers. For additional trips and a brochure, contact PO Box 1486, Valdez, AK 99686; (907) 835-2606.

Something Fishy Owned by Rik VanStone, this is one of the most popular saltwater fish guiding businesses in Valdez. Not only does Rik find fish, but he also neatly fillets them for you. For more information, contact PO Box 74, Valdez, AK 99686; (907) 835-5732.

Stan Stephens Cruises In business for 18 years, they offer day trips out to Columbia Glacier. They also run a tent camp on Growler Island, on the north side of Glacier Island, which faces Columbia. The name "growler" means any iceberg that presents a navigational hazard. The trip to Columbia Glacier, with stopover at Growler Island for lunch, takes 8 hours and costs $95. Stay overnight at their tent camp on Growler Island (adults $188, children $160) and spend the next day on a kayaking adventure with **Alaska Wilderness Sailing and Kayaking.** For more information, contact PO Box 1297, Valdez, AK 99686; (800) 992-1297.

FESTIVALS/EVENTS

Prince William Sound Theater Conference Held in mid-August, this conference draws hundreds of playwrights and theater buffs from around the country. The "godfather" of the event, Edward Albee—triple Pulitzer Prize winner—was joined in 1995 by Terrence McNally, author of the Tony Award–winning *Love! Valour! Compassion!* It's a chance for Alaska's own community theater organizers to rub elbows with New York City's finest. The conference features workshops, critiques,

BEACHCOMBING

*Spring is a great time for beachcombing in the Sound—
the time to see what the Gulf of Alaska has tossed out over the
winter. Winter storms in the Gulf are notorious, at times producing waves impersonating major mountain ranges.*

*Occasionally, shipping containers tumble off barges, their
contents spilling into the sea. Some of this stuff eventually
makes it to shore, sometimes in mass quantities. As a result,
Prince William Sound and Gulf Coast residents have found
their shorelines littered with everything from rubber ducky tub
toys to bundles of marijuana.*

*At Montague Island, driftwood piles alone tell the story
of the power of nature, not to mention the remodeling job
done by the Good Friday Earthquake in 1964. The kinds of
souvenirs you'll find here include wrecked boats and airplane
parts. In addition to unopened soda cans and plastic milk
containers, beachcombers have found whale bones, Japanese
glass floats, bottles with notes inside, and an abandoned
World War II mine. The Forest Service has 4 public-use cabins on the outer coast of Montague, available by reservation
for $25/night. The Log Jam Lake Cabin is the best of the
four. Decorated in a beachcombing motif, the cabin shelf
displays a fine collection of strange trophies. For reservations,
contact the U.S. Forest Service, Cordova Ranger District,
(907) 424-7661.*

*Perhaps the best beachcombing of all can be found at
Kayak Island, on the eastern edge of the Copper River Delta.
Because the island sits perpendicular to the wind and currents, it acts like a giant catcher's mitt. Booty found here includes rubber turtle tub toys, life rings, Japanese survival
rations with this message written in Japanese and English:
"Don't give up. But if all hope is lost, write down what you
think should be in this kit." People have found everything
from Skuffy the Tugboat, a toy with a warning not to use in
water, to Nike shoes. (A huge shipment lost in the Gulf had
people up and down the coast swapping shoes right and left
in an effort to find pairs that fit.)*

*Chartered boats or planes, which can land on beaches at
low tide, are your way out here.* **Fishing & Flying,** *(907) 424-
3324, out of Cordova has a great reputation, and its owners
are avid beachcombers themselves. A group of three can charter a plane to either island for about $440, round-trip.*

— Debra McKinney

and readings. The cost is $90 for the 5-day event. For information, call (800) 478-8800 or (907) 835-2681.

World Extreme Skiing Championships

Draws the world's most daring skiers to Valdez every year. The competition is at the end of March or beginning of April. Held at Thompson Pass, the event requires thrillseekers to pick the steepest and most dangerous run down death-defying slopes, around exposed rocks and over cliffs. A helicopter ferries competitors to the top. Judges award points for aggressiveness, form, fluidity, and control. Some consider the World Extremes a death-wish derby. Bring your binoculars. For information, call (907) 835-2108.

BEST RESTAURANTS

Mike's Palace Ristorante ★★

Owner Mike Panagis's menu runs the gamut from steak and seafood to lasagne, pizza, and enchiladas. While the pizzas are alluring and come with thin, thick, or really thick crusts, many diners swear by the lasagne. It's a cozy restaurant with a view of the harbor. The walls, covered with old newspapers, tell the history of Valdez. ■ *Directly across from the harbor; 201 N Harbor Dr, Valdez; (907) 835-2365; $$ (dinner entrees $10–$17); beer and wine; MC, V; local checks only; open 11am–11pm year-round. &*

Valdez

Restaurants

Oscar's on the Waterfront ★

While Oscar's serves three meals a day, it's breakfast that draws the crowd. The food is greasy, but the locals love it—and the eggs Benedict are the best in town. Another favorite is Klondike potatoes, which are homefries grilled with onions and blanketed with cheddar cheese. Grab a caffe latte at the Klondike Coffee Shop, 2 blocks away. ■ *A 2-block walk west from the harbormaster's office; 143 N Harbor Dr, Valdez; (907) 835-4700; $$ (breakfast $5.95–$7.95); MC, V; local checks only; open daily 4:30am–1am in summer, 5:30am–9pm in winter. &*

Pipeline Club Restaurant ★

This is where the tanker crews and fishermen head for steak and seafood dinners. The restaurant's speciality is "Pipeline Pu Pu," created by a chef from the Hawaiian Islands. In Valdez, the dish is made with sliced steak sautéed with onion, bell pepper, soy sauce, tomato, and seasoning, then served on bed of rice. Stick your head into the bar next door, where Captain Hazelwood had that famous scotch-on-the-rocks. Or was it two? ■ *Located in the town center, sandwiched between the Valdez Motel and the Westmark Inn; 112 Egan Dr, Valdez; (907) 835-4891; $$ (entrees $13–$20); full bar; MC, V, DC; checks OK; dinner daily. &*

BEST LODGINGS

Cliff House Bed and Breakfast ★★★★

This is Valdez's most elegant and expensive bed and breakfast. Nothing in town matches its space and views. Directly above the ferry terminal, 250 feet above sea level, it overlooks the fjord and port of

Valdez. The five-level home, built in 1967, has three guest rooms, all with private baths. Margie Lyon serves a breakfast of fresh fruits, smoked salmon, fresh fruit tarts, and soufflés. Playwright Edward Albee stays here when he comes to town for the annual theater festival. ■ *From Hazelet Ave, go to the top of Meals Hill Rd; PO Box 1995, Valdez, AK 99686; (907) 835-5244; $$$ (roughly $130–$140); MC, V; checks OK; closed mid-Sept–late May.*

The Lake House Bed and Breakfast ★★★ Like a country inn, far from the hustle of town, this home perches on a bluff and has wide decks overlooking Robe Lake. The setting is remote, yet only 10 minutes from downtown Valdez. Mountains can be seen from every window. Most rooms have private baths. Prices include a breakfast of muffins, pancakes, or scrambled eggs with fresh salmon. ■ *Mile 6 on Richardson Hwy; PO Box 1499, Valdez, AK 99686; (907) 835-4752; $$ ($80–$100); MC, V; checks OK; closed Nov–Feb.*

Best of All Bed and Breakfast ★★ In business for eight years, this place has a reputation for good, hearty breakfasts. Really early risers get continental breakfast with fresh fruit and bagels. But those who can stick around until 8am get treated to Sue Kennedy's crêpes, fancy pancakes, or waffles. A native of Thailand, Sue has decorated her home with a blend of Alaska and Thai art. She has three guest rooms, one with a private bath and spa. ■ *From the ferry terminal, drive up Hazelet Ave, turnoff for Mineral Creek Dr is near the end; 1104 Mineral Creek Dr; PO Box 1578, Valdez, AK 99686; (907) 835-4524; $$ ($75–$95 range); no credit cards; no checks; open year-round.*

Casa De La Bellezza ★★ Gerald and Lynn Bellezza got into the bed-and-breakfast business the year of the oil spill, and they're still at it. Lynn collects recipes and is known for serving one of the best hot breakfasts in town—ham, eggs, and biscuits or French toast. There are three guest rooms, two with queen beds. The Isabella Suite, named for Lynn's grandmother, is the most private with its own phone, mini-kitchen, and view of the mountains. Casa De La Bellezza is 12 blocks from the ferry dock and an 8-block walk from town. ■ *Follow Hazelet Ave from the ferry terminal to Oumalik St; 333 Oumalik St; PO Box 294, Valdez, AK 99686; (907) 835-4489; $$ ($75–$90); MC, V; checks OK; open year-round; sometimes closed Oct.*

Think Pink B&B A local character and self-styled historian, owner Dorothy Clifton has lived in Valdez since before the 1964 Earthquake. She is a packrat when it comes to memorabilia. Her five-bedroom house is full of historical files, maps, and old photos. She calls her place "Think Pink" because she wanted a pink house, but there were too many in her neighborhood, so she settled for a cream house. ■ *Head north from the ferry terminal on Hazelet Ave to Klutina. Turn left on Cottonwood. Follow Cottonwood to N Glacier Dr; 705 N Glacier Dr; PO Box 6, Valdez, AK 99686; (907) 835-4367; $$ (summer $85, winter $55); V, MC; checks preferred; open year-round.*

CORDOVA

Isolated and quaint, this fishing community is the hidden gem of Prince William Sound. The docks are lined with weathered canneries. The harbor brims with a fat fleet of mom-and-pop commercial fishing boats. The streets and hillsides are dotted with sun-worn bungalows. It's the kind of place where stray mutts wander down main street and everybody knows them by name. You won't need a car; everything is within walking distance.

Out Cordova's back door is the Copper River Delta, an immensely lush and diverse ecosystem fed by six glacial rivers. The town's history is rich with stories of trade and conflict between Natives, Russians, copper miners, and oil explorers. Cordova is strategically situated amid enormous runs of salmon and a bounty of shellfish. It was fish that reeled in the first Americans, who came to build a cannery here in 1889.

Michael J. Heney, a brilliant engineer, showed up a few years later to direct the building of the Copper River and Northwestern Railway, which winds alongside the Copper River 200 miles to McCarthy and Kennicott, towns built on the fortunes of copper and nestled in the Wrangell Mountains. Until the 1930s, Cordova thrived as a supply depot for the copper mines there and for the oil fields at Katalla, about 45 miles southeast of Cordova on the Gulf of Alaska.

About 2,500 people live here year-round, but the town nearly doubles when fishing starts in spring. It's an eclectic group of commercial fishermen, artists, intellectuals, Eyak Natives, and plain end-of-the-roaders. They live in bungalows clinging to steep slopes overlooking Orca Inlet or in old boathouses along Odiak Slough. The town has a reputation for making room for just about anybody, but at the same time it can become fiercely divided over any political issue. Everyone has an opinion. Just mention "the road." You'll get an earful.

Once upon a time, there were plans to build the Copper River Highway on top of the old railroad tracks that run up the Copper River to Chitina, where the road would link with the rest of Alaska. Construction began in the 1960s, but the 1964 Earthquake buckled the Million Dollar Bridge, bringing the project to a halt. In recent years, there has been talk of renewing that project. Those who like the isolation of the surrounding mountains and the sea don't want the road. Those who

Cordova

want it say it will bring new blood and a more reasonable cost of living.

In late April and early May, the town bustles with bird-watchers. They are followed by a wave of commercial fishermen who fish 24-hour openings, then return to Cordova, where you'll see them down in the harbor mending their nets and gearing up for the next opening. The season ends in late August, and the town is pretty quiet until spring rolls around again. It's mild but wet here, with an average of 15 feet of rain a year. If the sun shines, don't expect the shops to stay open.

Access

There are only two ways into Cordova, which is one of its beauties. You can fly in from Anchorage, Juneau, or Seattle on Alaska Airlines, (800) 426-0333, or you can take the **Alaska Marine Highway,** (907) 272-7116, ferry from Whittier or Valdez. From Whittier, it's about a 7-hour ferry ride. If you fly, the **Mudhole Smith Airport,** (907) 424-7151 (named for an early bush pilot), is located about 12 miles out of town and has a shuttle service.

Information

On weekdays, the **Cordova Chamber of Commerce's Visitors Center** (PO Box 99, Cordova, AK 99574; (907) 424-7260) is a wealth of information. It's on First Avenue in downtown Cordova, right next to **Orca Book & Sound,** also a good place for books, maps, and information.

THINGS TO DO

Mount Eyak Ski Area If the skies are clear and you can round up a group of six or so, the folks here will fire up the vintage chairlift to take you to the top of Mount Eyak. You'll have a spectacular view of Orca Inlet and miles beyond. Plus, you'll get to sit where Clark Gable and Marilyn Monroe once sat. This very same chairlift hoisted famous authors and movie stars such as Ernest Hemingway, Groucho Marx, Ingrid Bergman, Lucille Ball, and John Wayne to the top of the mountains in Sun Valley, Idaho, from 1936 to 1969. Alaska has it now. It's been in Cordova since 1974 and "You can't beat the view here," says David Bradshaw, local chairlift historian. For more information, call (907) 424-7766.

Mountain Bikes and Kayaks For rentals, try **Seaman True Value Hardware,** (907) 424-3647, or Leia and Jim Merritt at **Cordova Coastal Adventures,** (907) 424-3842. They rent double and single kayaks and will help you map out a kayak trip. **Wannabe's Bicycles,** (907) 424-5696, on Second Avenue, has bikes and inflatable kayaks.

Prince William Science Center An independent, nonprofit research facility housed down on the docks. Funded in part with settlement money from the 1989 Exxon oil spill, the work of the center focuses on the complex ecosystem of the Sound. Tours are available during business hours upon request. For more information, contact Prince William Science Center, PO Box 705, Cordova, AK 99574; (907) 424-5800.

DESTINATIONS OUT

Childs Glacier and the Million Dollar Bridge The bridge and glacier are 52 miles out of town, on the old Copper River Road. Impressive and close, the 300-foot wall of ice sits across the Copper River. Thunderous calving of ice off the glacier echoes from the steel beams of the bent bridge, which buckled during the 1964 Earthquake. You can still walk across the bridge. To get there, call **Copper River Northwest Tours,** (907) 424-5356, hitch a ride, or take a taxi.

Copper River Delta A rich, diverse ecosystem and breeding ground for all sorts of waterfowl, the Copper River flows 250 miles through the Chugach Mountains to the Sound. It is a strong, turbulent river that produces highly prized red salmon. Because of the firm, meaty flesh and layer of belly fat, Copper River salmon rank as the state's most delicious wild salmon. The best way to see the delta, the glacier, and the bridge is to call Becky Chapek at **Copper River Northwest Tours,** (907) 424-5356. She runs bus tours to the delta three or four times a week, and offers a narrative on the area's history and wildlife. Hardy bike riders can also jump on for a one-way ride to the glacier, peddling back at their own pace.

Wilderness Trails and Cabins The Cordova Ranger District of the Forest Service maintains about 37 miles of trails on the Copper River Delta and a dozen wilderness public-use cabins. For information and reservations, contact U.S. Forest Service, Cordova Ranger District, PO Box 280, Cordova, AK 99574; (907) 424-7661.

GUIDES/OUTFITTERS

Alaska Wilderness Outfitting Offers fly-in fishing trips. They have floating cabins in Simpson and Sheep Bays, cabins on shore, guided trips, and do-it-yourself trips where they'll set you up in a fully stocked cabin with motor boat, then leave you on your own. You bring only sleeping bags and fishing gear. Before dropping you off, they will fly you over the best fishing streams in the area. (They do leave you with a radio, in case of emergency.) You can even opt for a combo trip—3 days of saltwater fishing, then off to a remote camp in the Wrangell Mountains for freshwater rainbow and lake trout fishing. Costs for 5-day trips run $1,200 to $2,600. For more information, contact Alaska Wilderness Outfitting, PO Box 1516, Cordova, AK 99574; (907) 424-5552.

Fishing and Flying Offers flightseeing or drop-offs to the area's many remote Forest Service cabins or their own fishing

SHOREBIRD FESTIVAL

In early May, Cordova joyfully celebrates the return of the birds, as host of the Copper River Delta Shorebird Festival. The town is invaded by visitors in rubberized rain suits with notebooks in their pockets and binoculars around their necks. For 5 days, they take field trips and do lectures, workshops, and slide shows. All the while, they engage in species-speak and general bird adoration. In town, shorebirds are every-where—on signs, on T-shirts, and painted on store windows. Why the big whoop?

This is not just a few robins people are welcoming back. Waterfowl and shorebirds pass through the delta by the millions: Western sandpipers, Canada geese, trumpeter swans, sandhill cranes, fork-tailed storm petrels, red-faced cormorants—more than 240 species live or stop here. At times, they come in intense gusts—as many as 200,000 geese, swans, pintails, sandpipers, and other waterfowl have been known to pass overhead in the course of an hour.

Most birds traveling to or through Alaska funnel through the delta, where six glacial rivers rendezvous with the sea. This heavily braided, 50-mile-wide delta is a mecca of meadows, marshes, ponds, mud flats, and sloughs. In the bird world it's like a 24-hour diner, offering up an irresistible smorgasbord of fish and fly larvae after a nearly nonstop flight along the Gulf of Alaska's cantankerous coast. For most species, the last major rest stop was 900 miles back at the Stikine River in Southeast Alaska, or the Fraser River in southern British Columbia, more than 1,200 miles back.

As former Cordova mayor Kelly Weaverling once put it, "The birds have been having a festival here for thousands of years. It's only recently that we figured out there was a party going on." (For more information, call (907) 424-7260.)

—Debra McKinney

camps on the Katalla River and the Tsiu River. If you really want a bird's-eye view of the Sound, take their mail plane. They're "the postman" in Prince William Sound. It's a cheap way to fly over the area's glaciers and set down in some of the Sound's remote villages, such as Chenega. They don't fly every day, and there is room only for five passengers, so call ahead. They also offer day flightseeing trips to McCarthy. For more information, contact Fishing and Flying, PO Box 2349, Cordova, AK 99574; (907) 424-3324.

Sage Charters They will take you out fishing, birdwatching, or to watch sea otters. Rates depend on numbers of people and individual desires. The boat holds six people and costs $350 to $550 for a day charter. Scientists doing field work in the Sound often use this service. For more information, contact Sage Charters, PO Box 723, Cordova, AK 99574; (907) 424-3475.

FESTIVALS/EVENTS

Copper River Delta Shorebird Festival This festival draws hundreds of curious birdwatchers to Cordova every spring around the first of May to watch millions of migrating birds. In past years, the local chapter of the Audubon Society, (907) 424-7260, has sponsored a cruise with naturalists from Valdez to Cordova (see box).

Ice Worm Festival Held the first week of February, the festival is a week-long celebration and features a parade led by the guest of honor, a 100-foot-long ice worm. Some say the ice worm is only a mythological character. But what do they know? The true story is ice worms really do exist. As fanciful homework for the festival, read Robert Service's poem, *Ballad of the Ice Worm Cocktail.* All over Alaska, you'll find these midwinter carnivals and celebrations to dispel "cabin fever" and break up the long, cold winter. Tap into them. They are great for local color. For more information, contact Cordova's Ice Worm Festival, PO Box 819, Cordova, AK 99574; (907) 424-7260.

BEST RESTAURANTS

Cookhouse Cafe ★★★ All the charm that is Cordova can be found at this little cafe, nestled on the dock between weathered warehouses looking out over Orca Inlet. Once the mess hall of the old cannery, Cookhouse Cafe has been restored to wood beams, white walls, and the gray-and-red trim of the traditional cannery colors. In the old days, when the steam whistle blew, cannery workers gathered for "mug ups"—coffee and pastries. The cafe has revived the tradition. Mainly geared to breakfast and lunch, the cafe also has special evening events. ■ *Head north along First Ave until you spot the old canneries; 1 Cannery Rd, Bldg 7, Cordova; (907) 424-5926; $$ ($5.95–$8.95); V, MC; checks OK; open Mon–Sat till 3pm, Sun until 2pm; closed Oct–May.*

Baja Taco ★ This funky red school bus serves a mean burrito and scrumptious fish tacos. Its menu, featured on a surfboard, stands next to the bus. The owners spend enough time in Mexico each winter to know how to keep the food spicy. ■ *At the harbor; you can't miss it; Nicholoff St, Cordova; (907) 424-5599; $ ($3–$6); no credit cards; checks OK; open daily; closed Oct–April.*

Killer Whale Cafe ★ This little deli and coffee shop in the back of Orca Book & Sound is right in the center of town and a favorite espresso stop. It also serves hearty soups and bulky sandwiches. The cheesecake is a killer. The bookstore makes nice browsing, with its eclectic collection of fine literature and local art. ■ *Downtown Cordova; 507 First Ave; (907) 424-7733; $ ($3–$6); no alcohol; no credit cards; no checks; open Mon–Sat year-round.*

Reluctant Fisherman Inn A great place to drink up a view of the harbor, while sipping wine and lingering over halibut. Oscar, a friendly sea otter, swims nearby. The restaurant specializes in fresh Alaska seafood. Over the bar are brass plates listing all the local men and women lost at sea. ■ *Council St to Railroad Ave; 401 Railroad Ave, Cordova; (907) 424-7446; $$$ (entrees $15–$30); full bar; AE, DC, MC, V; checks OK; breakfast, lunch, dinner, daily; closed mid-Nov–Jan.* ⅄

BEST LODGINGS

Cannery Bunkhouse ★★★ Located above the Cookhouse Cafe, the old cannery bunkhouse has nine bed-and-breakfast rooms, austere and whitewashed. Showers are down the hall. The owners are still finishing the details, but their aim is to preserve the simple bunkhouse flavor. An added attraction is Cordova's massage therapist, who has an office near here. ■ *A little north of downtown; 1 Cannery Rd, Bldg 7; PO Box 120, Cordova, AK 99574; (907) 424-5920; $ ($35–$45 a person, a night); V, MC; checks OK; closed Oct–May.*

Cordova

Restaurants

▲

Cordova Rose Lodge ★★★ Permanently dry-docked in Odiak Slough next to an operating lighthouse, this old barge (now a lodge) is filled with nautical artifacts. Stay in the Captain's Quarters, the Officer's Quarters, or the Chief's Quarters. However, if you choose the Stowaway Room, the smallest and simplest, you're not allowed to complain. The joke is they follow the rules of the sea here. And you know what happens to stowaways. Because the barge is on the slough, it is popular with birdwatchers. ■ *A mile from downtown, go east on First; turn right on Whiteshed; 1315 Whiteshed Rd; PO Box 1494, Cordova, AK 99574; (907) 424-7673; $$ ($65/double); MC, V; checks OK.*

Reluctant Fisherman Inn If it's predictability and the conveniences of a standard hotel you are looking for, stay here. Ask for a room facing the harbor. You will pay about $20 more, but it's worth it. ■ *1 block from downtown; 401 Railroad Ave; PO Box 150, Cordova, AK 99574; (907) 424-3272; $$$ ($105–$125); AE, DC, MC, V; checks OK.* ⅄

WILDERNESS LODGES

Goose Cove Lodge An exclusive, educational retreat at Goose Cove for naturalists, wildlife photographers, and serious

ALASKA WILD WINGS

Pete and Belle Mickelson run Alaska Wild Wings, an educational retreat for naturalists, wildlife photographers, and birders, out at Goose Cove, 8 miles from Cordova, on the edge of the Copper River Delta. Between them, they have a doctorate and master's degrees in wildlife ecology, zoology, and environmental education. They can recite migration counts 20 years back and tell you everything from local lore to the mating rituals of the tanner crab. But, most of all, they are incurable birders.

So for them, Goose Cove is heaven. You see, the delta is one of the most spectacular shorebird migration rest stops in the world. Here, the Mickelsons and birds share gifts of the land. Like the bald eagle that one day flapped overhead and dropped a salmon on the beach. "What the heck?" they shrugged. They took it home and barbecued it.

Goose Cove Lodge, the Mickelsons' home, crouches among mountain hemlock and old-growth Sitka spruce. It's a human version of a nest, really, with one wall impaled by a spruce tree they couldn't bear to cut down. Living is Alaska Bush–style. In addition to the outhouse, there are composting toilets inside, well-stocked with reading material such as A Field Guide to Northwest Coastal Invertebrates.

Days are custom designed. You can poke around on the mudflats or photograph sea otters goofing around in pools left by outgoing tides. In addition to serious birding, guests fish, dig clams, pick berries, and barbecue seafood on the beach. There are also tours of marine mammal and seabird sanctuaries. For more information, contact Alaska Wild Wings, PO Box 325, Cordova, AK 99574; (800) 324-9464 or (907) 424-5104.

—Debra McKinney

bird watchers (see box). For information, contact Alaska Wild Wings, PO Box 325, Cordova, AK 99574; (800) 324-9464 or (907) 424-5104.

SUGGESTED READING

Alaska Geographic Society. *Prince William Sound.* Anchorage, 1993.

Armstrong, Robert H. *A Guide to the Birds of Alaska.* Anchorage: Alaska Northwest Publishing, 1989.

Crandall, Alissa. *Alaska's Prince William Sound: Paradise*

of the North. Anchorage: Alaska Art Print Co., 1993.

Davidson, Art. *In the Wake of the* Exxon Valdez: *The Devastating Impact of the Alaska Oil Spill.* San Francisco: Sierra Club Books, 1990.

Janson, Lone E. *The Copper Spike.* Alaska: Northwest Publishing Co., 1975.

Lethcoe, Jim and Nancy. *Cruising Guide to Prince William Sound* (a two-volume set). Valdez, Alaska: Prince William Sound Books, 1984.

Wheelwright, Jeff. *Degrees of Disaster: Prince William Sound: How Nature Reels and Rebounds.* New York: Simon & Schuster, 1994.

KENAI PENINSULA

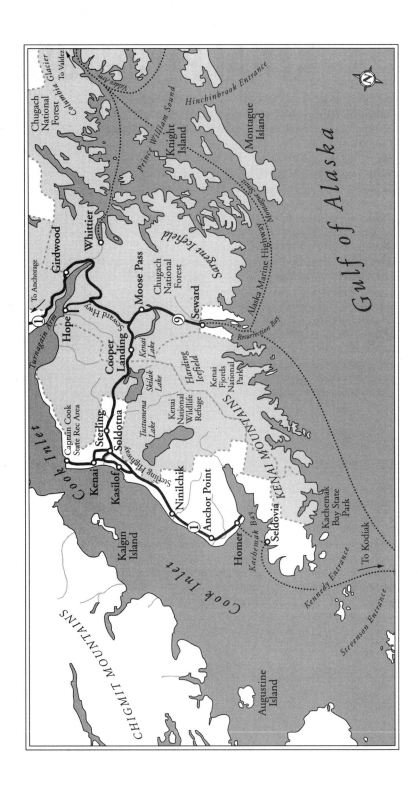

Kenai Peninsula

*Including Portage Glacier, Seward, Kenai Fjords
National Park, Exit Glacier, Kenai River, Homer,
Kachemak Bay State Park, and Seldovia*

Two hundred years ago, when the famous British navigator
Captain James Cook sailed into the waters that today bear his
name (Cook Inlet), he explored down Turnagain Arm in his
search for the elusive route to the fabled Northwest Passage.
Alas, he had to turn again. Hence the name of one of the most
dramatic bodies of water and scenery in all of Alaska. The road
down Turnagain Arm from Anchorage is your entry to Alaska's
greatest playground—the Kenai Peninsula.

The original Kenaitze people gave the land their name.
Then Russian fur hunters arrived. Their influence is reflected
today by other names—the little town of Ninilchik with its
onion-domed church, Kasilof near the mouth of the Kenai River,
Seldovia across Kachemak Bay. Little gold rushes sprang up.
The promise of a brighter day is laced into the names of all
those diggings, from the Resurrection Trail and Sunrise to the
little town of Hope itself.

After World War II, a whole new wave of adventurers arrived—the homesteaders. The road didn't go very far then. So
they picked a likely spot on the map, then hiked, rafted, or flew
into the wilderness to stake their claims and live off the land.
They built log cabins, planted vegetables, hunted moose, and
raised their families in the woods, near the ocean, or by the
rivers.

"In the beginning, we had just enough for a little grub-
stake," remembers Marge Mullen, one of the original homesteaders in Soldotna. "I found out what that meant—a few
cartons of groceries and a trusty rifle." The Mullens were the
first homesteading family on Soldotna Creek in 1947, and
around them grew up the town of Soldotna—today a town of
3,800 folks and a popular fishing destination for Kenai River
salmon fishermen.

Today, throngs of Alaskans and visitors (you'll recognize
them from the baseball caps pulled low over their brows and
the crazed look in their eyes) barrel down the highway to the
peninsula in summer for one big reason: FISH. Not just any
fish, but BIG fish—like king salmon and halibut. (The world
record king salmon was pulled out of this river in 1985, weighing 97 pounds.) Never mind that our poor finned friends have
eluded the nets of many foreign countries in their journey of
thousands of miles through the ocean back to their home
rivers to spawn, or that they've also swum out of the jaws of
larger fish and past the claws of hungry brown bears. No, for

now they face the final test: *combat fishing on the Kenai.* Things get so chummy on the banks of the rivers here that all those flying hooks don't necessarily nail your dinner; some nail your neighbor's nose or rear-end instead. The hospital in Soldotna has a marvelous mural of a fisherman covering one wall. Every painful hook pulled out from every body gets hooked up here in the same place it got yanked out. Just in case you're wondering, no place has been left unhooked.

Fishing folk have every right to be wild about the Kenai River. It's truly extraordinary. Not only is it gorgeous, but it's also home to the largest race of salmon (size-wise) to swim up any river in the world. It is phenomenally productive. No river in the world, crossed by bridges, with two cities on either side of it, has sustained such a run. That's the challenge. Today, the river's health is a hot topic and has all government agencies in the state pondering its growing problems: maintenance of clean habitat, integrity of streambanks, and control of waste water. If you fish and you love the Kenai, it is vital to educate yourself and do your part.

**Kenai
Peninsula**

Access

Lest you think fishing is the last word here, the Kenai Peninsula has a glorious spectrum of all that is wonderful about Alaska: sheer beauty, massive icefields, crystal-blue glaciers, dramatic fjords, dozens of hiking trails, and huge glacial-green lakes. The exquisite emerald waters of Kenai Lake tumble into the Kenai River, which then cascades through the canyon into Skilak Lake ("Lake of the Sky") and around Caribou and Frying Pan Islands. The lake waters flow back into the river again and on in grandeur down to Cook Inlet. A national park, a national forest, a lovely state park, and a huge wildlife refuge cover most of this peninsula. In between are a few towns and a handful of hamlets. With so much accessible beauty, you could happily spend an entire summer here and never come close to doing it all.

Access

Most people get to the Kenai Peninsula by car. If you are in a hurry, you can fly there from the Anchorage airport via smaller commuter airlines. Others come by ship, ferry, or fishing boat into the ports of Seward or Homer.

The Alaska Highway (Alaska 1) runs from Anchorage to Seward. Along the way is the Hope turnoff, which appears after about an hour and a half of driving. The road to Hope is about 17 miles long and makes for a nice round-trip bike ride from the highway into the little town of Hope. Two hours or so into your journey, the highway splits. If you go left, you will travel through Moose Pass and end up in Seward on Resurrection Bay. That takes about a half hour. If you go right, you're now on Sterling Highway (Alaska 9), which will take you past Kenai Lake, alongside Kenai River, through the mountains to the flats and into Soldotna. That takes about an hour. Farther south, toward the end of the road, are Homer and Kachemak Bay, 2 hours' drive from Soldotna. At the "Y" in Soldotna, turn right onto the Kenai Spur Highway and you'll pass the town of Kenai. At the end of that road, 35 miles later, you come to Captain Cook State Recreation Area on the shores of Cook Inlet.

Information

In Anchorage, **Alaska Public Lands Information Center** has reams of information on trails, forests, refuges, and parks and will help you plot your journey. You can find out here how to reserve public-use cabins on federal lands; for those on state lands, try the **Department of Natural Resources Public Information Center,** (907) 269-8400. There are also visitors centers in every town along the way, as well as park, forest, and refuge headquarters. Contact 605 W Fourth Avenue downtown; (907) 271-2737.

ON THE ROAD: ANCHORAGE TO SEWARD

The drive takes 3 hours. You cruise down Turnagain Arm, through Chugach State Park into Chugach National Forest, past the state's most popular glacier, into the mountains, and end up in Seward, headquarters for Kenai Fjords National Park.

En route, **Portage Glacier** and its iceberg-filled lake, an hour into your journey, is one of Alaska's treasures. With such proximity to the big city, it draws more tourists than any other attraction in the state. It even beats visitation to our highest mountain, Mount McKinley, in Denali National Park, by about 100,000 people a year. You can gaze from shore or take the **Portage Glacier Cruises,** (907) 783-2983, from May to September (weather and ice conditions permitting). They run five 1-hour tours daily. The cost is $21/adults, half-price for children. If you have time, be sure to watch the short film, *Voices from the Ice,* inside the theater at the **Begich, Boggs Visitors Center,** (907) 783-2326. The finale is breathtaking. The visitors center is open daily in summer and for long weekends in winter. In winter, the glacier takes on a severe and even eerie quality. Icebergs, some as big as ships, freeze into the lake, forming giant blue sculptures.

From here, you wind into the mountains and cross **Turnagain Pass,** a popular skiing and snowmobiling area in winter. The cut-off to **Hope** is a nice side trip, particularly by bicycle, if you have time. The road, 34 miles round-trip, is not heavily traveled. Hope is a sweet little collection of wood buildings at the edge of Turnagain Arm.

Farther on, after the road splits, you'll pass through **Moose Pass,** named for an ornery moose who wouldn't budge off the old dogteam trail that ran through here. If you have any

DRIVING TIPS

The drive is spectacular in all seasons. But be aware the word "highway" in Alaska really means "road" anywhere else. En route you will travel through park, forest, and refuge lands, and along glacially fed lakes and rivers. You'll curve around large bodies of salt water, through mountains and lowlands. Remember too that if you break down, you may be miles and miles from any help. This is particularly important in the winter. Carry emergency survival gear with you in the car. This means flares, flashlight, warm clothes, warm shoes, a sleeping bag, extra food, and water. Double-check that you have tools for changing your own tires. Good footgear cannot be overemphasized. Pumps and hose won't get you very far if you have to walk for gas in the middle of winter. Winter or summer, day or night, drive with your headlights on. And watch for animals. Every year people slam into moose and bears, especially at night. If you see moose on the side of the road, slow way down. They are apt to bolt over the road right in front of you, then get transfixed by your headlights.

knives, bring them and look for the water wheel on the right side of the road. A handwritten note says: "Moose Pass is a peaceful little town. If you have an axe to grind, DO IT HERE!" At least one four-star restaurateur we know from Anchorage sharpens his kitchen knives here on his way to Seward.

About 4 miles before you reach Seward, turn off to **Exit Glacier** at Mile 3.7. Nine miles of driving and half a mile of walking will take you to the foot of this impressive ice monster.

SEWARD

While the Kenai Peninsula is famous for fish, it's also a great place to see glaciers. Seward is the easiest and best place to do both.

The town was named after William Seward, secretary of state under President Andrew Jackson, who engineered the purchase of Alaska from Russia in 1867. His critics around the country were appalled. The United States had spent $7.2 million, they cried, for icebergs and polar bears. Cartoonists showed Seward amid glaciers and walruses. They claimed the new territory should more aptly be called "Walrussia" or "Seward's Folly." Asked at the end of his long and distinguished career about his single greatest achievement, Seward responded, "The purchase of Alaska! But it will take Congress and the American people a generation to find it out."

That original purchase price has been paid back thousands of times over in fur, gold, fish, timber, and oil. Ironically, now tourists come (and pay) to see icebergs, walruses, polar bears, and glaciers. While you'll see plenty of ice in Seward, you won't see walruses or polar bears this far south, unless you come for a strange event the third week of January, known as the **Seward Polar Bear Jumpoff Festival.** When everyone else is wearing parkas and wool hats, strange characters in costumes and capes—all for charity and the theater of the absurd—plunge into the frigid waters of Resurrection Bay and come flying back out. It's their entry fee to an elite and wacky club, the Polar Bear Club.

Resurrection Bay is the best of Seward, an inviting front yard, attracting boaters, birders, kayakers, fishermen, sailors, and whale watchers. Full of glaciers and incredible wildlife, all of the western coast of the bay is in Kenai Fjords National Park. Seward is the beginning of the railroad to Fairbanks and Mile 0 on the old historic Seward to Nome gold rush/mail route.

Information

Run by the Seward Chamber of Commerce, **Seward Visitors Information Center** (Mile 2, at the north end of town; (907) 224-8051) is open year-round. In summer, there's also a branch in an old Alaska Railroad car, permanently stationed at Third Avenue and Jefferson Street downtown.The visitors center for **Kenai Fjords National Park** is headquartered at the Seward small-boat harbor, close to the harbormaster, (907) 224-3175.

Seward

*Outdoor
Activities*

PLACES TO VISIT

Cruise the boardwalk filled with fishing charters and fjord tours. This is a great jumping-off place for both. Stroll the docks and look at the boats. Stop in at **Bardarson Studios,** a fun store filled with books, art, and interesting Alaska stuff. In the heart of downtown, scones and pastries await at **Ranting Raven Bakery** (228 Fourth Avenue; (907) 224-2228). While in town, visit a little renovated church for espresso and art, cleverly named **Resurrect Art** (320 Third Avenue; (907) 224-7161); the local environmentalist has an office in the old choir loft. In 1997, if all goes to plan, the **Alaska SeaLife Center,** a marine wildlife research center, will open its doors at the edge of Resurrection Bay downtown, giving scientists, students, and visitors "a window to the sea."

OUTDOOR ACTIVITIES

Hike Mount Marathon It was named for the marathon races up to its summit (4,603 feet). The first "mountain marathon" was in 1915, and the tradition continues every Fourth of July. You can recognize competitors by the mud and blood. Try climbing this conical mountain any clear day in summer for a grand view over ice, snow, glaciers, and fjords. You'll discover that for part of the climb you're reduced to all-fours. Then try to run down the mountain in as much time as it takes the winners to go both up and down (about 50 minutes total). The descent is half-airborne, flying and sliding down snowfields and scree slopes. Good luck. Mortal folk take about 3 to 4 hours round-trip.

Cruise Kenai Fjords National Park The immense Harding Icefield dominates the landscape of this park, the reservoir for a myriad of spectacular glaciers rumbling down the mountains to plunge into deep-water fjords. The best way to see the park is to take a flightseeing tour or—most popular—to take a day cruise from Seward down Resurrection Bay. You'll see calving ice, puffins, seals, whales, and great mountain and sea vistas. On cloudy days, the glaciers reflect deeper blues and the mists from the sea make the whole adventure that much more dramatic. Birdwatchers should take the tour that goes out to the Chiswell Islands, which rise out of the sea like floating honeycombs and swarm with life, from Stellar sea lions to colonies of puffins. Every ledge, at every altitude on the rock face, seems to hold a different species. Down near tideline are the graceful kittiwakes and funny oystercatchers. Up high, the clown-faced puffins hang-glide off their nesting sites. Several different operations will take you out for scenic cruises in the park; you'll find their offices at or near the small boat harbor. One of the oldest, established in 1974, is **Kenai Fjords Tours,** (800) 478-8068 or (907) 276-6249. **Mariah Tours and Charters,** (907) 224-8623, operating since 1981, has smaller boats for perhaps a more intimate view. **Alaska Renown Charters,** (907) 224-3806, takes passengers summer and winter. Headquarters for the park is right near the harbormaster's building at the Seward marina. For information, contact Superintendent, Kenai Fjords National Park, PO Box 1727, Seward, AK 99664; (907) 224-3175.

Visit Exit Glacier Drive to Exit Glacier, also part of the Kenai Fjords National Park, and walk up to the face of a glacier. Not too close, though: calving ice is dangerous. A tourist was killed here a few years ago, while standing under overhanging ice that broke off precisely at the wrong moment. Remember, glaciers are rivers of moving ice. There's a comfortable nature loop trail for easy walking, and a steep 3-mile scramble up the rock at the side of the glacier to an overlook of the Harding Icefield for more energetic hikers. Watch for bears. The road to Exit Glacier turns off the Seward Highway at Mile 3.7 and leads 9 miles to the ranger station and parking lot for the glacier. The road is closed in winter. Access to the glacier then is by cross-country skis or snowmobile. There is a public-use cabin available in winter.

Go Fishing There are dozens of charters for halibut and salmon fishing with little offices on the boardwalk or near the small boat harbor. If you're on a peanut-butter-and-jelly budget, fish from shore. You won't be alone. It seems nearly every mom-and-pop rig on the highway stops in at Seward to set up lawn chairs by the edge of the sea and wet a line.

Walk the Coastal Trail Caines Head State Recreation Area has a 4 1/2-mile cliff and beach hike from Lowell Point to North Beach. Be aware that a portion of this trail can be walked only at low tide. Pick up a tide table and directions from the Seward Visitors Information Center. The trail begins at the Lowell Point parking lot, a mile from downtown Seward, on the western side of Resurrection Bay.

BEST RESTAURANTS

Ray's Waterfront ★★★ If you've eaten in Anchorage, this is like the Simon and Seafort's of Seward—good appetizers, good seafood dishes, good wine list, good views, and good crowds. It's packed all summer. The mesquite salmon is excellent, as are the steamers, clams, and calamari. If you don't want to wait for a table, go to the bar for drinks and appetizers. Turn-over is fairly rapid. ■ *Overlooking the Seward Small Boat Harbor; 1316 4th Ave, Seward; (907) 224-5606; $$; full bar; AE, DC, MC, V; local checks OK; lunch, dinner daily (closed Nov–Mar).*

Apollo ★★ The pizza is great. The Greek salad is tasty. The waiters are spicy. And the décor is one of ruins and gods and goddesses. ■ *Fourth Avenue, downtown Seward; (907) 224-3092; $$; beer and wine; AE, MC, V; local checks only; lunch, dinner daily.*

A GOOSE-TONGUE ADVENTURE

Some years ago, an old-timer friend in Seward took me to her favorite tidal goose-tongue patch on Resurrection Bay. The wind was blowing so hard we could not stand or talk. So we got down on hands and knees and went picking the salty greens. The wind was quite cold. Suddenly, Lila started crawling toward her car. I picked even faster, thinking we'd have to leave. Continuing to pick, I looked back and saw her crawling back in my direction dragging two large quilts. Struggling wildly, she got one over me while holding the other one down. Then she crawled under it and together we crawled along the beach, filling our big basket with thousands of goose tongues, a delicious tidal plantain. At last, we crawled back to the car. I powered the door open and we squeezed in with all our gear. We were almost blown away. Sitting there for a moment, Lila, who was about 80 then, said, "Kid, we gottum."

—Joan Daniels

Seward

Restaurants

Le Barn Appetit Restaurant and Bakery ★★ This is a warm, hilarious, all-around family dining experience rolled into one. In addition, the food is delicious. Yvon, head chef and baker, was raised in Belgium. He has also sailed with Jacques Cousteau and has a few wild stories from that era. Ask about the shark skeleton in his bone museum on the second floor. If that isn't enough, Le Barn is also a health food store *and* a bed and breakfast. ▪ *Mile 3.5, Seward Hwy on Resurrection Rd; PO Box 601, Seward, AK 99664; (907) 224-8706; fax (907) 224-8461; $$; MC, V; local checks OK; open year-round.*

Harbor Dinner Club ★ This is old-time Seward, tucked into a quiet corner of downtown. If things are too swinging at the small boat harbor, you can find a peaceful evening here sipping wine and eating beer batter–fried halibut. ▪ *Downtown, at 220 Fifth Ave, Seward; (907) 224-3012; $$; full bar; AE, DIS, DC, MC, V; local checks OK; lunch and dinner daily.*

BEST LODGINGS

Best Western Hotel Seward ★ The best rooms in this recently renovated hotel are the bay-view rooms—there are 10 of them—which have a lovely bay window facing out to the waters of Resurrection Bay and the mountains beyond. Colorful Tiffany lamps are a bright accent to these spacious and elegant rooms. The hotel is open year-round. ▪ *Located in the center of town at 221 Fifth Ave, Seward; PO Box 670BC, Seward, AK 99664; (907) 224-2378 or outside Alaska (800) 528-1234; $$$; AE, DIS, DC, MC, V; local checks OK; no seasonal closures.* ⚐

ON THE ROAD: KENAI LAKE TO HOMER

(aka The Sterling Highway)

Presuming you took the right-hand fork of the "Y" (the left goes to Seward), you are now on the Sterling Highway, a continuation of Alaska 1 all the way to Homer.

The first part of the highway winds along a sparkling river to Kenai Lake. If it's a sunny day, pause at the lake and breathe in its beauty, like a turquoise-and-emerald jewel in the summer and pure gold in fall. The road soon hugs the mountains, with the Kenai River tumbling on the other side. You'll quickly pass through the hamlet of **Cooper Landing,** which is the best place to put in for floating or fishing the **Upper Kenai River** (far more peaceful and beautiful than the Lower Kenai). Great hiking abounds all around you.

Farther on, there's a road off to **Skilak Lake,** another great adventure and beautiful lake. A word of warning, though, to all paddlers on large lakes on the peninsula such as the Kenai, Skilak, and Tustumena: Pay attention. Winds can pick up, in the afternoons especially, and can fill these lakes with waves and turbulence as fierce as those of the ocean. Many unsuspecting boaters have drowned. Whatever you do, save the beer drinking for shore.

Shortly, you will descend out of the mountains onto the flats of muskeg and swamp spruce. From here, it's a long, straight shot into **Soldotna.** Beyond Soldotna, the drive is through rolling hills alongside steep bluffs overlooking Cook Inlet, with some gorgeous views of the mountains and volcanos (Redoubt and Iliamna) across the inlet. Visit the picturesque little Russian church sitting up on the bluff at the village of **Ninilchik**; then continue on past **Anchor Point,** another great fishing destination for saltwater fishermen, and on into Homer.

SOLDOTNA

Folks come here in droves to fish the **Lower Kenai River**. The community has no real "downtown," but the "Y" is often considered the center. The town grew up around the homesteaders, a special breed of folks who have plenty of stories to tell about the early days (which for this town were not so long ago). For an intimate and fun shopping experience, if you're looking for an upscale or humorous Alaska gift, stop in at **Northcountry Fair,** directly across the street from the Soldotna "Y." The "Y" is where you can turn right to the oil town of **Kenai** and the **Captain Cook State Recreation Area** at the end of the road, about 35 miles.

Soldotna

*Outdoor
Activities*

OUTDOOR ACTIVITIES

Fish the Kenai   Wherever you fish in Alaska, it is wise to come with respect. What seems like abundance today is also fragile and easily damaged by streambank erosion, development, overfishing, and pollution. You have only to think of the great rivers of the world to understand how unique the Kenai is. No river running through any city in the world has ever sustained the world-class run of fish that the Kenai does. But fishing on the Kenai in summer is intense. There are 300 to 400 fishing guides on this one river alone. Some are more ethical and conservation-minded than others. We encourage you to choose wisely. It has been suggested that, not far off in the future, the Kenai king salmon will be strictly a catch-and-release fishery. (See Wilderness Guides below.)

The most productive area for king salmon is the **Lower Kenai River** below Soldotna. It's also *the* combat fishing zone. Parties of anglers drift here in small and medium-sized boats, running up the river and drifting down. As one fisherman said, "King salmon are like cars on the freeway, moving in predictable patterns. They don't change lanes very often." But the human scene is like Coney Island. The first run of kings begins in late May, and each one averages more than 30 pounds. The

A MOOSE FOR WINTER

As fall begins its colorful show and berry harvesting winds down, it's time to dig potatoes and cut cabbages, and, for many Alaskans, time to bring in the winter meat.

In this age of packaged foods, many people look questioningly at the hunter who attempts the grueling task of pulling down a wild creature in the interest of feeding his or her family. Admire it or not, it falls into the realm of the romantic and the practical—eating foods native to your surroundings. For the homesteader or Bush family, hunting provides.

Actually, hunting a moose is not so difficult. It's the work of skinning, butchering, and packing the beastly thing out that is not so easy. He's big. He's really big. For instance, his liver overflows a dishpan. By a lot. A girlfriend of mine suggested we make an all-female hunting expedition. I said that would be fine if we didn't get anything. But, if we were successful, women's lib would have to go on the back burner. I want Conan and King Kong to help march moose haunches out of the woods. I've been flat on my face in the mud with a moose quarter on my back. You don't forget that!

After the kill, you must be sure the fellow is deadly asleep before opening him up to cool. Then begin the surgery. But first get a fire going; it's practical and a cheerful addition to the big job ahead. You can heat water, help ward off vampire bugs, and toast choice tidbits of fresh meat on a stick. You can also, in a pot or coffee can, melt down some fat and chew on some cracklings. (This is when you forget about eyelash enhancer. Only two things count: food and warmth.)

Among the "specialty pieces," I personally like the brains, so I always go after those enthusiastically. This is hard on some people. Gives them the creeps. Sometimes I make head cheese. It's rather a grisly business but the result will make you famous with old-timers who grew up eating it. It is very good. Later, on a stormy day before Thanksgiving, the whole cabin gets in an uproar with apples, sour cherries, cider, raisins, citrus peels, spices, and brandy in a hot and burbling mincemeat made from flavorful shoulder or neck meat. What a pie this makes!

Here's the part I don't like. The men never want to pack out the hide. It's so heavy. By the time all the meat is packed out, everyone is out of steam. I always try for the hide. I say it's good cut in little strips and deep fried. They look at me with disgust. I tell them it's rainproof and I'll make them a gun case with it. They say, "Right." I try everything. We usually leave the hide. A tanned moose hide is a prize—strong and beautiful with many uses.

> *Here's the part I love. When you eat a mooseburger, you know what real food tastes like. You don't wolf it down. You relish it. It tastes so good that when you go outside Alaska you want to come home because you miss it. This is the hearty food that allows you to skate by the meat counter; pass up all those questionable additives and distorted hormones; and head home with some garlic peppercorns and a good red wine for your moose bourguignon.*
>
> —Joan Daniels

second run usually arrives in late June or early July, with salmon averaging more than 40 pounds each. July is the most popular month for king salmon fishing on the Kenai. Regulations currently say anglers are allowed to keep two king salmon a season, although that could change in the near future.

For a different experience on the Kenai, fish the **Upper Kenai River**. It's more peaceful and far more scenic, with blue-green glacier waters sweeping through ice-streaked mountains. Here you can fish for salmon, but also rainbow trout, and Dollies. Plus, you fish from drift boats, with no motor, and can be rowed by guides down the river. Several companies offer the scenic combo, both rafting (including some white-water) and fishing on the upper Kenai. By far the best is **Alaska Wildland Adventures,** (800) 478-4100. If you are looking to enjoy fishing and combine it with natural history, this is the team to go with.

Soldotna

*Outdoor
Activities*

Float the Kenai River A great day outing is to float the Kenai River from Cooper Landing to Skilak Lake with **Alaska Wildland Adventures,** (800) 478-4100, based in Cooper Landing, Mile 51 on the Sterling Highway. They have a shorter trip, but you don't get the thrill of the rapids going through the canyon and then the grandeur of coming out into Skilak Lake. You're likely to see moose, coyote, wolves, and bears, if you're lucky. It's a beautiful trip, rain or shine. These guys do a great job. Trips depart daily in summer.

Hike Lots of good hiking takes off in this area. The start or finish of the Resurrection Trail, depending on your direction, traverses the mountains from Cooper Landing to Hope, about 35 miles of walking with public-use cabins for rent along the way. A madhouse in salmon season, the trail along the Russian River to Lower and Upper Russian Lakes is a lovely walk, once you get past all the fishermen. There are also cabins. At the Russian River Falls, in the right season, you can see those extraordinary salmon leaping up the falls. Cooper Lake is also a nice walk. Pick up a copy of *55 Ways to the Wilderness in*

Southcentral Alaska (see Suggested Reading, Anchorage and Beyond chapter). It's a marvelous guide to trails all over the Kenai Peninsula, around Anchorage, and in the Mat Valley, complete with detailed descriptions and directions. Or contact the Kenai National Wildlife Refuge in Soldotna; (907) 262-7021.

Picnic at Captain Cook State Recreation Area

Turn right at the "Y" in Soldotna and go to Mile 36 on the North Kenai Road. This state park is splendid for camping and picnicking right on the edge of the ocean bluff; you'll have the whole Alaska Range spread before you on a clear day. Walk the beach looking for agates, barbecue salmon high on the bluff while watching for beluga whales, and go to the campfire talks. Some of the old homesteaders are often there to tell their stories. It's a grand place. For more information, call Alaska State Parks in Soldotna at (907) 262-5581.

Visit the Kenai National Wildlife Refuge

The visitors center is in Soldotna and has lots of information and an interpretive trail that takes you, "with new eyes," down the trail to the lake and through the forest. (It's called "The Keen-Eye Trail.") The wildlife refuge itself covers about half of the Kenai Peninsula, and there are a multitude of outdoor recreational activities available, from hiking trails and canoe routes to hunting and fishing. For more details, call the visitors center at (907) 262-7021.

Send Your Kids to Camp Kushtaka

In a glorious setting on the edge of Kenai Lake, this camp is a great place for kids to spend a week in summer (while parents attend to business or pleasure elsewhere in Alaska). Kids live in cabins, paddle the lake, hike mountains, and take wilderness camping trips. The philosophy here is "It all happens on the trail"—new friendships, new songs, new secret places, new muscles, and sitting around campfires laughing and toasting "s'mores." The camp is run by the Alaska Council of Camp Fire Boys and Girls, 3745 Community Park Loop, Suite #104, Anchorage, AK 99508; (907) 279-3551.

WILDERNESS GUIDES

Alaska Wildland Adventures

This outfit rates at the top of the list. It's an impressive operation with an unusual focus on the Kenai River. They do natural history, some fishing, rafting, and scenic overland trips. The staff is enthusiastic, skilled, and knowledgeable. This tour company has as their headquarters a cluster of cabins on the banks of the Kenai River at Cooper Landing. They do river floats, drift fishing, "soft" adventures, and "senior safaris" (where you stay in a comfortable lodge at night). They also manage Denali Backcountry Lodge in Kantishna, so you can combine experiences on the Kenai

Peninsula and in Denali National Park. Contact HC 64, Box 26, Cooper Landing, AK 99572; toll-free (800) 478-4100 or direct (907) 595-1279.

Fishing Guides/Lower Kenai There are more than 300 fishing guides on the Kenai, but we are recommending only a few of the top guides—although this list is by no means inclusive—who have demonstrated through their guiding operations a concern for the health of the river and the resource, as well as the enjoyment of their customers. This is one of our concerns, and we hope it will be one of yours. For starters, before you hire someone, you might ask your potential fishing guides on the Kenai if they are members of the guides' association and what they do to help protect fish habitat. **Drift Boat Guides**: Rodbenders in Sterling, (907) 262-7671; Alaska Fish and Float in Soldotna, (907) 262-9439; Randa's Guide Service in Soldotna, (907) 262-9494; and Nick's Guide Service in Soldotna, (907) 262-3979. **Powerboat Guides**: King's Budget Charters in Soldotna, (907) 262-4564; Angler's Lodge and Fish Camp in Sterling, (907) 262-1747; Alaska Flaggs Kenai Charters in Soldotna, (907) 262-5426; Sourdough Charters in Soldotna, (907) 262-5300; and Big Boys, Inc. in Soldotna, (907) 262-1815.

BEST RESTAURANTS

Restaurants

Through the Seasons ★★★ This is a charming little restaurant tucked into the woods on a corner of the original Mullen homestead. A boardwalk leads you through the trees into a building designed to take advantage of its lovely natural setting. Locals love the raspberry chicken and the basil or peanut pesto fettuccine. Outsiders are particularly fond of the halibut baked in peppery Dijon sauce and the smoked salmon pâté. Everyone loves the warmth, homebaked bread, and gourmet aromas. For many years, this oasis in the heart of Alaska was called the Four Seasons Restaurant. But the "original" Four Seasons, back in New York City, apparently became so alarmed over this serious competition 6,000 miles away that they sent one of those humorless lawyer letters to "cease and desist," which is now framed and hangs on the wall, along with funny ruminations on choices for the restaurant's new name. ■ *On the west side of the Sterling Highway as you enter Soldotna (if you're coming from Anchorage), just north of the "Y." Look for the small wooden sign; 43960 Sterling Hwy, Soldotna; (907) 262-5006; $$; beer and wine; MC, V; local checks OK; in summer, open for lunch Mon–Sat and dinner daily; in winter, open for lunch and dinner Tues–Sat; closed Jan. ⅋*

Gwin's Lodge ★ This handbuilt log lodge was first opened for business in the 1950s. Situated across the road from the Kenai River in Cooper Landing, it's friendly and fun and a good homespun place to eat after a day's fishing or floating. A beer and

Gwin's Macho Nachos will just about do you in with total contentment. They have a whole range of hearty appetizers (none slimming, but definitely yummy) and a wide variety of omelets, fish, steak, and burger lunch and dinners. ■ *Mile 52, Sterling Hwy, Cooper Landing; (907) 595-1266; $$; full bar; DIS, MC, V; local checks OK.*

BEST LODGINGS

Kenai Princess Lodge ★★★★ Perched on the mountainside above the blue-green tumbling waters of the Kenai River, this is a grand wilderness lodge that caters to your romantic image of Alaska—rustic wood bungalows with wood stoves, a grand stone fireplace in the lobby, and outdoor decks with snow-capped mountains above and salmon-filled river below. The outdoor hot tubs are particularly fun on a star-filled evening after winter cross-country skiing. Princess Tours owns the operation, so the lodge (with 70 rooms and suites) is hopping with tourists in the summer. If you want a more peaceful time, try winter, or fall when the peninsula is ablaze with colors. ■ *Mile 47.7, Sterling Hwy and Bean Creek Rd; PO Box 676, Cooper Landing, AK 99572; (800) 426-0500 for reservations; (907) 595-1425 for hotel; $$$; AE, DC, MC, V; checks OK (closed Jan and Feb).* ♿

Soldotna Bed and Breakfast Lodge ★★★ With the charm of a Swiss chalet—carved window boxes filled with flowers at every window and the attention to detail that has made Swiss innkeepers so famous—this wonderful B&B sits on the banks of the Kenai River and has a lovely green garden out front and a gazebo down by the river's edge. Your hosts, Bill and Charlotte Ischi, came to Alaska from Bern, Switzerland, in 1960. This is a top-notch establishment. Six rooms have a river view. And if you're there from May to September for fishing, you can even have a full, hearty, hot breakfast beginning at 4:30am. They are open year-round, but they serve breakfast only in summer. No smoking. ■ *In Soldotna, right off the Sterling Hwy, on the banks of the Kenai River; 399 Lovers Lane, Soldotna, AK 99669; (907) 262-4779; fax (907) 262-3201; $$$; checks OK; rooms and continental breakfast available year-round (full breakfast only in summer); B&B open May–Sept.*

HOMER

Remember those friends from college who took off in the Volkswagen van with their guitars and dogs? Don't be surprised if you find them in Homer, a little town at the end of the road that has long been a haven for artists, writers, and counterculturalists. If you drive here, stop at the lookout point on the highway just before you descend into town and you'll see what all the fuss is about: a shimmering bay ringed by snow-

capped mountains and glacier-carved valleys. The Homer Spit,
an impossibly skinny wisp of land, stretches 4.5 miles into the
bay. Never mind that on summer weekends the end of the spit
looks like one giant RV park. Keep looking out over the bay—
the view is exquisite.

The town is named for Homer Pennock, a turn-of-the-century adventurer who expected to make a fortune in gold and
never did. Coal, woven through the bluffs, was king in the early
years. Now this town of 5,000 relies on commercial fishing and,
increasingly, sportfishing and tourism for its livelihood.

Known by one local sage as "Our Cosmic Hamlet by the
Sea," Homer gets its batteries charged every year by an influx
of young people who travel here for summer jobs in the fishing industry. Traditionally they camp on the Spit, and thus are
known as "Spit rats," which is not really a pejorative term. Every fall, some portion of them are so enchanted they stay the
winter. Eventually they become residents, mixing with the descendants of homesteaders and lending Homer a flavor of Bohemian hipness.

The Spit is the main draw here, and in summer the area
is a crowded hodgepodge of businesses catering to both visitors and the commercial fishing fleet. Halibut charter offices,
knickknack shops, and restaurants crowd the end of the Spit,
and some complain that the place looks more and more like Tijuana with each passing year. Still, there's no better place than **Homer**
the Spit for taking the pulse of the Kachemak Bay economy. A *Information*
stroll through the harbor will give you a good feel for it, or stop
in at the Salty Dawg, a dark little bar in a historic building with
sawdust on the floor. Commercial fishermen sit cheek-by-jowl
with visitors, and the place is so cramped that you'll have no difficulty striking up a conversation.

Access

Homer is quite spread out, so you'll probably need a car, although hitchhiking around town is acceptable. Most people
drive down from Anchorage, but flights are reasonable and National Car Rental has a few cars available at the airport, if
booked in advance.

Information

The **Homer Chamber of Commerce,** (907) 235-7740, can
send you maps and brochures. Even better, however, is **Central Charter** (4241 Homer Spit Road, Homer; (800) 478-7847
or (907) 235-7847). It's a booking agency that can make reservations for your adventures on charter boats and ferries and
with most B&Bs in town. Central Charters takes its cut from
the service provider, so you pay no more for the convenience.
The *Homer News,* the better of the two local weekly papers,
has extensive arts and entertainment listings, as well as fishing
information. It comes out on Thursdays.

PLACES TO VISIT

Pratt Museum Art, history, and marine life exhibits are nicely done. "Darkened Waters," a highly acclaimed exhibit about the *Exxon Valdez* oil spill, is not to be missed. It does a good job of conveying the enormity of the spill in easily understood terms. You can hear a recording of Capt. Joseph Hazelwood's first report to the Coast Guard that he'd run "hard aground." Located at 3779 Bartlett Street; (907) 235-8635.

Ptarmigan Arts This gallery features top-notch local artists and crafts people. It carries everything from jewelry to photographs, handmade clothes to handpainted silk. Located at 471 E Pioneer Avenue; (907) 235-5345.

Bunnell Street Gallery Bold exhibits of paintings done with oils and watercolors, as well as steel sculpture or group shows of mixed media—you never know what kind of cutting-edge art you might find at this nonprofit co-op. The Bunnell also offers special-event evenings of performance art at 106 W Bunnell Street; (907) 235-2662.

OUTDOOR ACTIVITIES

Homer

Places to Visit

Walks and Drives Homer has some nice walks. Bishop's Beach is one good example very near downtown. A drive out East End Road or Skyline Drive will be rewarded with spectacular views and perhaps a moose or two.

Kachemak Bay The bay is the best thing about Homer. It's teeming with marine life and provides an opportunity to see sea otters, harbor seals, porpoises, maybe even a whale. Unless it's stormy, some good ways to enjoy the bay are listed below.

Halibut Charter This is probably the most popular activity; however, there are dozens of outfits, many of which can be booked through **Central Charter**, (800) 478-7847. A word of caution: You really have to have the fishing bug to do this. Trips usually start early in the morning and go all day, often in rough water. Skippers won't turn around just because one of the party is horribly seasick. Still, many people gladly brave all this for the chance to reel in a 300-pound lunker.

Kayaking Offers an excellent way to get intimate with the sea. **True North Kayak Adventures** runs day trips for beginners from an island across from Homer. Book in advance through **Central Charter,** (800)478-7847, or through **Jakolof Ferry Service,** (907) 235-2376, which will taxi you to True North's island base. Kevin Bell and Alison O'Hara give a good beach lesson, then paddle around with you to various islands. You'll be back in Homer in time for dinner.

Boat Tours Homer has an embarrassment of riches here, but a few stand out. The *Danny J,* also known as the Kachemak Bay Ferry, is a brightly painted former fishing boat that makes two trips a day to Halibut Cove. The early departure, at noon, stops by Gull Island, a bird sanctuary crammed with all manner of winged things. For reservations call **Central Charter,** (800) 478-7847. St. Augustine Charters, (907) 235-6126, offers 2-hour cruises in its classic wooden sailboat. Scott and Susan, an affable couple, also offer tours specifically to see wildlife. Two large tour boats, the *Rainbow Connection,* (907) 235-7272, and the *Denaina,* (907) 235-2490, offer narrated day cruises to Seldovia, via Gull Island.

BEST RESTAURANTS

Cafe Cups ★★★★ When Cups opened in 1991, Homer's era of artsy chic arrived. The front of this whimsical building is overrun by giant tea cups and an assortment of gilded treasures. Inside, big colorful paintings compete with zany *objets d'art.* The place would be cool even if the food were only average. But it's not. The menu is eclectic, part California with Mediterranean influences and a twist of Alaska. Consider the delectable salmon carpaccio appetizer: cold lightly smoked salmon dressed with lemon, garlic, and capers. In winter, there are occasional readings by local authors. Good breakfasts, too.

■ *Downtown Homer, across the main drag from the library; 162 W Pioneer Ave, Homer; (907) 235-8330; $$$; beer and wine; MC, V; local checks OK; 7am–10pm daily March–Oct.*

The Homestead ★★★★ Chef Sean Maryott was also the founding chef of Cups, so if you dine at both you really get a sense of his genius. The Homestead, an old log-cabin restaurant that used to be a basic steak-and-potatoes joint, retains its traditional feel, but has new verve. Top-quality Alaska seafood is served with ginger, lime, and macadamia nuts, southwestern spices, mango salsa, or a variety of other tastes and textures. For the carnivorous, there's filet mignon and other tender steaks. The caesar salads, made at your table, are especially good. The service is very professional. ■ *Mile 8.2, East End Rd, Homer; (907) 235-8723; $$$; full bar; MC, V, AE; checks OK; dinner daily (closed Feb).* ♿

The Saltry ★★★★ This is more an experience than a restaurant. Take the *Danny J* ferry over to Halibut Cove, an impossibly cute community of artists and fishermen. No roads or parking lots here, just boardwalks and trails and docks. Houses are built on pilings and perched on rocks. The boat docks at the Saltry, which serves—what else?—seafood. You might start out with halibut ceviche, then try something like scallops and shrimp sautéed in spicy, fermented black beans. The restaurant concentrates on fresh everything, and many of the vegetables are grown out back. On a sunny day, the deck is nice, but cooler than you might expect. The *Danny J* schedule leaves enough time for a meal and a little stroll to

WILD THINGS (TO EAT!)

When foraging for wild foods, you'll need multiple containers for gathering. The easiest to use, I find, are a basket and some clear plastic bags. They're lightweight and you can identify your harvest instantly while keeping everything moist (unless the day gets too warm). A damp cloth or large cool leaves dipped in water laid over all will work. A small sharp knife and a little garden clipper are helpful. A few paper towels are good too. Woven-basket backpacks are great for carrying all your tools and treasures. Remember this: On the most casual walk, have a plastic bag or two in your pocket. Expect the unexpected. Keep different plants separate—they'll sometimes want separate treatment.

If you look on the nutrient chart, you'll find that dandelions make everything else you eat look like a major waste of chewing time. In picking dandelions, take as much of the root as possible. Wash it well and chop it along with the greens, or dry it in a basket for winter tea. It has enormous quantities of minerals. Many brave and vibrant greens grow in moist places near streams and in the mist of waterfalls. This is the water ouzel's garden. Beautiful little cress plants can be plucked, roots and all. The scallop-leaf saxifrage and the sourgrass (actually a sorrel with tender-tart leaves) can be easily cut by the clump. Violet leaves are tiny, but plentiful, and found along streams where moose forage when willow leaves first emerge. You'll find they are sweet and tender with oodles of vitamin C.

If you're terrified of trying wild mushrooms, halt that pronto. It spoils a lot of fun. Get a good book on Alaska mushrooms and get going. By following the rules and very simple tests, you'll find several indisputable varieties that are delicious. When you collect different types, keep them separate. Apparently they can be perfectly innocent and safe until they kiss another species. Then their little enzymes begin some devilish dance and can become very wicked.

Wherever you are, the smallest strip of unpaved ground will be growing something you can eat. Look at the surroundings and decide whether to pluck it. Go looking. If you garden, you'll be meeting all the relatives of your vegetables and herbs. Also, seek out people known for eating wild foods. They're your best resource.

—Joan Daniels

the art gallery along the one boardwalk open to the public. Reservations are crucial, particularly in summer. ■ *If you're in Halibut Cove, you can't miss it; (907) 235-7847 or (907) 296-2223; $$$; full bar; MC, V; local checks only; 1pm–9pm daily (closed Labor Day–Memorial Day weekend);* & *restaurant and outhouse only, but must get up ramp from boat to the dock; the pitch can get quite steep depending on the tide.*

Two Sisters ★★ A bakery and coffee shop not to be missed. You'll find terrific pastries, both sweet and savory, as well as Greek-style pizza. Feta and sun-dried tomatoes abound. The "Sisters" whip up a mean espresso, making this the best spot in town for a spot of breakfast. The atmosphere matches the food: bright and homemade. It's tiny, and very popular with the locals, so have patience if it's jammed. ■ *In the same building as the Old Inlet Trading Post, near Bishop's Beach; 106 W Bunnell, Homer; (907) 235-2280; $; no alcohol; no credit cards; checks OK; Mon–Sat, 7am–3pm.*

Smoky Bay Co-op Even Alaskans wear Birkenstocks, and this is where you'll find them. This natural food store has had its ups and downs, but the deli is a hidden gem. Excellent baked goods, such as blueberry tarts or large oatmeal chocolate-chip cookies, are made daily. Serve yourself good, stout coffee, brewed fresh and stored in thermal carafes. Midday, it's really more of a two-soup-and-daily-special lunch counter. The furnishings are hippieish, and the tie-dyed staff is pleasant and easy-going. Giant spools serve as tables on the porch. ■ *248 W Pioneer Ave, Homer (at the western end); (907) 235-7252; $; no alcohol; no credit cards; checks OK; store is open Mon–Fri, 8:30am–8pm; Sat, 9am–6:30pm; Sun, 10am–6pm. Deli is open 11am–3pm every day except Sun (slightly shorter hours in winter).* &

BEST LODGINGS

Island View Bed and Breakfast ★★★ If you want a taste of the real Alaska, stay in this beautiful, handbuilt cabin in the hills of Homer. The view is expansive across the horse paddock and down to the water and mountains beyond. A handsome woman with a merry laugh, Eileen Mullen grew up on a homestead on the banks of the Kenai River. She's a woman of impressive achievements—fisherwoman, captain, horsewoman, and cabin builder. Her robust breakfasts will get you to the top of any mountain. The little cabin is the most classic experience, but she also has a very warm and comfortable suite in the house. ■ *Up in the hills above Homer, 5 minutes' drive from downtown (call for directions); PO Box 1394, Homer, AK 99603; (907) 235-2265; $; DIS, MC, V; checks OK.*

Old Inlet Trading Post ★★★ All three rooms in this romantic bed and breakfast above an art gallery have beautiful views of the bay. Stay here long enough and you'll be overcome by an urge to write poetry or paint watercolors. Owners Kurt Marquardt and Asia Freeman have a finely tuned sense of beauty, resulting in a space that is spare and windswept. The location, in what was once central Homer, is a short walk to the shops of downtown, and even closer to Bishop's Beach. Monday through Saturday, breakfast is downstairs at the fabulous Two Sisters bakery. When the bakery is closed, Asia does waffles. Occasional concerts are a treat for all. ■ *At the corner of Bunnell and Main Sts; 106 W Bunnell, Homer, AK 99603; (907) 235-7558; $; no alcohol; no credit cards; checks OK.*

Magic Canyon Ranch ★★ Nestled in a lush green valley 5 miles east of town, Magic Canyon is a country-style bed and breakfast. Lots of homey antiques decorate the four rooms, and quilts abound. The 75-acre property has plenty of elbow room, so it's a great place for kids. Betsy and Davis Webb have an elementary school–age son (8 years old) who has a treehouse in a cottonwood grove. Four llamas live in the front yard. Great views, even from the indoor hot tub. ■ *At Mile 5.5 on East End Rd, turn left onto Waterman Rd, then follow the signs for about a mile; 40015 Waterman Rd, Homer, AK 99603; (907) 235-6077; $$; no alcohol; no credit cards; checks OK.*

Land's End Hotel If it weren't for its location, Land's End would be just a modern, charmless hotel trying for a nautical theme. But, perched as it is at the very tip of the Spit, it has appeal. If your room faces the bay, the beach begins practically at your bedside. Rooms facing the parking lot are slightly cheaper, but why bother? The "Port Wing" rooms on the bay side are a fair deal. They're basically small doubles, but with twin trundle and fold-down single, they'll sleep a tight-knit family. The two-story suites in the "Midship Wing" seem poorly designed, with window and deck too small to take advantage of the view. The deck's the best place in town to have a drink (but skip the food) and watch boat traffic in the harbor. ■ *The end of the Spit; 4786 Homer Spit Rd, Homer, AK 99603; toll-free in Alaska (800) 478-0400; (907) 235-0400; $$$; full bar; AE, DC, MC, V; checks OK; open year-round.* ♿

KACHEMAK BAY STATE PARK

The sheltered coves, spruce-tufted islands, and glacier-covered mountains of this park go on forever—actually, for 300,000 acres, along 200 miles of wild coastline, making this one of the largest coastal parks in the country.

Kachemak Bay itself is teeming with life, mammal as well as lower forms. Get out on the water and you might see sea otters, harbor seals, porpoises, or even whales. Hundreds of species of birds thrive in this coastal habitat, including bald eagles, loons, and mergansers. And the seabirds—well, just visit Gull Island, a rookery that's on the route for most of the tour boats and ferries out of Homer. Some 12,000 birds vie for space on this rock, including tufted puffins, cormorants, kittiwakes, and marbled murrelets.

The land is home to black bear, moose, coyote, and, on the rocky peaks, mountain goat. With all this, the park is heaven for humans of the outdoorsy variety, who might like to kayak, hike, pick berries, or photograph wildlife. Since this park can't be reached by road, getting here requires coordinating with one of the water taxis or ferries in Homer. Try **Central Charter,** (800) 478-7847 or (907) 235-7847, in Homer for reservations; or for more information, call the park office in Homer at (907) 235-7024. In summer, you can reach the ranger station in Halibut Cove at (907) 235-6999.

OUTDOOR ACTIVITIES

Hikes Poot Peak, the chocolate drop–shaped mountain prominent from Homer, can be climbed in a day, but it makes a much better overnight trip. Have a boat drop you off at the head of Halibut Cove Lagoon. If you reserve well enough in advance, you might be able to stay at the public-use cabin nearby. If not, hike to the lake and camp there. You can leave your pack behind and tackle the peak the next day.

Kachemak Bay State Park

Center for Alaskan Coastal Studies Knowledgeable naturalists lead excellent day programs at the center's field station on the south side of Kachemak Bay. You go over in the morning on the Rainbow Connection and spend all day studying tide pools, rain forest flora and fauna, or geology. The program varies depending on the interests of the group. This nonprofit organization is great for inspiring interest in marine science in children and adults. Call (907) 235-6667.

Alaska Coastal Journeys If hands-on marine education is your thing and you want a longer trip, opt for **Alaska Coastal Journeys,** (907) 235-2228. The outfit is owned by expert naturalists, and their base camp is in a spectacular location at the end of McDonald Spit. The 3- and 5-day trips include birdwatching, kayaking, and tidepooling. You'll sleep in wall tents, and food is provided.

BEST LODGINGS

Kachemak Bay Wilderness Lodge ★★★★ This is the most achingly beautiful place on the Kenai Peninsula. The hosts, Diane and Mike McBride, have been perfecting their lodge for 25 years, and the result is total luxury in a rustic setting. Each of the guest cabins has all the comforts of electricity and a full bathroom, but the ambience is rugged Alaska. The materials for the lodge, the dock, and many of the buildings were salvaged from wrecked ships. The sauna sprouts wildflowers and berries from its sod roof. The dining room chandelier is made of a boat hull that grounded on a nearby beach. The decorations are old floats and other treasures the McBrides found while beachcombing over the years. Here and there are finds from far away: a claw-footed bathtub, an antique concertina, and in the solarium, a 1915 cherry piano, a gift from a grateful guest. The McBrides are expert naturalists and dyed-in-the-wool conservationists, a walk-soft philosophy they live by but don't lay too heavily on the guests. The early morning yoga sessions Mike leads in the solarium are entirely optional. A soak in the hot tub, outdoors but shielded from the view of other guests, is, however, a must. The staff will take you by Boston Whaler for fishing or wildlife viewing on China Poot Bay or beyond. Kayaks are also available. There are plenty of hiking opportunities right from the lodge. There is a 3-day minimum stay, and it'll cost you. Guests arrive on Mondays and Thursdays. ■ *On China Poot Bay (the McBrides will reserve your seats on the MV Rainbow Connection); PO Box 956, Homer, AK 99603; (907) 235-8910; $$$$; no credit cards; checks OK; closed Oct–May.*

Tutka Bay Lodge ★★★★ This is a place of big, handsome cabins, on an isthmus between Tutka and Little Tutka Bays. It's high on comfort—the cabins have not only private bathrooms but also massage showerheads—and low on the funkiness factor. Everything is sturdy and well built, starting with the helipad just up from the boat dock. Some of the cabins are decorated with bear hides, and each has a copy of James Michener's *Alaska*. The owners, Jon and Nelda Osgood, are about as gracious as can be. Jon, a helicopter pilot, quit his federal career years ago, and Nelda left her school district job, so they could live here full time. They've been taking in guests for about a dozen years. They'll take you on a boat tour of Tutka Bay or to Seldovia. You can also hike or ride mountain bikes. For an extra charge, they'll arrange fishing charters, sea kayaking, or helicopter tours. They have a 2-night minimum stay and are open all year. ■ *9 water miles south of Homer in Tutka Bay; PO Box 960, Homer, AK 99603; (800) 606-3909 or (907) 235-3905; $$$; AE, MC, NOVUS, V; checks OK.*

SELDOVIA

Before the road connected Homer to the rest of the world, Seldovia was the economic hub of the Lower Kenai Peninsula. It was served by two steamship lines from Seattle, and the early Homer settlers told of rowing or sailing to the big city of Seldovia for mail and supplies. Now the roles are reversed, and it's Seldovia that's the sleepy little village.

Much of the town was built on boardwalks, but the land

sank some 4 feet during the 1964 Good Friday Earthquake, and a somewhat less quaint Seldovia was rebuilt. Still, a small portion of the old boardwalk, running along the Seldovia Slough, is enough to give you a feel of the town that was.

Tiny by comparison to Homer, Seldovia has in some ways more recreational opportunities for visitors. For hunter-gatherer types, the August crop of blueberries, salmonberries, and raspberries makes for easy picking. And the pebbly beaches on this side of Kachemak Bay are rife with butter and steamer clams, there for the taking if you have a sportfish license. There are several nice hikes and one terrific mountain bike adventure.

Everything about this town is small-scale. You will not need a car; a van service, the **Jakolof Bay Express,** will take you anywhere you need to go. Street addresses are, for the most part, fairly useless, as many streets aren't posted, and the locals may not agree on the name anyway.

Access

Several boats serve Seldovia daily in summer, such as the **Alaska Maritime Tours,** (907) 235-2490, **Rainbow Tours,** (907) 235-7272, and the **Jakolof Ferry Service.** It's also just a short hop from Homer by **Homer Air,** (907) 235-8591, and the center of town is an easy stroll from the landing strip.

PLACES TO VISIT

A hip coffeehouse on the waterfront, **The Buzz,** (907) 234-7479, is the place to get your espresso, as well as quiche, muffins, and pastries. The Buzz also rents mountain bikes and fishing gear and is the depot for the **Jakolof Bay Express** van, which will take you to the Jakolof Dock or anywhere else in town you need to go.

After you've copped your buzz, head next door to **Herring Bay Mercantile.** This gift store is a cute boutique of unusual Alaska-made treats with a few imports. Owner Susan Springer makes her own hand-rubbed, block-print cards right in the shop.

OUTDOOR ACTIVITIES

Halibut Fishing One advantage of taking a halibut charter out of Seldovia rather than Homer is that it's about an hour closer to the good fishing grounds. **Seldovia Fishing Adventures,** (907) 234-7417, can also put you up in their very homey B&B. The quarters are a bit cramped, but Peggy Cloninger's hearty meals will keep you well fortified.

Kayaking Guided day trips (and orientation) with Kirby and Lynn Corwin are available through **Kayak'atak.** Owner Kirby has a delightfully zany sense of humor. If you know your stuff and want to paddle on your own, Kirby is also the guy to see. He has a desk inside the Herring Bay Mercantile. Call (907) 234-7425.

Boat Tour You may have taken a boat to get here, but if you want more, try the **Jakolof Ferry noon passage to Halibut Cove.** You'll get a total of 2 hours on the water and 2 hours in delightful Halibut Cove, and you'll be back at the Jakolof Dock by 4pm.

Mountain Biking The premier mountain biking adventure in the area is the **Jakolof–Rocky River Road,** 15 miles of an old logging road that cuts across the very tip of the Kenai Peninsula. You can bring your bike on the Jakolof Ferry. From the Jakolof Dock, turn left and start pedaling. Strong cyclists can make it a day trip, but it's better as an overnighter. You can also rent bikes in Seldovia at The Buzz.

BEST LODGINGS

Harmony Point Wilderness Lodge ★★★★ Quiet reigns here. Guests are picked up from Seldovia's harbor in a 24-foot wooden dory for a 20-minute trip up the bay. The three simple cabins, heated with wood stoves and decorated with calico curtains, are well spaced. Honeymooning couples can gaze out over Seldovia Bay and pretend they are roughing it in the wilds, all alone. For extra Alaska authenticity, the cabins aren't plumbed or electrified. Each has its own outhouse—cute and clean—and is lit by kerosene lamps, though the summer days are so long you might not need them. The main lodge, built out of local Sitka spruce, serves up three meals a day, and is a cheerful place to read. Daily doings are geared for the eco-minded. Hosts Tim and Ila Dillon give you a half-day of guided adventure. You can learn to kayak, first with a beach lesson, then out in doubles or singles in the protected waters of Seldovia Bay. The next day you might want to use one of the Cannondale mountain bikes and ride up an old logging road. Hot showers are available all day at the bathhouse. The sauna is fired up at 4pm. There is a 3-night minimum stay. You might find a bit of flexibility for something shorter, but it'd be your loss. Harmony Point serves dinner to nonguests, too. It's far and away the nicest dinner in town. ■ *They'll pick you up in Seldovia; PO Box 110, Seldovia, AK 99663; (907) 234-7858; $$$; MC, V; checks OK; dinner for nonguests is served most days in summer (call by 3pm to reserve). You'll be picked up in Seldovia at 6:30pm; closed Oct–April.*

Dancing Eagles ★★ Quintessential Seldovia. This laid-back B&B is at the end of the old boardwalk, built on pilings over the water. The four-bedroom (shared-bath) house faces east, guarding the entrance to the slough, and the roomy cabin looks west over the harbor. The two are connected by a large deck, on which sits a wood-fired hot tub that's cranked up every night. The cabin is perfect for a family with kids. The place is run by a darling 20-something guy from Anchorage, Kris

Lethin, and his brothers. ■ *Walk the boardwalk to the end; 165 Main St (no street signs); PO Box 264, Seldovia, AK 99663; (907) 234-7627 in summer; (907) 278-0288 in winter; $$; MC, V; checks OK; closed Oct–May.*

Swan House South Bed and Breakfast ★★ Owners Judy and Jerry Swanson's B&B feels more like a modern little inn than somebody's home. It's sleek and adult and not the least bit funky. Three of the five rooms have private baths. The large, open living room with white pine trimmings gives the place a lodgelike touch, and there's a nice view of the historic boardwalk. The Swansons own a B&B in Anchorage, so the Seldovia operation is hosted by Judy's parents. ■ *From town, cross the bridge over the slough and make the first right; 175 Augustine Ave N, although you'll be hard pressed to find a correct street sign; for reservations, write 6840 Crooked Tree Dr, Anchorage, AK 99516; (800) 921-1900 outside Alaska; (907) 234-8888 in season; (907) 346-3033 all year; $$; AE, DIS, MC, V; checks OK; closed Sept–April.*

Across the Bay Tent & Breakfast Reminiscent of summer camp, this outfit is right on the beach and serves budget travelers who are willing to skimp on accommodations. As the name implies, guests stay in tents, but they're wall tents on raised platforms with beds and mattresses. Bring your own sleeping bags. The place is on Kasitsna Bay, an 8-mile taxi ride from Seldovia, but probably best reached directly by boat from Homer. Hot showers and a large wood-fired sauna are always available. Hosts Mary Jane and Tony Lastufka offer mountain bike rental and kayak tours for an extra charge. With beach fires and salmon bakes, this is a busy, convivial kind of place, with miles of beach. Breakfast is served in the main house; lunch and dinner are extra. A propane burner and a covered cooking area available for those who want to do for themselves. ■ *8 miles from Seldovia, on the Jakolof Bay Rd at Kasitsna Bay; PO Box RDO, Homer, AK 99603 in summer; PO Box 112054, Anchorage, AK 99511 in winter; (907) 235-3633 in summer; (907) 345-2571 in winter; $; no credit cards; checks OK; closed mid-Sept–mid-May.*

The Boardwalk Hotel Formerly Annie McKenzie's, this hotel is not on the old boardwalk, but it does have a good view of the harbor. The rooms are standard but it's a good bet for visitors who want a basic hotel, no frills. ■ *In town, just above the harbor; PO Box 72, Seldovia, AK 99663; (800) 238-7862 or (907) 234-7816; $$; no credit cards; checks OK; usually closes in winter.*

Seldovia Rowing Club Don't let the name fool you. This ain't no country club but a cute, funky B&B that accommodates only one party at a time. Like Dancing Eagles, it's on the old boardwalk, built on pilings over the water, scattered with antiques and nautical tidbits. Owner Susan Mumma, a school teacher, lives upstairs, so guests (up to five) have the entire main floor to themselves, including a kitchen. Susan goes all out on the breakfasts. ■ *On the boardwalk, on your left; PO Box 41, Seldovia, AK 99663; (907) 234-7614; $$; no credit cards; checks OK.*

KODIAK

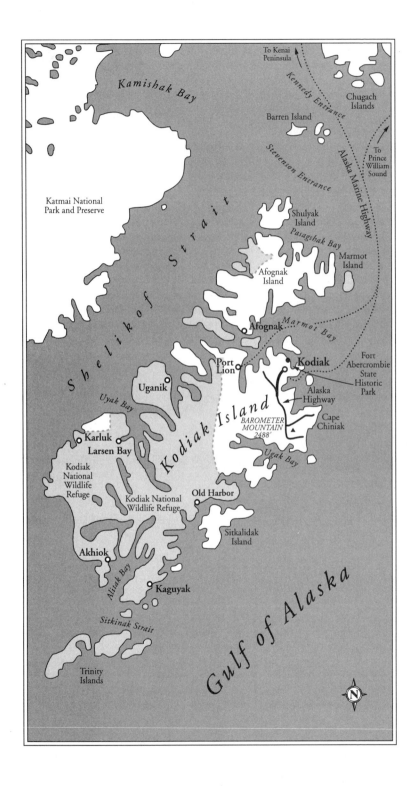

To Kenai
Peninsula

Kamishak Bay

Kennedy Entrance

Chugach
Islands

Barren Island

To
Prince
William
Sound

Alaska Marine Highway

Stevenson Entrance

Katmai National
Park and Preserve

Shulyak
Island

Pasagshak Bay

Marmot
Island

S h e l i k o f   S t r a i t

Afognak
Island

Marmot Bay

Afognak

Fort
Abercrombie
State
Historic
Park

Kodiak

Port
Lion

Uganik

Alaska
Highway

Uyak Bay

K o d i a k   I s l a n d

BAROMETER
MOUNTAIN
2488'

Cape
Chiniak

Karluk
Larsen Bay

Kodiak
National
Wildlife
Refuge

Ugak Bay

Kodiak National
Wildlife Refuge

Old Harbor

Sitkalidak
Island

Akhiok

Aliluk Bay

Kaguyak

G u l f   o f   A l a s k a

Sitkinak Strait

Trinity
Islands

N

Kodiak

Including the Town and the Island

Kodiak Island is often one of the last places discovered by visitors to Alaska. Unlike places on the state highway system or Southeast Alaska's extensive network of ferries, Kodiak isn't on the way to somewhere else. Few people just wander through Kodiak. A trip to "The Rock" is a commitment, but one that can bring many rewards.

Whether you arrive by boat or by plane, you're bound to be surprised by the sight of Kodiak's metropolitan appearance. Opulent homes line the cliffs and beaches that surround the city on three sides, and downtown Kodiak is a compact, bustling commercial center adjacent to one of the city's two harbors. Despite the island's isolation, residents enjoy a cosmopolitan lifestyle with access to uncrowded beaches, extensive wilderness trails, and easy mountain hikes.

Kodiak is the second largest island in the United States after the island of Hawaii. Situated in the northern Gulf of Alaska, just east of the Alaska Peninsula, the Kodiak Island Archipelago is home to 16,000 people, less than 100 miles of mostly unpaved roads, and 3,000 of the world's largest brown bears.

Salmon has remained an important source of income for the past 100 years, while other fish, such as crab, halibut, shrimp, pollock, and shellfish, have shown fluctuating abundance. The heady days of the rich king crab industry are gone, but may help explain some of the fancy homes in this wilderness outpost. Kodiak consistently ranks as the country's first or second most productive fishing port.

Access

For air travelers, **Alaska Airlines** flies jets from Anchorage and Seattle. Kodiak is an elongated city, 5 miles from end to end, and visitors will enjoy the freedom a rental car will afford. If you want to bring your own car or motor home to the island, this requires some planning. Call the **Alaska Marine Highway** at least a month in advance of your trip for reservations, (800) 642-0066. The ferry MV *Tustumena* departs from either Homer or Seward, and takes about 12 hours to get to Kodiak.

Information

A good source is the **Kodiak Island Convention and Visitors Bureau,** 100 Marine Way, Kodiak, AK 99615; (907) 486-4782. A visitors center is located at the ferry terminal and open year-round. The **Kodiak Daily Mirror** publishes every weekday.

Tips on the Town

In 1964, an earthquake centered in Prince William Sound created a huge wave that sucked most of downtown Kodiak out to

KODIAK BROWN BEARS

Kodiak Island is roughly the size of Connecticut, although two-thirds of the island is a national wildlife refuge and not accessible by road. The refuge is the domain of the Kodiak brown bear, the coastal relative of the grizzly and arguably the world's largest carnivore. In early summer, bears congregate along streams to fish for salmon. Most locals advise hikers not to explore trails outside town without carrying a firearm. But if it is not second nature to you to operate a gun, carrying one will cause you more trouble than not. Better opt for mace or cayenne pepper spray, which also have proven effective in discouraging bears.

Bear attacks are very rare. Only one person this century has been killed by a bear on Kodiak. If you spot a bear on the trail, do not turn and run. Do not run at all. The bear will think you're prey. A bear can outrun you easily. Band together with your hiking companions, make some noise, and back up slowly.

—Mark Gillespie

sea. As the city began to recover, planners redesigned the downtown into a series of closely spaced office buildings, known as "The Mall." Most of the city's shops are located either in the mall or less than a block away. **The Shire,** (907) 486-5001, a bookstore on the mall, is a good source for books about Kodiak. Here, you can also pick up a copy of the *Utne Reader* or the *Paris Review* before you head out to the Bush to hunt mountain goats. Across Center Street, in El Chicano Mall, is the **Northern Exposure Gallery and Frame Loft,** (907) 486-4956, which features a broad selection of prints and photographs from Alaska's leading artists.

During its boom years in the early eighties, Kodiak was famous for its ubiquitous bars and liquor stores, but that scene is quickly changing, as Kodiak's surprising number of espresso stands have now gained acceptance. **Harborside Coffee and Goods** (216 Shelikof Street; (907) 486-5862) could pass for a caffeine cache anywhere in Washington State or California, except for the fox pelt mounted to its wall. **Mill Bay Coffee** (3833 Melnitsa Lane; (907) 486-4411) is a short walk from Mill Bay Beach, a popular destination for joggers and bicyclists, and is accessible on an extensive paved trail that circles the east end of town.

THINGS TO DO

Kodiak may have its share of creature comforts, but many of the island's visitors do not arrive to nibble cinnamon rolls and look at art. It's the vast wilderness that draws them—the island beyond the city.

The mountains on Kodiak lie fairly low compared to others in Alaska. **Barometer Mountain,** a three-sided triangle that bookends a long ridge, stands only 2,488 feet high, while the island's tallest mountains barely exceed 4,000 feet. (Barometer Mountain is so named because one can tell if the weather is worsening or improving by watching the cloud ceiling move along Barometer's sides.) The peaks of Kodiak's mountains are easily climbed in an afternoon. On a warm day, hikers can be spotted against the bare, grassy mountainside making their way to the top for a view of the Pacific or the mainland's snow-capped peaks across Shelikof Strait.

Summers in Kodiak are cool, with temperatures most often between 50°F and 65°F. A thermometer reading of 75°F will tempt pale, sun-starved locals to don bathing suits for a dip in the frigid ocean. Summer is the time for the best sports-fishing in the world. Many people prefer Kodiak's relatively unspoiled streams to the crowded, combative atmosphere on the Kenai River. Kodiak salmon can be just as large as their Kenai Peninsula cousins, with king salmon sometimes weighing in at more than a hundred pounds.

The prize fish of the region is halibut, a flatfish that feeds on the bottom of the ocean until it reaches sizes in excess of 300 pounds. Several halibut charter boats, including the *MV Ten Bears,* (907) 486-2200, offer day tours and supply gear and assistance for hauling in these monsters. Don't be alarmed if your skipper draws a gun or a baseball bat and deftly puts the beast out of its misery. This precaution is to keep a struggling fish from sending hapless passengers overboard.

Kodiak tour guides have now altered their usual slate of hunting and fishing expeditions to accommodate the tastes of the new "eco-tourists." One of the first to jump into the fray was **Kodiak Wilderness Tours,** (800) 556-8101, a floatplane charter company that provides tours of the **Kodiak National Wildlife Refuge** and **Katmai National Park**. Kodiak Wilderness Tours looks for brown bears on its flightseeing tours. They also arrange raft trips down the Karluk River, which traces the girth of the island. **Wavetamer Kayaking,** (907) 486-2604, is another excellent charter company. They arrange instruction and short trips in the area's popular sea kayaks. Kayakers paddle out to watch sea lions and whales. No other mode of transportation brings a person closer to the marine wildlife of Kodiak.

WINTERTIME ACTIVITIES

In the winter, Kodiak is one of the warmest cities in Alaska. Islanders often take delight in calling their relatives in Dubuque or Charleston, who are shivering with subzero temperatures, and informing them that the high temperature that day is 45°F and sunny. Winters are not all fun, however. Sometimes the temperature drops to 20 below and the island's famous wind storms can cross the 70mph mark, literally soaking low-lying areas with seawater. The winter freeze-thaw cycle is hard on local roads, which are often rife with potholes.

Kayaking Winter kayaking is actually a popular pastime on the island. When the wind isn't blowing and the moon is out, one may paddle through luminescent algae and reflections of stars. The ambient air temperature on these days is usually right around freezing. **Wavetamer Kayaking,** (907) 486-2604, often holds winter tours on the full moon. Tours are especially recommended in March and April, when migrations of gray whales skirt along Kodiak's coast.

PLACES TO VISIT

There are not many roads to explore in Kodiak, but the landscape these roads take you to is unparalleled in Alaska. Sheer cliffs emerge from the ocean, giving way to lush green hillsides that Irish tourists swear look just like home to them. Puffins skim the water along wide sandy beaches, while eagles circle overhead.

Five miles north of town, **Fort Abercrombie State Historic Park,** with its rugged coastline and lovely woods, displays a cannon once mounted on a high bluff overlooking miles of open sea. The park also holds summer tours of the **Miller Point bunker,** a former underground concrete residence for watchmen who patrolled the horizon for signs of enemy ships. Elsewhere in the park are small concrete pillboxes, which are mere turrets with slits facing seaward. When one stands inside, it's impossible to imagine the amount of concentration servicemen had to have to be alert and watchful in the cold, windy weather of the North Pacific.

Four roads branch off from Rezanof Drive, Kodiak's primary boulevard. To the north, Rezanof becomes Monashka Bay Road and ends 11 miles later, at one of the island's few white sand beaches. (Most of Kodiak's beaches are composed of black-slate sand.) A system of trails leads for several miles into a majestic Sitka spruce forest. Hikers will appreciate the spongy texture of the mossy forest floor. This area is called **Termination Point.**

To the south, Rezanof Drive becomes the Chiniak Highway. You quickly pass the western edge of the island's spruce forest. The hills are now covered with alpine grasses and flowers. You'll see jagged mountain ridges, windy seaside cliffs, and river valleys, which provide pasture for horses, cattle, and domestic buffalo. At the end of the road is **Chiniak,** populated mostly by people who think even Kodiak is getting too big for comfort. Only one business in the area caters to visitors:

THE CRAB FESTIVAL

Twenty years ago, this rite of spring was celebrated as the "Kodiak King Crab Festival" in honor of the rich harvests of king crab. But the kings have disappeared from the waters around Kodiak.

The festival was quite bawdy in its early years. Now, the emphasis is on family fun, complete with carnival, vendors, races, and barbecues. Today's Crab Festival is not without strange events, however. Watch for swimmers in bright red neoprene suits lining up for the annual **Survival Suit Races.**

Survival suits, also known as "full-immersion suits," insulate stranded mariners from the frigid waters of the North Pacific Ocean. Without such protection, a person can die within minutes from hypothermia. In the race, a team of four swimmers dashes 100 yards to water's edge, correctly zips themselves into survival suits, and plunges into the water for a 300-yard swim to a life boat anchored in the harbor. The race is meant to simulate a real-life emergency and gives non-fishermen a taste of what the fishing fleet must be prepared to handle.

The race assumes new meaning when watched on the last day at the main event, **"The Fishermen's Memorial Service."** *The service is held in front of Fishermen's Hall on Marine Way at a monument bearing the names of Kodiak fishermen lost at sea. The names of each man or woman who has perished that year are read as a bell tolls from the Holy Resurrection Orthodox Church. Kodiak awaits the year when the bell will be silent.*

The Crab Festival lasts from the Thursday before Memorial Day until the following Monday; (907) 486-5557.

— Mark Gillespie

Road's End Restaurant and Lounge, (907) 486-2885, a popular greasy spoon famous for its huge hamburgers (served on French bread) and homemade pies. Road's End used to open in March at the first sighting of the gray whales' migration and close in October after the first snow, but because of a recent boom in logging, both the restaurant and bar are currently open year-round.

Branch right on the Chiniak Highway to travel along **Anton Larsen Bay Road,** which snakes up between **Barometer and Pyramid Mountains** and down to a long shallow inlet. In the summer, Anton Larsen Bay is so thick with salmon you can see one jump just about every 5 seconds. The trip is short (about 11 miles) but quite spectacular.

Pasagshak Road forks to the right from the Chiniak

Highway, 30 miles to the south of Kodiak, and leads to Pasagshak River and Pasagshak Bay. The road ends at **Fossil Beach,** a dream for rock hounds.

All of Kodiak's outlying roads are unpaved and often in poor condition. Most of the land on either side of the roads is privately owned. While owners usually don't object to public use of the land, visitors should check first with the **Kodiak Visitors Bureau,** (907) 486-4782, about specific stretches of roadside.

NIGHTLIFE

As an old saying goes, "In Kodiak, Alaska, there are more bars than churches." But this might not be the case anymore since the **Salvation Army** bought a notorious strip joint called the Beachcomber's Bar and converted it into a place of worship. Ironically, many of the same musicians who played at the original Beachcomber's return to the building each Saturday for alcohol-free rock-and-roll nights sponsored by the church. Another bar conversion happened to the Ship's Bar downtown. A hairstylist has moved in and cleverly renamed the establishment **"The Ship's Barber."**

It would be a mistake to say all of Kodiak's bars have gone the way of the now scarce king crab, though. Billing itself as "Alaska's Largest Navigational Hazard," **Tony's,** (907) 486-9489, on the mall, is a throwback to the glory years of Alaska fishing, with a loud jukebox and a big pool table in the center of the room. This is the headquarters for community stunts such as the **Pillar Mountain Golf Classic,** a late-March, cross-country golf event that has been featured nationally on ABC Sports and in *Sports Illustrated.* The course is one hole at par 70. Golfers use bright orange balls for better visibility in the alpine snow. The rules specifically forbid the use of dogs to find lost balls or power tools to remove brush from the fairway.

BEST RESTAURANTS

Second Floor Restaurant ★★★ Many Kodiak Islanders believe the community's civilization quotient increased several points when the Second Floor Restaurant opened downtown, serving traditional Japanese cuisine. Second Floor serves excellent tempura dishes. Don't pass up the home-grown "Kodiak Roll," sushi made from locally caught seafood. The restaurant offers a good selection of imported beers, including Japanese brands. ■ *(907) 486-8555; $$$; beer and wine; MC, V; local checks; open daily.*

Chartroom Grill ★★ The Chartroom Grill, located on the second floor of the Westmark Hotel, affords a spectacular view of St. Paul's Harbor and the mountains beyond Chiniak Bay. The Chartroom offers wonderful entrees of locally caught seafood and thick steaks. The breakfast menu is especially good. ■ *236 W Rezanof Dr (a half block west of the downtown Y-intersection* with Lower Mill Bay Rd); (907) 486-5712; $$; full bar; AE, DC, DIS, MC, V; local checks OK.

Eagle's Nest ★★ Located in the Buskin River Inn, this is the place to come for king crab legs shipped fresh, in season, from the Bering Sea. The restaurant pre-cuts the legs and the claw (for the uninitiated) and provides lots of butter and lemon for dipping. The staff keeps fresh bread coming as you eat. This is a nonsmoking dining room, but the adjacent bar is separated by a sliding door that admits smoke; if you're bothered, sit close to the kitchen. ■ *395 Airport Way (at the state airport entrance); (907) 487-2700; $$; full bar; AE, DC, DIS, MC, V; checks OK.*

El Chicano ★★ "El Cheez," as the locals call it, offers heaping helpings of familiar Mexican dishes. Don't let your eyes be bigger than your stomach. The "License-Plate Burrito" really is as big as a license plate. Pace yourself through the generous entrees so you'll have room afterwards for traditional flan or fried ice cream, which arrives crisp and smothered with chocolate syrup. El Chicano often features a live mariachi band during Mexican holidays such as Cinco de Mayo. ■ *(907) 486-6116; $$; full bar; AE, DIS, MC, V; checks accepted with ID; open daily.*

Mimi's Deli ★ This is a seriously well-stocked Italian-style delicatessen featuring freshly made sandwiches and salads, including pasta concoctions such as smoked salmon fettuccine and sun-dried tomatoes, prosciutto, and pine nuts. Mimi's is on the way to some excellent beachcombing territory and specializes in gourmet box lunches. ■ *About 3 miles north of downtown; 3420 E Rezanof Dr; (907) 486-2886; $$; MC, V; checks accepted; open Mon–Sat.*

Beryl's A short-order grill and candy shop tucked away in the mall, Beryl's (rhymes with "curls") serves cold-cut sandwiches, hamburgers, and delicious homemade soups. Fresh pies and cakes are often available, as well as a good selection of espresso drinks. The co-owners make frequent trips to Russia, and you can buy souvenirs such as lavishly decorated tea services, hand-painted Ukrainian Easter eggs, or colorful nesting dolls. ■ *(907) 486-3323; $$; no alcohol; MC, V; checks accepted; open daily.*

BEST LODGINGS

Kodiak is not a four-star town, so if you're expecting valet service and a mint on your pillow, you could be in for a big letdown. Kodiak's two major hotels, **The Westmark** (236 W Rezanof Dr; (907) 486-5712) and the **Buskin River Inn** (near the airport; (907) 487-2700), provide serviceable accommodations. Expect to pay from 30 to 50 percent more in Kodiak than you would for similar lodgings in the Lower 48. There are few bargains on this remote island.

An alternative—typically less expensive and sometimes more luxurious—is one of Kodiak's bed and breakfasts. Most are in private homes, some with spectacular views of the water. The **Kodiak Visitors Information Center** in the ferry terminal maintains lists of bed and breakfasts and remote wilderness lodges. Contact them at 100 Marine Way, Kodiak, AK 99615; (907) 486-4782.

DENALI NATIONAL PARK & THE PARKS HIGHWAY

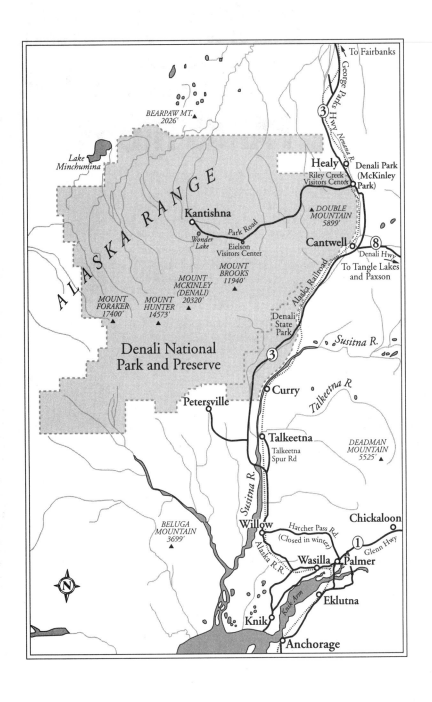

Denali National Park & The Parks Highway

Including Wasilla, Knik, Hatcher Pass, Talkeetna, Denali State Park, the Denali Highway, and Denali National Park

While you may think the Parks Highway was named for the parklands that surround the extraordinary massif of Mount McKinley (Denali National Park and Denali State Park), it was actually named for George Parks, one of the territorial governors of Alaska in the early 1900s. Officially it's known as the George Parks Highway, but everyone refers to it simply as the Parks Highway. It runs from the Matanuska Valley just south of Palmer north to Fairbanks, a journey of 324 miles. Paralleling the Susitna and Chulitna Rivers and the Alaska Railroad, the route wends its way up a broad glacial valley. The land here is dotted with swamp spruce, lakes, old homesteads, cabins, a multitude of bars, little roadhouses, and a small assortment of whistlestops and towns all framed by incredible mountain ranges in the distance. It's also dog-mushing country.

WASILLA

Twenty years ago, the town was little more than an airstrip and a charming grocery near the old railroad section house. But it boomed with strip malls during the pipeline construction years of the late 1970s, and big money was liberally laced with questionable taste. The wild feel of the place is gone. But never fear. It lives on in the woods and foothills a stone's throw away.

FESTIVALS/EVENTS

"Re-Start" for the Iditarod Trail Sled Dog Race The best of Wasilla happens in March during "Iditarod time" at the official re-start, which has its ceremonial beginnings on Fourth Avenue in Anchorage the first Saturday of every March. After racing from Fourth Avenue to Eagle River, mushers and handlers truck their teams to Wasilla for the "re-start" the next day. This is as festive as the first day of the race. For spectators, there's more room to get a really good view of this extraordinary event. And mushers and dogs are just darned glad to get out of the booby traps of civilization and onto the real trail to Nome.

Dancing Bears Dance Camp Another one of the best annual events in the region occurs at King's Lake Fine Arts Camp off Fishhook Road in Wasilla every Memorial Day weekend at Dancing Bears Dance Camp. The motto with this fun-loving group is "dance 'til you drop"—three days of nonstop clogging, squares, contras, swing, old-time fiddling, and calling with guest callers and musicians from all over Alaska and the United States. Dance workshops start early in the morning, run all day, and are followed by dancing and music all night. It's a joyful rite of spring. Except for summer, dances and workshops are held monthly in Anchorage. For a schedule, contact Dancing Bears, PO Box 200366, Anchorage, AK 99520-0366, or call the "Bear Phone" at (907) 248-BEAR.

KNIK

This is a journey into Iditarod country. Or at least a glimpse into the modern-day lore of the Iditarod Sled Dog Race. The historic Iditarod Trail runs out of Knik. A lot of dog-mushers live down here, and it's also the site of the big log cabin **Iditarod Trail Sled Dog Race Headquarters and Visitors Center,** (907) 376-5155, at Mile 2.2 on the Knik Road. It's open daily in summer. Stop in and steep yourself in characters and stories. If you want to volunteer on the next race, contribute money, or buy a seat in the sled bag of one of the starting mushers for a $500 ride down Fourth Avenue come race day, this is where you can do it.

THINGS TO DO

Iditarod Trail The founder of the race, Joe Redington, Sr., is 80 years old and still mushing. He's raced the race nearly every year except for the last four, when he's guided tourists with their own dog teams down the trail. When he started his latest escapade, Alaskans just shook their heads and grinned. They thought he was nuts, but hey, this is the guy who also mushed his dogs to the top of Mount McKinley. Redington calls his tour, appropriately, "**The Joe Redington, Sr., Iditarod Challenge**." This is an extreme adventure of the grand sort with one of Alaska's legendary characters. He takes nine mushers for $15,000/person on a 3-week journey in March following the Iditarod racers down the trail. This is not for the unfit or feeble-hearted. Temperatures can get to 60° below zero, and mushing over the Alaska Range can be harrowing. Do not let Joe's age fool you. He's as tough as they get in Alaska. If you want a lesser thrill, Joe or one of his handlers will take you on an hour-long sled-dog ride around Knik, winter or summer. Call his home at "Husky Haven," at Mile 13 on the Knik Road, which turns off the Parks Highway in Wasilla at the old railroad section house. Call (907) 376-5622 for an appointment.

HATCHER PASS

Hatcher Pass is beautiful, with alpine meadows and streams; a narrow, winding dirt road; ruins of old gold mines; and looming mountains with names like Microdot, Skyscraper, and Government Peaks. **Hatcher Pass Road** from the Palmer side to the Willow side is a fun trip in summer, but closed to the Willow side in winter. The easiest way to get to Hatcher Pass is to drive past Palmer on the Glenn Highway, turn left on Fishhook Road, and follow it all the way to Hatcher Pass.

THINGS TO DO

Explore Independence Mine State Historical Park The best things to do in summer at Hatcher Pass are explore the old mine buildings and the main building, which are preserved today as an historical park. Call (907) 745-2827.

Alpine Hiking Located above treeline, this is a wonderful area for alpine hiking in all directions. Pick your ridge and go for it, or follow one of the established trails. The trail to Reed Lakes is a popular day hike.

Rent a Llama There are also some unusual ways to journey to Hatcher Pass. One of the most unusual is to rent llamas and an artist for a day with **Llama Buddies Expeditions,** (907) 376-8472. The llamas carry your paint, palette, and gourmet lunch, while you hike from one beautiful spot to the next with an Alaska artist who helps stir your imagination to translate it all onto paper and canvas. They cater to non-artists, too. (Cost is $150/person.)

WINTERTIME ACTIVITIES

Backcountry Skiing In winter, Hatcher Pass is a backcountry ski haven. It usually has skiable snow long before and long after many other places near Anchorage. Folks come here to cross-country ski on set track ($5/day for use of trails); or to forge their own trails up the mountains with cross-country, mountaineering, or telemark skis or snowboards.

Avalanche Education Do not trip lightly into these mountains. Avalanches have buried several backcountry travelers here in past years. If your skills and knowledge are thin in this area, you're in luck because Hatcher Pass is the teaching arena for the best avalanche education/training program in the country, provided by the internationally renowned **Alaska Mountain Safety Center,** run by Doug Fesler and Jill Fredston. Their team of experts conducts weekend avalanche and mountaineering workshops during the winter and launches people into summer with a sea-kayaking workshop out of Seward in Resurrection Bay. For a schedule of classes, contact 9140 Brewsters Drive, Anchorage, AK 99516; (907) 345-3566.

Hatcher Pass

*Wintertime
Activities*

Hatcher Pass Lodge In winter, ski all day and stay overnight in one of the cozy little A-frames run by Hatcher Pass Lodge. The lodge, while quite small, is a fun place to eat, and the food is quite tasty too. You can get hot liqueur and coffee drinks from the bar, espresso, Swiss cheese fondue, gourmet pizzas, and a variety of soups, salads, and sandwiches. Contact PO Box 763, Palmer, AK 99645; (907) 745-5897.

TALKEETNA

If you're looking for "an end-of-the-road experience" or you want to take a flight around Mount McKinley on a clear day, turn off on the Talkeetna Spur Road just past Mile 98 on the Parks Highway It's 14 miles to the little village with Alaska's most famous mountain rising as its backdrop. Nowhere else on earth does a massif rise so dramatically from nearly sea level as McKinley. If measured from base to summit, it is the tallest mountain in the world. In 50 miles, the land rises from 350 feet (Talkeetna) to 20,320 feet (the summit of McKinley).

The history of Talkeetna (pop. 260) has spanned old bachelor gold miners, feisty dames, daring bush pilots, back-to-the-earth flower children, dog mushers, hippies, wild mountain guides, and every year an international onslaught of climbers bound for the summit of Mount McKinley. With such a diverse mix of locals comes an eclectic mix of architecture. As renegade English professor Ed Craver, who lived here for many years along the banks of the river, once wrote: "One of the first things a traveler notices in Talkeetna is the bazaar of construction. There are A-frames and timber frames, domes and teepees, log cabins and plywood shacks . . . enough turrets and towers for a medieval village and even a shoe-shaped home for the old woman."

THINGS TO DO

Fly Around Mount McKinley On a clear day in Talkeetna, take a flight around Mount McKinley, soar over the summit, or land on one of its glaciers. The pilots here are some of the best in the world. They routinely fly hundreds of climbers to the mountain in late spring and early summer, landing most of them at Kahiltna Glacier base camp, at around a 7,000-foot elevation. It's a spectacular flight. For flight tours, call **Hudson Air Service,** the oldest air service in Talkeetna, (907) 733-2321; **Doug Geeting Aviation's McKinley Flight Tours & Glacier Landings,** (800) 770-2366 or (907) 733-2366; and **K2 Aviation,** (800) 478-2291 or (907) 733-2291. All are top-notch.

Climb the Mountain If you're looking for a more intimate view of Mount McKinley or one of the other mountains in the Alaska

Range, perhaps even a summit bid, you could hire no finer guides than **Alaska Denali Guides**. Brian and Diane Okonek have been guiding on Denali for years and are highly respected for their wilderness savvy and attention to safety and detail. They're wonderful human beings to boot! For more information, contact the Okoneks at PO Box 566, Talkeetna, AK 99676; (907) 733-2649; fax (907) 733-1362. **Mountain Trip** is another highly respected guiding outfit in the high mountains. For more information, contact PO Box 91161, Anchorage, AK 99509; (907) 345-6499.

DENALI STATE PARK

Denali State Park is one of Alaska's best-kept secrets because most travelers continue north to the more popular (and populous) Denali National Park. With a little effort, hikers can easily climb out of the thick vegetation and emerge onto beautiful alpine tundra ridges. The park is about half the size of Rhode Island and runs on both sides of the Parks Highway. On the east side, two ridges—**Curry and Kesugi**—provide the backbone of the park and run 35 miles north and south. They offer stupendous views of Mount McKinley and surrounding peaks. Hiking here is also a sure way to avoid crowds.

Information

In downtown Anchorage, **Alaska Public Lands Information Center** (605 W Fourth Avenue, (907) 456-0527) is the best place for displays and information on Denali State Park. Or you can call **Alaska State Parks Information** at (907) 762-2261.

THINGS TO DO

Backpacking Little Coal Creek is a short day hike or first stop for an overnight backpacking trip. It is also the quickest access to get above treeline in that section of mountains. Three miles into the hike on a clear day, enjoy a "forever" view of mountains and glaciers on the other side of the Chulitna River. If you're a strong hiker, you can get there in less than an hour. The trail is not particularly steep. Vegetation is thick en route, so make lots of noise to let bears know you're in the area. Black bears are common.

Fishing/Car Camping Byers Lake is a great stop for car camping, especially for those folks with fishing poles in hand. Fish for grayling, burbot, rainbow, lake trout, and whitefish. The state campground has 66 sites and charges $10 a night. If you want to get a little farther away from civilization, pack your tent and hike to a more remote campground about 2 miles away.

Denali State Park

Things to Do

THE DENALI HIGHWAY

*(Note: Mile markers on the Denali Highway read east
to west and west to east. We have chosen to take you from
east to west, from Paxson on the Richardson Highway
to Cantwell on the Parks Highway.)*

The Denali Highway offers one of the most scenic drives in
Alaska. From Paxson on the Richardson Highway it is 135
miles to Cantwell on the Parks Highway. The road is primarily gravel, except for the first 21 miles out of Paxson. The ride
can be rough, dusty, and hazardous to your tires. Be sure to
bring mounted spares. Potholes and other rough spots in the
road require you to keep your speed well below 50 mph and actually closer to 30 mph. Four hours is a quick trip. Take your
time and you will be rewarded with fabulous vistas and maybe
wildlife sightings.

When the Denali Highway opened in 1957, it provided a
route from the Richardson Highway to what was then Mount
McKinley National Park, today Denali National Park. Before
that, visitors could reach the park only by train, plane, or
dogsled. The road that led from the entrance of the park to
Wonder Lake was already in use, so visitors often sent their vehicles to the park via rail. After the George Parks Highway was
built, more than a decade later, the Denali Highway became a
destination in itself. Today, it is a popular road for bikers,
hunters, skiers, and sightseers.

▼

**The Denali
Highway**

▲

In the summer, there are a few inns along the way that offer some amenities, but you should come prepared with extra
water and food for emergencies. Also be prepared for changes
in weather. The day may start out sunny and warm and change
dramatically to cold, rain, wind, and even snow, any month of
the year. The road is not plowed in the wintertime.

You can camp anywhere along the highway. There are any
number of beautiful spots. However, if you want a few amenities, there are three Bureau of Land Management (BLM) campgrounds along the highway, with a total of 46 campsites. These
include (note: the mile markers on the road are calculated from
Paxson).

Tangle Lakes Campground, Mile 21.5. Water pump, toilets, boat launch, picnic area. This is the starting point for a 3-
day river trip (see below).

Tangle River Campground, Mile 21.7. Water pump, toilets, boat launch. You can launch a boat here for an extended
wilderness canoe trip on the upper Tangle Lakes. Note: There
is a 1.5-mile portage to the Gulkana River drainage. The country is covered with numerous lakes.

Brushkana River Campground, Mile 104. Firepits, water, toilets, tables, trails, and 17 campsites.

On both sides of the highway, a series of beautiful lakes—

Tangle Lakes—connected by the Tangle River are a popular destination. Round Tangle, Long Tangle, and Lower Tangle Lakes are on the north side of the road, and Upper Tangle Lake is on the south side of the road. The name Tangle comes from the maze of lakes and streams in this drainage system. The lakes offer good fishing, even from shore. Catch trout, grayling, or burbot. Be sure to check state fishing regulations and have a fishing license in hand before you wet a line.

The Tangle Lakes are also terrific for birding. With a little luck you might see Arctic warblers, Smith's longspurs, gyrfalcons, or ptarmigan. Canoeists can paddle across any of the lakes and instantly find themselves in remote Alaska wilderness with tundra hiking in any direction. Be sure to wear rubber boots though, because some of that hiking is wet. You can rent a canoe for $3 an hour from Tangle River Inn, Mile 20.

Experienced paddlers looking for a longer trip can paddle across Round Tangle and Long Tangle Lakes to reach the **Delta River,** designated as a Wild and Scenic River. This 30-mile trip is best done in a leisurely 3 days. At the end of Long Tangle Lake, you'll have to portage a half-mile around a waterfall. The 1.5 miles of river just below the falls is notorious for demolishing canoes, since the water moves swiftly and the river is very rocky. To paddle this section, you should know how to maneuver through rapids rated Class III. (Class II rapids have small waves that you can paddle right through. Class III rapids require some maneuvering.) Generally, this trip is done in a raft or a canoe. Takeout is at Mile 212 on the Richardson Highway.

Between Mile 17 and Mile 37, there are more than 400 archeological sites. Designated the **Tangle Lakes National Register Archeological District,** this area contains some of the earliest evidence of human occupation in North America.

As you continue driving west on the Denali Highway, on a clear day you'll have spectacular views the whole way. Keep a sharp eye on ponds and lakes. Swans and other migratory waterfowl nest in these areas and can be easy to spot.

The second highest point on Alaska's road system is **Maclaren Summit** (4,086 feet). (The highest is Atigun Pass (4,800 feet) on the Dalton Highway.) Just before Maclaren Summit, catch a panoramic view of the Alaska Range, including Mount Hayes (13,832 feet) and the Maclaren Glacier. A short trail to Maclaren Summit takes off across the tundra at Mile 37. This is alpine tundra, home to ground squirrels and arctic rodents called pikas.

At Mile 43.5, you might want to mountain bike or hike the **Maclaren River Road** as it follows along on the west side of the Maclaren River for 12 miles to the Maclaren Glacier. After 4 miles, you must ford the west fork of the Maclaren River, a glacial stream that can be dangerously high after heavy rains.

**Denali
National Park
& The Parks
Highway**

▼

**The Denali
Highway**

Lodgings

▲

That is followed by 5 miles of good trail, a half-mile of willow thicket, and another 3 miles of good trail.

Continuing on your route, you'll drive over the **Susitna River,** a major drainage in this area. Eventually, the Susitna turns west, flows through the Talkeetna Mountains, and empties into Cook Inlet. Don't think about floating that section of river. Between the bridge and the outlet is the dangerous **Devil's Canyon,** which is not runnable because of huge rapids. Only a handful of expert kayakers have ever tried it, and some have died trying.

Caribou routinely migrate through the area past the Susitna River, so keep an eye peeled for bands of them. At Mile 93.8, a 5-mile trail leads into **Butte Lake,** a popular local fishing hole. Trout, grayling, and burbot are in the lake. The beauty of the Denali Highway is that you can take off hiking in any direction.

Floating the **Upper Nenana River** is a beautiful wilderness canoe trip beginning at Mile 117 (or Mile 18 coming from Cantwell), where the Nenana River flows right next to the Denali Highway. Launch a canoe or raft here and spend the day floating swift but flat water through the Reindeer Hills. The river leaves the road and cuts through the mountains, making its way about 20 miles to the Parks Highway. Takeout is at the Nenana River bridge north of Cantwell, at Mile 215.7 on the Parks Highway. The access road to the bridge is just south of there, at Mile 213.9 on the Parks Highway. The only disruptions to the peacefulness of the trip are the jetboats, or worse, airboats, which take visitors to the Brushkasna River. Boat pilots are generally courteous, however, and slow down when approaching canoes. The trip takes 4 to 6 hours, but may be faster at higher water.

BEST LODGINGS

Gracious House ★ Gracious House has been serving travelers along the Denali Highway for 38 years. The name comes from the owner's last name, Butch Gratias. For a break from the dusty road in summer, check into a motel room here. The restaurant primarily serves short orders. Drivers can buy gas here, get flat tires repaired, or find a tow for disabled vehicles. If you're looking for a little adventure, Gracious House Flying Service offers scenic flights. Butch is also a registered guide and offers guided hunts. ▪ *Mile 82, Denali Highway; summer: Box 88, Cantwell, AK 99729; (907) 822-7307 (this is a radiophone, so let it ring); winter: 859 Elaine Dr, Anchorage, AK 99504; (907) 333-3148; $; full bar; no credit cards; checks OK; restaurant open daily; closed Oct–May.*

Maclaren River Lodge ★ This is the only lodge open year-round on the Denali Highway. Snowmobilers and dog mushers visit regularly during winter months. Those in training for the 1,100-mile Iditarod Trail Sled Dog Race in March will stop here for lunch while doing training runs in the area. The lodge has rooms for 30 people, plus a couple of cabins that sleep five people. Lodge rooms cost $70 each. The cabin beds cost $35 apiece. ■ *Mile 42, Denali Highway; PO Box 3018, Paxson, AK 99737; (907) 822-7105; $; beer and wine; V, MC; local checks only; breakfast, lunch, dinner daily; open year-round; ⅙ main lodge only.*

Tangle Lakes Lodge ★ Originally known as "Butcher's Hunting Camp," this lodge, built in 1952, is now owned by Rich and Linda Holmstrom. Rich is a falconer, and you can see him working his falcon in the fall hunting season. The area is tundra with low bushes so there are lots of ptarmigan and spruce hens, which makes it a good area for falcons. The lodge has log cabins that sleep four people. You can rent canoes for the Tangle Lakes ($30 for 24 hours or $5/hour). Rich can also guide you to good fishing or hiking. Cabins with wood-stove heat are available for rent in the wintertime, but no other services are offered during that season. In winter, bring your own food and water. ■ *Mile 22, Denali Highway, 1 mile past the end of the pavement; PO Box 670386, Chugiak, AK 99567; (907) 688-9173; summer only: (907) 822-7302; $; full bar; V, MC; checks OK; breakfast, lunch, dinner, daily; closed Oct–May.*

Tangle River Inn ★ Overlooking Tangle Lakes, this inn features homestyle cooking and boasts the only karaoke bar along the Denali Highway. For about $25/person, you can stay in one of the 5 motel rooms, 3 cabins, or log bunkhouse. The bunkhouse is good for family reunions or parties who plan to float the Delta River the next day. The inn advertises the cheapest gas in 100 miles and guarantees that its lodgings are less expensive than any in the nearest towns—Delta Junction and Glennallen on the Richardson Highway. ■ *Mile 20, Denali Highway, overlooking Tangle Lakes; summer: Mile 20, Denali Highway, Paxson, AK 99737; (907) 822-7304; answering service, Mon–Fri, (907) 895-4439; winter: Box 783, Delta Junction, AK 99737; $; full bar; V, MC; checks OK; breakfast, lunch, dinner daily; closed Oct–May.* ⅙

DENALI NATIONAL PARK

Ah, the magic of Denali! It's no surprise thousands of people travel here every year. A wilderness area roughly the size of Massachusetts, this is home to some of the most magnificent creatures on earth. It is all framed by a range of breathtaking icy peaks leading up to the highest mountain on the North American continent—Mount McKinley. Memories here are not soon forgotten: the sight of a moose calf wobbling behind its mother, a wolf relentlessly digging for a ground squirrel, or a blond grizzly bear loping over the tundra. While most visitors

Denali
National Park
& The Parks
Highway

▼

Denali
National Park

▲

RAY GENET: MOUNT MCKINLEY'S FIRST GUIDE

"To the summit!" was the rallying cry of Mount McKinley's first and most colorful guide. A boisterous Swiss-American, Ray Genet made mountaineering history in Alaska. He was part of the first successful winter expedition on McKinley in 1967 on which he earned a lifelong nickname, "The Pirate." Dave Johnston of Talkeetna and Art Davidson of Rainbow were with him on the summit and later were trapped by winter storms in an ice cave on the descent where the temperature with windchill dropped to 148°F below zero. Davidson wrote a gripping account of that journey in his book Minus 148°.

In the next 12 years, Genet summitted McKinley more than 30 times, guiding other climbers to the top, often in the most unorthodox ways. In the fall of 1979, after four summer expeditions on the mountain, including the Joe Redington, Sr.–Susan Butcher Mount McKinley Sled Dog Expedition, he climbed to the top of Mount Everest in Nepal, the highest mountain in the world. Beneath the summit, he froze to death on a bivouac. But his legend lives on. (His son, Taras Genet, followed in his famous father's footsteps, becoming, at age 12, the youngest person to summit the mountain in 1991. That record was broken only in 1995, when a young girl, Merrick Johnston, just a couple of months younger at the time, became the youngest on top of the mountain.)

McKinley is an arena of "firsts." Appropriately, the first to set foot on the top of the highest mountain in North America was a young Athabascan-Irish lad, Walter Harper, part of the Hudson Stuck expedition in 1912. Barbara Washburn in 1947 was the first woman to climb McKinley and still holds the record for climbing both the North and South Peaks in a single expedition. In 1970, the famous Japanese world adventurer Naomi Uemura made the first successful solo ascent. In February 1984, Uemura returned to the mountain for the first solo winter summit bid. Tragically, he died upon descent. Following in Uemura's footsteps, mountain guide Vern Tejas in 1988 became the first to reach the summit alone in the winter and return alive.

World-class climbers have met their match on McKinley. This mountain is sometimes called "the coldest mountain in the world" for its proximity to the polar region. Temperatures in summer can plummet to –50°F with winds gusting to 100 mph. Many have died in their bid for the summit. Two renowned British mountaineers, Douglas Scott and Dougal Haston, who had both climbed Mount Everest, were a very respectful pair when they summited McKinley in 1976.

> *Haston wrote: "We had climbed . . . forever into a revived
> storm and relentless wind. Everything was cold, even our souls.
> Frostbite was waiting to jump at the slightest weakness. . . .
> We were drawing heavily on all our Himalayan experience
> just to survive. . . ."*

will see bears and some will see caribou or a wolf, this is not a
zoo. Sighting of animals takes patience, persistence, and constant looking, looking, looking. Denali is home to 161 species
of birds, 37 species of mammals, and 450 species of plants.

If weather cooperates during your visit, you may even see
the top of Mount McKinley, rising 20,320 feet above sea level.
During summer months, this imposing peak creates its own
weather system and may be clearly visible only a third of the
time. When the mountain is "out," there is no mistaking which
peak is McKinley. It looms dramatically over every other
mountain on the horizon.

A prospector dubbed the mountain "McKinley" in 1896, in
honor of William McKinley of Ohio, who became the 25th president of the United States. Long ago, Athabascan Indians called
it *Denali,* which means "the high one." Debate continues today
over whether the name should be officially changed to Denali.
Meanwhile, most Alaskans call it simply "The Mountain."
More than 1,000 climbers attempt to scale McKinley every
year. Only half succeed. To date, nearly 100 have died trying
to reach the summit. Climbing McKinley is serious business
and can often take 20 to 30 days. The mountain not only is high,
but can be bitterly cold. Severe storms may hit without warning, and winds can easily gust to 150 mph.

**Denali
National Park**

*Park
Information*

In 1922, only 22 tourists came to admire the wonders of
this newly created park. By 1939, there were 2,200 visitors. In
1971, visitors numbered 44,528. In 1994, numbers soared to
490,311 visitors. The best season to come is May, when snow
is still melting, through September, when the tundra turns red
and gold. In between, the flowers bloom in June, mosquitoes
attack voraciously in July, and rains often hit in August. Snow
may fall at any time. Each season holds its own charm. One
road leads into this magnificent wilderness, and private vehicle traffic is restricted.

PARK INFORMATION

Visitors Center   The first building on your right as you enter
the park is **Riley Creek Visitors Center,** (907) 683-2294, where
you can buy tickets for the bus into the park, get backcountry
camping permits, or learn about easily reached hiking trails.
Video programs cover everything from bear safety to how to

safely ford a river. Rangers give programs twice daily and lead moderate-to-strenuous hikes through backcountry wilderness. There is also a visitors center near the end of the park road at Eielson.

Entrance Fees In addition to campground fees and shuttle-bus fees to ride into the park, each visitor must pay an entrance fee. A 7-day pass for an individual is $3 and for a family, $5.

Backcountry Permits The park is divided into 43 units. To preserve a wilderness experience for backpackers, the number of people allowed into any given area is limited and by permit only. Sometimes units close due to wildlife activity, such as a curious grizzly bear. During the peak summer rush, they may be booked for days. Be flexible. Permits are issued one day in advance. (Reservations are not accepted.)

Camping Permits are required to camp at any of the park's eight campgrounds except Morino campground, at the entrance to the park. In addition to the campground fee, add the park entrance fee and a $4 reservation fee per site. The only campgrounds you can drive to are Riley Creek, Savage River, and Teklanika. All others are reached by bus. **Riley Creek** is the first campground past the park entrance, open year-round. **Morino Backpacker Campground,** Mile 1.9, is for backpackers only. **Savage River** is at Mile 13. **Sanctuary River,** Mile 23, is for tents only. **Teklanika River,** Mile 29, has a number of sites for both tents and RVs. **Igloo Creek,** Mile 34, is for tents only. And **Wonder Lake,** Mile 85, is for tents only.

PARK ACCESS

Whether you're coming from Anchorage or Fairbanks, there are economical ways to get to Denali National Park, if you're not driving a vehicle.

Moon Bay Express Daily round trips in summer between Anchorage and Denali. Departs Anchorage Youth Hostel at 7th and H Streets early morning. Returns in the afternoon. Five hours one way. $60 round trip, $10 extra for bicycles. Call (907) 274-6454.

Fireweed Express Departs Fairbanks Visitors Center early morning daily and arrives Denali National Park Visitors Center about 2 hours later. Returns to Fairbanks early evening. $45 round trip, $25 one way, $5 bicycles. Call (907) 452-0521.

Parks Highway Express Shuttle bus 6 days a week between Fairbanks and Anchorage. Nine-hour trip. One way costs $40. Bus will drop you off anywhere in between. Call (907) 479-3065 for times.

In the Park

Front Country Shuttle Bus Once you are in the Denali Park area, you can use the free "Front Country" shuttle bus to get from hotels to places inside and outside the park. Bus stops are clearly marked with schedules. Check with your hotel.

Shuttle Bus Into Park   A trip into the park along the park road costs between $12 and $30, depending on how far you travel. Some tickets may be reserved up to 5 days in advance. Otherwise, you will need to reserve a seat at the visitors center. The buses leave the visitors center every half hour, from early morning to late afternoon. They begin operating the Saturday before Memorial Day and end the second Thursday after Labor Day. Reserve a seat ahead of time by calling (800) 622-7275. In Anchorage or outside the U.S., call (907) 272-7275.

Wildlife Tour   This narrated tour goes to Toklat at Mile 53 or, if the mountain is "out," to Stony Hill at Mile 62. A box lunch is provided for the 7-hour trip. Cost: $51. Denali Park Resorts, (800) 276-7234.

Natural History Tour   This narrated tour goes to Primrose Ridge at Mile 17, making interpretive stops along the way to places such as the Savage Cabin, an historic patrol cabin. A 3-hour trip. Snack is provided. Cost: $28. Denali Park Resorts, (800) 276-7234.

Camper Bus   This special bus carries travelers, their backpacks, and camping gear to campgrounds inside the park, particularly Sanctuary, Igloo, and Wonder Lake Campgrounds, which do not allow vehicles. Backpackers with backcountry permits generally travel on this bus and stay in a campground their first night. Be sure to reserve and pay for a seat when you pick up your backcountry permit. Call (800) 622-7275; in Anchorage or outside the U.S., call (907) 272-7275.

Private Vehicle   You can drive the park road in your own vehicle as far as Teklanika, before the buses start running on Memorial Day weekend and after buses stop running at the end of the season, if weather permits and the road is open. During summer months, private vehicle use is restricted to "inholders," those who own property inside the park at Kantishna. Generally, Kantishna resort owners insist visitors ride a specially provided bus to each resort rather than drive a personal vehicle.

Off-Season Visits   July is the busiest time at Denali. Recreational vehicles that have driven north from the Lower 48 arrive in force by then, and campgrounds and hotels are usually booked. The "shoulder" seasons—May and September—are some of the best times to visit, if you want to avoid crowds. Park workers begin plowing the park road in March and, in an average year, the road is open to the public as far as Savage River Bridge (Mile 15) in early April and as far as the Teklanika River rest stop and overlook (Mile 30.3) in early May. This is a great time to load up the bicycle, drive to either one of these spots,

▼

Denali
National Park

*Park
Access*

▲

**Denali
National Park
& The Parks
Highway**

▼

**Denali
National Park**

*Park
Access*

▲

and enjoy a traffic-free bike ride on the park road. Expect cool temperatures—often below freezing—and be aware that the road could close again at any time due to snow.

Road Lottery For 4 days each fall, beginning the second Friday after Labor Day, the park allows 400 vehicles per day to drive the length of the park road. Permits are weather permitting and if road conditions allow. No one got to use their permits in September 1992, when 3 feet of snow fell on September 12, closing the park road for the season. Permits are good for 1 day. To earn this privilege, mail a self-addressed, stamped envelope to the park headquarters (PO Box 9, Denali National Park, AK 99755) between July 1 and July 31. List your choice of dates in order of preference. Permits are assigned by a drawing held in early August. Only one application per person is allowed.

Kantishna Day Trips Travel the length of the park road with an experienced naturalist guide and eat a buffet lunch at the Kantishna Lodge, before returning the same day. The special Kantishna bus leaves from park-entrance hotels at 7am. It arrives at Kantishna at noon, and you are allowed enough time for lunch, gold panning, relaxing, or exploring. Leave Kantishna at 3pm to return to the park entrance in time for dinner. Cost: $99 per person. To make reservations, write PO Box 81670, Fairbanks, AK 99708, or call (800) 942-7420.

*THINGS TO DO
Travel the Park Road*

A journey into Denali National Park is a journey into the heart of wilderness. From the time you board the bus at the visitors center until you reach Wonder Lake 5 hours later, you'll pass through forest and tundra and, if you're fortunate, see some of the animals who live here.

The first 15 miles of road are home to many of Denali's moose. By early fall, the bulls are showing off their massive antlers and butting heads to vie for the affections of cow moose waiting nearby. They can be spotted either in the forest along the road or as the trees give way to open tundra.

The first glimpse of the mountain comes just about 8 miles into the park as you pass from the forest into tundra. At that point, it looms large even 72 miles away. As the road dips and turns, you'll lose sight of it periodically. It will disappear when you drop into the **Savage River** drainage and come into view again 8 miles later at the top of a hill called **Primrose Ridge,** then again at **Sable Pass.** The first place you can see the full mountain, including its base, is at **Stony Hill** at Mile 62. Here, the mountain is 37 miles away.

Most of the park is above timberline, which in Denali

THE ALASKA RAILROAD

*Heading north out of Anchorage on the Alaska Railroad
toward the majestic peaks of the Alaska Range and its crown
jewel, Mount McKinley, you'll travel along the broad Susitna
River Valley and through the old railroad stops that motorists
never see. Most were named by old gold prospectors. Their
names alone reflect hope, nostalgia, and a hankering for
home and warmer climes: Gold Creek, Sunshine, Colorado,
and Honolulu. The view is especially dramatic in spring during breakup, when huge chunks of ice float down the Susitna
River. Chances are good for seeing bald eagles, moose, and
caribou, so keep a lookout.*

*The railroad, which extends from the ice-free port of Seward
to the Interior gold-rush town of Fairbanks, was built in the
1920s to open up the rich Interior for development. Today, the
railroad carries coal, gravel, logs, petroleum products, and half
a million passengers every year. It is North America's last "full-
service" railroad, offering both freight and passenger service.*

*In summer, the train runs daily between Anchorage and
Fairbanks with a stop at Denali National Park. The An-
chorage-to-Fairbanks run takes 12 hours; Anchorage to
Denali takes 8. Package deals are available through the railroad, (800) 544-0552.*

*In winter, the railroad provides a special service called
"The Hurricane Turn," mainly for Alaska homesteaders,
cabin dwellers, and wilderness folks. The name comes from
Hurricane Gulch, 170 miles north of Anchorage, where a
dramatic bridge spans an even more dramatic canyon. The
northbound train from Anchorage turns around there and
heads south again.*

*This is the last "flag-stop" service in the United States. Of-
ficially, waiting passengers along the tracks are supposed to
wave a white flag, but the train crew usually slows to a halt
at the wave of a hand. Other trains will not stop in the summertime. The Hurricane Turn uses special, self-propelled silver "Budd" cars that have their own engines so they don't
need a locomotive to pull them.*

*Regularly scheduled passenger trains stop only at Wasilla,
Talkeetna, and Denali. In the winter, weekend passenger
trains can be flagged down. Passengers generally include
Alaskans traveling to their remote cabins or homesteads for
a weekend or adventurers beginning multi-day wilderness
cross-country ski trips. Many enjoy a long weekend by riding
the Hurricane Turn out of Anchorage on Thursday, then
catching the southbound train back to Anchorage on Sunday.*

—Kris Capps

**Denali
National Park
& The Parks
Highway**

▼

**Denali
National Park**

*Things
to Do*

▲

starts at 2,700 to 3,000 feet; you get above timberline about 10 miles into the trip. The trees on the tundra include dwarf birch, willow, and alder.

Caribou can be seen almost anywhere along the park road. They are usually moving or grazing on sedges and grasses. Sometimes they can be seen on snowfields, where they flee in order to escape harassing insects, particularly warble flies and nose flies. The easiest animals to find are Dall sheep, bright white spots on mountain slopes. **Igloo Canyon** is a good place for sheep viewing.

Sable Pass, at Mile 39, is home to the Toklat grizzly bear, and this area has been closed to hiking and camping since 1955. But grizzly bears can be seen anywhere along the park road, digging for roots, strolling through the tundra, or snoozing on a sunny hillside. Many are blond in color, easily blending in with fall's golden and red tundra.

The grandeur of the park is evident at the top of **Polychrome Pass,** Mile 45.9. There, you can revel in the spectacular view of a broad valley, lined with tendrils of glacial streams flowing from distant mountains. Turn around and you may be surprised to see Dall sheep on the hillside behind you.

On the other side of Polychrome, you'll pass over the **Toklat River.** Early conservationist Charles Sheldon lived on the Toklat River the winter of 1907–1908. His stay inspired him to campaign to preserve the area as a national park.

The road continues to undulate through valleys and over hills. At Mile 58.3 is **Highway Pass,** the highest point on the park road, at 3,980 feet. Just a little farther is **Stony Hill Overlook** and the first full-frontal view of The Mountain to the west.

From **Eielson Visitors Center,** at Mile 66, visitors can ogle the mountain from the warmth of the glass-enclosed building. This is also where you can change buses and continue on to Wonder Lake, if seats are available. Naturalists offer tundra walks here at different times each day. Eielson is named in honor of pioneer Alaska bush pilot Carl Ben Eielson.

Just past Eielson, weather permitting, you can see the 1-mile-wide **Muldrow Glacier,** the longest glacier on the north side of the Alaska Range. As the road heads west, it drops onto rolling tundra and the land becomes flatter and wetter.

You're getting closer to the mountain, and at **Wonder Lake Campground,** the mountain is only 27 miles away. Wonder Lake is 4 miles long and about 280 feet deep. It is home to lake trout, burot, arctic char, and ling cod. Beaver cruise along near shore, caribou wander by, and moose commonly wade in for an aquatic lunch.

Beyond Wonder Lake lies **Kantishna,** once an active mining district, now home to four luxury resorts, open only to guests who make arrangements in advance.

Float or Paddle the Nenana River

Denali Outdoor Center Located outside the entrance to Denali National Park, at Mile 238.9 on the Parks Highway, the center offers inflatable-kayak trips for full or half days, whitewater instruction in hardshell kayaks, and paddle raft trips or oar raft trips down the nearby Nenana River. This is the only company offering inflatable-kayak trips, which even beginners can safely enjoy. Participants need to bring warm clothes, preferably pile, fleece, capilene, polypropylene, or wool (no cotton), and their enthusiasm. The center provides full drysuit and paddling gear, including helmet, wetsuit booties, gloves, lifejacket, and paddle. The drysuit has latex gaskets at the ankles, wrists, and neck to keep water out and keep paddlers dry. The water is very cold—in the 40-degree range—so it is important to dress appropriately. An experienced guide takes paddlers down the river on half- or full-day trips, usually through Class II and III rapids. The inflatable kayaks are stable and maneuverable. They also are self-bailing, so water that sloshes in flows back out on its own. If you tip over, you just flip the kayak right side up again and crawl back in. Custom, multiday trips on the Nenana River and other rivers are also available. If you are a paddler new to the area and looking for either a paddling partner or information on Nenana River rapids, check in here. This has become *the* center for whitewater paddlers. ■ *For more information, contact PO Box 170, Denali National Park, AK 99755; (907) 683-1925; open May–Sept.*

Denali Raft Adventures They have been running the Nenana River for more than 20 years and offer a variety of trips. You'll be outfitted in either rain gear or mustang flotation suits on chilly days. The suits are like snowmobile suits with flotation and can be cinched tight at the wrists, feet, and neck to protect from water. Trips range from the scenic 2-hour Mount McKinley Float to a thrilling 2-hour trip down Wild Canyon Run, 11 miles of big waves and vertical canyon walls through rapids with names like "Coffee Grinder" and "The Narrows." The 4-hour Healy Express Run is a combination trip. ■ *For more information, contact Drawer 190, Denali National Park, AK 99755; (907) 683-2234.*

Go Horseback Riding

Beaver Lake Meadow Creek Ranch Trail Rides Get a slightly different perspective on sightseeing from the back of a horse. No experience is necessary to enjoy this leisurely walk up Carlo Creek or into the Yanert and Nenana River Valleys. A 1-hour ride is $55; a 90-minute ride is $60. Longer rides, up to 8 hours, are also available. Reservations are suggested, but drop-ins for the half-day and full-day trips are welcome. ■ *Office is next to Salmon Bake, Mile 238.5, on the Parks Hwy; PO Box 73, Denali National Park, AK 99755; (907) 683-1699.*

Denali National Park

Things to Do

NIGHTLIFE

Alaska Cabin Nite Dinner Theater Definitely for tourists, but folks love it. The cast members have lovely singing voices, and the 40-minute performance tells the story of Kantishna, an early mining town at the west end of the park road, through the lives of real-life pioneer Fannie Quigley and a cast of other characters. Dinner is delicious—Alaska salmon, barbecued ribs, side dishes, rolls, and dessert, all chuckwagon style. The servers are also the performers. ■ *Down the hill from the McKinley Park Chalets, at Mile 238.9, Parks Hwy. Follow the signs; (907) 683-2215; winter: McKinley Chalet Resort, Denali Park Resorts, PO Box 202516, Anchorage, AK 99520; (800) 276-7234 or (907) 276-7234; $$; beer and wine available by bottle; MC, V; checks OK; performances nightly, 5:30pm and 8:30pm; closed Oct–May.* ﾖ

FESTIVALS/EVENTS

Nenana River Wildwater Races A 20-year-old festival of whitewater rodeos and slaloms down the Nenana River, usually held on the weekend following the Fourth of July. (See box.)

McKinley Park Fourth of July Celebration Held the Saturday closest to the Fourth of July, this fund-raising event for the local fire department features two main events: a dog weight-pull and a dog-cart race. Here, local residents and visitors compete against the likes of Iditarod champion Jeff King, who also happens to be fire chief of the McKinley Volunteer Fire Department. Two dogs hook up to each cart and run a 2-mile stretch of highway. Dogs who compete in the weight-pull generally come from all over the state. One year, Brutus the Saint Bernard pulled 3,000 pounds. When judges ran out of cinderblocks for weight, spectators were recruited to stand shoulder to shoulder on the cart. For information, call (907) 683-2570.

BEST RESTAURANTS

Lynx Creek Pizza ★★ The opening and closing of this restaurant unofficially marks the beginning and end of the summer season. This is a popular spot for locals. Every year, Lynx experiments with new pizza recipes. A favorite is the New Yup Pie, topped with sun-dried tomatoes, garlic, olive oil, artichoke hearts, mushrooms, onions, and cheese. There are veggie pizzas, Oriental pizzas, and pizzas made with spinach, garlic, and jalapeños. (Save your receipts; eight receipts can be traded in for a free pizza.) ■ *Mile 238.6, Parks Hwy; (907) 683-2547; $; beer and wine; V, MC, AE, DIS; checks OK; 11am–11:30pm; closed Oct–May.* ﾖ

Chalet Center Cafe Make sure to sneak into this sandwich shop at the McKinley Chalet Resort before the "Wildlife Tour" buses return with hungry travelers, or you'll have to wait in a

NENANA WILDWATER RACES

The Nenana River Wildwater Races are traditionally held the weekend after the Fourth of July. Started in 1976, this is the longest-running whitewater river festival in Alaska. The 2-day festival attracts kayakers, canoeists, and rafters from all over the state, as well as visiting paddlers. Events include a downriver race, a slalom race, and a whitewater rodeo, which are all easily viewed from the Parks Highway.

The Nenana is a powerful river, with big, splashy waves and pushy current. The races are held at the beginning of the Nenana River Canyon, where the river narrows and flows between a canyon wall on one side and the Parks Highway and a cliff on the other side.

The downriver race begins with a colorful mass start at Jonesville Bridge, the first bridge north of the entrance to Denali National Park. Paddlers dash for their boats, hop in, and furiously race 4 miles downstream through big waves and swirling hydraulics to the finish line at Twin Rock Rapid.

Twin Rock Rapid is where the real action happens on this day. At this rapid, water curls back on itself to create a churning "hole." If safe water levels allow, this is also the site of the Whitewater Rodeo. To compete, expert boaters deliberately paddle into the hole and do tricks such as surfing, rolling over and over inside the hole—on purpose, not accidentally—and "enders." An ender is when the river throws a kayak straight up into the air. The person who has the most controlled ride with the most paddling tricks wins.

The Slalom Race takes place at Rooster-Tail Rapid, at Mile 239 on the Parks Highway. This is a rapid with a line of big, surging diagonal waves. Before race day, participants spend 2 days stringing wire across the river, then hanging poles from the wire to create "gates" for paddlers to negotiate as they make their way downstream. Paddlers must go through some gates facing upstream and others facing downstream, without hitting poles on either side. The person who goes through all gates the fastest, with the least number of hits, wins. Inevitably, kayakers flip over and have to "Eskimo roll" to get upright again. This is a great spectator sport. ■ Race headquarters is the Denali Park Paddling Center, Mile 238.9, on the Parks Highway, (907) 683-1925. Or call race organizers at (907) 683-2781 or (907) 474-8508.

—Kris Capps

long line. Some folks rave about the rotisserie chicken. We like the sandwiches and ice cream. Afterwards, browse the Goose Lake Gallery and visit with local artist Donna Gates and her husband Jeff King (1993 and 1996 Iditarod Sled Dog champion). Donna's artwork focuses on Alaska wildlife, lifestyles, and dog mushing. ▪ *In the center court, near the swimming pool; Mile 238.9, Parks Hwy; (907) 683-2215 ext 244; $; V, MC, DIS, AE; local checks only; dinners to 10:30pm; closed mid-Sept–mid-May.*

BEST LODGINGS

Denali Princess Lodge ★★ The lodge has everything, including outdoor hot tubs overlooking the Nenana River. Rooms are clean and comfortable, and employees are friendly. Many people staying here are on package tours with Princess Cruise Tours, (800) 426-0442, but the hotel offers a great price during the "shoulder" seasons. A large deck overlooks the Nenana River, and landscaped walkways line the river bluff, a good spot for an evening stroll. If it's windy or too chilly, just move inside and enjoy the same view from the comfort of the lounge. ▪ *Mile 238.5, Parks Hwy; 2815 2nd Ave, Ste 400, Seattle, WA 98121; (800) 426-0500; $$$; lounge with full bar; V, MC, AE, DC; checks OK; fine dining room and cafe; closed Oct–early March.* &

McKinley Chalet Resort ★★ Everything you want is right here: a comfortable room, two restaurants, a lounge, a gift shop, a swimming pool, an art gallery, and an espresso stand. High on a bluff overlooking the Nenana River, this hotel is totally self-contained. You can catch buses into the park from here. Talk to the travel desk for tickets to Alaska Cabin Nite and other activities. A new wing down by the river has rooms with views. ▪ *Mile 238.9, Parks Hwy; Denali Park Resorts, 241 West Ship Creek Ave, Anchorage, AK 99501; (800) 276-7234 or (907) 276-7234; $$$; lounge with full bar; MC, V; checks OK; complete restaurant, plus separate cafeteria-style restaurant; closed Oct–mid-May.* &

Denali Grizzly Bear Cabins & Campground ★ Jack and Ede Reisland homesteaded this chunk of land along the banks of the Nenana River back in 1958 and now welcome summer visitors. Cabins nestle in a birch and spruce grove along the Nenana River. Each one is unique. Fisherman Cabin has a pair of hip waders and a net nailed over the door. The Sourdough Cabin has a handpainted scene of the northern lights. Some of the cabins date back to the early 1900s in Fairbanks. Jack dismantled them in Fairbanks, then reassembled them at the campground. You can also stay in your own tent near the river, in surprisingly secluded settings. Recreational vehicles park on the other side of the campground, near the highway.

Coin-operated hot showers are available. ■ *Across the highway from McKinley Village Lodge, at Mile 231, Parks Hwy; summer: PO Box 7, Denali Park, AK 99755; winter: 910 Senate Loop, Fairbanks, AK 99712; (907) 683-2696; $; V, MC, DIS; traveler's checks only; closed mid-Sept–mid-May.* ⟁

WILDERNESS LODGES

Camp Denali ★★★ The first wilderness camp at Denali National Park was founded by Celia Hunter and Ginny Wood. Both were World War II pilots who first flew north in order to ferry military planes to Alaska. Originally outside park boundaries, Camp Denali became an island of private land when the park expanded in 1980. The tent camp has grown every year, with a lodge and permanent chalets eventually built to replace the tents. Today, it accommodates up to 40 guests in log or frame guest cabins, each with a view of Mount McKinley. Cabins sleep from two to six and come with small wood-burning stoves for heat and propane lights. A gas hot plate for heating water is available in each building. Guests may use outhouses or a central bathhouse that is a short walk from each cabin. Resident naturalists lead guests on hikes and teach natural history. The hikes range from short interpretive walks to 12-mile hikes. Two or three of these are offered every day. Camp Denali is allowed day use of the park road, so guests can spend a long time observing wildlife. Evening programs and special workshops featuring visiting experts focus on all aspects of Denali, such as birds, the aurora borealis, nature photography, or tundra ecology. There is no extra cost for the sessions. ■ *Denali National Park Wilderness Centers, Ltd, Box 67, Denali National Park, AK 99755; (907) 683-2290; fax (907) 683-1568; $$$$; no bar, but you may bring your own bottle; no credit cards; personal checks OK; closed mid-Sept–early June. Minimum stay is 3 nights: $285/adult, $214/children under 12 (per person, double occupancy, plus tax). Families get 10 percent discount if three or more occupy the same cabin. Prices include round-trip transportation from park rail station, lodging, all meals, guided activities, natural history interpretation, evening programs, use of recreational equipment such as bicycles or canoes, and park entrance fee.*

North Face Lodge ★★★ A sister lodge to Camp Denali, this wilderness outpost rests near the remains of an old log cabin. Grant Pearson, an early superintendent of the park and the original owner of the lodge, staked out the property in 1957. Located a mile away from Camp Denali, the lodge has 15 guest rooms, private baths, and, of course, a view of Mount McKinley. Both lodges are now run by Denali National Park Wilderness Centers, Ltd. ■ *Denali National Park Wilderness Centers, Ltd, Box 67, Denali National Park, AK 99755; (907) 683-2290; fax (907) 683-1568; $$$$; no bar, but you may bring*

Denali National Park

Wilderness Lodges

your own bottle; no credit cards; personal checks OK; closed mid-Sept–early June. Minimum stay of 2 nights: $285/adult, $214/children under 12 (per person, double occupancy, plus tax). Families get 10 percent discount if three or more occupy the same cabin. Prices include round-trip transportation from park rail station, lodging, all meals, guided activities, natural history interpretation, evening programs, use of recreational equipment such as bicycles or canoes, and park entrance fee.

Denali Wilderness Lodge ★★★

This lodge is not actually in Denali National Park, but rather lies a short flight east of the park. Once owned by a well-known Alaska hunting guide, the lodge has been transformed into a haven for tourists who want to shoot wildlife with a camera instead of a gun. Located in the Wood River Valley, on the shore of the scenic Wood River, the lodge features gourmet meals, charming cabins with private baths, and an impressive wildlife museum (once the trophy room of the former owner). Now the museum serves as a gathering spot for guests to relax. You won't see Mount McKinley from here, but the country is spectacular. Visiting experts present special evening programs. It is possible to fly out just for the day. ■ *PO Box 50, Denali National Park, AK 99755; (800) 541-9779; $$$; full bar; all credit cards OK; traveler's checks only; closed mid-Sept–mid-May; $275 a night per person includes plane flights in and out, accommodations, meals, and activities such as horseback riding, guided naturalist hikes, and evening programs.* &

Kantishna Roadhouse ★★★

The historic Kantishna Roadhouse once provided comfort to miners and travelers in the early 1900s. When gold was discovered in the Kantishna Hills, so many miners flocked to the area that whole towns grew. They had names such as Glacier City, Diamond, Roosevelt, and Square Deal. Kantishna was once called Eureka and had a population of 2,000 people in 1905. In the mid-1920s, gold fever ebbed. Today, Kantishna landowners mine tourism, not gold. Doyon Native Corporation is the new owner of the Kantishna Roadhouse. The lodge provides resident naturalists for guided hikes, natural history programs, or activities such as panning for gold or mountain biking. ■ *PO Box 81670, Fairbanks, AK 99708; (800) 942-7420 or (907) 683-1475; $$$$; full bar; V, MC, DIS, AE; personal checks OK; closed mid-Sept–early June; approx $540 for two per night; cost includes round-trip transportation from the park entrance area, all meals, guided hikes, programs, horse-drawn wagon rides, gold panning, and mountain biking.* &

SUGGESTED READING

Davidson, Art. *Minus 148°: The Winter Ascent of Mt. McKinley.* Seattle: Cloudcap Press, 1986 (first published in '69). A mountaineering classic!

Greiner, James. *Wager with the Wind.* New York: St. Martin's Press, 1974. The story of one of Talkeetna's legends, bush pilot Don Sheldon.

Jettmar, Karen. *The Alaska River Guide: Canoeing, Kayaking, and Rafting in the Last Frontier.* Seattle: Alaska Northwest Books, 1993. Descriptions of more than 100 different trips for beginners to experts.

Krakauer, Jon. *Eiger Dreams: Ventures Among Men and Mountains.* New York: Lyons & Burford Publishers, 1990. A marvelous series of essays on mountain climbing from the Devil's Thumb in Southeast Alaska to Mount McKinley and the Himalayas.

Sherwonit, Bill. *To the Top of Denali: Climbing Adventures on North America's Highest Peak.* Seattle: Alaska Northwest Books, 1990.

Washburn, Bradford, and David Roberts. *Mount McKinley: The Conquest of Denali.* New York: Harry N. Abrams, Inc., 1991. This stunningly beautiful book of photographs by the premier photographer and early explorer of this great mountain, Brad Washburn, is co-authored by David Roberts, an avid mountain climber and outdoor writer.

FAIRBANKS AND THE INTERIOR

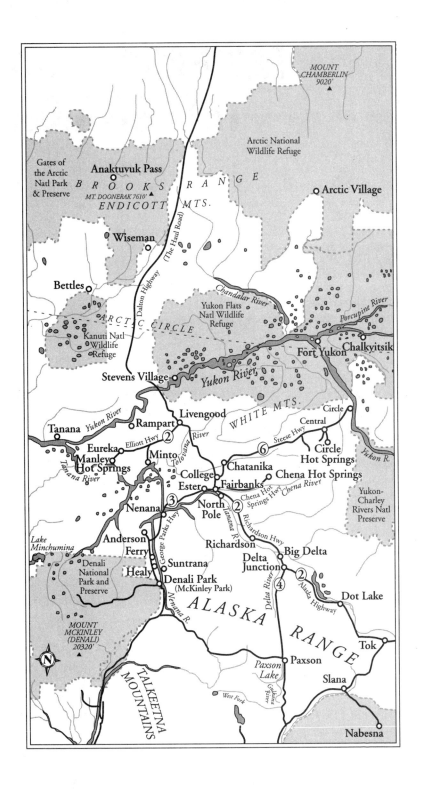

Fairbanks and the Interior

Including Fairbanks, with Nenana and Ester
to the south, and Circle to the north

Think of the Interior as the "outback" of Alaska, where asphalt is rare, and where locals still fight to keep roads unpaved. The few roads that do exist are rebellious. They buck and squirm in an effort to remain untamed. Their resistance (or freeze-thaw action) creates vehicle-launching waves in the pavement called "frost heaves." If you're at all prone to motion sickness, look out.

In the Interior, the major "highways" are the rivers. The smaller ones, like the Chena running through Fairbanks, are the side streets. The larger ones—the Tanana, the Koyukuk, the Yukon—are the freeways. Native people have depended on these waterways for food and transportation for centuries. Today, these rivers still feed the people and connect their villages by boat in summer and by snowmobile and dog team in winter.

Lured first by gold in the 1890s, then by the opportunity for self-reliance, the "sourdoughs" of the Interior tend to be seasoned souls who'd rather take their chances carving a living out of the land than punching a time clock in exchange for a pension. They love elbow room. They hate regulations. They are miners, trappers, hermits, socialites, teachers, artists, scientists, climbers, dog mushers, and general wilderness junkies. You'll find condo dwellers whose idea of "the great outdoors" is the space between the front door and the carport. You'll find cabin dwellers whose idea of "the big city" is any place with a gas pump. People of the Interior are as diverse as the weather. They grow some of the most impressive gardens in some of the most unlikely places. They seem to possess more household goods held together by duct tape than any other demographic group in America.

It's the land that encourages them to do things differently. Something about it says follow your heart. Be wide open, daring, and wild. There are rolling boreal forests as far as the eye can see; great meandering rivers; ponds and lakes reflecting overcast skies like beads of scattered mercury. This is land with no fences.

In the fall, the land shakes its subtle beauty and gets outright loud. Stop-light reds. Emergency yellows. Golds more gold than nuggets. There's nothing more stunning than tundra the color of spawned-out salmon.

Well, there is one thing: a clear winter night when the northern lights shimmer across the sky like curtains of light fluttering in a breeze. Entire barrooms have been known to empty out on nights like these, their patrons pouring onto the streets to hoot and howl at the heavens.

The sky here makes such great theater in part because it's so darn big. The Interior comprises about a third of the state with the Brooks Range at its northern border, the Alaska Range at its southern, and the city of Fairbanks right about in the middle. More than 99,000 people live within the boundaries

▼

The Interior

▲

THE NORTHERN LIGHTS

The mystery of the night—the aurora borealis—may be the Interior's most alluring quality. Some nights there is only a single streak of green. Other nights, the sky explodes with streamers of light like colorful confetti. They shimmer, spiral, and pulsate. They do the hula. They play crack-the-whip. The Interior is the ultimate domed theater, with the ideal latitude, enormous skies, and long, dark winters. Of all the skies Alaska has to offer, scientists from the University of Alaska's Geophysical Institute chose to set up shop here in the Interior, 30 miles north of Fairbanks at Poker Flats, where they shoot rockets into the atmosphere to learn more about the aurora.

This polar phenomenon occurs when solar winds slam into the earth's magnetic field, causing electrons to react with atmospheric gases. The impact sends them into a major uproar, lighting them up like neon signs. This all happens 50 to 200 miles overhead. Color depends on the height of the interaction, due to the varying composition of atmospheric gas. Green, the most common color, comes when the impact is low, around 60 miles above the earth's surface. Reds occur around the highest impact zone. In the winter of 1958, the reds were so intense in the Fairbanks area that residents thought the surrounding hills were on fire.

Too bad there's a logical explanation. The legends are far more fun. One Eskimo tale says the lights are the pathway to heaven, lit by departed souls holding torches to the world beyond. In another, spirits are playing ball in the sky, kicking up colorful cosmic dust.

No matter how many times you may have seen this chorus line of lights, it never gets old. People will rouse each other from deep sleep without a hint of apology. The best time to see the aurora is on a clear dark night around 2am. The lights make dashing to the outhouse at 40 below a little more thrilling.

—Debra McKinney

of this 192,660-square-mile region; 12 percent are Indian and Eskimo. That amounts to almost 2 square miles per man, woman, and child.

In summer, the midnight sun rules. Vegetables become giants. And normally ho-hum people act like Tasmanian devils on caffeine. It's not uncommon to forget to go to bed.

The opposite problem occurs in winter. People forget to get up—or at least they'd like to. With less than 4 hours of daylight in Fairbanks, the body tends to slide into hibernation. Add weather inversions, dead car batteries, and freezing-cold outhouse seats, and you'll see why Interior winters aren't for everyone.

The highest temperature ever recorded in Alaska was in the Interior—100°F in Fort Yukon on June 27, 1915. So was the lowest. It plummeted to minus 80°F at Prospect Creek up the Dalton Highway on January 23, 1971. The thing about the weather here is that you can get both extremes in the course of a day. Warm winter winds called "chinooks" can raise the temperature from 25 below to 25 above in a few hours.

The point is, when you visit the Interior, dress in layers and be prepared for all of the region's various moods. Because when it's good, it's very, very good, and when it's bad, it's horrid.

NENANA

At the confluence of the Nenana and Tanana Rivers, this village of less than 400 folks was originally an Athabascan fish camp before its conversion to a transportation center. Now it's home port to a tug and barge fleet that supplies villages along the Tanana and Yukon Rivers.

It's also the home of **The Annihilator,** one of Alaska's toughest 10K runs. Held in June, this potentially bloody run starts at the railroad tracks and basically goes straight uphill for 1.5 miles. That's the easy part. The descent is so steep, runners start coming down off the mountainside on a fixed rope.

The town's name comes from a Native word meaning "good place to camp between two rivers." These days, it's a good place to stop for gas, a bite to eat, and a stroll back in time. Look for fish wheels in action and their catches drying in the sun during salmon run season. The white crosses across the river mark graves at a Native cemetery.

It was here in Nenana that President Warren G. Harding, the first United States president ever to visit Alaska, drove in "the golden spike," symbolizing the completion of the Alaska Railroad between the ice-free port of Seward and the Interior city of Fairbanks. The old **Nenana Railroad Depot** is on the National Register of Historic Places.

All this aside, the main attraction in town is the **Nenana Ice Classic.** A tripod is set up in the middle of the river after freeze-up, and participants guess the exact day, hour, and minute the river ice will start breaking up in the spring. The first stirring dislodges the tripod, which sets off a siren, which tips a meat cleaver, which cuts a rope, which pulls a cotter pin, which stops a clock, which determines the winner or winners. This annual event goes back to 1917, when Alaska Railroad surveyors pooled $800 in prize money to bet among themselves. Since then, the jackpot has grown to more than $330,000, divided among winners, the town till, and tax collectors. The earliest breakup was April 20, 1940, at 3:27pm; the latest was May 20, 1964, at 11:41am.

Information

Housed in a quaint log cabin with a sod roof is the **Nenana Visitors Center** on the Parks Highway at the Nenana turnoff. You can buy tickets there for the Nenana Ice Classic at $2 a guess (see above). The center is open daily from Memorial Day through Labor Day. For information, call (907) 832-9953.

BEST RESTAURANT

The Monderosa ★ This roadside bar and grill has a reputation with locals for having the biggest and best hamburgers in the Interior. As one Nenana resident put it, "They're huge. Not those shoe-leather, processed things, but the kind your mom would make." ■ *Mile 309, Parks Hwy; (907) 832-5243; open summers, 10am–10pm, daily; bar is open until midnight, depending on the crowd. Winter hours are shorter.*

Nenana

BEST LODGINGS

Finnish Alaska Bed & Breakfast ★ Think of it as a three-story present wrapped in silver paper (insulation) and tied with a big red bow. That's how the owners like to think of it. Carl and Gerrie Jauhola have been building out of pocket or, as they say, "on the 17-year, pay-as-you-go plan." Inside, however, all is finished with warm wood paneling, including some antique planks salvaged from old shipyards along the Nenana River. Décor is a cross between Alaskana and country. A large Finnish sauna is the centerpiece of the family complex. Breakfasts typically include Finnish cardamom biscuits or sourdough pancakes. ■ *Mile 302.1, Parks Hwy; PO Box 274, Nenana, AK 99760; (907) 832-5628; $; MC, V; checks OK; open year-round.*

ESTER

With two gold booms under its belt, Ester was quite the boisterous little miners' mecca in its day. The first boom came with the discovery of gold on Ester, Cripple, and Eva Creeks around the turn of the century, which drew prospectors by the hundreds. The second came in 1936, when the Fairbanks Exploration Company built Ester Gold Camp to support its nearby dredge operation. The camp shut down in the 1950s, and most of the miners moved on. Today, about 250 people live in houses and cabins scattered throughout the woods. It may be the peace and quiet that attracts residents now, but it's the town's former wild ways that lures tourists. The old gold camp has become one of the most popular tourist attractions in the Interior.

PLACES TO VISIT

Ester Gold Camp The gold camp, on the National Register of Historic Places, draws more than 20,000 visitors a season. Entertainment revolves around the restaurant and the Malemute Saloon, after which you can sleep off all the effects at the bunkhouse. Locals say this is the best all-you-can-eat Dungeness crab buffet ($21.95) in the Interior. The camp's hefty feed trough also includes halibut fillets baked in a light wine sauce and reindeer stew. If you can still move, waddle on over to the Malemute Saloon, complete with swinging doors, an antique mahogany bar, a player piano, beer-barrel tables, and a sawdust floor that spills out the front door. The bar specializes in drinks with names like "Moose Milk," "Iceworm Cocktail," and "Dog Bite." *Service With a Smile*, a musical revue heavy on Robert Service, features costumes, songs, and stories from the gold-rush era. The camp offers free shuttle service from most major hotels and campgrounds in Fairbanks. ■ *Follow signs from the Ester turnoff to the Ester Gold Camp; (800) 676-6925 or (907) 479-2500; open late May–early Sept; reservations advised.*

Ester

*Places
to Visit*

Golden Eagle Saloon Just up the road from this tourist complex is where the locals hang out. But don't expect the appeal to be obvious the moment you walk in the door. An assortment of local dogs snooze on the floor. The sign on the front door says "No animals allowed." But the dogs can't read. You'll find them hanging out with their owners, especially during winter months. One Friday night not long ago, two of the local dogs got into a fight. Then their owners started going at each other. (Yeah, there was beer involved.) The four of them made such a ruckus, the bartender got fed up and laid down the law. "That's it! No more dogs!" A hush went over the crowd. "What? No more dogs??" "No more dogs," he hollered, "on Friday nights." Saturday through Thursday is still OK, though.

You're bound to meet some colorful folks here, if you're willing to put in the time and don't mind second-hand smoke. Like the guy who lives across the road, who leaves his front window open year-round. Not for health reasons, though. If someone rings the bell, indicating a free round, he wants to be able to hear it, dash over, and slip in the back door. ■ *Across the road from Ester Gold Camp; (907) 479-0809; open daily, year-round.*

We may as well get this right out in the open. Fairbanks was a mistake. Much to the delight of the state's largest city (Anchorage), the state's second-largest city (Fairbanks) exists only due to one man's error in judgment and the subsequent stroke of somebody else's luck.

Before we launch into that tale, you should know that rivalry between Alaska's two biggest cities is rather animated. Fairbanks may call itself "the golden heart" of Alaska, but to "Los Anchorage" residents it is, and always will be, "Squarebanks." While Fairbanks is the "city on the edge of nowhere," Anchorage is the "city on the edge of good taste."

Now, back to that mistake known as Fairbanks. Athabascans were here first—living, hunting, and fishing up and down the shores of the Chena and Tanana Rivers. Then, in August 1901, a trader from Ohio, one E. T. Barnette, found himself marooned on the banks of the Chena with $20,000 worth of goods, about 200 miles short of his destination.

Fortunately for Barnette, along came an Italian immigrant named Felix Pedro, who hit gold in the hills above his cache in 1902. In the right place at the right time, Barnette set up shop in time for the ensuing gold rush, eventually becoming the town banker. He led the campaign to name the town after Charles W. Fairbanks, a United States senator from Indiana who became vice president under President Theodore Roosevelt. At one point, Barnette was reportedly worth millions.

By 1910, Fairbanks was Alaska's most cosmopolitan city, while Anchorage was still muskeg and swamp. The United States Census counted 3,542 residents that year, with another 7,000 others, mostly miners, in camps nearby.

During Fairbanks' formative years, Barnette ruled—until word got out that he'd served 18 months in an Oregon prison 20 years prior for grand larceny. In 1911, when his bank went bankrupt, the locals were convinced he'd cheated them out of their life savings and ran him out of town. For years, no one knew what had happened to him. There were rumors of his squandering away the town's money, living in style in Mexico. There were rumors he'd died. Well, he did die, but not until 1933. Fairbanks' founding father fell down a flight of stairs in Los Angeles, cracked his skull, and died at the age of 70.

Fairbanks has drawn every kind of personality imaginable, as well as some unimaginable—from hard-driving entrepreneurs to free spirits who followed the Grateful Dead to Alaska in 1980, fell in love with the state, moved north, and never left. Its history is peppered with people such as the late Hulda Ford, who slept on the street and died of malnutrition in 1957 while holding title to something like a half-million dollars in real estate.

Fairbanks is the birthplace of the Alaskan Independence

Party, which has called for secession from the Union. It's also the location of the main campus of the University of Alaska and home to the supercomputer and Alaska's Geophysical Institute. Scientists come here from all over the world to study everything from the center of the earth to the center of the sun.

While Anchorage may have better packaging, Fairbanks is the type of place that challenges visitors to look beyond the obvious. Fairbanks sits on the banks of the Chena River and is surrounded by rolling hills that turn practically fluorescent in the fall. In summer, the Interior is where other Alaskans come for sun. Sure, it can get to 40 below in the winter, but it can also get to 90°F in the summer (the average in July is 63°F). Just a few miles outside Fairbanks, you can be alone in the wilderness hiking, fishing for grayling, panning for gold, or pondering the trans-Alaska oil pipeline with its 1.8 million barrels of oil a day gushing its way to oil tankers in Valdez.

Incidentally, according to one Denali National Park employee, the dumbest question in Alaska asked about the pipeline was this: "All them barrels of oil rolling down the pipeline, don't that make an awful lot of noise?"

Access

You can get to Fairbanks by driving the **Alaska Highway,** the **Richardson Highway,** or the **Parks Highway**. Or you can take the **Alaska Railroad** from Anchorage. Or even quicker, you can fly. There are several scheduled flights a day, starting with **Alaska Airlines**. Once you get to town, there's a **public bus system,** (907) 459-1011. **G.O. Shuttle & Taxi Service,** (907) 474-3847, will haul you around to the major tourist attractions. The **Chena River Shuttle,** (907) 458-8458, runs between Golden Heart Park downtown and the Chena Pump House, for $2 per stop.

▼
Fairbanks
▲

SKINNY DICK'S HALFWAY INN

You already know about the stuff flowing through the trans-Alaska oil pipeline. This place specializes in the other kind of Alaska crude. Notorious for its sleazy name, copulating bears logo, and raunchy jukebox tunes, Skinny Dick's is probably not the kind of place a Sunday school teacher would appreciate. For starters, the joint is a bar, not an inn at all. Dick, however, IS skinny and the place IS about halfway between Nenana and Fairbanks. Décor includes dollar bills stuck to the walls and bikini undies and boxer shorts emblazoned with those infamous mating bears. Skinny Dick is especially known for his Bloody Marys. "B.S. is my other good point," he says. ■ *Mile 328, Parks Hwy; (907) 452-0304.*

One company making the trip up the Dalton Highway is **Trans-Arctic Circle Treks,** (907) 479-5451 or fax (800) 479-8908, which takes you to Prudhoe Bay on a 3-day tour for $588, including meals and accommodations. **Van Go Custom Tours,** (907) 235-5431, offers off-the-beaten-path tours of the Fairbanks area, as well as fly-outs to Native villages.

Information

Stop first at **Fairbanks Visitors Information Center** (550 First Avenue; (800) 327-5774 or (907) 456-5774). Open daily in summer and weekdays in winter. Save yourself a lot of trouble by stopping at **Alaska Public Lands Information Center** (250 Cushman Street, Fairbanks, AK 99701; (907) 456-0527) second. You'll find maps, brochures, articles, and log books on hiking, rafting, canoeing, skiing, camping, photography, hunting, fishing, gold panning, scenic drives, and more. Parks, refuges, Wild and Scenic Rivers—all are featured here. There's also a naturalist program covering songbirds, bear mythology, and edible plants in the forest. The center is open daily in summer and Tuesday to Saturday in winter. Located in the basement of the old Fairbanks Courthouse.

Tips on the Town

▼

Fairbanks

Access

▲

Shoes Many private homes and bed and breakfasts will ask you to leave your shoes at the door. Don't take it personally. It's an Alaska thing.

Bugs Our advice on bug dope: don't leave your room without it, June through August. The mosquitoes can be wicked.

Views For the best view of the city, head to Hagelbarger Turnout on Hagelbarger Road, off the Steese Highway. The best view of Denali (also known as Mount McKinley) can be seen from the west ridge of the University of Alaska Fairbanks campus. For the best view—period—give a call to **Midnight Sun Balloon Tours,** (907) 456-3028, or **Advanced Balloon Adventures,** (907) 455-7433, and take in the sights from about 1,000 feet up.

THINGS TO DO

Hiking If there's one thing the Interior has in abundance (besides mosquitoes), it's hiking—from a 2-mile stroll on Creamer's Field Nature Trail to potentially epic expeditions. Here are two of our favorites.

For a short hike, try **Angel Rocks Trail.** This 3.5-mile round trip takes you along the North Fork of the Chena River, through the forest and up into a maze of granite pinnacles that could pass as castle ruins. The highest point is 1,750 feet, atop a rock overlook. These outcroppings, called "tors," were formed millions of years ago when molten rock pushed upward, but cooled and solidified before breaking ground. The trail begins at Mile 48.9 of the Chena Hot Springs Road.

For a long hike, try **White Mountains Summit Trail.** On a clear day, panoramic views of the Alaska Range, Minto Flats, and the White Mountains may find you bursting into a Julie Andrews impersonation. From the trailhead at Mile 28 on the Elliott Highway, the 20-mile trail climbs just under Wickersham Dome 7 miles in, follows ridges, drops into forest, and climbs to the highest point, 10 miles in, at 3,100 feet. The trail ends at Beaver Creek, where there's good fishing, camping, and even a cabin to rent. For reservations, call (907) 474-2251.

Biking Our favorite mountain bike ride is **Ferry Trail.** This ride begins in Ferry, a small mining town about 100 miles south of Fairbanks, and goes through the historic Liberty Bell Mining District for as many miles and sidetrips as you can peddle. Go at least 9 miles, as far as Boot Hill. For years, local miners have tossed their worn-out shoes and boots upon this mound, creating a footwear graveyard that's a hoot to see. There's no sign for Ferry, which is about a mile off the Parks Highway, at Mile 259.4. Ask locals.

Rock Climbing You'll find routes with names like "Ministries of Silly Walks," "The Nose Knows," "Fat and Fuzzy," "I Am a Climbing God," and "Teenage Wasteland." To find out more about them, pick up a copy of the *Fairbanks Area Climbing Guide* by Stan Justice, available at local sporting goods stores. Or call Stan and the **Alaska Alpine Club** at (907) 479-5017; he can also steer you in the right direction and may be able to hook you up with climbing partners.

Boating The Alaska Public Lands Information Center is an oasis of information for river travelers. In addition, there are "river logs" containing the comments of boaters who've made various trips. Ask for a copy of the BLM's *Alaska River Adventures,* which has descriptions of rivers, including Beaver Creek, Birch Creek, the Delta River, Fortymile River, Gulkana River, Squirrel River, and Unalakleet River. The **National Weather Service**'s "River Information Program," (907) 456-0247, provides information on river conditions and water-level updates, May through October.

Fishing Rivers and lakes of the Interior are a fisherman's dream. You'll find Dolly Varden, arctic char, pike, sheefish, arctic grayling, rainbow trout, five different species of salmon, and more. You don't even have to go very far. The Chena River offers catch-and-release for grayling and fishing for salmon. If you're in the market for a guide, consider **Alaska River Charters,** (907) 455-6827, which offers multiday fly-in fishing, rafting, and backpacking excursions, including the remote Melozi Hot Springs and Iniakuk Lake Lodge in the Brooks Range. **Bob Elliott's** Fly-In Wilderness Fishing, (907) 479-6323, run by long-time pilot and guide Bob Elliott, offers fly-in overnight trips to remote lakes within a 35-minute to one-hour flight of Fairbanks. Elliott has cabins and boats at six lakes, and will supply everything from hipwaders to sleeping bags.

GUIDES/OUTFITTERS

Alaska Wilderness Recreation and Tourism Association A group of more than 200 outdoor-oriented businesses. A directory is available by mailing $5 to AWRTA, PO Box 22827, Juneau, AK 99802; (907) 463-3038; or visit their Web site, http://www.alaska.net/~awrta.

Backcountry Logistical Services For those who'd prefer to lead their own remote trip, but need help with gear and logistics. A self-guided, 10-day raft trip on Beaver Creek with all gear (rafts, tents, cookstoves, etc., but not food or sleeping bags) and an emergency locator transmitter costs around $425 per person, including fly-out. For information, call (907) 457-7606.

PLACES TO VISIT

So you want to get the most Alaskan experience out of this little expedition to Fairbanks as possible? And in the shortest amount of time? You want to take in history, Native culture, wilderness, and dogs? You want to experience the thrill of a gold strike, the chill of a harsh winter, the spasm of innards as you come nose to nose with a perturbed bear as big as your house? But you want to do it from the safety and comfort of a bar stool? No problem. Fairbanks has got you covered. Read on.

Alaskaland This 44-acre pioneer theme park was built to commemorate the 100th anniversary of the purchase of Alaska from Russia. While entrance to the park is free, some attractions come with a fee. Alaskaland is home to some of the state's most precious relics. Among them is the SS *Nenana*, the largest wooden-hull sternwheel river steamer ever built west of the Mississippi. You'll find museums, a famous and posh railroad car, the Palace Theatre & Saloon, the Alaska Salmon Bake, and more. ■ *Located at the intersection of Airport and Peger Rds; PO Box 71267, Fairbanks, AK 99707-1267; (907) 459-1087.*

Alaska Salmon Bake/Palace Theatre & Saloon The best way to fully appreciate this musical journey down gold-rush lane is to go to the Alaska Salmon Bake first and arrive at the theatre with a full stomach. Rick Winther owns both attractions, so the two were meant for each other. They're both at Alaskaland. The salmon bake offers steak with all the trimmings or all the salmon, halibut, and barbecued ribs you can stomach for $20. The show at the Palace ($11) is a musical revue featuring turn-of-the-century costumed performers telling tall tales laced with 20th-century humor. The Alaska fashion show is a hoot. Greasy carharts. Breakup boots. Parkas adorned with glow-in-the-dark duct tape. ■ *Located at Alakaland, at the intersection of Airport and Peger Rds; Alaska Salmon Bake, (907) 452-7274; Palace Theatre & Saloon, (907) 456-5960; mail for both: 3175 College Rd #1, Fairbanks, AK 99709; V, MC, DIS; checks OK; open mid-May–late Sept.* &

Riverboat Discovery The moment you board this sternwheeler, you begin an adventure into the history of the Interior, the lives of Native people, the Chena and Tanana Rivers, and all the creatures and personalities along the riverbanks. You'll float past a fish wheel, a Native fish camp, and the home of Iditarod champion Susan Butcher and her husband, Dave Monson, winner of the Yukon Quest Sled Dog Race. Either they or one of their handlers gives a sled-dog demonstration. Captain Jim Binkley, whose father was one of the original riverboat pilots during the gold-rush era, began in the excursion business in 1950 with a 40-foot motor launch. Binkley now has three sternwheelers, the largest being the *Discovery III,* a tripledecker capable of carrying more than 900 passengers. This is a family business if ever there was one. Of the 20 members of the Binkley family, all but three work in the business, "and those three aren't renegades," he says, "they're just not old enough." ■ *Turn right at Dale Rd exit off Airport Rd and follow signs; (907) 479-6673; mid-May–mid-Sept; twice-daily departures; $37/adults.*

Alaskan Tails of the Trail with Mary Shields Mary Shields may be a wonderful and gentle storyteller, but her sled dogs are the stars of the show: Happy, Kid-O, Big Boy, Little Girl, Flopsy, Uproar, Captain, Rita, Jay, and Solo. "They upstage me constantly," she says. The first woman to finish the Iditarod Sled Dog Race, Mary Shields is the author of five books, including *Sled Dog Trails,* and is the subject of the PBS film *Season of the Sled Dog,* which has aired in 17 countries. In this tour, she opens her home to visitors interested in taking a peek at how Alaskans live. After introducing her dogs and talking about training, racing, breeding, and the like, she turns her dogs loose and they race around, frolic, and get their social hierarchies all straightened out; then she calls for order again. Only she's made a game of it. The dogs know they can sleep in any doghouse they want. So when she hollers, they dash for their favorites. Visitors howl as two or three dogs play king of the mountain on the roof of the most coveted accommodations. Afterward, there's time up at Mary's home, a log house with a sod roof, for refreshments, stories, and photos. ■ *Contact Mary at PO Box 80961, Fairbanks, AK 99708; (907) 455-6469; mid-May–mid-Sept; $17/adult, $10/children, 12 and under; no credit cards; checks OK.*

Ester Gold Camp   The Ester Gold Camp, listed on the National Register of Historic Places, is the place to be for history and peanuts. (See section on Ester for more detailed description.)

Gold Dredge No. 8   This is the best opportunity in Alaska to see an historic gold dredge in all its former glory. Between 1928 and 1959, this iron monstrosity gobbled up millions of ounces of gold from Goldstream and Engineer Creeks near Fairbanks. In addition to mining equipment and tailings galore, you'll see a collection of mammoth tusks and other prehistoric bones found in the area. ■ *Mile 9, Old Steese Hwy; (907) 457-6058; open daily in summer; tours begin every 45 minutes; $10 admission includes guided tour and gold panning (you keep what you find); admission free for children 8 and under.*

El Dorado Gold Mine   Nobody goes away without gold, the owners promise. They make sure you get at least a few specks by keeping their panning area stocked with pay dirt. But first, this 2-hour tour takes you on a narrow-gauge train ride into a permafrost tunnel, where you learn about underground mining techniques and see prehistoric bones up to 30,000 years old. Though the tunnel smells a bit like a pair of 30,000-year-old socks, it gives you not only a sense of being deep underground but also a knowledge of how gold is formed and how it gets to where miners find it. This is another Binkley family venture. It's also a working mine. ■ *Mile 1.3, Elliott Hwy; (907) 479-7613; open mid-May–mid-Sept; train tours depart morning and afternoon; $25/adults, $20/children under 12.*

Creamer's Field Migratory Waterfowl Refuge   This is a gold-rush era dairy farm. The buildings are historic. And the land now belongs to the birds. Each spring, snow buntings blaze the migration trail as early as mid-March, followed by Canada geese, tundra swans, pintails, golden plovers, sandhill cranes, peregrine falcons, and others. Some of the more rare sightings include snow geese and the Eurasian wigeon. The refuge has observation platforms, a 2-mile trail, and guided nature walks. Bring binoculars and bug dope. Early mornings and late evenings are best for spying moose. ■ *Trail guides available at the Alaska Department of Fish and Game near the trailhead at 1300 College Rd; (907) 459-7307; guided walks offered at 7pm on Tues and Thurs; Farmhouse Visitors Center open 10am–5pm Tues–Fri and 10am–3pm Sat.*

Large Animal Research Station   This is more popularly known as the "Musk Ox Farm." Once extinct in Alaska, musk oxen are stout, prehistoric-looking creatures resembling wool-bearing refrigerators on hooves. Yet beneath that shaggy exterior lies the softest and finest fiber produced by an animal. The underhairs or *qiviut* are warmer and softer than cashmere. Operated by the University of Alaska Fairbanks' Institute of

Arctic Biology, this is home to the largest group of captive musk oxen and caribou in the world and draws researchers from all over the world. During summer months, viewing is best in early morning or late evening, after temperatures have cooled and the animals aren't hiding in shade. Bring binoculars. ■ *From the university area, head north on Farmers Loop, then turn left on Ballaine and right on Yankovich; (907) 474-7207; guided tours offered June–Sept. Call for times.*

Otto William Geist Museum Perched atop a ridge overlooking the Tanana Valley, this museum is considered one of the best in the state. The most famous of its exhibits is Blue Babe, a restored 36,000-year-old bison, found in the permafrost by local miners. She was so well preserved that she even had most of her hide. The museum features exhibits on the natural history and cultural heritage of the Interior, as well as the state's largest display of gold nuggets. ■ *Located on the University of Alaska Fairbanks campus; (907) 474-7505; open year-round.*

Georgeson Botanical Gardens Do not leave town without visiting the veggies. Under the spell of the midnight sun, they grow into giants. While you're at it, check out all the other marvels of Alaska agriculture, including the brilliant, jumbo-size flowers. Since this is an experimental farm, there are new things in the garden every year. ■ *Located on Tanana Loop, 1 mile west of the lower University of Alaska Fairbanks campus; (907) 474-7200; free public tours every Fri at 2pm, June–Sept.*

Fairbanks
Nightlife

Santa Claus House, North Pole Heading south? Go find North Pole. Don't be alarmed if you mysteriously find yourself humming "Jingle Bells." This is a town with a serious Santa fixation. Each holiday season, North Pole (pop. 1,600) gets deluged with children's letters to Santa, as well as grown-ups' letters requesting North Pole postmarks on their Christmas cards. Everywhere you look, there are businesses such as "Santa's World Travel" and "Santa's Suds" Laundromat. Light poles resemble giant candy canes, and streets have names like "Kris Kringle Drive" and "Rudolph Lane." But the name of this city was no accident. Back in the early 1950s, when it was being incorporated, the townsfolk considered names like Moose Crossing and Mosquito Junction, but voted for North Pole instead. That sealed its fate as a theme town. The 30-foot Santa out front is a clue you've arrived at Santa's trading post. ■ *Off Richardson Hwy, 14 miles south of Fairbanks; 101 St. Nicholas Ave, North Pole, AK 99705; (907) 488-2200; open daily winter and summer.*

NIGHTLIFE

The Howling Dog Saloon This Alaska classic is so legendary it has been written up in the *New York Times* more than once. One step inside the rustic log saloon and you'll see why. The

Dog is one of the city's hottest dancing spots. Décor by committee hangs from the ceiling—everything from moose antlers to hundreds of hats from the heads of people all over the world. The Dog is also known for its animated, all-night volleyball games out back. If all this recreating finds you low on oats, drag yourself over to the Dawghouse Performance Pizza counter for some of the best pizza in Fairbanks, "made by real Italians from New York." The bar features 17 micro-brews on tap. ■ *2160 Old Steese Hwy, in Fox, about 11 miles north of Fairbanks; (907) 457-8780; AE, MC, V; local checks OK; open nightly, year-round, 5pm–5am.*

The Marlin "This is where all the cool people come," as one loyal Marlin fan put it, himself included. So check your plastic pocket protector at the door. Co-owner and musician Adam Wool of the Groove Diggers and the Hot Licks Jazz Band got into this business for the right reason. "All musicians want to start their own clubs, so they can play," he says. With live mu-sic 6 nights a week, this place gets hopping. The club features jazz 2 nights a week, rhythm and blues 2 nights a week, acous-tic 1 night a week, and rock or alternative 1 night a week. The bar serves Guinness on tap and rotates 5 microbrews. There's a nonsmoking section and yummy pizza to soak up the beer. ■ *3412 College Rd, Fairbanks; (907) 479-4646; MC, V; local checks OK; open nightly, year-round, 5pm–5am.*

▼
Fairbanks

Nightlife

▲

Alaska SaloonTours There's a species of wildlife here in Fair-banks that the tourist brochures fail to mention. It's a noctur-nal creature known for its voracious thirst and tendency to dance with wild abandon with or without members of the op-posite sex. Those who wish to see this phenomenon, but who don't have a clue where to go, call **G.O. Transportation Ser-vices,** (800) 478-3847 or (907) 474-3847. They will serve as your designated driver as you tour the city's most popular nightlife haunts. Cost is $25 a head.

BEST ESPRESSO

Mocha Dan's Espresso On the corner of Geist Road and Fair-banks Street stop at the most popular drive-up coffee wagon in town (mostly because of Dan).

FESTIVALS/EVENTS

Midnight Sun Baseball Game They say people do strange things on account of the moon. Here, it's the sun that messes with your mind. This annual baseball game, played on summer solstice (June 21), begins at 10:30pm and lasts until 2am, with no lights. The game dates back to 1906, when it was originally played between "The Drinks" and "The Smokes," so called be-cause the local newspaper refused to identify their sponsors and give them free publicity. Incidentally, The Drinks won after 10 innings. For more information on the game, call (907) 451-0095.

Golden Days This 2-week festival in mid-July is not only Fairbanks' biggest bash, it's an opportunity to end up in jail. In addition to all the normal stuff like races, contests, and parades, you can buy a warrant for $5 and give the sheriff and his band of thugs a name and address, and off they'll go, guns a-blazing, with their roving slammer—a set of bars pulled around town by a 1-ton truck. Your victim's sentence could be 5 minutes or 25 minutes. It all depends on how good a sport you are. Golden Days commemorates the discovery of gold near Fairbanks in 1902. There's a Felix Pedro look-alike contest (Pedro being the prospector who started all this), a hairy legs contest, a beard and mustache contest, and the Rubber Ducky Race, in which 5,000 rubber duckies are tossed into the Chena River. The first ducks to reach the finish line downriver earn prize money for their ticket holders. For information, call (907) 452-1105.

Fairbanks Summer Arts Festival This is the art community's gift to the people of Fairbanks. The annual event is a study-performance festival, with up to 65 guest artists from around the world sharing their talents in theater, music, opera, dance, ice-skating theater, and visual arts. There are workshops and free performances. The festival is held on campus at the University of Alaska Fairbanks at the end of July and beginning of August. For information, call (907) 474-8869.

World Eskimo Indian Olympics You've never seen anything like it. For 4 days in mid-July, Native athletes, dancers, and artisans from around the state gather here to play traditional games, perform dances, and test their strength and skills in a variety of events, including high kick, knuckle hop, ear-pull, and white man vs. Native women tug-of-war. With the exception of the latter (which white men never seem to win), all the games originate from a lifestyle that demanded (and still demands) extraordinary skill and agility to survive. For information, call (907) 452-6646.

Athabascan Old Time Fiddlers Festival That's right: Athabascan fiddles, as in violins, played with an attitude. Along the Yukon River, 19th-century French, Canadian, and Scottish fur traders left behind a taste for old-time fiddle tunes and the dances they inspire. This November festival of performances and dances is one of the biggest winter gatherings in the Interior. For information, call (907) 456-7406.

Festival of Native Arts Native people from all over Alaska gather in Fairbanks in late February to sing, dance, and hold drumming circles at the University of Alaska. Arts and crafts tables fill the Great Hall. Native artists and crafts people sell everything from ivory carvings to dance fans and beaded mukluks. For information, call (907) 474-7181.

Yukon Quest International Sled Dog Race This is the epic of all sled dog races. Blasting off in mid-February, competitors say this 1,000-mile, international race over gold-rush and mail routes is colder and tougher than the more well-known Iditarod Sled Dog Race between Anchorage and Nome. Starting points alternate each year between Fairbanks and Whitehorse in the Yukon Territories. For information, call (907) 452-7954.

Ice Alaska And you thought ice was meant for gin and tonics? During this annual festival in March, carvers take huge blocks of clear blue ice and create a frozen art gallery, with some pieces so delicate you'd hate to sneeze. This international ice sculpting competition draws sculptors from all over the world. Eighty to 100 teams participate. For information, call (907) 451-8250.

Chatanika Days Witness cabin people unwinding after a long, dark winter the second weekend of March. In addition to a pool tournament, a band, and general merrymaking, this celebration of spring includes an outhouse race from the Chatanika Gold Camp to the Chatanika Lodge. Located at Mile 28 on the Steese Highway; (907) 389-2164.

BEST RESTAURANTS

Let's face it. Fairbanksians are not food snobs. In fact, they'll eat just about anything that doesn't eat them first. The restaurants listed below serve food ranging from pretty-darn-good-most-of-the-time to exceptional-more-often-than-not. Some are recommended above all for their atmosphere.

Bun on the Run ★★★ You walk up to the window of this trailer, order a sandwich, a snack, or a cinnamon bun, and away you go. Bun on the Run. Get it? The bakers are sisters Gretchen Petersen and Ingrid Herreid, who spent much of their childhood in the Bush and learned to bake from their mom. The pastry line-up includes a variety of scones, sour-cream cakes, coconut bars, crème de menthe brownies, and "The Ultimate." Sandwiches ($4) feature turkey, cheeses, and locally grown veggies slathered with fresh pesto and arranged on freshly baked buns. On a warm summer day, outdoor seating is available, so you don't have to take your bun and run.
■ *In the parking lot between Beaver Sports and the Marlin, on College Rd; $; open daily except Sun, May–Oct, depending on weather.*

The Thai House ★★★ This place practically has a cult following among the Fairbanks dinner crowd, particularly those who travel and know a good phad Thai when they see one. Among local favorites are the red, green, and yellow curries, the leg of lamb marinated in a special blend of spices, the

Paramgai, and a chicken dish with spicy peanut sauce. All the important stuff is there: friendly service, consistently tasty food, an assortment of hot oils and spices for turning up the heat when there's a request for "blistering hot." ■ *526 5th Ave, Fairbanks; (907) 452-6123; $$; no alcohol; no credit cards; local checks OK; lunch and dinner, daily (closed Sun).*

Two Rivers Lodge ★★★ There are enough antlers, pelts, bear-skin rugs, and rusty old traps in this place to get a Friends of Animals patriot frothing at the mouth. Built of burnished logs and rough-cut lumber, Two Rivers features a menu of seafood dishes, steaks, game dishes such as pheasant and quail, and some surprises, including the tail meat of an alligator flown in fresh from Louisiana. Grapefruit Pie, a light cream pie made of ruby-red grapefruit, was awarded "Grand Champion" at the Alaska State Fair. In addition to fine dining, Two Rivers also offers fine drinking in the Trapline Lounge. Limousine service, with a television, bar, and sun/moon roof, is available to and from the restaurant for a $125 flat rate, round trip, with an optional aurora borealis–watching tour for $50 extra. ■ *Mile 16, Chena Hot Springs Rd; (907) 488-6815; $$; full bar; V, MC, DIS, DC, AE; checks OK; dinner nightly, lunch on Sun.* &

The Edgewater ★★ Tucked inside the Princess Hotel, this restaurant has the classiest dining atmosphere in town. Though most patrons are tourists, this is the kind of place you'd spend your anniversary. Lunch includes a seafood pasta; a prime rib sandwich, and an open-face seafood melt. Dinner entrees include Alaska king crab, and beef tenderloin topped with Alaskan crab. ■ *4477 Pikes Landing Rd, Fairbanks; (907) 455-4477; $$; full bar; MC, AE, DC; local checks OK; lunch and dinner, daily.* &

Gambardella's Pasta Bella ★★ This downtown Italian eatery has a surprisingly warm, urban atmosphere for a city full of establishments sporting moose antlers and other decorative body parts. Highly recommended for its aromatherapy value alone—it's filled with the smell of fresh bread and Italian spices. They make their own sausages, breads, and even cheeses such as ricotta and mozzarella. Don't miss the focaccia, an Italian flat bread made with virgin olive oil, fresh garlic, olives, and fresh rosemary. They have a wicked-good lasagne with four Italian cheeses, the best pizza in the Interior, and homemade cheesecake. ■ *706 2nd Ave, Fairbanks; (907) 456-3417; $$; beer and wine; V, MC, AE; local checks OK; open daily.*

Pike's Landing ★★ On a warm, sunny day, there's no finer place for lunch than on Pike's deck overlooking the Chena River, as water-skiers, canoeists, and families of ducks pass by. Pike's elegant dining room overlooks the river, so reserve a table by the window. You'll find such entrees as Alaska king salmon, sautéed garlic prawns, and seafood baked "en croute"—crab, scallops, shrimp, and cheeses served in a puff pastry. The crab bisque with aged Kentucky whiskey is excellent. After the main courses, you may find yourself seduced by the decadent dessert tray. Succumb. ▪ *4438 Airport Way; (907) 479-6500; $$$; full bar; V, MC, DIS, DC, AE, JCV; checks OK; lunch and dinner; open year-round.* &

The Pump House Restaurant & Saloon ★★ The exterior of this restaurant looks like a tin workshed because it once was one. The original Chena Pump House was part of a vast system of pumps, sluiceways, ditches, and flumes built by the Fairbanks Exploration Company to support its gold dredging operations. Reconstructed as a restaurant and bar in the late 1970s, today the Pump House has the most colorful atmosphere of any restaurant in the city. The inside is full of antiques, old photographs, and relics. It has a solid mahogany bar and a pressed-tin roof. Belly up to the oyster bar or hunker down to a game of backgammon in the bar. ▪ *796 Chena Pump Rd, Fairbanks; (907) 479-8452; full bar; V, MC, AE; checks OK; lunch and dinner, daily.*

The Vallata ★★ Patty and Sam Galindez are the heart and soul behind this wonderfully warm, sunny log restaurant in the Goldstream Valley. The octagon-shaped building is full of windows and has a rare, natural elegance, particularly with candlelight reflecting off the logs. In addition to all the Italian favorites, the Vallata offers filet mignon, pepper steak, savory veal dishes, halibut, lobster, and crab legs. For those who like it hot, there's Linguine Fradiavolo. "Diavol" means devil in Italian, so keep the fire extinguisher handy. ▪ *2190 Goldstream Rd, Fairbanks; (907) 455-6600; $$; full bar; V, MC, AE, DIS, DC; local checks OK; dinner nightly (closed Mon).* &

Whole Earth Grocery & Deli This natural food store has a loyal following that includes everyone from organic latte lovers to local dog mushers. It's not unusual to see a dog team hitched out front during winter months. Meals include the No Bull Burger, a meatless burger with all the trimmings; the Natchester, a spread made of organic pinto beans and three cheeses on homemade bread; Tortilla Wrap, a chapati stuffed with beans, chiles, jalapeño Jack or soy cheese, sour cream, and salsa. ▪ *1157 Deborah St, Fairbanks; (907) 479-2052; $; no alcohol; MC, V; checks OK; open daily.*

BEST LODGINGS

A Cloudberry Lookout ★★ It took Suzi Lozo and Sean McGuire 8 years to build their post-and-beam, three-story home on 40 acres. On a knoll overlooking a lake, surrounded by boreal forest, the Lookout is stunning. This log-frame home is loaded with glass and topped by an aurora borealis–viewing tower. To get there, you climb spiral steps notched into a 196-year-old spruce log. Partway up is an aerial library stocked with natural history and Alaska books. You then keep going another floor to the aurorium. The Lookout also has a third-story outdoor walkway, a solarium on the south side of the house, and a music room with a grand piano (Suzi is a piano teacher). Skiing and nature trails are nearby, and dog-mushing tours can be arranged. ■ *PO Box 84511, Fairbanks, AK 99708; (907) 479-7334; $$ (you can rent the entire house for $375 a night); MC, V; checks OK; children over 13 welcome; open year-round; no smoking.*

Fairbanks Princess Hotel ★★ Without a doubt, this is Fairbanks' finest. On the banks of the Chena River, this tastefully decorated 200-room hotel is also Fairbanks' newest. A large, terraced river-side deck and lovely flowerbeds make it worth staying put on a warm, sunny day, watching canoeists and ducks paddle by. The deluxe rooms are elegantly decorated, with light wicker furniture and goose-down comforters on the beds. During summer, a boat shuttle stops at the dock and will take you sightseeing or drop you off at one of the river-side restaurants. ■ *4477 Pikes Landing Rd, Fairbanks, AK 99709; (800) 426-0500 or (907) 455-4477; $$$; V, MC, AE, DC; checks OK; free airport shuttle.*

Forget-Me-Not Lodge/Aurora Express ★★ The "Aurora Express" is the name of a train sitting in Sue and Mike Wilson's front yard. A real train. The Wilsons started their bed-and-breakfast business inconspicuously enough in their custom-built home on 10 acres with a great view. Then, in a dream, Sue's dearly departed Irish grandmother told her to get a caboose. No fooling. So she did. "When my grandmother speaks to me, I listen," she explains. The "Golden Nellie," formerly Caboose #1068, has a golden ceiling, heavy velvet drapes, and original chairs re-covered in brocade. A ladder leads up to the covered observation deck. The caboose looked so lonely in the front yard, Sue added two Pullman sleeper cars and a water tanker on 400 feet of winding track. The cars have been renovated with queen-size beds, private baths, and themes ranging from "Billie's Gold Mine" to "The Immaculate Conception," a room with an arched ceiling painted as a blue sky full of fluffy clouds with angel and cherub motif. If you'd prefer something more traditional, the Wilsons' 5,000-square-foot home has several lovely guest rooms as well. ■ *PO Box 80128, Fairbanks, AK 99708; (907) 474-0949; $$; MC, V; checks OK; Aurora Express is open June–mid-Sept; Forget-Me-Not Lodge is open year-round.*

A Taste of Alaska Lodge ★★ This wonderful log home, full of antiques and Alaska artifacts, is situated on a 200-acre family homestead, once an old potato and wheat farm staked in 1946, overlooking the city and the Alaska Range. The 10-acre field out front draws sandhill cranes that stick around all spring and summer. The owners rent cabins on their property and recently completed a 7,000-square-foot lodge that can be rented for weddings and other special events. There are gold panning, hiking, and hot tubbing. Buffet breakfasts include quiche, crêpes, bacon, sausage, yogurt, fresh fruit, muffins, Danishes, granola and more. The owners can arrange sled dog rides and other adventures. ■ *5 miles up Chena Hot Springs Rd; 551 Eberhardt Rd, Fairbanks, AK 99712; (907) 488-7855; rates are $70–$200; AE, DIS, V, MC; checks OK.*

Captain Bartlet Inn ★ If you want a hotel that's truly Alaskan, look no further; this one comes complete with totem poles. Never mind that it's the Southeast coastal Indians who carve totems rather than Interior Athabascans; they still look cool. The main lobby is log, decked with old photographs and rustic doodads. The hotel restaurant, Slough Foot Sue's, has an old-roadhouse atmosphere, including a huge stone fireplace. All 197 guest rooms and suites have a turn-of-the-century feel with four-poster beds, hardwood furniture, and warm-colored wallpaper throughout. Outside, there's a large patio and flowerbed. ■ *1411 Airport Way, Fairbanks, AK 99701; (800) 478-7900 (AK); (800) 544-7528 (outside Alaska); (907) 452-1888; $$; summer, $140/double; winter, $99/double; V, MC, DIS, AE, DC; checks OK.*

▼
Fairbanks
Lodgings
▲

BED & BREAKFAST SERVICES

The **Visitors Information Center** keeps an entire forest-worth of brochures on local bed and breakfasts, as well as a two-volume binder with descriptions and photographs of the homes, owners, and rooms. Or try the **Fairbanks Association of Bed & Breakfasts** (PO Box 73334, Fairbanks, AK 99707-3334; (800) 327-5774 or (907) 456-5774), or the **Bed & Breakfast Reservation Service** (PO Box 71131, Fairbanks, AK 99707; (800) 770-8165 or (907) 479-8165). Not all bed and breakfasts are created equal. Some are handsome log houses that radiate "Alaska," while others could just as well be in suburban Detroit. Some can hook you up with friends offering sled dog rides. Some have hiking right outside their front doors.

WILDERNESS LODGES

Denali West Lodge One hundred miles from the nearest highway, this stunning hand-hewn log lodge on the shore of Lake Minchumina is a visit to another world. It's not a seasonal outpost for Jack and Sherri Hayden; it's their home. They're located on the western border of Denali National Park and Preserve, and Mount McKinley is practically in their laps. Guests stay in cozy log cabins with sod roofs, wood stoves, and birch log beds, and have access to custom guide service 8 hours a day. The list of options includes fly-in fishing at the base of Mount Foraker, hiking, canoeing, wildlife photography, and birding excursions. You can fish for northern pike in front of the lodge. During winter season, the Haydens offer sled dog expeditions on historic trapline, mail, and gold-mining trails, followed by a stint in the sauna back at the lodge, if you so desire. Dinner features fresh salmon or game dishes, barbecued or cooked on a wood stove. The lodge accommodates 6 to 10 guests. ■ *PO Box 40 #ABP, Lake Minchumina, AK 99757; (907) 674-3112; $$$$; MC, V, DIS; checks OK; open Feb–mid-April and late May–mid-Sept.*

Tolovana Lodge The old Tolovana Roadhouse, on the National Register of Historic Places, is one of the last of the original roadhouses in Alaska. Abandoned for 25 years, it was sinking into ruin when Doug Bowers and Kathryn Lenniger bought it in 1984. After rescuing it, they restored the roadhouse using old photographs as a guide. They even painted the outside yellow, just like in the old days, which makes it look quite cozy. Located on the Tolovana and Tanana Rivers, the lodge serves as a base camp for guided fishing and canoeing trips in summer, and dog sled adventures in the winter. Its location next to the Minto Flats State Game Refuge makes this a prime spot for birders. ■ *55 miles west of Nenana, on the Tolovana and Tanana Rivers; Box 281, Nenana, AK 99760; (907) 832-5569; $$; no credit cards; checks OK; open mid-May–early Sept and Nov–April.*

CHENA HOT SPRINGS ROAD

Tacks' General Store, Mile 23.5 If you get a sweet-tooth cramp about halfway up the road, stop here for a slab of killer pie. Try the strawberry-rhubarb with apple-crisp crust. It's big enough to share, but why would you want to do that?

Chena River State Recreation Area, Mile 26 to Mile 53 The Chena Hot Springs Road bisects a 254,080-acre playground of marshes, sloughs, rolling boreal forest, alpine tundra, and turretlike granite pinnacles. Within its boundaries are some of the region's best hikes, as well as opportunities for rock climbing, horseback riding, river running, fishing, and wildlife viewing in summer months, and ski touring, dog mushing, snowmobiling, and snowshoeing in winter months. **Angel Rocks Trail,** at Mile 48.9, is a pretty excursion and a favorite hike among locals. **Granite Tors Trail,** Mile 39, is Angel Rocks squared, with large pinnacles of quartz, diorite, and granite poking out of the ground. The 15-mile loop, with a high point of 3,300 feet, offers access to alpine tundra and "The Tors," a favorite local rock-climbing haunt. The trail begins at the Tors Trail Campground, near Mile 39 of the Chena Hot Springs Road. Seven miles in, the trail is less developed. Keep an eye on the weather; fog makes it tricky to keep track of the trail markers. **Chena Dome Trail,** at Mile 50.5, is a 29-mile, 3-day loop that circles the Angel Creek drainage area and is mostly on tundra ridgetops. The highest point is Chena Dome, a flat-topped ridge at 4,421 feet. On a clear day, the views are awesome, as is the tundra in July, when it's covered in wildflowers, and in late August and early September, when it's aglow with autumn colors. You'll find the trailhead on the left side of the road, at Mile 50.5 of the Chena Hot Springs Road. **Angel Creek Cabin** is a public-use cabin, accessible by a 1.5-mile side trail (22.5 miles in). It's available for rent, but you must make reservations well in advance through the Alaska Division of Parks & Recreation. As a day hike, it's 3 miles to timberline, and another 6.2 miles from there to Chena Dome. To reserve the cabin, call (907) 451-2695.

The Resort at Chena Hot Springs, Mile 58 Your muscles will be thanking you profusely, long after you've dried and gone back to Fairbanks (an hour and 15 minutes away). The spring-fed, indoor swimming pool is kept around 98°F in a building with floor-to-ceiling windows and three hot, hotter, and hottest tubs. The very hottest is a tub kept at 104 degrees, which sits outside on a 2,800-square-foot redwood deck. The dining room, with log walls and a stone fireplace, specializes in beef, seafood, and pasta. During winter, the resort offers cross-country skiing, dog sled tours, guided snowmobile rides, horse-drawn sleigh rides, ice skating, and aurora borealis watching. In summer, there's horseback riding, hiking, and mountain bike rentals. ■ *Mile 58, Chena Hot Springs Rd; (800) 478-4681 or (907) 452-7867; PO Box 73440, Fairbanks, AK 99707. The resort has three seasonal rate structures: the highest is Dec 21–April 15, the lowest Sept 16–Dec 20. In summer, hotel rooms start at $85/double; cabins with no running water, $50. V, MC, AE, DIS, DC, JCV; local checks OK; open year-round.*

THE STEESE HIGHWAY

Built in 1927 to connect Fairbanks with Circle on the Yukon River, this mostly gravel road has been open year-round since 1984, though some maps won't tell you that. The first 44 miles are paved with some nasty frost heaves. The gravel stretch is in better shape, although it can get a little muddy around Twelvemile and Eagle Summits. There's fishing, gold panning, rustic lodges, and great hikes, as well as a motley mix of roadside attractions, such as the **Trans-Alaska Oil Pipeline Visitors Center.**

Opportunities for fishing abound between Mile 29 and Mile 40 on the Chatanika River. At Mile 86, you'll reach **Twelvemile Summit,** elevation 2,980 feet. Then on to **Eagle**

Summit, 3,624 feet, 20 miles up the road. Winds can be strong enough here to rip up road signs, so watch your hat. Down the other side, the mountains give way to hills, which give way to the **Yukon Flats**. When you hit a slab of pavement, you'll know you've reached the town of **Central,** hub of the Circle Mining District, one of the oldest and most active in the state. This hard-working, no-sniveling type of town is home to miners, homesteaders, and others with little use for city ways.

A hard right takes you to **Circle Hot Springs.** If you continue straight, the road narrows, gets windier, and finally dead-ends at the **Yukon River** in **Circle** (pop. approx. 95), which began as a mining supply town in 1887 and was so dubbed because it was thought to be on the Arctic Circle. To check winter road conditions, call (907) 451-5204.

Chatanika Gold Camp, Mile 27.9 Built in 1921, the old gold camp is on the National Register of Historic Places. For 30 years, the complex provided room and board to miners. Now it does the same for travelers and Fairbanksians escaping the city. The camp itself is like an old ghost town. There's a bunkhouse, cabins, a bar, and an Alaskana restaurant with an enormous antique wood stove. The breakfast buffet on Sundays features fluffy sourdough biscuits. The camp is seriously into winter sports and offers bus service to Cleary Summit Ski Area, as well as cross-country skiing, snowmobiling, sled dog rides, and aurora borealis watching. ■ *Mile 27.9, Steese Hwy; 5550 Steese Hwy, Chatanika, AK 99712; (907) 389-2414; rooms $55/double, cabins $50–$65; open year-round, 7 days a week, noon "until the last person leaves." The restaurant serves a breakfast buffet on Sun.*

Chatanika Lodge, Mile 28.6 You'll find this rustic log lodge decked to the teeth with quintessential Alaskana—diamond willow, moose antlers, totem poles, and a satellite dish. You'll find all kinds of things inside to gawk at, too, including a shrine to the owner's Harley Davidson, the best salt and pepper shaker collection in all of Alaska, and donated dollar bills coating the walls. ■ *Mile 28.6, Steese Hwy; (907) 389-2164; rooms $50/double; breakfast, lunch, and dinner daily; open year-round.*

Pinnell Mountain National Recreation Trail, Mile 85.6 or Mile 107.3 This trail offers stunning views of the Alaska Range to the south and the Crazy Mountains and Yukon Flats to the north. The entire trail follows treeless, tundra-clad ridge lines for 27.3 miles, starting and ending on the Steese Highway at Eagle Summit (Mile 107.3) and Twelvemile Summit (Mile 85.6). The trail is defined by wooden posts and cairns. Allow at least 3 days and be prepared for summer temperatures that can range from 20° to 80°F and high winds that can whip up anytime. Keep your eyes open for caribou and the occasional moose or bear. Wildflowers are jamming from mid-June to mid-July. The terrain is a little kinder if you begin at the Eagle Summit Trailhead. ■ *For a recorded trail-condition update, call (907) 474-2372; 2 small cabins, 10 miles from each trailhead, are available on a first-come, first-served basis.*

Tom's Used Bookstore Tent in Central, Mile 127.5

Proprietor Tom Lavender runs his little shop out of a large wall tent with a dirt floor, a wood stove in the corner, and a plywood office tacked on front. Books here start at one thin dime. If Tom's not there, go in and browse. If you find a book you'd like to buy, just leave the money in the drawer in the office. Central may be the last holdout for that sorely missed business virtue known as "trust." ■ *Near the Central Motor Inn, in Central; no address, no phone; open during summer season; hours are whenever to whenever; just ask around for Tom.*

Circle Hot Springs, Mile 8.3, Circle Hot Springs Road

At this hot springs, there's nothing between you and the stars but your bathing suit. As the story goes, the hot springs were "discovered" in 1893 by a hunter tracking a moose. When the hotel first opened in 1930, miners could get a bed, three square meals, and a hot bath for $3 a day. The dining area is so informal you could wander in for breakfast in your robe and slippers and not feel awkward. Be sure to ask about the ghost. In the winter, there's a network of trails for cross-country skiing and snowmobiling. Summer attractions include fishing, gold panning, hiking, and mountain biking on old mining trails. ■ *From Central, Mile 8.3, Circle Hot Springs Rd; PO Box 254, Central, AK 99730; (907) 520-5113; resort has 28 rooms in the old hotel and 12 cabins for rent; hotel rates: $50/single; $75/double; cabins/$110 for two; V, MC; checks OK; dogs allowed in the cabins; open year-round.*

THE ELLIOTT HIGHWAY

It may seem like all roads out of Fairbanks lead to hot water, and it's almost true. This former gold trail dead-ends at Mile 152 (mileage begins in Fox) at **Manley Hot Springs** (pop. 100). This tidy old trading-post town is what you're likely to envision when you think of Bush Alaska. It has log cabins surrounded by great gardens, houses made of salvaged building materials huddled among the trees, and an historic roadhouse serving as the town's community center. You'll meet mushers, miners, trappers, fishermen, and other folks carving a living out of the land. There's fishing for northern pike in the Manley Hot Springs Slough and for salmon in the Tanana River.

Built in 1906, **The Manley Roadhouse** is a National Historic Site and offers room and board and a lot of antiquities, including some of the bar's regulars. For information, call (907) 672-3611. Before heading out on the Elliott, stop about a quarter mile out of Fox and fill your water bottles at **Fox Springs,** which has pure artesian spring water that runs year-round. This is where many locals living without running water come to fill their jugs. The first 28 miles of the highway are paved; the remaining 124 are not. Watch for moose and other wildlife, including spruce hens attempting self-sacrifice in the middle of the road. The road is wide and hard-packed up to its rendezvous with the Dalton Highway, west of Livengood. From then on, it narrows and gets into a little roller coaster action.

In addition to hot springs, the Elliott offers access to fishing spots, hikes in the **White Mountains National Recreation Area,** a local rock-climbing spot called **Grapefruit Rocks** at Mile 38.5, and a side-trip at Mile 110 to the Athabascan village of **Minto,** at the edge of **Minto Flats State Game Refuge.**

Blixt Public-Use Cabin, near Mile 62
This is a 12-by-20-foot log cabin with a loft that sits on a hillside overlooking the Tolovana River Valley, on the east side of the Elliott Highway. The cabin is accessible year-round, due to its close proximity to the road. There's a wood stove, bunkbed, and an outhouse. Spring water is available nearby, but you'll need to treat it. You'll also need all your camping gear. Use of the cabin is through reservation only ($20/night). To reserve, contact the Bureau of Land Management, 1150 University Avenue, Fairbanks, AK 99709; (907) 474-2250.

Tolovana Hot Springs, Mile 93
In an effort to keep the setting serene, use of the natural hot springs is by reservation only. The 11-mile trail is miserable in the summer, since part of it goes through a swamp. It is strenuous in the winter because of major gains and losses in elevation and sometimes icy trail conditions. Winter weather can be severe and wickedly windy. After the ski or mush in, however, the hot springs will be nirvana. Transportation during winter can be arranged by dog team or snowmobile. ■ *Tolovana Hot Springs, PO Box 83058, Fairbanks, AK 99708; (907) 455-6706; 2 cabins are available for rent on weekends, $50–$100/cabin (in peak season, mid-Feb–May, rates are higher); no credit cards; checks OK.*

Hutlinana Warm Springs, Mile 129.3
About 500 yards east of the Hutlinana Creek Bridge, Mile 129.3 on the Elliott, you'll find a well-defined trail running north along the creek for 8 miles to the warm springs, an undeveloped pool about 3 feet deep and lined with rocks. There's room for tents nearby.

Lost Creek Ranch, Eureka Pioneer Access Road
Les and Norma Cobb built their horse ranch in the Minook Valley, 140 miles northwest of Fairbanks, more than 20 years ago. A weekend stay at Lost Creek Ranch is $400 per person and includes 2 full days of trail riding, fishing, and gold panning, and a dip

in natural hot springs. Meals and lodging are sometimes on the trail and other times back at the lodge. Norma's known for her moose stew and sourdough pancakes made from starter that's more than 50 years old. ■ *Take the Eureka turnoff and go 11 miles along the Eureka Pioneer Access Rd; Lost Creek Ranch, PO Box 84334, Fairbanks, AK 99708; (907) 672-3999; week-long pack trips available.*

Manley Hot Springs Resort, Mile 152   The Manley Hot Springs Resort isn't much of a resort, but it's about as Alaskan as it gets—a cross between quaint and funky. The restaurant and bar are in a log building, while the hot-springs swimming pool and hot tub are in a cement-block pool house with a plastic roof. ■ *Manley Hot Springs Resort, Manley Hot Springs, AK 99756; (907) 672-3611; rooms, $80/double; open daily, year-round.*

WILDERNESS/VILLAGE GUIDES

Several tour companies offer culturally sensitive, quality trips to remote Native villages. Many of the tour leaders are village people themselves. Remember always that villages and fish camps are people's homes, not a theme park. Listen. Be respectful. Ask before you take photographs. You are in somebody else's home.

Yukon Star Enterprises   Offers scenic tours of the **Yukon River** out of the village of Tanana for up to six passengers. Lifelong Alaskan Paul Star is an Athabascan and a certified master river pilot who will show you firsthand the land he loves, stopping at friends' fish camps along the way. ■ *Contact PO Box 126, Tanana, AK 99777; (907) 366-7251. The cost is $150 per person for a full day, not including airfare to Tanana, plus $75 per couple for optional overnight.*

Athabasca Cultural Journeys   Fly to the village of Huslia, home to about 250 Athabascans living in the Koyukuk National Wildlife Refuge. You'll be greeted by members of local families who will serve as your guides. You'll experience life in a fish camp. You'll taste Native foods. You'll go boating and hiking, and you'll learn traditional crafts, such as beadwork and sewing skins. You'll learn to read animal signs and how to pick a fish net. You'll hear stories, myths, and folklore. Guests stay in tents in a fish camp during their 3-day, 3-night visit. ■ *PO Box 72, Huslia, AK 99746; (800) 423-0094 or (907) 829-2261; cost for 3 days is $1,650, including airfare, food, lodging, and guide service; no credit cards, postal money orders preferred; tours are June–Aug; in fall, villagers lead hunting trips.*

Arctic Village Tours   The Venetie Tribal Government invites visitors to Arctic Village in the heart of the Brooks Range, as well as to Venetie on the Chandalar River in the Yukon Flats.

When you step off the bush plane in either village, it's like entering a different nation, explains Ben Boyd, who helped put the tours together. "We had to do this to control the influx of people. We don't want to become like that Denali Park. We still live from hunting." If you feel strongly about oil drilling in the Arctic National Wildlife Refuge, the Arctic Village is the tour for you. Whether you're pro or con, you'll get the chance to hear how the Gwich'in people, who depend on the Porcupine Caribou Herd, feel about the subject. Canoe trips, hikes, and fishing trips can be arranged with local Indian guides. ■ *PO Box 82896, Fairbanks, AK 99708; (907) 479-4648 or call Fairbanks Visitors Center. Summer trips to Arctic Village; airfare is $250 round trip from Fairbanks; food, lodging, equipment, and guide service is $150/day. Winter trips only to Venetie, sled dog and snowmobile excursions; airfare is $260 round trip from Fairbanks; food, lodging, equipment, and guide service is $150 day. Credit cards OK; postal money orders preferred.*

Yukon River Tours The Athabascan people of Stevens Village, on the banks of the Yukon River, invite people to visit one of their fish camps. Guests take a bus up the Dalton Highway to the Yukon River Bridge, where they board a boat and head upriver to a working fish camp in the Yukon Flats Wildlife Refuge. At camp, where men once cut wood to fuel the old sternwheelers, you'll see villagers fishing with nets and fish wheels and cutting salmon for drying or smoking, as they have done for generations. Guests also visit a cultural center, put together by the village elders to learn about life on the Yukon and the Native people's annual subsistence cycles. The center includes artifacts, old photographs, and a display of traditional subsistence tools. The tour lasts about 1 1/2 hours, although visitors can arrange to spend the night in one of the wall tents at the fish camp for an extra $10, if they like. You'll need to bring your own sleeping bag and some food, though chances of being offered a chunk of salmon are good. The village itself is about 20 more miles upstream, and special tours can be arranged, as well as tours of the Rampart Canyon. Shuttles for private river trips are also available. ■ *Yukon River Tours, 214 Second Ave, Fairbanks, AK 99701; (907) 452-7162; $; V, MC; checks OK; tours June 1–Sept 1.*

Fairbanks

*Wilderness/
Village
Guides*

SUGGESTED READING

Cole, Terrence. *E. T. Barnette: The Strange Story of the Man Who Founded Fairbanks, Alaska.* Anchorage: Alaska Northwest Publishing Co., 1981.

Huntington, Sidney. *Shadows Along the Koyukuk: An Alaskan Native's Life Along the River* (as told to Jim Rearden). Seattle: Alaska Northwest Books, 1993.

Lund, Annabel, and Kelley, Mark. *Heartbeat: World Eskimo Indian Olympics.* Juneau: Fairweather Press, 1986.

Stall, Chris. *Animal Tracks of Alaska.* Seattle: The Mountaineers Books, 1993.

THE ARCTIC

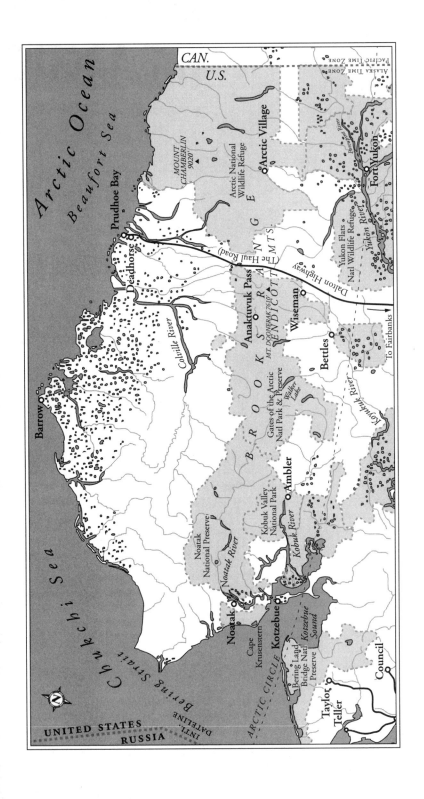

The Arctic

Including Barrow, Kotzebue, The Haul Road, The Brooks Range, and Arctic Parks and Wildlife Refuges

Stretching north of the Arctic Circle (66°33' north latitude) is a wilderness of spare *taiga* forest ("land of little sticks") and *tundra* ("a flat or rolling, treeless plain"). The Brooks Range, that "range of blue light" described by early explorer Robert Marshall, sweeps across the Arctic, separating the forests from the 80,000 square miles of tundra known as the North Slope. Rivers south of the mountains flow into the Yukon River, which empties into the Bering Sea; northern rivers flow into the Arctic Ocean.

The Arctic is a frigid zone, with cold winters and short, cool summers. With less than 10 inches of precipitation per year, it is really a cold desert. Temperatures range from 80°F in summer to minus 60°F and colder in winter. Permafrost underlies much of the region, in places to a depth of up to 3,000 feet. These frozen soils account for the countless lakes and ponds that dot the coastal plain. Thirty percent of its surface is covered by fresh water. Pingos, steep-sided mounds with ice cores, and polygons, patterned ground caused by ice wedges, are distinctive surface features related to permafrost.

Arctic, from the Greek *arctos* for bear, refers to the two constellations—Ursa Major (Great Bear) and Ursa Minor (Little Bear)—that rotate around Polaris, the North Star, the one fixed point in the sky. These constellations contain the easily recognized Big and Little Dippers. As one travels north, the bears loom higher and higher in the night sky. The seasonal change in daylight, which limits available energy, is the single most important physical characteristic of the polar region.

On June 21, summer solstice, the day when the sun is at its greatest distance from the equator, the sun does not set at the Arctic Circle and, due to refraction, appears not to set for 4 days. In Barrow, the farthest north American city, the sun does not set for 84 days, from May 10 to August 2. On winter solstice, December 21, the sun does not rise at all at the Arctic Circle. In Barrow the sun remains below the horizon for 67 days, from November 18 to January 24.

No large cities and only a few large villages dot the region. Barrow is the largest community and a regional trade center. Prudhoe Bay is the industrial center, with its wealth and jobs flowing out statewide. Most communities are small and isolated, with subsistence-based economies. The 414-mile-long Dalton Highway, built as the trans-Alaska pipeline haul road, bisects the Arctic north to south and parallels the pipeline. All other access to the region is by aircraft.

AMONG THE PEOPLE

First-time travelers to the Bush are often surprised by conditions in rural communities. Dilapidated cabins stand next to modern houses; satellite dishes sprout next to racks groaning under the weight of walrus meat; yards seem full of junk snowmobiles and rusting barrels. But it is the lack of fresh, clean water and modern sanitation that most shocks tourists: "Honey Buckets? Gross!"

An Inupiat guide in Barrow once said that the hardest question she has to answer from tourists is: "Why is this community here?" They see a lack of industry, agriculture, and trade. They notice the pockets of poverty and unemployment, and the incredibly high cost of goods and services. Born and raised in Barrow, the guide has no satisfactory answer for visitors.

Alaska Natives have a rich and varied cultural heritage tied to the land. Until a very short time ago (a few decades really), the people lived in small family bands or tribal groups and moved seasonally from one choice subsistence site to another. Some followed caribou; others relied on marine mammals. They all collected and cured furs, fish, berries, roots, and plants. Starvation, privation, and hardship were facts of life.

Life began to change forever around the turn of the century when European adventurers, prospectors, whalers, and missionaries began arriving. Change was rapid—and, in many cases, devastating. People began to settle near missions and whaling stations. Kaktovik, on Barter Island, grew up around a trading post. Barrow would eventually grow into the largest community in the north. Traders brought modern implements, a cash economy, religion, and science. Disease, alcohol, deceit, and prejudice were also part of the package.

The raison d'être for the existence of Barrow, as well as other villages in the "next-to-nowhere," may elude some visitors, but in reality the same question can be asked of many towns and cities in decline in the rest of the country. Gone are the mills, factories, and trade routes that caused many such places to spring up. Perhaps only in the stark reality of the Arctic is the incongruity of location so obvious.

Permafrost and remoteness are major, almost insurmountable hurdles to sewage treatment, safe water distribution, and trash and garbage disposal. Everything costs much more in remote places. Unemployment is high, with poverty as the result. Nutrition, health care, and education suffer in isolation. A subsistence way of living may not mean life or

> *death to the people now, but it renews cultural pride and adds immeasurably to the quality of life in places where a can of soup costs $6.*
>
> *While many villages offer cultural performances for visitors, village life is not a tableau enacted for tourist season. Things seen are often not what they seem. One person's "yard full of junk" may be another's collection of spare parts. Hauling drinking water by hand is both a necessity and hard work, not a photo opportunity. The lined face of an aging Nunamiut woman may clearly convey wisdom and strength of character, but she isn't a photographer's model who can be rudely approached. No matter how humble, village homes and property should be respected by visitors and not stared at as if they were part of some Disney-ish "Arcticland." Poverty is not quaint. Uniqueness is not carte blanche for photographic intrusion. The people of the Arctic have survived in a cold land of darkness and hardship for centuries. They deserve respect.* —Tom Walker

Inupiat Eskimos predominate in the region. Nunamiut Eskimos—*The People*—live in Anaktuvuk Pass. Athabascans, both Gwich'in and Kutch'in, also live in the region. The Gwich'in live just north of the Arctic Circle in Arctic Village, the Kutch'in along the southern edge.

Seasonal abundance of wildlife is characteristic of a region marked by long, hard winters. Much of the region's wildlife is migratory and transient. Two large herds of caribou, the Western Arctic Caribou Herd and the Porcupine Caribou Herd, attract wildlife watchers from around the world. The smaller Central Arctic Caribou Herd sometimes frequents Prudhoe Bay.

The Arctic is the last great stretch of wilderness on the face of the earth. As Justice William O. Douglas said in 1960, "The Arctic has a call that is compelling. The distant mountains make one want to go on and on over the next ridge and over the one beyond. This last American wilderness must remain sacrosanct."

The Midnight Sun

Here's the chance to experience a whole new life, unrestrained by clocks and darkness. Forget 9-to-5 and the traditional times to eat. Go on "Eskimo Time." Get up at noon. Stay up until 4am. Don't sleep at all. Continuous light has a tremendous impact on our "natural rhythms." Living unrestrained by clocks and darkness can have a profound effect upon a person.

Access

One road takes you from Fairbanks into the Arctic—the Dalton Highway, also known as the old "Haul Road." (See below.) The airlines with scheduled flights to and within the Arctic are as follows. **Alaska Airlines,** (800) 426-0333, has jet service to Barrow, Deadhorse/Prudhoe Bay, and Kotzebue. **Cape Smythe Air,** (907)852-8333, in Barrow can take you to coastal villages and other destinations. **Frontier Flying Service,** (907) 474-0014, in Fairbanks regularly flies to Anaktuvuk Pass, Bettles, and Kaktovik. **Larry's Flying Service,** (907) 474-9169, in Fairbanks flies to Anaktuvuk Pass and Arctic Village. **Warbelow's Air Ventures,** (907) 474-0518, in Fairbanks goes to Ambler, Kobuk, and Shungnak and also flies charters and tours. **Wright Air Service,** (907) 474-0502, in Fairbanks flies to Anaktuvuk Pass, Arctic Village, and Bettles.

Those who fly strictly air charters are **Arctic Air Alaska,** (907) 488-6115, with Sandy Hamilton in Salcha, Alaska, but with charters to all Brooks Range destinations; **40-Mile Air,** (907) 474-0018 at the Fairbanks International Terminal and (907) 659-2344 at Deadhorse Airport, with charters and North Slope Tours; and **Yukon Air Service,** (907) 479-3792, with Don Ross in Fairbanks, who has made the Arctic National Wildlife Refuge a specialty.

Ambler Air Service, (800) 720-2121 in Alaska or (907) 445-2157, is the very best small-town air service, especially if you are flying to Kobuk National Park. It is located in the small Inupiat village of Ambler. David Rue has been running this flight service since 1976. He knows the area along the Kobuk River as well as anyone. His pilot, Scott Jones, is affable and unflappable—just the qualities that make for a good bush pilot. These folks fly on floats, wheels, and skis and do a lot of support work for river rafters, fishermen, and government agencies. They charter and also have limited scheduled service to Kobuk River villages and Fairbanks. They offer very competitive rates.

Note: Many Bush villages ban alcohol importation and possession. Check with air carriers before transporting alcohol in any quantity. "Any quantity" means more than a few days of personal use.

BARROW

More than 300 miles above the Arctic Circle, this is the northernmost settlement in the United States, and it feels like it. Take a ride out to Point Barrow and you've gone as far north as dry land will allow. The 1,300 miles still separating you from the North Pole is ocean, clogged with ice and populated by polar bears, whales, walrus, seals, and other mythic critters. This is not just the end of the road, it's the absolute edge of the planet.

POLAR BEAR ALERT

While you rest in your hotel room, check out the message channel on the television (Channel 20). It displays local notices and advertisements while the radio station (KBRW, 680 AM) provides the audio. It never hurts to tune in before you go for a long walk on the beach, just in case there's a polar bear warning in effect. Roughly half the world's 20,000 polar bears pay an occasional visit along Alaska's Arctic coast. Spring and fall are their favorite seasons to drop in on Barrow, and the police always maintain a bear patrol on Halloween to protect little trick-or-treaters.

Speaking of bears, how would you like to join the Polar Bear Club? You don't have to stare down the Arctic's most fearsome critter at close range to qualify. No, just find an opening among the ice floes and dive in. Fran Tate, owner of Pepe's North of the Border Restaurant, will arrange to verify your total submersion in the Arctic Ocean. She'll also call the paramedics if you don't rocket back to the beach. For your pain and suffering (and a small fee), you will earn a certificate, an embroidered patch, and lifetime membership in one of the most exclusive clubs in America.

—David Harding

Barrow

Visitors to Barrow encounter reminders of this marginal planetary location at every turn. Satellite dishes seem to point at the ground as they track communications satellites in orbit over the Lower 48. Tour companies issue parkas to arriving guests in mid-July. Even the concepts of "day" and "night" must be renegotiated out here on the edge. When you're sitting on top of the world, 84 days pass between a single sunrise in May and the next sunset in August.

The Inupiat Eskimos have inhabited the Arctic coast for more than a millennium. Even with the advent of a cash economy, hunting remains an essential cultural activity. The most important hunt of all occurs in the spring and fall, when bowhead whales migrate along the coast. The **Nalukataq Festival** in June celebrates a successful spring whaling season. The Inupiat equivalent of Christmas, it attracts relatives from the outlying villages and can last for several days.

The Inupiat have pursued economic development with the same aggressive pride that keeps their traditional customs and language alive. In response to the discovery of America's largest oilfield at Prudhoe Bay, the Inupiat formed a regional government, the North Slope Borough, to guarantee their voice in development decisions.

Information

The North Slope Borough's **Public Information Office,** (907) 852-0215, can give you accurate information on the schedule of local events.

THINGS TO DO

Extreme Tours Gets you out of town on the back of a four-wheel-drive, all-terrain vehicle. Guided rides along the coast cover birds, bones, and botany of the area. Call (907) 852-2375.

Arctic Mushing Tours Offers dogsled rides year-round. Call (907) 852-6874.

Border Ventures Has bikes for rent, if cycling on gravel roads is your thing. Call (907) 852-2010.

BEST RESTAURANTS

Pepe's North of the Border Restaurant ★ A stop here is *de rigueur*. Mexican and American food are on the menu, but the

ESKIMO ETIQUETTE

Do's.

If you can manage a few words of the Inupiaq language, you're assured a warm smile in return. Try these words for starters: Maktak *(pronounced "muk-tuk") is the thick skin and a few inches of fat from the bowhead whale. It is a staple of the Inupiat diet.* Quyanak *(koy-ah-nuk) means "thank you." Or get fancy with* Quyanakpak *(coy-ah-nuk-puk), "thank you very much."* Uutukuu *(oo-tuh-koo) is a good word to know in case you are offered a helping of maktak dipped in seal oil. It means "just a little bit."* Aari-gaa *(ah-dee-gah) means "that's good!"*

Don'ts.

It's not polite to be offended by the dead animal parts drying on racks or lying around people's yards. Depending on the time of year, you're liable to encounter slabs of whale or walrus meat, strips of caribou, whole seals, or strings of ducks. Keep in mind that animals represent much more than food here. If you're a die-hard animal rights activist, it's best to swallow your opinions. An elder once described her first visit to a zoo in the Lower 48. She was a child at the time, and she couldn't understand why all the animals were caged. "It's not right," she said. "Someone should take them home and eat them." She felt much more comfortable when she visited a farm. At least there the animals had a useful purpose.

—David Harding

real pizazz at Pepe's is its owner, Fran Tate. Approaching the age when most folks retire, Fran is a dynamo in a mini-skirt. She's also a consummate promoter of Barrow, which landed her on the *Tonight Show* a few years back. During her 15 minutes of fame, she presented an *oosik* to Johnny Carson. "What's an oosik?" Johnny asked, as he beheld the 2-foot-long bone. Fran replied, "Let's just say every male walrus has one." In town.

Brower's Cafe For a good view and sense of history, stop in at Brower's Cafe, located in a historic building on the far side of town, an area called Browerville. It's the site of the whaling and trading station operated before the turn of the century by Charles Brower, a Yankee whaler who settled here in 1882, learned the language, married a local woman, and established what has become one of the largest Eskimo families in Barrow. Brower's Cafe has a nice ocean view, and after your meal you can photograph the arched whale jawbones and *umiak* (traditional whaling boat) out front. In town.

BEST LODGINGS

Top of the World Hotel ★★ It's not the only hotel in town, but it has the best location and serves as the hub of visitor activity. Ask for a room in the new wing. Even better, snag Room 150 for the best ocean view. Walking maps and lists of activities are available at the front desk. The hotel operates local sightseeing excursions year-round, and in the summer months hosts a daily Inupiat cultural presentation of song, dance, games, and crafts in a large tent on the beach. Even if you're fairly independent, the hotel's package is still the best way to get oriented. Call (800) 882-8478.

Kotzebue

KOTZEBUE

A regional service hub, Kotzebue (pop. 3,000) is located on a 3-mile-long spit jutting into Kotzebue Sound. This predominately Inupiat village serves as the trade center for 10 northwestern villages. Summer tours see Eskimo blanket tosses and other cultural activities. The **NANA Museum of the Arctic** in Kotzebue is a highlight. The best large museum anywhere north of the Arctic Circle, it features Northwest Coast Inupiat cultural history, displays, dioramas, and live performances unmatched statewide, (907)442-3747.

Best lodgings are at the **Nullagvik Hotel,** Box 336, Kotzebue, AK 99752; (907) 442-3331. The best tours are with **NANA Tour Arctic,** (907) 442-3301. While in town, tune in to the local public radio station, KOTZ, 720 khZ; PO Box 78, Kotzebue, AK 99752. The *Arctic Sounder* is the biweekly regional newspaper serving western Alaska, PO Box 290, Kotzebue, AK 99752.

Expect high prices throughout the Arctic. Air charter and

scheduled flights provide access to Kotzebue, surrounding villages, the eastern Brooks Range, Kobuk Valley National Park, Noatak National Preserve, Cape Krusenstern National Monument, and Selawik National Wildlife Refuge.

THE JAMES DALTON HIGHWAY

aka The Haul Road

If you want to drive to the Arctic, there's only one way. Head north along the old North Slope Haul Road, originally built in 1974 as part of the construction of the 800-mile-long trans-Alaska oil pipeline, running from Prudhoe Bay to the port of Valdez. Officially opened to the public in 1995, the route is now called the Dalton Highway, although most Alaskans still call it "The Haul Road."

The road begins in forested rolling hills at Mile 73 on the Elliott Highway, crosses the inclined bridge over the Yukon, and runs 414 miles from the Yukon River over the Brooks Range to Prudhoe Bay on the Arctic coast. The highway was named for James William Dalton, an engineer involved in pioneer Arctic oil exploration. The only services and fuel stops between the Elliott Highway and Prudhoe Bay are located at the Yukon River, **Yukon Ventures Alaska,** (907) 655-9001, and at Coldfoot, Mile 175, where **Coldfoot Services and Arctic Acres Inn,** (907) 678-5201, has the best truck stop, albeit the only truck stop, north of the Arctic Circle.

Road travelers should be well prepared for emergencies and carry food and survival gear, two *mounted* spare tires, extra gasoline, and spare parts. The Dalton Highway alternates between mud and thick dust. Drive slowly and with headlights on at all times. Give way to large trucks. *Watch for flying rocks and tire blowouts!*

The road north from Coldfoot traverses the Brooks Range and the North Slope tundra and has phenomenal vistas of mountains, tundra, and wildlife. Moose are commonly seen south of the mountains, Dall sheep in Atigun Pass, and caribou, grizzlies, musk oxen, waterfowl, and occasionally wolves in the north. Even though the road opened "officially" to the public in 1995, streams along the road have long been overfished. Fish in frigid Arctic waters grow slowly and are never in overabundance. One fish caught near Toolik was *46 years old*, and it was a midget by Alaska standards. *(Note: Catch-and-release should be the byword here.)*

Interesting stops north of Coldfoot are numerous and include **Wiseman,** turnoff at Mile 188.6; **Mount Sukakpak,** best view from a pond at Mile 207.5; the **Chandalar Shelf,** Mile 237.1; **Atigun Pass,** Mile 244.7; and almost anywhere from the first **Atigun River** crossing, at Mile 253.1, to **Slope Mountain Camp,** at Mile 305.7 (492 km). Watch for wildlife all the way to **Prudhoe Bay,** Mile 414.

The last 90 miles into **Deadhorse** is often very rocky and dusty. Deadhorse/Prudhoe Bay is the end of the line, where the road meets the ice of the sea. Access to the oil fields at Prudhoe Bay and Kuparuk is tightly controlled. Check at hotels for oil-field tours: **Prudhoe Bay Hotel,** (907) 659-2449, and **Arctic Caribou Inn,** (907) 659-2368.

Although in many Alaskans' opinions the pipeline paralleling the road is Alaska's greatest eyesore, marring an otherwise beautiful landscape, one has to admire the 800-mile-long, $8 billion project as an engineering marvel. On average, 1.8 million barrels of oil pass through the pipeline each day.

If you don't have the time or the vehicle to go all the way, but want to experience part of the road, go on the best little driving tour to the Arctic Circle around, offered by **Northern Alaska Tour Company** in Fairbanks, (907) 474-8600. A narrated drive in small vans along the old haul road provides travelers with limited time a look at the sub-arctic forests and tundra, a visit to an Athabascan fish camp, and a ceremonious crossing of the Arctic Circle. They also have a 3-day trip all the way up the road to Prudhoe Bay, as well as flying and cultural tours.

THE BROOKS RANGE

Including Arctic national parks and wildlife refuges

Stretching from the Yukon border almost to the Chukchi Sea, these mountains separate the muskeg and forest of Interior Alaska from the treeless tundra expanses of the Arctic Coast. The peaks and valleys of this northern extension of the Rocky Mountains, with elevations from 4,000 to 9,000 feet, spawn numerous spectacular rivers and streams, flowing both north and south, and support fish and wildlife in, at times, astonishing numbers.

Impressive peaks include **Mount Igikpak** (8,510 feet), the highest point in the western Brooks Range; and **Mount Chamberlin** (9,020 feet) and **Mount Michelson** (8,855 feet), the two tallest peaks, which are located in the eastern Brooks Range and within the Arctic National Wildlife Refuge. The **Arrigetch Peaks,** along with **Mount Doonerak** (7,610 feet), are impressive spires in the central range. **Boreal Mountain** and **Frigid Crags,** rising on either side of the North Fork of the Koyukuk, are Robert Marshall's **"Gates of the Arctic."**

Temperatures vary from about 85°F in summer to minus 60°F in winter. Summer offers 24 hours of daylight, wind, and mosquitoes. Winter offers 24 hours of darkness, wind, and ice. This is real wilderness, with miles of great, uninhabited expanses. Bush travelers should be self-reliant and skillful. Those who come prepared can choose from a plethora of activities,

MOSQUITOES

The Arctic from mid-June to early August is a good place to avoid if you fear mosquitoes. Mosquitoes are often thought of as tropical, but some of the densest concentrations are found in northern regions. Permafrost traps water on the surface, providing prime insect hatcheries. How bad are the mosquitoes? In July 1995, one scientist near Toolik slapped the back of another, killing in a single blow 270 mosquitoes!

A biologist estimated that the North Slope's summer mosquito population outweighs the biomass of all its other living creatures. At least 27 species of mosquito are found in Alaska, measuring from an eighth- to a quarter-inch long. Only female mosquitoes bite; males buzz around looking for mates. The constant humming of mosquitoes, beating their wings more than 300 times a second, disturbs some people more than actual bites. Mosquitoes are capable of flying at 30 mph, but are fragile and easily grounded, even by a light breeze. Cold weather also grounds or kills them. Warm, still mornings and evenings are prime time for mosquitoes.

Female mosquitoes need blood protein to manufacture eggs. They home in on their prey by using their twin antennae to sense warm, moist air rising from the body. When they bite, they inject saliva that contains a chemical to prevent blood clotting and improve blood flow. It is the victim's allergic reaction to saliva that makes mosquito bites itch. Once her abdomen is full, the female mosquito flies off—often before the victim can feel the bite. She then rests for several days, digesting the meal, before laying between 75 and 500 eggs. In summer, campers, hikers, floaters, and fishermen will have intimate contact with mosquitoes, but even those on tours to places such as Barrow, Kotzebue, and Prudhoe Bay will encounter at least some biting insects.

Mosquito sprays, lotions, and pumps containing the active ingredient DEET are the most effective and widely used repellents in Alaska. However, formulas containing 100 percent DEET (short for N,N diethyl-m-toluamide) may pose some neurological risk to humans, especially children and infants. Experts are divided on the actual risk. Many health experts recommend using only repellents with formulations of less than 30 percent DEET. DEET-free repellents made from citronella are growing in use. Naturapel is a popular alternative. Some people swear by Avon's Skin-So-Soft bath oil, which contains pennyroyal. Mosquito coils made of pyrethrum, Buhach powders, and citronella candles are also widely used. "Bug jackets" or bug suits are the choice of a few trekkers. Headnets, gloves, and long-sleeved shirts offer time-tested protection.

> *Casual travelers to larger villages or destinations need to take along nothing more than a small bottle of repellent or perhaps a lightweight headnet. However, no one should venture cross-country without ample protection. Mosquitoes are capable of "hearing" and detecting motion as well as sensing warmth and moisture. Hot, sweaty backpackers staggering across uneven tundra or through brushy terrain are ideal targets. On one such trek, a friend took a picture of me in a "fur coat." The "coat" was made of bugs.*
>
> —Tom Walker

ranging from river rafting to mountain climbing.

There are far more parks and refuges in the Arctic and in the Brooks Range than listed here—and each is a gem. Whole books have been written about the parks, rivers, and refuges and the exquisite country that surrounds them. The following is a small sample of some of the most popular. Even then, it will be a rare day when you see anyone else of the human species.

Information

The best places to obtain initial information on the Arctic's national parks and wildlife refuges are the **Alaska Public Lands Information Centers** in Anchorage, at 605 W Fourth Avenue, Suite 105, (907) 271-2737; and in Fairbanks, at 250 Cushman Street, (907) 456-0527.

GATES OF THE ARCTIC NATIONAL PARK AND PRESERVE

Astride 200 miles of the central Brooks Range, this park covers about 8.4 million acres of mountains, valleys, and rivers, an area four times the size of Yellowstone National Park. Access is via plane from Bettles, Fairbanks, or Kotzebue. Road access is via the Dalton Highway.

Unlike most parks, this park, established in 1980, is completely undeveloped. There are no visitor facilities of any kind within the park. Visitors must seek their own trails and adventures. But those who do will enjoy pristine territory in which to camp, canoe, climb, fish, photograph, river raft, and view wildlife. Winter activities include cross-country skiing and dog mushing.

Hiking often is difficult. The tundra is covered with grass tussocks, knots of Arctic cottongrass that twist and turn under foot. River crossings can be dangerous and difficult. Frostbite in winter and hypothermia in summer are real threats. It is important to check in with park rangers in Bettles, Coldfoot, or Fairbanks prior to embarking. Consult with those who have local knowledge and file a trip plan—you'll be glad you did,

▼

The Brooks Range

Gates of the Arctic

▲

should a search and rescue operation be necessary. ■ *For more information, contact Superintendent, Gates of the Arctic National Park and Preserve, PO Box 74680, Fairbanks, AK 99707; (907) 456-0281.*

WILDERNESS HIKE

North Fork of the Koyukuk to the Village of Anaktuvuk Pass via Ernie Creek
Ernie Creek was named by Robert Marshall for Ernie Johnson, a Finnish prospector and trapper who explored much of the region just after the turn of the century. This trek is for the *hardy* and *capable* who want to sample the essence of the Brooks Range. Novices are advised to hire a guide. The trip can begin at a fly-in drop-off point near Gates of the Arctic National Park and end in Anaktuvuk Pass or vice versa. The route traverses **Ernie Pass** and **Valley of the Precipices.** Expect to see Dall sheep and to encounter bears, perhaps even wolves. Contact the national park office listed above.

WILDERNESS LODGES

Iniakuk Lake Wilderness Lodge
This beautiful lodge on the shores of Iniakuk Lake is the best in all the Arctic. It is small, with 12 guests maximum. Guests enjoy fishing, hiking, canoeing, wildlife watching, flightseeing, birding, and photography, or simply relaxing in the hand-crafted lodge. Long-time Alaskan and owner Pat Gaedeke offers gourmet meals and fresh-baked goods. Pat also offers guided and unguided stays at two well-maintained cabins on the Alatna River within Gates of the Arctic National Park. River rafting is also available. This lodge is fly-in only and accessible by a 30-minute flight from Bettles, Alaska. ■ *Iniakuk Lake Wilderness Lodge, PO Box 80424, Fairbanks, AK 99708; (907) 479-6354; Email 102021.3553 @compuserve.com; rates are $450/day at the main lodge, $275/day for guided cabin stays, and $195/day for unguided river cabin stays; airfare not included.*

KOBUK VALLEY NATIONAL PARK

The Kobuk River flows through a wide, forested valley between the Baird and Waring Mountains. The river meanders through spruce, birch, and aspen forests and past several Inupiat villages before emptying into Kotzebue Sound. The boundaries enclose 1,726,500 acres of undeveloped parkland.

Just 75 miles east of Kotzebue, this park boasts two Wild and Scenic Rivers: the Kobuk and the Salmon. Villagers along the river are dependent on subsistence hunting and fishing for much of their livelihood, so visitors are often surprised to find that hunting continues within the boundaries of this park. Private property along the river should be respected. Sport fishing for grayling, pike, char, and sheefish is often outstanding. The vast Western Arctic Caribou Herd crosses the Kobuk in early September en route to southern wintering grounds. Floaters have found themselves amid large herds swimming the river. ■ *For information, contact Kobuk Valley National Park, PO Box 1029, Kotzebue, AK 99752; (907) 442-3890.*

The Great Kobuk Sand Dunes, which cover 25 square miles, inland from the south bank of the river, are the park's most notable feature. These dunes, up to 125 feet high, would look more at home in an Edward Abbey novel than they do in Arctic Alaska. Travelers can hire local guides with boats, float down the Kobuk on their own, or be dropped off by plane. The dunes are accessible from the river by a short hike up Kavit Creek. Watch for bears. ■ *For information, contact Superintendent, Kobuk Valley National Park, PO Box 1029, Kotzebue, AK 99752; (907) 442-3890.*

ARCTIC NATIONAL WILDLIFE REFUGE

Truly America's Serengeti, the most northern of all our national refuges has been much in the news lately. Essentially, there are those who are fighting fiercely to protect it and those who want to drill for oil on it. It is a priceless treasure. Rivers flow clear and pure and the land embraces musk oxen, moose, polar bears, black and brown/grizzly bears, wolves, and the great Porcupine Caribou Herd. Part of the refuge is mountainous with limited tree cover, but much of it is tundra and marsh. Refuge winters are long and severe, summers short and intense. The brief summer growing season, with its attendant insect plague, supports minimal plant growth. A white spruce tree growing at the northern treeline may take 300 years to achieve a base diameter of 5 inches. Both Inupiats and Gwitch'in subsist off refuge lands. Visitors enjoy summer float trips, hiking, photography, climbing, fishing, and hunting. The main lure for many people is viewing the spectacular caribou migrations and post-calving aggregations. ■ *For information, contact Refuge Manager, Arctic National Wildlife Refuge, Federal Building and Courthouse, Box 20, 101 12th Ave, Fairbanks, AK 99701; (907) 456-0250.*

RIVER FLOAT TRIPS
(Also see Guides/Outfitters below)

Central Brooks Range It is very difficult to pick one *best* float trip because Gates of the Arctic National Park offers so many great trips on wonderful rivers north and south of the divide. Perhaps the best choice is the Kobuk River float, from its headwaters at Walker Lake to Kobuk Village. Plan an overnight stay at the lake to enjoy the mountain setting before traveling between the Baird and Waring Mountains 125 miles to Kobuk. There are two sets of rapids to portage, but mostly the trip is a peaceful 6- or 7-day run that requires no extraordinary boatmanship, just common sense and camping experience.

Eastern Arctic Float trips in the Arctic National Wildlife Refuge have exploded in popularity over the last decade. Two outstanding trips are down the Kongakut and Hulahula Rivers. Both, depending on the timing of the trip, offer exceptional views and encounters with the 175,000-strong Porcupine Caribou Herd. Dall sheep, bears, golden eagles, waterfowl, and small mammals are commonly encountered. Musk oxen are also sometimes seen. Neither trip is particularly hazardous, but experience in wilderness travel is very important. Guided trips are recommended for novices and the inexperienced. Access is via air from Kaktovik and Arctic Village.

Central North Slope The Colville River flows north to the Arctic Ocean past cliff-nesting falcons, hawks, and eagles; fossilized remains of Pleistocene mammals visible in sloughing permafrost bluffs; and tundra mammals, large and small. The 428-mile-long Colville, seventh longest in the state, begins in the De Long Mountains of the Brooks Range and runs to the coast. It is slow-moving and easy to run but is extraordinarily remote. Umiat is about 230 miles from the headwaters. Travelers need to be prepared and experienced in wilderness trekking. Access is via Barrow, Bettles, Umiat, or Deadhorse.

Western Brooks Range A float down the Wild and Scenic Noatak River through the Noatak National Preserve begins near Mount Igikpak and, if desired, can terminate almost 400 miles later in Kotzebue Sound. From the headwaters to the village of Noatak takes about 15 days or so, but shorter trips are possible, depending on pickup or drop-off points. The mountains around the headwaters are spectacular, as is the only-slightly hyperbolic "Grand Canyon of the Noatak." There are several Class II rapids along the river, but altogether it's a fairly easy float. Again, this is a remote wilderness river, and the inexperienced should consider guide service. The river is becoming an ever more popular destination. Access is via Bettles for the headwaters and via Kotzebue for the lower river.

FLIGHTSEEING TRIPS

Central Brooks Range Two trips to recommend: the Arrigetch Peaks, just west of the Alatna River; and through the Gates of the Arctic. The granitic, Teton-like spires of the Arrigetch are a favorite visitor attraction, but my personal favorite is a flight up the North Fork and by Frigid Crags and Boreal Mountain to Mount Doonerak. Inspiring country at any season, but indescribable at the peak of fall colors. Bettles is the most economical place to begin a flight. Road travelers should check at Coldfoot to see if charter service is available there now.

Eastern Brooks Range Circumnavigate Mounts Chamberlin and Michelson. These are some of the only glaciated peaks in the eastern Arctic, and on a summer "night," they glow with

SHOOTING TIPS FROM A MASTER PHOTOGRAPHER

1) *When photographing any large animals, especially bears and moose, a long telephoto lens, preferably 400mm or longer, is a necessity. These often slow-moving animals are capable of lightning speed when aroused, and a photographer needs to keep his or her distance. Never approach bears; always photograph from a distance. Use caution around small animals such as foxes and squirrels. Rabies is endemic to Arctic Alaska, and any animal that unwarily approaches or behaves erratically should be avoided.*

2) *To stop action on flying birds or running mammals, use the fastest shutter speed possible, usually 1/500 of a second.*

3) *Arctic wildflowers are a beautiful challenge for photographers. A macro lens (meaning one that allows close focus) is a must for close-up work. Pros favor special lenses, such as the 100mm or 200mm macro, for this type of work. Good pictures also can be made using the 50mm macro lenses or normal lenses aided by an extension tube. (Pros like the longer macro lenses because their use increases the distance from subject to film. An extension tube fits between the body and lens to allow close focusing.)*

4) *The Arctic is windy, so a medium-speed film, 100 ISO, along with solid support such as a tripod, are necessary to help stop camera movement. When doing close-up work, the critical technical element to control is depth of field. Depth of field is defined as that area from near to far that is in focus. Depth of field is affected by : a) the lens in use; b) the distance from subject to film; and c) the aperture (f/stop) choice. Therefore, for the best close-ups of tundra flowers, use the longest macro lens or extension-tube-equipped lens available (this increases the distance from subject to film). Or use the smallest aperture opening possible, f16 or f22, and a cable release and tripod to minimize camera movement when photographing at slow shutter speed.*

5) *Whiz-bang cameras seem to experience battery failure at the moment of peak action. Always carry extra batteries.*

6) *Always provide waterproof protection for camera equipment, summer and winter.*

—Tom Walker

The Brooks Range

Flightseeing

golden rays of the midnight sun. It's an expensive flight from almost all access points, notably Kaktovik and Arctic Village; therefore, it's best arranged as an adjunct to another trip.

Western Arctic Fly from Kotzebue, early or late in the day, along the coast 10 miles to Cape Krusenstern. From this altitude the traveler can best appreciate the starkness of the Chukchi Sea coast and this landscape that has supported people for 6,000 years. Flying services in Kotzebue offer flightseeing here, as well as around Kotzebue Sound and to local villages.

GUIDES/OUTFITTERS

The trend in wilderness travel seems to be toward older clients and longer stays. Not all guides are appropriate for all clients. Client-guide relationships are volatile. One client may swear by one guide, while another may swear *at* that same guide. Check references and clearly spell out desires and expectations. Some of these guides offer very similar trips but have different perspectives on the same areas and adventures. This list is not to be considered inclusive. Some great guides work for large organizations. Veteran Arctic guide and photographer Wilbur Mills, for example, sometimes guides for the Sierra Club.

Best Alpine Guide Alaska Wildtrek specializes in alpine treks especially suited for European travelers. While the multilingual Chlaus Lotscher also offers float trips and treks of all kinds, his climbing adventures to places like Mount Chamberlin and Mount Michelson combine Swiss-style climbing with wildlife viewing, rafting, and wilderness camping. An internationally published photojournalist, Lotscher will assist photographers in obtaining high-quality images. ■ *Chlaus Lotscher, Alaska Wildtrek, PO Box 1741, Homer, AK 99603; (907) 235-6463.*

Best Birding Adventure Lisa Moorehead has been a wilderness guide for 15 years and holds a master's degree in cultural anthropology. Bob Dittrick, a biologist, has been guiding 11 years and birding for 27 years. Together, they offer birders the chance to explore via raft and to backpack wilderness areas missed by most serious birders. Two special offerings are a raft/hike in the Arctic National Wildlife Refuge during the caribou migration and a Nome beach-house birding trip. ■ *Contact Bob Dittrick and Lisa Moorehead, Wilderness Birding Adventures, PO Box 103747, Anchorage, AK 99510-3747; (907) 694-7442.*

Best High Arctic Guide Service The son of legendary bush pilot Bud Helmericks, Jim Helmericks lives on family property on the Colville River delta, just a few miles from the Arctic Ocean. The ponds and tundra around the Helmericks' modern home are a family wildlife refuge and an exciting place for birders to visit. Helmericks is an outstanding bush pilot and can custom-tailor trips of all kinds for birders and adventurers. The Helmericks family's natural history museum is exceptional. Standing in stark contrast to the tussock-covered coastal tundra, the Helmericks property is a true oasis for a select, limited number of guests. Lodging, family meals, and air and boat logistical support are provided by the host. ■ *Contact Jim and Teena Helmericks, Golden Plover Air, Colville Village via Pouch 340109, Prudhoe Bay, AK 99734; (907) 659-3991.*

Best Hunting Guide Born and raised in Alaska, Te Tiffany made his first successful hunt at age 10. A licensed registered guide, Tiffany offers traditional fair-chase hunts from comfortable tent camps established in the Brooks Range and on the Koyukuk River. ■ *Contact Alaska Perimeter Expeditions, Henry D ("Te") Tiffany IV, PO Box 329, Ester, AK 99725; (907) 456-4868.*

Best River Runners Ramona Finnoff has been guiding river travelers for more than 16 years and has extensive experience in whitewater kayaking, rock and ice climbing, skiing, dog mushing, and mountaineering. Two special offerings are a raft and backpacking combination during the caribou migration in the Arctic National Wildlife Refuge and Ramona's favorite, the Noatak River float and backpack. Both are good bets for folks who will make only one trip to the wilderness of Arctic Alaska. ■ *Contact ABEC'S Alaska Adventures, Ramona Finnoff, 1550 Alpine Vista Ct, Fairbanks, AK 99712; (907) 457-8907.*

Best Natural History Adventure Macgill Adams' goal is to see and visit *all* of the Arctic National Wildlife Refuge; his guided treks, therefore, are not limited to "the same old routes." Each trip offers some portion that is unique as well as open to opportunity. The refuge's great glory lies in the ability to observe wildlife in undisturbed settings. Adams, ably assisted by Dee Dee Van Vliet, works hard to ensure that Arctic novices learn to appreciate not only the smack-in-the-face beauty of the Brooks Range but also the glorious subtleties of the plain and coastal lagoons. ■ *Contact Wilderness Alaska, Macgill Adams, PO Box 113063, Anchorage, AK 99511; (907) 345-3567.*

Alaska Wilderness Recreation and Tourism Association Also try this group of more than 200 outdoor-oriented businesses. A directory is available by mailing $5 to AWRTA, PO Box 22827, Juneau, AK 99802; (907) 463-3038; or visit their Web site, http://www.alaska.net/~awrta.

SUGGESTED READING

Brower, Charles. *Fifty Years Below Zero.* Fairbanks: University of Alaska Press, 1994. A lifetime of pioneer adventure.

Crisler, Lois. *Arctic Wild.* New York: Harper and Brothers, 1973. The wolf, caribou, and wilderness adventures of film makers Herb and Lois Crisler.

Kauffmann, John. *Alaska's Brooks Range: The Ultimate Mountains.* Seattle: The Mountaineers Books, 1992. A celebration of the range's natural history and beauty. Eloquently written.

Lopez, Barry. *Arctic Dreams: Imagination and Desire in a Northern Landscape.* New York: Bantam Doubleday Dell, 1996. A celebration of the northern landscape—its elements, cycles, and history—and its sometimes magical effect on man and beast.

Marshall, Robert. *Alaska Wilderness—Exploring the Central Brooks Range.* Berkeley: University of California Press, 1970. The adventure of exploring the last great wilderness in America.

Marshall, Robert. *Arctic Village.* Fairbanks: University of Alaska Press, 1991. An intimate look at the collision of cultures in Wiseman Village on the upper Koyukuk River in the 1930s.

Murie, Margaret. *Two in the Far North.* Anchorage: Alaska Northwest Publishing Co., 1978. Natural history and frontier life, as experienced by pioneer conservationists Margaret and Olaus Murie.

Wright, Billie. *Four Seasons North.* New York: Harper and Row, 1973. A cerebral, almost mystical account of life in a remote Arctic cabin.

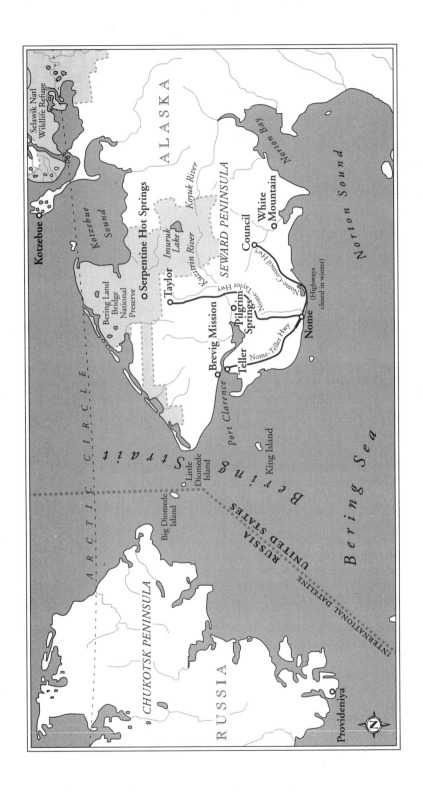

Nome

At first glance, Nome seems a bit disheveled. Even homely. But it gets cold here—like 50 below or colder. So it's best to think of Nome as unpretentious. The houses serve their purpose. The water is safe to drink. Function rules.

Nome is on the Seward Peninsula, 102 miles below the Arctic Circle, with its back to the hills and its face to the sea. People work hard here. The land demands it. They play hard, too. Rituals tend to be unusual. In spring, they dig out bathing suits and plunge into the icy Bering Sea. In fall, they race down Front Street in bathtubs on wheels.

The people of Nome know how to have a good time. They can celebrate with wild abandon. Any excuse will do—anniversaries, divorces, their birthdays, their dogs' birthdays, the bars being open—it doesn't matter. As reported in the *Wall Street Journal*: "Every night is Friday night in Nome, Alaska. Except Friday night—which is New Year's Eve."

A hundred years ago, the town was only wind-swept tundra. Then, gold was discovered on the black sands of Cape Nome, and within months there sprang up a tent city of 20,000 hopeful gold-seekers. It was known as the poor man's gold rush, because gold lay all over the beaches just for the taking. Gamblers, con men, prostitutes, and other characters straight out of a B-rated western flocked to the north. They entertained themselves in high style. The legendary lawman and gunslinger Wyatt Earp even owned a saloon here. At one time, Nome had a French lingerie shop and piano-moving businesses. Although fires and storms have wiped out nearly all the remnants of this colorful era, Nome still identifies heavily with its past.

Today, the city is home to about 4,500 people and is the hub of Northwest Alaska. There is no road *to* Nome. But there are about 300 miles of roads *around* Nome. The city is located 539 air miles north of Anchorage, and the only way to reach it is by air or sea or sled dog team. Nome is most famous today in Alaska and around the world not for its gold but for being the end of The Last Great Race, the thousand-mile winter dash by sled dog team down the Iditarod Trail from Anchorage every March.

Access

Regularly scheduled flights to Nome are available through **Alaska Airlines,** (800) 426-0333, and **Frontier Aviation** from Fairbanks, (800) 478-0074. Nome also has van service to the Eskimo village of Teller (72 miles northwest of Nome), taxi cabs, and several businesses that rent vehicles. More than 300 miles of well-maintained gravel roads head out of Nome in a variety of directions. They're open May to October, depending on snowfall. Unleaded gas runs about $2 a gallon. Cars may be rented from **Stampede Rent-A-Car,** (907) 443-3838; **Budget Rent-A-Car,** (907) 443-5598; and **Alaska Cab Garage,** (907) 443-2939.

Information

Nome's friendly **Convention & Visitors Bureau** on Front Street has historical photos and scrapbooks on Nome; bird lists; flyers on fishing and wildlife; and information on lodging and tours. Contact Nome Convention & Visitors Bureau, PO Box 240, Nome, AK 99762; (907) 443-5535.

THINGS TO DO

Watch the End of the Iditarod For lots of activity, March is the best time to visit. As the finish for the Iditarod Trail Sled Dog Race, Nome draws mushers, media, and groupies from all over the world. Iditarod time is something to behold, with everything from Native dancing and drumming to golfing on the frozen Bering Sea. You'll also find a whole ream of sports going on, from the 2-mile Businessmen's Sled Dog Race to Iditabasketball tournaments, drawing more than 50 teams from all over the state.

Go Road Tripping In the summer, what Nome really has to offer that no other place in Bush Alaska has is the rare chance to travel deep into the country by road. Nome has more than 300 miles to explore with unique opportunities for hiking, fishing, skiing, boating, birding, wildlife viewing, and other adventuring. Birding is big, with more than 180 species found on the Seward Peninsula from late May through July, including Asiatic birds rarely seen in North America.

Mush Dogs Richard Burmeister and his son Aaron are both Iditarod veterans. They can take you on a half-hour sled dog ride for $25 or arrange lessons and longer rides, even multiday trips. In the summer, the sled dogs pull you on wheels rather than runners. Flat Dog Kennels, PO Box 1103, Nome, AK 99762; (907) 443-2958.

Go Gold Panning Pick up a pan at one of the local stores and hit the beach. Gold panning is allowed on a 2-mile stretch east of Nome, between town and the Fort Davis Roadhouse. If you want to do it as part of a tour, call the visitors center on Front Street, (907) 443-5535.

Visit Russia: Tours to Provideniya A Bering Air Piper Navajo was the first American aircraft to fly through the "Ice Curtain" between the United States and Russia in May 1988. Now, hundreds of flights later, Bering Air offers a 3-day, 2-night whirlwind tour of Nome's sister city of Provideniya in the Russian Far East. After a 1½-hour flight, travelers stay with host families, take tours of the city, enjoy Russian songs and dances, indulge in a Russian feast, and maybe take a traditional sauna. Plans must be made well in advance because of all the paperwork. You also need a valid passport. Bering Air will help make arrangements for required invitations and visas. The cost is $999 per person. Bering Air can also arrange fishing and kayak tours in the Chukotsk Region. Contact the Russian Travel Desk, Bering Air, Inc., PO Box 1650, Nome, AK 99762; (907) 443-5620.

GUIDES/OUTFITTERS

INUA Expeditions Inua means "spirit." Guides Keith and Annie Olanna Conger introduce their clients to that spirit of the land and the people whose lives are intertwined with it. The Congers are teachers in the Eskimo village of Brevig Mission. They spend their summers running a bike shop and guiding out of Nome. INUA arranges custom adventures—anything from visiting reindeer herders to telemark skiing along the road system in late spring. They also offer package trips such as an easy 1-day paddle down Pilgrim River to the hot springs ($150) or a week-long kayak trip in the Imuruk Basin, where you visit beautiful, wild country, as well as the summer fish camps of their neighbors from Teller and Brevig Mission ($1,600). In summer, contact Box 1333, Nome, AK 99762; (907) 443-4994. In winter, contact Box 65, Brevig Mission, AK 99785; (907) 642-4161.

Nome Custom Adventures This company specializes in small, custom tours arranged to your interests. If you'd like to pan for gold, visit an Eskimo village, or go berry picking, dog sledding, fishing, canoeing, bicycling, or birdwatching—all this is possible for under $250 a day, split among your group. Contact PO Box 480, Nome, AK 99762; (907) 443-5134.

Yaayuk Tours Captain Jim Stimpfle (U.S. Coast Guard–certified), who named his business after his King Island Eskimo wife, caters mostly to visitors on a mission, such as film crews and photographers on major photo expeditions. Custom services start at $250/day, plus expenses. In the winter, he can arrange snowmobile expeditions. In summer, travel is by boat. Contact PO Box 729, Nome, AK 99762; (907) 443-2002. (No credit cards; checks OK.)

Alaska Wilderness Recreation and Tourism Association A group of more than 200 outdoor-oriented businesses. A directory is available by mailing $5 to AWRTA, PO Box 22827, Juneau, AK 99802; (907) 463-3038; or visit their Web site, http://www.alaska.net/~awrta.

DESTINATIONS OUT

Three major roads lead out of Nome, opening up a whole array of recreational possibilities, from fishing to mountain biking. Though gravel, they are well maintained during summer and fall. There are no services—no gas, no food, no lemonade

THE IDITAROD TRAIL SLED DOG RACE

The Iditarod race commemorates the old dogteam trail across Alaska from one gold rush to another. The town of Iditarod was once a booming inland empire of gold, built in an unbelievably mosquito-infested swamp (even by Alaska standards) halfway between Anchorage and Nome in the early 1900s. Today, it's a ghost town. The gold and mail trail, covered by dogteam in the winters, ran from Seward on the coast to the fabled gold town of Nome, more than 1,000 miles away over two mountain ranges, up the frozen Yukon River, and across the frozen Bering Sea.

Nome's glory days were fading when gold was discovered in the country surrounding the Iditarod River. So a spur route from the Seward-to-Nome trail was cut to the new boom town of Iditarod. Gradually, the whole route became known as the Iditarod Trail.

On the first Saturday of every March, men, women, and dogs test their mettle against the elements and mush down Fourth Avenue in Anchorage in a ceremonial start to the thousand-mile Iditarod Sled Dog Race, run from Anchorage to Nome. The race is the brainchild of Joe Redington, Sr., known affectionately in Alaska as the "Father of the Iditarod." Because of his love of dogs, challenge, and adventure, he struggled against enormous criticism to create the race, which today is famous around the world as "The Last Great Race."

stands. Keep your eyes open for reindeer, musk oxen, bears, and foxes, as well as abandoned gold dredges. Be prepared to do battle with mosquitoes. If you don't want to rent your own vehicle, **Strom Cab Service,** (907) 642- 2047, and **Sherman Transportation,** (800) 478-3767 in Alaska or (907) 642-3767, make regular runs between Nome and Teller for $40 each way. They also do custom tours and drop-offs all along the road system.

The Nome–Teller Road   About 40 miles out of Nome, you'll see a road wandering off toward the sea to Cape Woolley, a fish camp formerly used by King Island Natives during summer months. The road dead-ends 72 miles northwest of Nome in the Inupiat Eskimo village of Teller, a community of 300 people on the sea between Grantley Harbor and Port Clarence. Joe Garney, Iditarod musher, lives in Teller. Look for the yard with 40 or so dogs. During summer months, many families head upriver, through Imuruk Basin and up the meandering Kuzitrin River, to fish camps at Mary's Igloo. **Grantley Harbor Tours,** run by Kenneth and Emily Hughes, are custom-designed to help you get deeper into the country, whether you're on a photo safari, fishing, or meeting a local ivory carver. Contact Box 586, Teller, AK 99778; (800) 478-3682 in Alaska or (907) 642-3682.

The Nome–Taylor Highway More popularly known as the Kougarok Road, this 85-mile road does lead to Taylor, but Taylor is a private mining operation and not open to the public. At the Kuzitrin River Bridge, the road becomes more like a trail and it's time to turn around. About 8 miles out of Nome, there's good fishing in the Dexter Valley. About 38 miles out, Salmon Lake is a beautiful spot for fishing, camping, or a picnic. About 50 miles out, take the left-hand turn to Pilgrim Hot Springs, 7 miles off the main road. Don't miss it. **Pilgrim Hot Springs** is an interesting historical site with a wooden hot tub for soaking (it's free). Once it was a Catholic mission, boarding school, and orphanage. During the flu epidemic of 1918, the mission was overwhelmed by Native children who'd lost their families. The Jesuits ran the orphanage for 23 years, until it was closed in 1941.

The Nome–Council Road This road follows the coast for about 30 miles before wandering inland toward Council, 72 miles northeast of Nome. Cape Nome, about 13 miles out, has a sweeping view of the Bering Sea. About 34 miles out is the ghost town of Solomon. Just before Solomon you'll see the old gold-rush train, "The Last Train to Nowhere." About 65 miles out, you'll see a rare sight for the Seward Peninsula—trees! Council is another former gold-rush town with a summer population of 40.

The Anvil Mountain Road A short 5-mile jaunt out of Nome takes you to the top of Anvil Mountain and a view of Nome and the Bering Sea. Take Bering Street north to the Nome–Beltz Highway. Once you pass Icy View, Nome's one and only suburb, you'll see a right-hand turn. Take it. About 2 miles up, turn left and continue until you reach the top.

FESTIVALS/EVENTS

Iditarod Trail Sled Dog Race This world-famous, 1,049-mile sled dog race begins in Anchorage the first Saturday of March. The race commemorates the diptheria serum run between Nenana and Nome in 1925. The winning time for the first Iditarod, held in 1973, was 20 days. With improved breeding, training, and equipment, and good trail conditions, it was run in 9 days in 1995. The Iditarod Awards Banquet is usually held on the Sunday following the winner's arrival. Accommodations fill up quickly at Iditarod time, so book early. Once everything is full, a call goes out to the community for spare rooms, even floor space for rent. Contact the Iditarod Trail Committee, PO Box 870800, Wasilla, AK 99687; (907) 376-5155.

Bering Sea Ice Golf Classic Held in mid-March at Iditarod time, this is a six-hole fund-raising tournament played on the frozen Bering Sea, with bright orange golf balls and coffee cans sunk into the ice as holes. Golfers tee off outside the back door of one of the bars after the prerequisite number of drinks. They ham it up for this one, wearing plus fours and outfitting their huskies as caddies. Contact the Bering Sea Lions Club, PO Box 326, Nome, AK 99762; (907) 443-5278.

Polar Bear Swim A rite of spring held each Memorial Day. Stir-crazy Nomeites plunge into the icy Bering Sea, where the water is so cold and invigorating it could kill them were they to linger. Those who fully submerge receive a certificate to prove to their friends how deranged they are. For information, contact Rotary Club of Nome, PO Box 275, Nome, AK 99762; (907) 443-5549.

Nome River Raft Race Held in mid to late June, the race begins at Mile 13 of the Kougarok Road. Homemade rafts—basically anything that floats—race downriver. The victorious team claims the distinctive trophy, a fur-trimmed honey bucket. (FYI: "Honey bucket" is a polite term for a bucket used in the Bush in lieu of a "loo.") Contact the Bering Sea Lions Club, PO Box 326, Nome, AK 99762; (907) 443-5278.

Bathtub Race An annual Labor Day spectacle, with bathtubs mounted on wheels rattling down Front Street. The rules state the tubs must be full of water and bubbles and that the "bather" must wield a bar of soap, a towel, and a bath mat while being propelled by teammates down the course. Tubs must have at least 10 gallons of water left at the finish line to win. Contact Leo Rasmussen at the Music Mart, PO Box 2, Nome, AK 99762; (907) 443-2798.

BEST RESTAURANTS

Fort Davis Roadhouse ★★ The Roadhouse is the closest thing Nome has to fine dining (weekends only). Chef Hatto Eberl, an Austrian, has cooked on cruise ships, has run his own restaurants, and is now running the kitchen here after coming to Nome with his wife, a public health nurse working in the villages. Eberl is giving Nome diners something to talk about. Friday night's seafood buffet features fresh halibut, Alaska king salmon, shrimp, crab soufflé, and a variety of other seafood dishes. Saturday night, it's prime rib. Sunday brunch ($16) includes crêpes, Belgian waffles, eggs Benedict, and other goodies. Upon occasion, the lounge upstairs offers live music and dancing. ■ *Straight out Front Street in Nome, 2 miles out of town; (907) 443-2660; V, MC; checks OK; open Fri and Sat eves and Sun brunch.*

Fat Freddie's Cheeseburgers, grease, and lots of them make Fat Freddie's Nome's most popular hangout. Plus, it's located next to the Nugget Inn, is open year-round, and has nice windows looking over the Bering Sea. Call (907) 443-5899.

Lucky Swede No, it's not a casino, just a cozy shop with coffee and fresh flowers. Named for "The Three Lucky Swedes," the first to find gold here, the shop serves flavored lattes, cappuccinos, espresso, and Ibarra chocolate, a spicy Mexican version of hot chocolate. In summer, they serve Hot Licks Ice Cream, made in Fairbanks. ▪ *On the corner of Front and Bering Sts in Nome; (907) 443-3828; open daily, winter and summer.*

BEST LODGINGS

Nome Nugget Inn ★ The Nugget, in the heart of town, has the most character and class. The famous burl arch for the finish line of the Iditarod stands right outside. During the race, it's like Grand Central Station. Anybody who's anybody is in and out of here. The Gold Dust Lounge, with friendly bartenders, gold-rush character, and a view of the Bering Sea, is a pleasant place to trade stories and wild rumors of mushers and the trail. Rates are about $100 for a double. ▪ *In downtown Nome; PO Box 430, Nome, AK 99762; (907) 443-2323; $$.*

Betty's Igloo Michael and Betty Hannigan have a tidy two-story home a block from shore, with a view of the Bering Sea. If you're there at the right time, they'll take you out to pull in the crab pots. The Hannigans live upstairs and rent three rooms downstairs. Continental breakfasts. ▪ *PO Box 1784, Nome, AK 99762; (907) 443-2419; $.*

Château de Cape Nome This could be the biggest house on the Seward Peninsula—a two-story, 4,400-square-foot home with a stretch limousine parked in the garage. The proprietors, Cussy Reardon, city comptroller, and Bob Kauer, chief of police, run their bed and breakfast in a home full of gold-rush memorabilia and hunting trophies, off and on throughout the year, when they aren't too busy guiding bear hunters. You're most likely to find rooms available June though early September and mid-October through the end of March. ▪ *PO Box 715, Nome, AK 99762; (907) 443-2083; $.*

WILDERNESS LODGES

White Mountain Lodge This lodge, 70 miles east of Nome, caters to visiting fishermen and is also a retreat for locals. It's located in the middle of White Mountain Village. Most visitors come by air, a 30-minute flight from town. Fishing can be out of this world. Last fall, one of the owners went out ice fishing and got 300 tomcod in 2 hours. The lodge operates like a bed and breakfast and can sleep up to 30 people. Bed and breakfast is $120 a night per person in the summer, and $85 in the winter season (except during Iditarod time in mid-March, when it's $120). A full day of fishing via jet boat is an additional $125.

■ 70 miles east of Nome, in White Mountain Village; PO Box 149, White Mountain, AK 99784; (907) 638-3431; open year-round.

BERING LAND BRIDGE NATIONAL PRESERVE

This national preserve is one of the most remote and least visited national parks in the country. It has no visitor facilities and no roads. Yet it is the remains of a major highway. Today, Siberia is 55 miles across the Bering Sea. But during the Pleistocene Ice Age, much of the earth's water was locked in ice. The level of the seas fell, exposing a broad bridge of land—1,000 miles wide—between Asia and North America. Most anthropologists believe this is how the First Peoples came to the Americas thousands of years ago.

The Bering Land Bridge is a primitive landscape, with extensive lava flows, low sand dunes, and craters that have since become lakes. The people who live here follow a traditional subsistence lifestyle. Some are reindeer herders. The area is home to musk oxen, grizzly bears, moose, reindeer, wolves, wolverines, and foxes. In winter, polar bears cruise the coastline and sometimes come ashore. You can get to the preserve by boat or bush plane in the summer or by ski plane, snowmobile, or dog team in the winter.

THINGS TO DO

Serpentine Hot Springs A natural hot springs within the preserve, this is a truly magical place. The steaming hot springs are surrounded by a circle of granite spires, once a place of power used by shamans for training in traditional medicines. There's a short airstrip, an old bunkhouse, and a small bathhouse with a wooden pool. It's free and open to the public. In winter, access is by snowmobile or dog team. For more information, contact Bering Land Bridge National Preserve, PO Box 220, Nome, AK 99762; (907) 443-2522.

SUGGESTED READING

Alaska Geographic. *Nome: City of the Golden Beaches.* Vol. 11, No. 1. Anchorage. The colorful history of Alaska's most famous gold-rush town told in hundreds of rare black-and-white photos.

Jones, Tim. *The Last Great Race.* Seattle: Madrona Press, 1982. The story of the early days of the Iditarod Sled Dog Race across Alaska from Anchorage to Nome.

Riddles, Libby, and Jones, Tim. *Race Across Alaska.* Harrisburg, Pennsylvania: Stackpole Books, 1988. The first woman to win the Iditarod Race tells her story in a highly readable and dramatic fashion.

SOUTHWEST ALASKA

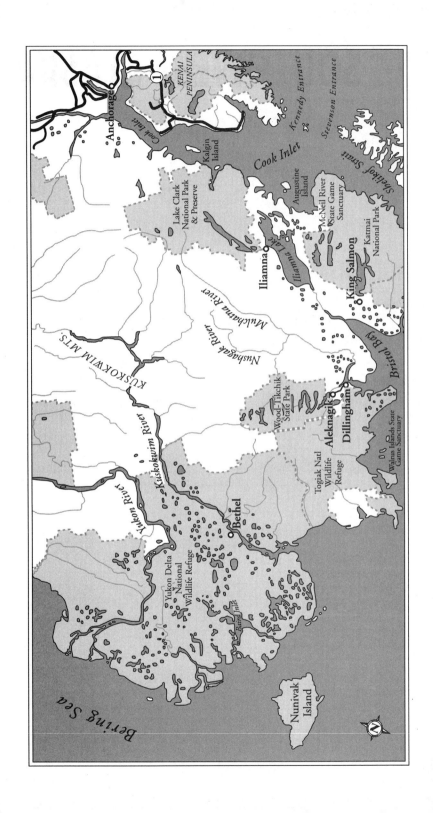

Southwest Alaska

*Including Lake Clark National Park and Preserve, McNeil
River State Game Sanctuary, Walrus Islands State Game
Sanctuary, Katmai National Park and Preserve, Wood-
Tikchik State Park, Yukon Delta National Wildlife Refuge,
Bethel, Iliamna, Dillingham, and King Salmon*

Southwest Alaska is best defined by its wildness and biologi-
cal diversity. The region stretches from Lake Clark down to
Bristol Bay, then up the coast to the Yukon-Kuskokwim Delta.
It is North America's largest nesting and breeding area for migratory waterfowl. The world's densest population of brown
bears and greatest salmon runs are here. More than 60 communities dot the landscape, most of them small, remote villages whose Athabascan and Yup'ik residents continue to lead
subsistence lifestyles heavily dependent on the region's abundant wildlife. Most villages have fewer than 200 people. There
is only one paved "highway," 15.5 miles long. Few other roads
connect villages. Access is by air, boat, or snowmobile in winter. Scheduled airlines serve only four of the region's towns: Iliamna, King Salmon, Dillingham, and Bethel. Local air taxis fly
to villages. Fishing is the main work. Bristol Bay, the world's
largest sockeye salmon fishery, generates millions of dollars
each summer.

This is an angler's paradise—salmon country and rainbow
heaven. For the well-to-do, there are luxury fishing lodges
($3,000 to $5,000 per week). If you're not so spendy, do what
most Alaskans do—pack your gear and go camping. There's a
wealth of areas from which to choose: two national parks, two
national wildlife refuges, several Wild and Scenic Rivers, two
state game sanctuaries, and the largest state park in the country. Not only do these water-rich habitats sustain incredible
salmon migrations, they support two of the world's great gatherings of brown bears—at McNeil River State Game Sanctuary
and Brooks Falls in Katmai National Park—with densities
of up to 1.4 brown bears per square mile, greater than even
Admiralty and Kodiak Islands. The Yukon Delta refuge is seasonal home to the one of the world's largest nesting populations of geese, ducks, and swans. And thousands of male
walrus gather on islands within Bristol Bay.

Though overshadowed by the region's wildlife and fisheries, several of Alaska's most fascinating landscapes occur
here. There's the remote Yukon-Kuskokwim Delta and two
separate lake regions—Lake Iliamna and Lake Clark in the
west and the lakes of Wood-Tikchik State Park farther east.
Katmai National Park includes 15 active volcanoes and the
Valley of Ten Thousand Smokes, site of the largest volcanic

eruption in Alaska's recorded history. In summer, visitors can expect wet, cool weather with temperatures around 55° F, overcast skies, and occasionally fierce storms.

LAKE CLARK NATIONAL PARK AND PRESERVE

Located on the western side of Cook Inlet, this park and preserve is the quintessential Alaska parkland. Here, wilderness seems to stretch forever, rich with mountains, glaciers, wildlife, wildflowers, forests, tundra, lakes, rivers, and rugged coastal cliffs. There are two active volcanoes, including Mount Redoubt (10,197 feet), visible from Anchorage, which last erupted in 1989. The Aleutian and Alaska Ranges join to form rugged peaks, still mostly unclimbed and unexplored. Several major rivers and lakes offer world-class sport fishing for rainbow trout and all five species of Pacific salmon. Lake Clark, a narrow, 42-mile-long body of water, is the sixth largest lake in Alaska and the jewel for which the park was named. It is one of the state's least known and least appreciated national parks, in large part because access is only by air. There are no campgrounds, no maintained trails, no visitor centers. But of wildness, there is plenty.

Access

From Anchorage, **Lake Clark Air,** (800) 662-7661, provides daily commuter flights. Once in Port Alsworth, travel is by foot, boat, or air taxi to outlying areas.

Information

For information, contact Superintendent, Lake Clark National Park and Preserve, 4230 University Drive, Suite 311, Anchorage, AK 99508; (907) 271-3751.

Tips on the Park

Field headquarters for the park is at Port Alsworth, a small community (pop. 65) on Lake Clark's southeastern shore. The park has no other public facilities, although rangers are often seasonally based at Twin, Telequana, and Crescent Lakes. Among the first settlers were bush pilot Leon "Babe" Alsworth and his wife Mary, who homesteaded 160 acres, built an airstrip, and gave this tiny town its name. Visitors exploring the backcountry should plan to be totally self-sufficent and understand how to behave around bears.

THINGS TO DO

Float the Tlikakila, Mulchatna, or Chilikadrotna Rivers (each of them officially designated a Wild and Scenic River). **Fish** for salmon, rainbow trout, or Dolly Varden. Beautiful lakes to explore by **kayak** are Lake Clark and Telequana, Turquoise, and Twin Lakes. **Backpack** from Turquoise to Twin Lakes. Tuxedni Bay, along the coast, is also quite special.

Lake Iliamna, Alaska's largest lake and another area known for world-class sport fishing, is located just south of the park. Much of the Mulchatna and Chilikadrotna, two popular fishing and floating rivers, lie outside park boundaries. They feed into the Nushagak River, also a popular **river-trip** destination.

GUIDES/OUTFITTERS

Guided river trips, as well as hiking opportunities, are offered by **Alaska Adventures,** (907) 345-4597, and **Alaska Pathways and Wilderness Journeys,** (907) 349-2964, while **Northward Bound,** (907) 345-2891, guides mountaineering, backpacking, and hiking trips. **Ouzel Expeditions,** (907) 783-2216, provides fishing and river trips. Park headquarters has a complete list of Lake Clark's guide and travel services. Also try **Alaska Wilderness Recreation and Tourism Association**, a group of more than 200 outdoor-oriented businesses. A directory is available by mailing $5 to AWRTA, PO Box 22827, Juneau, AK 99802; or call (907) 463-3038.

WILDERNESS LODGES

Alaska's Wilderness Lodge Nestled among the aspen and spruce on the shores of Lake Clark at Wilderness Point, this lodge specializes in fishing adventures with guided trips into the park. Guests stay in private cabins. Gourmet meals are served in the main lodge. No more than 12 guests at a time for week-long visits ($4,500/person for the week with fly-out fishing included). For information, contact Tim Cudney and Lisa Shaw, PO Box 190146, Anchorage, AK 99519; (800) 835-8032.

▼

**Lake Clark
National Park
and Preserve**

*Wilderness
Lodges*

▲

Farm Lodge In Port Alsworth, the Farm was built by homesteaders Babe and Mary Alsworth in the 1940s and has been operated as a lodge since 1977 by their son Glen and his wife Patty. The main lodge (also their home) originally resembled a big, red barn, but now is cedar-sided. Homecooked meals feature wild game, salmon, and vegetables from their garden. The Alsworths also provide flying services (through Lake Clark Air), guided fishing, backpacking drop-offs, or river trips. Full lodging with three meals a day is $75/person; bed-and-breakfast rates are $50/person. For information, call toll-free (800) 662-7661.

Koksetna Wilderness Lodge Located on Chulitna Bay, on the shores of Lake Clark, guest accommodations include the main lodge, two cabins with wood stove for heat, two bathhouses, and a steam bath. Accessible by plane, the lodge is a family affair, hosted by Jonathan, Juliann, and Drew Cheney. During the 6-day, 5-night stay ($1,500/person) activities range from fishing, bird watching, and wildlife viewing to boating and hiking. Guests also may stay in the cabins and provide their own meals at a lower cost. For information, call (907) 781-2227, June to August, or (916) 458-7446, September to May.

Wilder House B&B Located right on the airstrip, this B&B has a cedar-sided cabin or rooms for rent in Dave and Jacque Wilder's house. There's a boat for fishing and exploring Lake Clark. Hiking trails are nearby. The Wilders also own Lake and Peninsula Airlines and will drop people off in the backcountry (for an extra fee, of course). For information, contact Wilder House B & B, 3323 Dry Creek, Port Alsworth, AK 99653; (907) 781-2228.

MCNEIL RIVER STATE GAME SANCTUARY

Created in 1967, McNeil River Sanctuary, located 200 miles southwest of Anchorage, is intended to protect the world's largest gathering of brown bears. The main focus is McNeil Falls, where bears come to feed on chum salmon returning to spawn. During the peak of the chum run (July to August) dozens of brown bears congregate at the falls. As many as 106 bears, including cubs, have been observed along the river in a single day. No more than 10 people a day, always accompanied by one or two state biologists, are allowed to visit bear-viewing sites during the permit period, June 7 through August 25. Because demand is so high, there is an annual drawing to determine permit winners.

▼

Lake Clark National Park and Preserve

Wilderness Lodges

▲

The bears begin to arrive at the sanctuary in late May or early June, along tidal mud flats, where they graze on sedges. From mid- to late June they also feast on sockeye salmon that spawn in Mikfik Creek, a neighboring stream of McNeil River, also within the sanctuary. June visitors make daily guided visits to Mikfik to watch the bears. Mikfik's salmon run ends in late June, and the action shifts to McNeil Falls, where humans are restricted to two gravel viewing pads. Located about a mile above the mouth of the river, the falls is actually a series of small waterfalls, pools, and whitewater rapids. One of the great thrills is to watch these magnificent creatures close at hand. It's not uncommon for the most tolerant bears to eat salmon, take naps, or even nurse cubs within 10 feet of the falls' viewing pads.

Access

Located near the northern end of the Alaska Peninsula, along Cook Inlet's western shore, McNeil is accessible by either boat or plane, but nearly all visitors fly into the sanctuary on floatplanes. Most arrange for air-taxi flights out of Homer, a coastal community on the lower Kenai Peninsula. The two most commonly used are **Kachemak Air Service,** (907) 235-8924, and **Beluga Lake Floatplane,** (907) 235-8256. Once in the sanctuary, all travel is on foot.

Information

For information, contact **Alaska Department of Fish and Game,** Division of Wildlife Conservation, 333 Raspberry Road,

MCNEIL RIVER BEARS

Brown bears—the coastal equivalents of grizzlies—are solitary creatures by nature. For them to gather in large numbers and close quarters, as they do at McNeil Falls within McNeil River State Game Sanctuary, is exceptional. That they do so while viewed by humans is even more remarkable.

The sanctuary manager for the past two decades, Larry Aumiller, attributes this phenomenon to several factors: (1) the presence of salmon, an abundant and reliable energy-rich food source, (2) the lack of good fishing nearby, (3) the presence of McNeil Falls, which acts as a barrier to the chum salmon, making them easy prey for the bears, and (4) the region's high bear density.

The final piece of the puzzle is people management. Visitors are told: "The bears come first at McNeil River. All human use is of secondary importance." That philosophy led to the sanctuary's highly successful permit system, limiting the number of people at the falls each day. Since the state enacted visitor restrictions, the number of bears visiting the falls has increased dramatically. Even more significant: no bears have been killed in self defense, and no humans have been injured by bears. This despite thousands of bear-human encounters, often at close range.

"It's widely assumed that bears and people don't mix," says Aumiller. "But here, we've shown that they can mix, if you do the right things. To me, that's the most important message of McNeil: humans can coexist with bears. The first day people come here, many are fearful, because of things they've heard or read about bears. But after they've seen a few bears up close and the bears go about their business, people begin to relax. The transformation is almost universal." Instead of irrational fear, visitors learn tolerance and healthy respect. They also learn to understand what Aumiller means when he says, "McNeil is an example of what could be."

—Bill Sherwonit

Anchorage, AK 99518-1599; (907) 267-2179.

Tips on the Sanctuary

Permit applications are available from the Alaska Department of Fish and Game. They must be postmarked no later than March 1 and accompanied by a $20 nonrefundable fee. The permit drawing occurs on March 15 of each year. Permits are for 4-day periods. As many as 3 people may apply as a group. Visitors pay an additional user fee for the sanctuary—$100 for Alaskans and $250 for nonresidents.

All visitors stay in a designated tent-camping area that also has a wood-fired sauna. Food is stored and cooked in a cabin. Bring sturdy camping gear and be prepared for wilderness conditions. Note that the hike to the falls is 4 miles round trip and is strenuous. Visitors spend approximately 6 to 8 hours viewing bears each day. Weather at McNeil Sanctuary is often foggy or rainy, and coastal storms are common. Visitors should be prepared for travel delays when planning their trip.

WILDERNESS LODGE

Chenik Camp Located on Kamishak Bay within McNeil River State Game Refuge (which borders the sanctuary), the camp was established in 1978, intended for visitors who wanted to watch and photograph brown bears gathering at Chenik Creek, about 6 miles north of McNeil River. The rustic camp has room for 8 guests in 3 cabins (without indoor plumbing or electricity), a sod-roofed sauna, bath house, and small lodge with dining area, fireplace, library, and picture windows that overlook the ocean. Gourmet meals are served 3 times daily, including fresh halibut, salmon, and crab. Run by Michael and Diane McBride (who also own Kachemak Bay Wilderness Lodge near Homer), Chènik Camp is open from early June through early August. Five-day packages are $2,250/person, (907) 235-8910.

WALRUS ISLANDS STATE GAME SANCTUARY

Each year, in spring and summer, thousands of male walrus gather on this group of seven islands in Bristol Bay. The females and young travel north to spend their summers in the Bering and Chukchi Seas. Scientists still aren't sure exactly why males stay behind. However, what is clear is that the walrus bulls use these islands as resting places in between food binges. Because of their importance to these creatures, the seven Walrus Islands and adjacent waters were given special "protected" status in 1960. The centerpiece of the sanctuary is Round Island, a small (2 miles long by 1 mile wide) and rugged piece of ground where thousands of walrus congregate in spring as the pack ice begins its annual retreat. For the next 7 months, these huge fellows (some weigh up to 2 tons) spend their time alternately gorging on invertebrates such as clams and snails, then hauling out on the rocks and resting up for the next binge.

Access

Round Island is located about 30 miles from the mainland. Most visitors get there by chartering a boat ride with Don Winkelman's **Round Island Charters,** (907) 493-5127, based at the Togiak Fisheries cannery. To reach the cannery, take a plane from Dillingham to either Togiak or Twin Hills. Several airlines and air-taxi operators fly between Dillingham and

Togiak, including **Peninsula Airways,** (800) 448-4226, **Tucker Aviation,** (907) 842-1023, and **Yute Air,** (907) 842-5333. The boat ride takes 1 to 3 hours, depending on the seas. Once at Round Island, visitors are met by sanctuary staff, who assist in transferring people and gear to shore. Travel on the island is entirely by foot.

Information

For permit applications and information, write **Alaska Department of Fish and Game,** Division of Wildlife Conservation, PO Box 1030, Dillingham, AK 99576-1030; (907) 842-2334.

Tips on the Sanctuary

Round Island has by far the largest gathering of walrus of all the islands. The best time is June through August. Only 12 people at a time are allowed to camp on Round Island. Permits are on a first-come, first-served basis. Applications must be sent to the Alaska Department of Fish and Game, accompanied by a $50 fee.

Round Island is a rugged, often stormy place, and anyone who goes there should be in good physical condition, prepared for wilderness conditions. Visitors should also anticipate weather delays when making travel plans. Visitors are required to bring their own camping gear. Tents should be expedition quality, capable of withstanding 60 mph winds. Two wildlife technicians are stationed on the island to conduct research and enforce sanctuary regulations. They are not tour guides. Visitors should be prepared to fend for themselves. Visitors are expected to stay on the island's trail system and within designated viewing areas. Beaches are off-limits to minimize disturbances to resting walrus.

Katmai National Park and Preserve

KATMAI NATIONAL PARK AND PRESERVE

Declared a national monument in 1918 to preserve the "living laboratory" of a violently explosive 1912 volcanic eruption, Katmai—upgraded to national park status in 1980—is perhaps now best known for its abundance of brown bears. The park's premier attractions are the Valley of Ten Thousand Smokes and Brooks Falls, where up to two dozen bears may be observed fishing for sockeye salmon. The salmon start arriving in early July, bound for spawning grounds in Brooks Lake. As they near the end of their journey, they face one final obstacle: 5-foot-high Brooks Falls. Following the salmon to the falls are brown bears, the coastal equivalents of grizzlies. As many as 35 to 40 brown bears inhabit the Brooks River drainage in July, although only rarely do more than a dozen fish the falls at any one time.

The bears, in turn, attract humans. Hundreds of people come daily from mid-June through early September to Brooks

BEARS AND HUMANS

Nearly all of Alaska is "bear country." When traveling in the state's backcountry areas, several steps can be taken to minimize surprise meetings with bears.

Given a choice, bears will almost always avoid people. To prevent sudden, close encounters, walk in open country during daylight hours. If you must pass through forested areas or thick brush with limited visibility, make noise. Sing. Talk loudly. Or clap your hands. Some people wear bells. Keep alert and look for signs of bears, such as fresh tracks, bear scat, matted vegetation, and partly consumed salmon. Leave the family dog at home. Dogs can provoke encounters. Traveling in groups is recommended because more people make more noise.

When setting up camp, stay away from hiking trails, animal trails, salmon-spawning streams, and berry patches. Avoid areas where scavengers such as ravens have gathered. A bear's food cache may be nearby. Bears aggressively defend their food supplies. It's especially important to be a "clean" camper. Cook meals at least 100 feet from tents. Store all food away from tents and camp. If possible, hang it high in the trees. If you've been fishing, change your clothes before entering your tent, and store clothes away from camp. Avoid odoriferous foods. Wash up after cooking and before sleeping. Store garbage in an airtight container or burn it and pack out the remains.

If you meet a bear, talk to it. Don't yell. And don't run. Running from a bear triggers a bear's predatory instincts. He'll probably chase you. Instead, back away slowly. If possible, give the bear an escape route. If you're dealing with a female that has cubs, avoid getting between the mother and her young. As a general rule, bigger is better with bears. Try to increase your size. Raise your arms above your head. Stand side by side with two or more people. Climb a tree. Only be aware that black bears and young grizzlies can also climb.

In the extreme, a bear will charge. Most are bluff charges. But if a bear makes contact, the best thing to do is fall to the ground and play dead. Lie flat on your stomach or curl into a ball, hands behind the neck. Remain passive. The one exception to this rule is when a bear shows predatory behavior. Instead of seeming upset or charging, a hunting bear will show intense interest, while approaching you at a walk or run, or circling you. If you're certain that you're being treated as prey, fight back. Understand that such circumstances are exceedingly rare and most involve black bears.

The question of carrying a gun is a personal choice. Carry a gun only if you know how to use it. Also be aware that guns are not allowed in certain areas of the national parks (check park regulations). One possible alternative is red-pepper spray (which comes in aerosol cans). Because the canisters sometimes leak, it's best to store bear sprays in airtight containers. Users are also cautioned to notify pilots when flying into backcountry areas. If the spray leaked into the cockpit, it could cause a crash.

A summary of bear-safety tips is available in a free brochure titled "Bear Facts." Pick one up at the Alaska Public Lands Information Centers in Anchorage, Fairbanks, Ketchikan, or Tok. Another excellent source is Stephen Herrero's book Bear Attacks: Their Causes and Avoidance.

—Bill Sherwonit

Falls and nearby Brooks Camp, which is a park field station, campground, and wilderness lodge. They come to see bears and to fish. If time, there's an interesting side trip to the Valley of Ten Thousand Smokes, formed by the giant volcanic eruption of Novarupta and subsequent collapse of Mount Katmai in 1912.

▼

**Katmai
National Park
and Preserve**

Information

Despite the monument's volcanic wonders, Katmai received little attention until the 1940s, when entrepreneur and early bush pilot Ray Petersen established 5 remote sport fishing camps. The largest was Brooks. Now, as then, Brooks Camp and Brooks Falls remain the focal point of Katmai tourism. Most visitors come to see bears. Largely overshadowed by Brooks' bears is the rest of Katmai National Park and Preserve, which includes hundreds of miles of rugged, pristine coastline, 15 active volcanoes belonging to the "Pacific ring of fire," 2 officially designated Wild and Scenic Rivers—the Nonvianuk and Alagnak—and a series of large, connected lakes that form a kayak and canoe route called the Savonoski Loop.

Access

Located at the northern end of the Alaska Peninsula, Katmai National Park and Preserve is 300 miles southwest of Anchorage. Most visitors fly into the park through King Salmon. There are several air-taxi operations, including **Branch River Air,** (907) 246-3437, **C-Air,** (907) 246-6318, **Egli Air Haul,** (907) 246-3554, and **Katmailand,** (800) 544-0551.

Information

For permits and information, contact Superintendent, Katmai National Park and Preserve, PO Box 7, King Salmon, AK 99613; (907) 246-3305. There's a **campground, visitors center,** and **ranger station** at **Brooks Camp,** as well as viewing platforms to watch the bears at Brooks Falls and the lower Brooks River. The remainder of the park, however, is undeveloped (with the exception of a few privately owned lodges). Camping is by permit only, within 5 miles of Brooks Camp. Sites at the Brooks campground are determined by lottery. Wilderness travelers may camp anywhere in the park, but are asked to pick up a backcountry permit at park headquarters. Clean camping is particularly important in bear country.

Tips on the Park

Prime-time bear-viewing is in July and September. Camping at Brooks Camp is by permit only. Contact park headquarters for permit information (see above). With the notable exception of Brooks Camp and a 23-mile road to an overlook of the Valley of Ten Thousand Smokes, Katmai is wilderness with no public facilities. Visitors going beyond Brooks must be self-sufficient and prepared for wilderness travel. A brochure, *Traveling the Katmai Backcountry*, is available from park headquarters. The Katmai region has one of the world's highest densities of brown bears, and visitors should understand the do's and don'ts of bear encounters.

THINGS TO DO

Watch bears. Attend naturalist programs, staged nightly at Brooks Camp. Fish for salmon and rainbow trout. Hike through the Valley of Ten Thousand Smokes. Hike up to Dumpling Mountain (2,440 feet), accessible from Brooks Camp. Canoe or kayak the Savonoski Loop. Float the Nonvianuk and Alagnak Rivers.

GUIDES/OUTFITTERS

Guided hiking and/or river-running trips are offered by **Alaska River and Ski Tours,** (907) 595-1422; **Alyeska Wilderness Guides,** (907) 345-4470; and **Ouzel Expeditions,** (907) 783-2216. **Katmailand,** (800) 544-0551, and **Joseph Van Os Photo Safaris,** (206) 463-5383, do photography trips, while **Lifetime Adventures,** (907) 746-4644, offers biking, bear viewing, kayaking, and climbing packages. Three dozen companies and lodges offer guided fishing services, including **Alaska Trophy Adventures,** (907) 246-8280; **Fox Bay Lodge,** (907) 246-6234; and **Morrison Guide Service,** (907) 246-3066. A complete list of guide services and air-taxi operators is available from Katmai headquarters. Also try **Alaska Wilderness Recreation and Tourism Association,** a group of more than 200 outdoor-oriented businesses. A directory is available by mailing $5 to AWRTA, PO Box 22827, Juneau, AK 99802; or call (907) 463-3038.

WILDERNESS LODGES

Katmailand Katmailand operates three fly-in lodges within Katmai National Park. **Brooks Lodge** was built in the 1940s as a fishing camp, though today most of its guests come to see the brown bears that fish for salmon at nearby Brooks Falls. The lodge looks out over Naknek Lake, with 16 small cabins around it that sleep 4 guests each. Visitors fish for salmon or rainbow trout, watch and photograph bears, or take the day trip to the Valley of Ten Thousand Smokes. The lodge operates from June to September. Prices range from $419/person for a 1-day tour to $1,140/person for 5 days. **Kulik Lodge,** on the Kulik River, offers premier fishing for rainbows and salmon. The spruce-log lodge has a large stone fireplace and bar. Multiday packages include transportation from Anchorage and cost between $2,500 and $6,500/person. **Grosvenor Lodge,** on the stream that connects Colville and Grosvenor Lakes, is another sport fishing lodge. There is room for only six guests in three guest cabins with shared bathhouse. Prices range from $1,625 to $2,575/person. The Katmailand office is located in Anchorage. For more information, call (800) 544-0551.

Katmai Wilderness Lodge   Owned by the Russian Orthodox Church, this lodge is located on Kukak Bay along Katmai's remote outer coast. Brown bear viewing, sea kayaking, and fishing for halibut or salmon are the main attractions. Up to 6 guests stay in a log cabin. The 3-night "wilderness package" costs $1,800, including round trip from Kodiak, lodging, meals, guided bear viewing, and fishing. Open June through mid-Sept. Prime time for bears is August. For more information, call (800) 488-8767.

WOOD-TIKCHIK STATE PARK

Despite its inland setting, this is a water-based park dominated by the Wood River and the spectacular Tikchik Lakes. Snow-capped mountains, low tundra, and interconnected clearwater lakes, some 45 miles long, characterize the region. Everything from grizzlies and moose to porcupines, river otters, and loons inhabits the park's forests and tundra, but best known are the fish. Lakes and streams here provide critical spawning habitat for the five species of Pacific salmon. They also support healthy populations of rainbow and lake trout, arctic char, grayling, and pike. This has long been known as a fisherman's paradise. Today it is becoming increasingly popular with water adventurers, such as kayakers and rafters, who travel its interconnected river and lake systems.

Access

Located in the Bristol Bay region, 325 miles southwest of Anchorage, Wood-Tikchik is easiest to reach by plane through Dillingham. Flying into the park are **Bay Air,** (907) 842-2570; **Tikchik Airventures,** (907) 842-5841; **Starflight,** (907) 842-2486; and **Yute Air,** (907) 842-5333. Once in the park, the easiest way to get around is by boat via the Wood River and Tikchik Lakes systems.

Information

In summer, contact Wood-Tikchik State Park, PO Box 3022, Dillingham, AK 99576; (907) 842-2374. From October to May, write or call Wood-Tikchik State Park, 3601 C Street, Suite 1200, Anchorage, AK 99503; (907) 345-5014.

Managed as a wild area, Wood-Tikchik has no trails and only four "developed" camping areas with a total of 12 sites. Most are very primitive. A backcountry ranger cabin is located near the mouth of Lake Beverly.

THINGS TO DO

You can **float** either the Wood River or Tikchik Lakes systems and **fish** for rainbow trout and salmon. The park's most popular fly-in float trip is the 85-mile journey from Lake Kulik to Aleknagik, a Yup'ik Eskimo village east of Dillingham. Though it can be done in less than a week, paddlers are advised to give themselves at least 10 days to 2 weeks. The other popular trip begins at Nishlik Lake and ends at at Tikchik Lake, a distance of about 60 miles. Those who float the Nuyakuk River below Tikchik Lake should use extreme caution; portages are necessary to get past the Nuyakuk Rapids and Nuyakuk Falls.

▼
Wood-Tikchik State Park

Information

▲

GUIDES/OUTFITTERS

Outfitters that run guided river trips through Wood-Tikchik include **Alaska Pathways and Wilderness Journeys,** (907) 349-2964; **Alaska River Adventures,** (907) 595-2000 in summer and (907) 276-3418 in winter; and **Wilderness Birding Adventures,** (907) 694-7442. **Alaska Fishing Adventures,** (907) 278-9607, and **Alaska Recreational River Guides,** (907) 376-8655, offer guided fishing trips. Also try **Alaska Wilderness Recreation and Tourism Association**, a group of more than 200 outdoor-oriented businesses. A directory is available by mailing $5 to AWRTA, PO Box 22827, Juneau, AK 99802; or call (907) 463-3038.

WILDERNESS LODGES

Royal Coachman Lodge Another floatplane-accessible fishing lodge in the heart of the nation's largest state park. It lies at the outlet of Tikchik Lake, on the Nuyakuk River. Guests stay in comfortable cabins. Experienced fishing guides take guests to streams and lakes throughout the Wood-Tikchik park and Togiak refuge, but there's also excellent fishing right at the lodge. No more than 12 guests at a time are hosted for a week's stay. Cost is $4,250/person. For information in summer, call (907) 842-2725; (907) 346-2595 the rest of the year.

Tikchik Narrows Lodge Located on a narrow peninsula between Nuyukuk and Tikchik Lakes, with a view of the ruggedly beautiful Kilbuck Mountains. More than 50 miles from the nearest road and accessible only by floatplane, this fishing lodge sits deep within Wood-Tikchik State Park. Guests stay in cabins. The main lodge has a stone fireplace and a panoramic view of the surrounding park. Meals include freshly baked breads and pastries, and entrees ranging from sautéed halibut to roast beef with Yorkshire pudding. Guests fish the waters of this parkland, as well as neighboring Togiak National Wildlife Refuge. The week-long stay includes daily guided fishing trips and costs $4,600/person. For information, call (907) 243-8450.

YUKON DELTA NATIONAL WILDLIFE REFUGE

Each spring, millions of birds return to the Yukon-Kuskokwim Delta, where they nest and raise their young on the wetlands. Birds come from all over North America as well as from continents that border the Pacific Ocean. Most notable are brant, geese, ducks, and swans. This is the nation's largest refuge. Most of it is tundra, interwoven with countless ponds, lakes, sloughs, marshes, and meandering streams, including Alaska's two longest rivers: the Yukon and Kuskokwim. One-third of the refuge's acreage is water. Not surprisingly, given the abundance of fish, birds, and other wildlife, the delta has been home to Yup'ik Eskimo people for thousands of years.

Access

The only companies with permits to operate air taxis in the refuge are **Yukon Aviation,** (907) 543-3280, and **Hageland Aviation Services,** (907) 543-3800. **Kusko Aviation,** (907) 543-3279; **Yute Air,** (907) 543-3003; and **Craig Air,** (907) 543-2575, offer transportation from Bethel to outlying villages.

Information

There are no visitor facilities within the refuge itself. For further information, contact **Yukon Delta National Wildlife Refuge,** PO Box 346, Bethel, AK 99559; (907) 543-3151.

Tips on the Refuge

The prime time to visit the delta is mid-May to late June, when the weather is best and breeding season is at its peak. Fishing and river floating are best from June to September.

Some villages, such as Chevak and Emmonak, are starting up cultural tours that may include trips into the refuge. Contact the refuge for more information. Mosquitoes and biting insects can sometimes be intolerable, especially in lowland areas, during midsummer.

PLACES TO GO

Besides the Yukon and Kuskokwim, other rivers popular with boaters, anglers, and wildlife watchers are the Kisaralik River, a Kuskokwim tributary, and the Andreafsky River, a Yukon tributary. Nunivak Island offers opportunities to see musk ox, reindeer, marine mammals, and birds.

GUIDES/OUTFITTERS

Among the outfits who provide guided hunting, birding, or wildlife viewing/photography trips are **Kuskokwim Wilderness Adventures,** (907) 543-3900, and **Nunivak Island Experiences,** (907) 827-8512.

BETHEL

This is not the picture-book part of Alaska with green forests and snow-capped mountains, nor is it part of the popular tourist circuit. The Yukon-Kuskokwim Delta is flat and almost treeless. But the longer you are there, the more extraordinary you'll find its beauty.

This is the home of the most traditional Native population in Alaska—the Yup'ik Eskimos. From Platinum to Kotlik, from Stony River to Tuntutuliak, from Grayling to Emmonak, they live in 46 villages scattered over 76,000 square miles. It is a vast, wet expanse of land with twisted, convoluted rivers and streams, myriad lakes, and soggy tundra. For anyone outside the culture, the names of many of the villages are often unpronounceable—words such as Chuathbaluk, Kwigiumpainukamiut, and Mamterillermiut. The last is the original Eskimo name for the town we know today as Bethel.

**Yukon Delta
National
Wildlife
Refuge**

Bethel (pop. approx 5,000) is the hub of the region—a ramshackle assortment of buildings on the right bank of the Kuskokwim River. Next to the Yukon River, the Kuskokwim is the second longest river in Alaska. This is bird country, and subsistence fishing is a way of life. In 1885, the Moravian Church sent missionaries to the area to establish a church and school here. They took the name Bethel from the Holy Scriptures. In Hebrew, it means "House of God." But, once here, the missionaries ignored the advice of the local shaman about the siting of their mission. He warned them that the riverbank would fall away underneath their home and the water would sweep it downstream. They thought this was only superstition. But, rather, it was the forces of nature, correctly interpreted—weather, wind, and water. Consequently, over the past 100 years, Bethel residents have been dragging their homes away from the banks of the river on a consistent basis, and the town has moved farther and farther inland.

Until about 1984, the most modern attempt at controlling this erosion was to take junked cars and push them over the bank to make a type of bulwark. It, too, ultimately failed. But the sight of 1959 Ramblers and Willy's jeeps tilted on the bank at 50-degree angles, as if some phantom were about to drive them into the river, made an unforgettable picture. The present seawall, constructed by the Army Corps of Engineers, is more sturdy, but Bethel lost some of its charm with the departure of the junkers.

The river defines the way of life here. Most Native folks spend time at fish camps along its banks in the summer, go duck hunting on the delta in spring, pick berries in the fall, and take their skiffs upriver to hunt moose for the winter. Traditional clothing is still worn.

Access

Regularly scheduled daily flights are available, winter and summer, to both Bethel and Aniak on **Alaska Airlines,** (800) 426-0333.

Information

Tune into public radio station **KYUK–640 AM,** (907) 543-3131, for local color and events. And definitely visit the new **Yugtarvik Museum and Cultural Center.**

GUIDES/OUTFITTERS

Wilderness Experiences A warm-hearted, no-nonsense, burly fellow, **Lamont Albertson,** former mayor of Aniak, is the best sport-fishing guide in the Aniak-Bethel-Kuskokwim region. He has fished, lived, raised his family, and taught school in this part of Alaska for more than 30 years. His guided fishing trips have a naturalist/educational bent to them with strong emphasis on catch-and-release. His tent camp, 45 miles up the beautiful little Aniak River, is reached by jet boat from the village of Aniak. All five species of Pacific salmon and the most northern population of naturally occurring rainbow trout in the world swim here, as well as Dollies, arctic char, and grayling. Bears, moose, and caribou wander close to camp—sometimes right through. First you fly to Aniak, home of "The Half-Breeds." (No fooling, that's the name of their basketball team. Basketball is big time in village Alaska, and this village straddles the line between Athabascan and Eskimo country. A former city manager took the job out here because of the team name: "I love a town that has a sense of humor about itself.") The big Kuskokwim is not a good river for sport fishing, but the little Aniak is sport-fishing heaven. Not only that, but with Lamont's wife Sheryll doing the cooking, you'll eat like a king—salmon, king crab, wild game, and a vast array of local blueberry dishes. Fishing is good mid-June to September. Cost is $250–$400/person per day. For information, contact Lamont Albertson, PO Box 91, Aniak, AK 99557; (907) 675-4380 (March to Oct); (706) 547-6264 (Nov to Feb).

FESTIVALS/EVENTS

The Kusko 300 Held every year at the end of January, this is one of the most popular sled dog races in Alaska and a qualifier for the Iditarod Race. It starts in Bethel, runs a course down the Kuskokwim River, turns around in Aniak, and dashes back. With a purse of $100,000, it is the second richest long-distance dog race in the world, next to the Iditarod. For more information, call headquarters near race time; (907) 543-3300.

Camai Dance Festival Held the last weekend of March, this is a welcoming festival of dances. In the Yup'ik language, *Camai* means "hello." This is a regional festival of special importance. Despite the efforts of missionaries to suppress this traditional form of expression, it never disappeared in Southwest Alaska. In the past 15 years, it has seen a resurgence with many villages sponsoring youth dance groups led by village elders who teach the songs, drumming, and movements. The festival takes place in the Bethel High School gym, which is filled to capacity during the 3 days and nights of dancing. Each village gets an hour to perform. This is not actors pretending to demonstrate a culture; this is the real thing. It is not done for tourists. It is for the enjoyment and celebration of the locals. Count yourself lucky if you get to witness this festival. For more information, call (907) 543-2911.

BEST RESTAURANT

Diane's Cafe While the majority of customers are Yup'ik Eskimo, and tend to order fare such as steak and potatoes, which is more akin to their traditional foods, you can also order such dishes as pasta primavera or chicken Dijon. The cafe is small—eight tables—and built much like a solarium, with lots of plants and windows. ■ *1 1/2 miles from the airport, near the hospital; 1220 Hoffman Hwy; (907) 543-4305; $$; no alcohol; AE, DIS, MC, V; checks OK; open year-round for breakfast, lunch, and dinner.* &

BEST LODGINGS

Bentley's Porter House Bed and Breakfast Bentley's overlooks the Kuskokwim River and is a block from downtown. From the second floor, you can see the famous "Bethel seawall," the river, and the start of the Kusko 300, if you're there in the right season. A big, friendly place with 18 rooms, Bentley's serves family-style breakfasts, with good food and plenty of it. Choose rooms upstairs for the best views and light. ■ *Downtown, on the river; 624 First Ave; PO Box 529, Bethel, AK 99559; (907) 543-3552; $$ (includes "government rate"); no bar; AE, DIS, MC, V; checks OK; open year-round.*

Pacifica Guesthouse This hotel is a mile or two out of town, on the way in from the airport. There's a simple, northern European feel to it. There are 35 rooms, some with private bath. If you really want to be luxurious (by bush standards), go "Las Vegas" in one of their 10 new suites ($135/double). Each has a private bath and sitting room with furnishings from the Las Vegas Hilton. ■ *1 1/2 miles from the airport, toward downtown;*

1220 Hoffman Hwy; PO Box 1208, Bethel, AK 99559; (907) 543-4305; $$$; no bar; AE, DIS, MC, V; checks OK; open year-round. &

ILIAMNA

Iliamna is an Indian word meaning "big ice" or "big lake." Iliamna Lake is Alaska's largest lake and gives the name to the town on its shores. About 90 people live here year-round. In summer, anglers from around the world come to fish for salmon, Dolly Varden, and especially rainbow trout. The Kvichak River, which flows out of Iliamna Lake, is famous for the largest rainbow trout in the world. The Iliamna–Lake Clark watershed is considered the most important spawning habitat for sockeye salmon in the world and is the major contributor to Bristol Bay's commercial sockeye fishery. Fishing and hunting lodges have operated in the Iliamna Lake region since the 1930s.

Access and Information

Located about 100 miles from King Salmon and 225 miles southwest of Anchorage, Iliamna is reached only by air. Scheduled passenger service is provided by **ERA Aviation,** (800) 866-8394. **Iliamna Air Taxi,** (907) 571-1248, provides local charters.

Iliamna is a short flight from both Lake Clark and Katmai National Parks. A gravel road connects Iliamna to the neighboring Native village of Newhalen, as well as the Newhalen River, a popular sport-fishing stream. Much of the land surrounding Iliamna Lake is privately owned by individuals and Native corporations. **Iliamna Natives Ltd.,** (907) 571-1246, allows camping on its land, but charges a fee.

Iliamna

Lodgings

For information, contact **Iliamna Village Council,** PO Box 286, Iliamna, AK 99606; (907) 571-1246.

BEST RESTAURANT

Gram's Cafe The best restaurant in town, Gram's is known for its desserts. The dining room overlooks Lake Iliamna. ▪ *In the middle of town, about 2 miles from the airport; (907) 571-1463.*

BEST LODGINGS

Airport Hotel For those who cannot afford the thousands of dollars for a fishing lodge, here is a moderately priced option. It has 10 guest rooms and shared bathrooms and offers complimentary rides to the Newhalen River for fishing. ▪ *Iliamna, AK 99606; (907) 571-1276; $$.*

Iliaska Lodge Iliaska caters particularly to fly-fishers. On the edge of the lake, the lodge has private guest rooms for 12 people who come to fish from 3 to 7 days. Guests are flown out daily with experienced guides to the best fishing for rainbows, salmon, grayling, and arctic char. Chief pilot, guide, and owner

Ted Gerken has been flying for more than a quarter-century and "tying flies for over 40." Cost is from $2,300/person for 3 days to $4,700 for a week. ■ *On the edge of Lake Iliamna; 6160 Farpoint Dr, Anchorage, AK 99517-1261; (907) 571-1221, May 1–Oct 1, and (907) 337-9844 the rest of the year.*

DILLINGHAM

Commercial fishing has been the heartbeat of this town for more than a century. Bristol Bay's first cannery was built in 1884 at the site of present-day Dillingham, and several more were constructed over the next 17 years. Dillingham's population more than doubles in summer with the arrival of Bristol Bay's world-famous salmon runs. The harbor holds more than 500 boats, and the city-run dock handles more than 10,000 tons of fish and freight annually. Traditionally a Native village, Dillingham's year-round population (2,100) includes a mixture of Eskimos, Aleuts, Athabascans, and non-Natives. About 55 percent of the population is Native. Residents retain subsistence lifestyles consisting of hunting, fishing, trapping, and berry picking. The largest community in the Bristol Bay region, Dillingham has eight churches, a hospital, a health clinic, a public library, a community college, four restaurants, several hotels and bed and breakfasts, five taxi companies, nine air-taxi operators, and nearly 200 businesses. The region's climate is maritime, and the weather is often foggy, windy, and wet.

Access

Alaska Airlines, (800) 426-0333, and **Peninsula Airways,** (800) 448-4226, have regularly scheduled flights from Anchorage, an hour's flight away. Several local air-taxi operators offer access to the region's parks, refuges, and villages; among them are **Bay Air,** (907) 842-2570; **Yute Air,** (907) 842-5333; **Tucker Aviation,** (907) 842-1023; **Starflight,** (907) 842-2486; and **Tikchik Airventures,** (907) 842-5841.

Information

The **Samuel K. Fox Museum,** (907) 842-5610, features contemporary and traditional Native arts, crafts, and artifacts and occasionally hosts traveling exhibits (limited hours). The **Peter Pan Cannery,** (907) 842-5415, schedules daily tours when in operation. For further information, contact **Dillingham Chamber of Commerce,** PO Box 348, Dillingham, AK 99576; (907) 842-5115.

Tips on the Town

Dillingham is a jumping-off point for many backcountry destinations, including Wood-Tikchik State Park, Togiak National Wildlife Refuge, Round Island, several popular spots for river running, and numerous fishing lodges. A 22-mile gravel road connects Dillingham with Aleknagik Lake, the lowermost lake in the Wood River chain. The airport is located about 2.5 miles from downtown Dillingham. An espresso bar in Dillingham also serves sandwiches; it's named "Just Because."

KING SALMON

King Salmon was a U.S. Air Force base during World War II and remained a major military installation until 1994, when the base closed down. Now, only a skeleton maintenance crew of nonmilitary people remain. But the community that grew up around the base continues to do just fine, thanks to the superior runway. People stop here en route to other villages or backcountry destinations in nearby parks and refuges.

Fewer than 400 people live here year-round (about 15 percent are Alaska Natives). Most are employed by government or transportation agencies, such as the Alaska Department of Fish and Game, U.S. Fish and Wildlife Service, National Park Service, National Weather Service, and Federal Aviation Administration.

The nature of the town changes dramatically in summer, when seasonal workers arrive to work in Bristol Bay's fishing or tourism industries. From June through September, thousands of tourists come here from around the world, bound for fishing, hunting, wildlife viewing, river floating, and backcountry trekking adventures in nearby wilderness areas.

Access

Located along the Naknek River, about 20 miles from Bristol Bay and 290 miles from Anchorage, King Salmon is served year-round by two airlines: **Peninsula Airways,** (800) 448-4226, and **Reeve Aleutian Airways,** (800) 544-2248. **Alaska Airlines,** (800) 426-0333, flies to King Salmon during the summer season.

Once in King Salmon, it's possible to rent a car, catch a cab, or walk. Most everything in town is within walking distance. Several air-taxi operators offer transportation to outlying villages, as well as nearby parks and refuges. Charters can be arranged with **Branch River Air Service,** (907) 246-3437; **C-Air,** (907) 246-6318; **Egli Air Haul,** (907) 246-6119; and **King's Flying Service,** (970) 246-4414. For those going to Brooks Camp, **Katmai Air Service,** (907) 246-3079, offers regularly scheduled summer flights.

Information

Located at the airport, the **King Salmon Visitors Center** is open daily in summer. For more information, contact PO Box 298, King Salmon, AK 99613; (907) 246-4250.

Tips on the Town

Make reservations for airlines and hotels well in advance. King Salmon's three hotels are often filled in summer. The same is true for planes.

A paved road connects King Salmon with Naknek (15 miles away), as well as Naknek Lake, which offers boat access into Katmai National Park and Preserve. Boats can be rented locally.

BEST RESTAURANTS

Quinault Landing Resort ★ With large windows looking out at the Naknek River, the restaurant offers the most formal and elegant dining experience in King Salmon. White tablecloths, wine lists, gourmet meals, daily specials, advance reservations—everything you'd expect in a big city. It's also seasonal, open only in summer. Fresh fish and other seafood are served daily, in both appetizers and entrees. ■ *Located along the Naknek River, a short walk from the airport; (800) 770-FISH or (907) 246-6200 (summers only); fax (907) 246-6200; $$$; full bar; AE, DC, MC, V; local checks only; breakfast, lunch, and dinner daily in summer; closed Oct–April.* &

Eddie's Fireplace Inn Eddie's is a King Salmon institution. The walls are decorated with mounted fish, artificial flowers, Christmas trees with white lights, and a portrait of owner Eddie Oakes and family. It's small, loud, and smoky—a bit like walking into a cave in summertime. But in winter, there's the fireplace. The menu features potato salad, hickory-smoked ribs, and burgers, which include the Belly Buster and the Fireplace, "the burger that made the Fireplace famous." ■ *Located in downtown King Salmon, a block from the airport; (907) 246-3435; $$; full bar; AE, MC, V; checks OK; open daily, 8am–10pm.*

BEST LODGINGS

Mike Cusack's King Salmon Lodge Located on a grassy bluff that overlooks the Naknek River, just a short distance from the King Salmon airport, this has evolved into one of the region's premier fishing lodges. Gourmet meals include fresh salmon, Alaska king crab, filet mignon, duck, pheasant, or quail, plus a selection of premium wines. The dining room has views of both the Naknek River and Mount Katmai. Guests may choose to participate in guided fishing trips. Anglers are flown out to world-class fishing streams and lakes anywhere within a 200-mile radius. The lodge offers a 1-week package for $5,700/person. ■ *King Salmon, AK 99613; (800) 437-2464; open mid-June–Oct.*

SUGGESTED READING

Alaska Geographic Society. *Katmai Country.* Anchorage, 1989.

Alaska Geographic Society. *One Man's Wilderness.* Anchorage, 1973. In photos and words, this is an account of Dick Proenneke's life as a homesteader in the Lake Clark region.

Aumiller, Larry, and Walker, Tom. *River of Bears.* Minnesota: Voyageur Press, 1993. A coffee table–style photo-essay book on McNeil River Sanctuary.

Bledsoe, Thomas. *Brown Bear Summer.* New York: E. P. Dutton, 1987. Describes research done at McNeil River Sanctuary in the early 1970s.

Bodeau, Jean. *Katmai National Park and Preserve.* Anchorage: Alaska Natural History Association, 1992.

Fierstein, Judy. *The Valley of Ten Thousand Smokes.* Anchorage: Alaska Natural History Association, 1984.

Hubbard, Bernard. *Cradle of the Storms.* New York: Dodd, Mead & Co, 1935.

Lenz, Mary, and Barker, Jim. *Bethel: The First 100 Years: Photographs and History of a Western Alaska Town.* Bethel, Alaska: Tundra Press, 1985.

Squibb, Ron, and Olson, Tamara. *Brown Bears of Brooks River.* Salt Lake City, Utah: Lorraine Press, 1993.

ALASKA PENINSULA AND ALEUTIAN ISLANDS

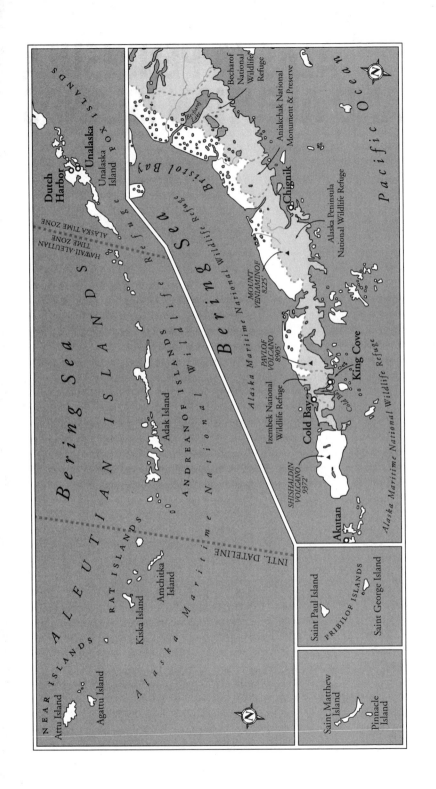

Alaska Peninsula and Aleutian Islands

Including the Pribilof Islands

Sweeping away from Alaska's mainland, the Alaska Peninsula and Aleutian Island Chain stretch more than 1,500 miles toward Siberia, separating the North Pacific Ocean from the Bering Sea. Mere dots in the vast waters of the Bering Sea are the Pribilof Islands, a tiny volcanic archipelago whose geologic origins are tied to the peninsula and the Aleutian Chain. All are part of the Pacific basin's "Ring of Fire."

The region encompasses some of Alaska's most remote, inaccessible, and rugged country. Volcanoes, earthquakes, wind, and oceans carve the landscape. From a seismic and volcanic perspective, this is one of the most turbulent regions in the world. More than 70 volcanoes have been identified, many of them active. Among the most active are Akutan, with 33 eruptions; Shishaldin, which has erupted 35 times; and Pavlof, 41 times. Pavlof is on the lower Alaska Peninsula, while the other two are in the Aleutians. The Aleutian and Pribilof Islands are actually the tops of large, submerged mountains. Among the most spectacular volcanic landforms in the region are the Aniakchak Caldera, the Aghileen Pinnacles, Ukrinek Maars (craters), and the mountains Pavlof, Veniaminof, and Peulik.

This is the traditional home of the Aleut people, distant cousins of the Eskimos. Many still supplement their income with subsistence lifestyles, dependent on the harvest of fish, wild game, berries, and other foods from the sea. There are few roads (all of them local and isolated, and none more than 50 miles long) and no paved highways. Of the region's two dozen villages, 15 have fewer than 200 year-round residents. The largest community, Unalaska/Dutch Harbor, has a population of less than 4,000.

Biologically, the waters of the North Pacific, the Bering Sea, and Bristol Bay are among the richest on earth. They support a billion-dollar fishing industry (though a growing number of scientists, conservationists, and Natives of the region fear overfishing is taking its toll on the region's sea life). A few coastal villages boom dramatically in summer, as fishermen and cannery workers from Outside arrive for the lucrative salmon and bottomfish harvests. King Cove's population more than doubles during the fishing season. Egegik, on the shores of Bristol Bay, jumps from 120 residents in winter to more than 1,000 in summer. The other main employer since World War II (until recently) was the military. (The Aleutians were the site of one of the bloodiest battles in the Pacific.)

Wildlife, too, arrives in spectacular numbers, all dependent on the ocean's bounty. Forty million seabirds are seasonal residents. The coastal cousin of the grizzly—the brown bear—grows to enormous proportions on a high-protein diet of salmon, which spawn in vast numbers in the clear lakes and streams of the peninsula. The sea coast boasts an abundance of marine mammals—sea lions, seals, sea otters, whales, and porpoises—yet there are distressing signs that even the rich North Pacific–Bering Sea ecosystem is under stress. Two once-plentiful species—sea lions and harbor seals—have experienced dramatic declines in recent decades.

Access to Towns

The principal means of travel is by air. **Alaska Airlines,** (800) 426-0333, **Reeve Aleutian Airways,** (800) 544-2248, and **Peninsula Airways,** (800) 448-4226, provide regularly sched-

WORLD WAR II IN ALASKA

Many people today are surprised to learn that the United States was occupied by enemy forces during World War II in a far-off corner of Alaska.

The front-page headline in the New York Times *on that fateful day—June 4, 1942—read: "Japanese Bomb Dutch Harbor, Alaska, twice!" The Japanese landed forces on Attu and Kiska, two tiny islands at the end of the Aleutian Chain, and the Rising Sun flag flew on American soil. It took the United States more than a year and hundreds of lives to liberate those islands. On Attu, fighting was in the mountains. They say it was grim. The Japanese had retreated just above the fog line and continued to pick off hundreds of American soldiers down below. But the United States forces outnumbered them 10 to 1.*

The Japanese who didn't get killed in that final charge died by holding hand grenades to their chests. After the battle, the Americans found the diary of a young Japanese lieutenant. This was his final entry: "The last assault is to be carried out . . . Only 33 years of living and I am to die here. I have no regrets. Banzai to the Emperor! . . . Good-bye, Tasuka, my beloved wife."

Next to Iwo Jima, Attu was the second bloodiest battle of the war in the Pacific.

uled passenger service to Chignik, Cold Bay, Sand Point, and Dutch Harbor. Round-trip costs average $500 to $800. **Aleutian Air** offers charter service to neighboring islands, including the Pribilofs.

For those with flexible schedules, the state ferry *MV Tus-tumena,* known as "The Trusty Tusty," has service from Homer and Kodiak from March through October, which takes 3 to 4 days, depending on where you embark. En route it stops at five towns—Chignik, Sand Point, King Cove, Cold Bay, and Dutch Harbor. For reservations, call (800) 642-0066.

Tips on Travel to Parks and Refuges

Anyone traveling to this region must be prepared for **weather delays,** sometimes lasting several days. Weather can often be violent and stormy. **Brown bears** are abundant throughout much of the Alaska Peninsula. Take precautions to avoid unwanted encounters. (See "Bears and Humans" box in the Southwest Alaska chapter.) Boil or filter **water** before drinking to prevent giardia, an intestinal disorder caused by a waterborne parasite. Parks and refuges within this region generally have **no visitor facilities.** If you plan to explore the backcountry, come prepared for wilderness camping and travel.

Large acreages within some refuges or parks have been conveyed to Native corporations or individuals. Respect **private property.** Get permission if passing through private lands and contact the refuge or park headquarters if uncertain about land status. Use **low-impact camping** techniques whenever traveling in the backcountry. Avoid camping on fragile vegetation. Carry out all garbage. Never cut trees. Keep a clean camp. Use biodegradable soaps, and wash at least 100 feet from water sources. Dig holes for human waste and burn or carry out toilet paper. Avoid building fires.

UNALASKA/DUTCH HARBOR

The history of this far-flung community mirrors the history of Alaska. Many centuries ago, the ancestors of the Aleuts arrived in this new land. Much, much later, in the 18th century, Russian fur hunters discovered a rich treasure chest here in the soft, black, velvety fur of the playful sea otter. By the turn of the century, whales and gold had lured waves of fortune-hunters and ships to sail north along this coast.

For a long time, the village of Unalaska on Unalaska Island, with its charming onion-domed church, was the main town on the Aleutian Chain. But during the gold-rush era, its little neighbor, Dutch Harbor, swelled with thousands of hopeful gold-seekers. Some called her "the bawdy queen of the Alaska Gold Coast." As the gold began to taper off, though, "Dutch" was left almost a ghost town. Business boomed again during World War II, when it became a strategic naval base. After the war, it lay deserted. Not so today. Beginning with the rich and dangerous king crab industry, which took off in the 1960s, the pendulum of history has swung back again. Today fortunes are mined from beneath the sea.

The big money is in fish and crab. The City of Unalaska and the International Port of Dutch Harbor (Unalaska/Dutch Harbor) is the number one fishing port in the United States, measured in both pounds of fish processed and total dollar value delivered. Unalaska is a working town with an international flavor. On any one day, Russian, Japanese, and Korean vessels are waiting in the harbor to pick up fish products and cargo to freight back home.

For many visitors, the military aspect is perhaps the most interesting. There's a partially sunken war ship in one of the bays left over from World War II. Old trails zigzag up the sides of the mountains, leading to former defense garrisons. (The zigzagging was to avoid strafing by Japanese war planes.)

Weather is characterized by wind and water, fog and ferocious gales. Clear blue skies on the average happen about 10 days out of the year. During the war, American forces in the Aleutians lost two men to weather and frostbite to every one killed by enemy gunfire. As the soldiers stationed out here used to say, "It doesn't rain in the Aleutians. It rains in Asia and blows over."

▼

**Unalaska/
Dutch Harbor**

▲

Information

For local information on fishing excursions, birding, sightseeing tours, historical tours, hiking, flightseeing, hotels, restaurants, and special events, visit **Unalaska/Dutch Harbor Convention & Visitors Bureau,** (907) 581-2612; fax (907) 581-2613.

THINGS TO DO

Church of the Holy Ascension A National Historic Landmark, this Russian Orthodox cathedral has been a symbol of Unalaska and part of its distinctive charm since its construction in 1895. The first church here was built under the sharp eye of Father Veniaminov in 1826. Later canonized as Saint Innocent, he was a singularly impressive fellow who mastered the baidarka so that he could paddle a thousand miles through the Aleutians to tend his flock. Although the cathedral is undergoing extensive renovation, tours are available by appointment. Call (907) 581-6001.

Remnants of World War II Bunkers, pillboxes, tunnels, the remains of old Quonset huts, zigzag trails all over the hills, and a sunken batttleship in the harbor are visible reminders of the military presence here and the fierce battle for the Aleutians. Hike up Bunker Hill, visit Memorial Park, walk along Unalaska

Lake. Visit the small historical museum of wartime memorabilia, including old weapons, photos, and field gear. The museum is open weekdays at Marine Works near the airport. Call (907) 581-1749.

Hiking the Mountains On Unalaska there are no bears, no trees to block your vision, and bugs tend to get blown away by the sea breezes. The island does have lots of bald eagles and red foxes and a profusion of wildflowers, birds, and berries. Salmonberries are ripe in August, followed by blueberries, which can be picked as late as November some years. **Mount Makushin** (6,680 feet), a steaming volcano, is the highest mountain on the island. Some of the more popular hikes close to town are **Pyramid Peak** (2,136 feet), rising to the south, and **Mount Ballyhoo** (1,589 feet), on the Dutch Harbor side. They say this mountain was named by the famous writer Jack London on his way to the gold fields in Nome around the turn of the century. Every Fourth of July, there's a rigorous scramble up to its summit called the **Ballyhoo Run.**

Most of the land on the island is privately owned by the Native people. In order to hike, ski, bike, or camp on the land, please first obtain a permit from the **Ounalashka Corporation,** (907) 581-1276, at Margaret Bay, near the Grand Aleutian Hotel. Topo maps (as well as an espresso bar) are located at **Nicky's Place** on the Front Beach, (907) 581-1570. Open every day, with the exception of "exceptionally sunny days," they will also open after hours "for coffee emergencies and for those who work late or fish hard."

Unalaska/ Dutch Harbor

Guides/ Outfitters

Fishing The Iliuliuk River, which runs out of Unalaska Lake into Iliuliuk Harbor, teems with salmon in the summer. As it flows past the onion-shaped domes of the cathedral, it is in full view of bald eagles sitting atop the spires, watching their dinner passing by on the fin. Fish from shore or charter out. Charter operations that offer trips in the summer include **Far West Outfitters,** (907) 581-1647; **Grand Aleutian Tours,** (907) 581-3844; and **Volcano Bay Adventures,** (907) 581-3414. Fishing licenses may be purchased at the local grocery or fish supply shops.

Renting a Bicycle Unalaska has 38 miles of gravel road. Some may be paved by the time you get there. You can rent a bicycle through the City of Unalaska, Department of Parks, Culture, and Recreation.

GUIDES/OUTFITTERS

Aleut Tours Offers a 2-hour bus tour with an emphasis on Aleut and Russian history. Call (907) 581-6001.

Equinox Wilderness Expeditions Guided backpacking and sea kayaking trips around Unalaska and neighboring islands. Call (907) 274-9087.

Volcano Bay Adventures   Guided salmon and trout fishing; hiking and birdwatching. Call (907) 581-3414.

Grand Aleutian Tours   Offered through the Grand Aleutian Hotel, this group provides a whole array of trips, from charter fishing on the 32-foot *Grand Aleutian* to historic, cultural, and bird-watching tours. They also arrange guided hiking, biking, and kayaking trips. Call (907) 581-3844.

Far West Outfitters   Marine tours, fishing charters, and sightseeing on the 32-foot boat *Suzanne Marie*. Call (907) 581-1647.

Alaska Wilderness Recreation and Tourism Association   Also try this group of more than 200 outdoor-oriented businesses. A directory is available by mailing $5 to AWRTA, PO Box 22827, Juneau, AK 99802; (907) 463-3038; or visit their Web site, http://www.alaska.net/~awrta.

BEST RESTAURANTS

The Chart Room ★★★   Located in the Grand Aleutian Hotel with windows overlooking Margaret Bay, the Chart Room is quite posh and no more expensive than a nice restaurant in Anchorage. Get a happy start to your evening with a drink by the fireplace in the Cape Cheerful Lounge. It's no big surprise that from this island's vantage point, facing out to the ocean with the Bering Sea in its backyard, halibut, salmon, shrimp, squid, and other fish and shellfish are star players in the Chart Room's "North Pacific Rim cuisine." The wine selection is quite good and reasonably priced. ■ *In the Grand Aleutian Hotel on Airport Beach Rd; (907) 581-3844; $$$; full bar; AE, DC, DIS, MC, V; local and traveler's checks; dinners daily, Sun brunch; open year-round.* 占

Stormy's   Although this is not a big or fancy place (there are perhaps only a dozen tables, complete with plastic tablecloths), Stormy's menu is enormous and ethnically diverse. It has a full sushi bar and a sushi chef. But it can't quite make up its mind whether it is Japanese, Chinese, Mexican, Italian, or your basic American hamburger joint. All are represented here. The lunch buffet is particularly impressive and largely Chinese. ■ *Located on the Unalaska side, near the church; (907) 581-1565.*

BEST LODGINGS

The Grand Aleutian ★★★   Some call it "The Grand Illusion"— a fancy hotel seemingly at the end of the world and in another time zone. But it is fancy without pretension, and certainly the most comfortable place in Unalaska. From its opening in 1994, it quickly became the hangout for all the local movers and shakers. Here's where you'll find the big muckety-mucks in the fish business. It's also perfect for tourists who want familiarity. Most nights, there is live music and dancing. All rooms have a view of Margaret Bay, Unalaska Bay, or Ballyhoo Mountain.

Their tour operation—Grand Aleutian Tours—offers a selection of excursions, such as charter fishing, birding, nature hikes, island tours, marine tours, and mountain biking. ■ *Five minutes from the airport on Airport Beach Rd (at Margaret Bay); Pouch 503, Dutch Harbor, AK 99692; (800) 891-1194 or (907) 581-3844; fax (907) 581-7150; $$$; full bar; AE, DC, DIS, MC, V; local and traveler's checks; open year-round.* ♿

Carl's Bayview Inn ★ On the Unalaska side of town, a stone's throw from the Russian church, this is a roomy and comfortable inn with homey touches and a well-connected host. Carl Moses is the state legislator in the Alaska House of Representatives with a district that covers Bristol Bay through the Aleutian Islands. With a view over Iliuliuk Bay (when it's not too foggy), the inn is next door to Carl's general store, which is as general a store as you've ever been in. You can buy anything here from a fishing boat to a thimble. The inn has about 30 rooms. Prices vary: $90 for a basic room with shower; $125 for a studio with kitchenette; and $150 for a suite with kitchen, like a small apartment. The inn also has a live band, playing country and rock and roll, 6 nights a week. ■ *On the Unalaska side, near the church; 606 Bayview; PO Box 730, Unalaska, AK 99685; (907) 581-1230; $$; full bar, Bayview Lounge; DIS, MC, V; checks OK; open year-round; ♿ one room only.*

THE PRIBILOF ISLANDS

Five tiny volcanic islands way out in the Bering Sea make up the Pribilofs. The two largest, 40 miles apart, are inhabited—St. Paul (pop. 750) and St. George (pop. 170). Most of the people are Aleut. In the late 1700s, Russians forcibly moved several hundred Aleut people here to harvest fur seals. When the United States purchased Alaska in 1867, relatively little changed out here except the flag. The Aleuts were considered wards of the state. It was only on October 28, 1983, on the long coattails of the civil rights movement, that they gained total autonomy, and that is the day they celebrate. Though their lives have revolved around the fur seal harvest for nearly 200 years, residents are now dependent on two other industries: tourism and commercial fishing. The fur seal harvest today is for subsistence only.

This is as remote as you can get, but the treasure chest of wildlife is rich indeed. Hundreds of visitors come here annually—to watch seals and birds. The islands are part of the Alaska Maritime National Wildlife Refuge. St. Paul is home to the largest northern fur seal colony in the world. More than 800,000 seals gather here annually. St. George has a smaller population, but nearly a quarter of a million fur seals still arrive on its shores every summer.

The seals spend their winters at sea. They begin arriving in the Pribilofs in May. Large male "beachmasters," weighing about 600 pounds, show up first, quickly establishing their territories and building their harems (sometimes up to 100 females). Pregnant females don't arrive until June. They usually give birth to a single pup within 48 hours, then mate again within a week, while still nursing their newborn.

The Pribilofs have often been nicknamed "Islands of the Seals," but they could just as easily be called "Islands of the Birds." This remote Bering Sea archipelago is widely recognized as a birder's paradise.

The best time to visit is mid-May through August, when migratory birds and marine mammals are most abundant. Each month "is a season of its own," say locals. The best time for birders interested in a glimpse of the accidental Asian songbird blown off-course by westerly winds is mid-May to early June. Best time for viewing both seals and seabirds is June through August. And the most colorful time, the peak of the wildflower blooms, is late June through mid-July.

Access

Located 300 miles from mainland Alaska and nearly 800 miles from Anchorage, St. Paul and St. George are accessible by air or boat. But nearly all visitors fly due to the distances involved and island-tour arrangements. The largest of the Pribilofs, St. Paul is served by **Reeve Aleutian Airways,** (800) 544-2248. **Peninsula Airways,** (800) 448-4226, flies to both islands. Round-trip airfare is about $800.

**The Pribilof
Islands**

Information

For package tours to St. Paul, contact **Reeve Aleutian Airways,** (800) 544-2248. For tours on St. George, contact **Joseph Van Os Photo Safaris,** (206) 463-5383. Contact the City of St. Paul by writing PO Box 901, St. Paul, AK 99660, or call (907) 546-2331; to contact the City of St. George, write PO Box 929, St. George, AK 99591, or call (907) 859-2263.

Tips on the Islands

Be sure to bring foul-weather clothing. Temperatures in summer rarely rise above 60°F. Plan for **weather delays,** both coming and going. **No camping** is allowed anywhere on St. Paul or St. George Island.

The majority of visitors to both St. Paul and St. George Islands come with guided tour groups, but it's possible to explore the islands on your own, if planning is done well in advance. St. George is much less frequently visited. While it has a hotel, there is no restaurant. But there is a kitchen available for use and two stores for groceries. Those not on tours need to get special permission to visit seal rookeries from refuge headquarters in Homer, (907) 235-6546. On St. Paul, vehicles may be rented from the **Tanadgusix (TDX) Native Corporation,** (907) 546-2312; independent travelers may also join daily guided tours of the island.

With its 45 miles of volcanic-cinder roads, an excellent way to explore St. Paul is by **mountain bike,** as well as by car. No rentals are available, but bikes can be brought on airlines as excess baggage.

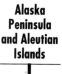
THINGS TO DO

St. Paul Island Tours   Tours of St. Paul Island are arranged through **Reeve Aleutian Airways,** (800) 544-2248. Packages range from 3 days/2 nights to 8 days/7 nights, offered from late May through late August. Prices range from $800 to $1,500. Tour price includes round-trip transportation from Anchorage, guide services, ground transportation on St. Paul Island, sightseeing, and shared accommodations at the hotel. Meals are not included. Tour participants are escorted to both seal and seabird rookeries.

Individual Activities   Watch St. Paul Island's fur seals from viewing blinds—a couple are within walking distance of town. Participate in the village's many summertime cultural events, including Aleut dances, parades, and Native games. Smell the flowers—dozens of species bloom here each summer. Look for birds—more than 200 species have been sighted on St. Paul. Watch for the island's small reindeer herd, transplanted here decades ago.

Joseph Van Os Photo Safaris   Runs tours to St. George Island in July. A week-long package that begins and ends in Anchorage includes 5 days on the island, with visits to seabird and fur seal rookeries. The cost of $2,395 includes meals, lodging, round-trip airfare from Anchorage, guide service, and island transportation. Call (800) 669-6768 or (206) 463-5383.

BEST RESTAURANTS AND LODGINGS

King Eider Hotel on St. Paul Island   This is the only hotel on the island, with 25 rooms, many of them reserved in advance during the summer season by tour groups. It's located in the middle of the village, about 5 miles from the airport. The **King Eider Restaurant** is a short walk from the hotel and serves meals cafeteria-style, to suit the schedule of the tours. Call (907) 546-2477 for reservations.

St. George Tanaq Hotel on St. George Island   A national historic landmark, this, too, is St. George's only hotel. With 10 rooms, it can accommodate up to 18 people. Advance reservations are especially encouraged in July. The hotel has four shared bathrooms and a shared kitchen as there is no restaurant on the island. The hotel is located 5 miles from the airport. Call (907) 272-9886 for reservations.

ANIAKCHAK NATIONAL MONUMENT AND PRESERVE

This is one of the nation's wildest and least-visited parklands. On the Alaska Peninsula, 450 miles southwest of Anchorage, its principal feature and attraction is the **Aniakchak Caldera.** Six miles across, the caldera was created thousands of years

DON'T PACK A BIG EGO

The blood pulsed across my temples. My mouth went dry. A shiver of excitement rippled down my spine. A massive brown bear stood less than 40 feet from us. There was nothing between the bear and ourselves save the ominous tension between predator and prey the second they become aware of each other.

Grizzly. Brown bear. The names evoke a vast array of emotions—fear, admiration, respect.

I am a professional big-game guide. Most importantly, I have learned to respect these tremendous creatures. Bears saunter over countless miles of mountains and tundra with natural ease and confidence. The forearm of a mature boar (male) is the circumference of a large man's thigh, and in a short burst he can travel up to 35 mph. His sense of smell borders on the supernatural. To witness his power, speed, and intelligence is wonderful and sobering. Whether looking at bears through binoculars, a camera lens, or a rifle scope, it is a unique experience and the highlight of anyone's trip to Alaska. There are about 37,000 brown bear/grizzlies in this far northern land—the best viewing anywhere in the world.

If you choose to experience brown bears through hunting, prepare yourself. Here is some of what it takes: patience, more patience, and good physical condition. You can spend days "glassing" for bears—scanning with binoculars while you sit waiting and watching from a hill or ridge. You can spend days walking miles over rugged terrain carrying a 40-pound pack and later, if successful, return carrying a bear hide and skull that can weigh up to 130 pounds.

But the most important preparation is mental.

Do not come with a large ego or sense of superiority packed in your suitcase—bears can easily crush both! Remember, you booked a hunt, not a kill. The kill may be the climax, but the hunt is the real experience. If you are prepared to return home without a trophy and still consider the adventure a rewarding success, then you are ready to go on a brown bear hunt. No matter what the outcome, you will have memories to last a lifetime.

—Henry "Te" Tiffany

ago by the collapse of a large volcano, following an eruption geologists say was much larger than the one at Mount St. Helens. Still active, Aniakchak last erupted in 1931.

When first viewed from a plane, the caldera looks like a moonscape, bleak and desolate. But, surprisingly, with a closer view, one finds a myriad of life—plants, mammals, and birds. Sockeye salmon swim up the **Aniakchak River** into the caldera through a break in the crater wall called "The Gates." They then spawn in the blue-green waters of **Surprise Lake.**

Even in midsummer, weather in the Aniakchak Caldera may become violent. The caldera creates its own microclimate, and its interior is subject to severe windstorms and heavy rains. Campers have had their tents ripped apart from 100 mph gales, and high winds may stir up volcanic ash clouds to an elevation of 6,000 feet.

If you visit the caldera, you're likely to have it all to yourself. Less than 100 people visit it annually (not including flightseers). Because of its remote location and fly-in access, Aniakchak is expensive to reach. Park staff discourage solo travel. All visitors are advised to file a trip plan with the National Park Service at park headquarters. **Aniakchak National Monument and Preserve Headquarters,** PO Box 7, King Salmon, AK 99613; (907) 246-3305.

THINGS TO DO

The best things to do are to explore the caldera—**climb Vent Mountain** (3,350 feet), a splatter cone formed 1,500 years ago and located inside the caldera; or **float Aniakchak River,** which flows out of Surprise Lake within the caldera and offers Class II to Class IV whitewater, as it rushes past sharp volcanic boulders in its upper 13 miles. Officially designated a Wild and Scenic River, the Aniakchak offers easier floating and excellent salmon fishing in its lower 14 miles, before emptying into the Pacific Ocean. Floatplane pickups can be made along the coast.

Air taxis serving the monument include **Egli Air Haul,** (907) 246-3554; **Katmai Air Service** c/o Katmailand, (800) 544-0551; and **Aleutian Specialty Aviation,** (907) 246-3030. **Ouzel Expeditions,** (800) 825-8196, offers 8-day wilderness float trips down the Aniakchak River. The cost is $3,600, which includes the flight into Aniakchak, rafts, camping gear, meals, and guiding expertise.

ALASKA PENINSULA/BECHAROF NATIONAL WILDLIFE REFUGES

These two refuges stretch along the Alaska Peninsula and encompass towering volcanic mountains, broad valleys, rugged coastal fjords, rolling tundra, and glacially formed lakes. Fourteen major volcanoes are located here, including nine that have erupted in historic times. **Mount Veniaminof** last erupted in

LOOK BACK TO THE FUTURE

The most unusual feature of the islands that lie at the end of the Aleutian chain—Attu, Kiska, Shemya, and Amchitka—will occur for the first time in recorded history on December 31, 1999.

If it weren't for the United States–Russian Convention signed in 1867 during the United States purchase of Russian America, these islands would be west of the International Dateline, which lies at 180 degrees longitude. This is the demarcation line separating today from tomorrow.

That old agreement called for bending the dateline so that the tip of the Aleutians would be considered part of North America in reckoning time. Adventurers reluctant to leave the Second Millennium as it slips into history can use Shemya or Attu as viewing stations for looking north, south, east, or west from the year 1999 into the year 2000 and the Third Millennium. If the Russians or Japanese are so inclined, they too can use the far-out Aleutians, so close to their homelands, to look from the year 2000 back into 1999.

It will be another thousand years before the next time warp comes to look forward or back to the future millennium.

—Ed Fortier

▼
Alaska
Peninsula/
Becharof
National
Wildlife
Refuges

▲

1993. The refuges are best known for sport fishing and trophy hunting. **Becharof Lake,** 35 miles long, is Alaska's second largest lake (next to Lake Iliamna) and is the nursery for one of the world's largest runs of salmon. **Mount Peulik, Ukinrek Maars,** and **Gas Rocks** offer a glimpse into the region's volcanism. **Ugashik Lakes** are famous for salmon and trophy grayling (the world-record grayling, nearly 5 pounds, was caught at Ugashik Narrows in 1981). The coastline offers rugged scenery and abundant wildlife, although it's often stormy or shrouded in fog. The land is dense with brown bears, and caribou migrate through here annually.

Most visitors fly in from **King Salmon,** located about 10 air miles from Becharof's northern corner. Air-taxi services include **Branch River Air,** (907) 246-3437; **Egli Air Haul,** (907) 246-3554; **King's Flying Service,** (907) 246-4414; and **Katmai Air Service** c/o Katmailand, (800) 544-0551.

Some of the top wilderness lodges for hunting and fishing in the refuges are **Blue Mountain Lodge,** (907) 688-2419, in the Ugashik Lakes region; **Cinder River Lodge,** (907) 522-1164, an hour's flight from King Salmon, which emphasizes big-game trophy hunting; **Painter Creek Lodge,** (907) 344-5181, which is exceptional for sport fishing—rainbows, salmon, arctic char, Dolly Varden, and grayling; and **Ugashik**

Lakes Lodge (907) 248-3012, which specializes in both sport fishing and trophy hunting.

Contact the Refuge Manager, Alaska Peninsula and Becharof National Wildlife Refuges, PO Box 277, King Salmon, AK 99613; (907) 246-3339.

IZEMBEK NATIONAL WILDLIFE REFUGE

An international crossroads for migrating waterfowl and shorebirds, Izembek is Alaska's smallest national wildlife refuge. It's also one of the oldest. Visitors normally fly into the town of Cold Bay on regularly scheduled airlines, then arrange transportation into the refuge.

The heart of the refuge is Izembek Lagoon, 30 miles long, which contains one of the world's largest eelgrass beds. Hundreds of thousands of waterfowl converge on the lagoon each fall, including the entire world population of black brant, which feed on Izembek's eelgrass before heading south to warmer climates. Brown bears fish salmon-rich streams. Caribou feed on tundra plants. Among the year-round residents are tundra swans, the only nonmigratory wild population of this species in the world.

Two of the most prominent features of the land are **Frosty Peak** (6,000 feet), accessible from the Cold Bay road system, and **Aghileen Pinnacles,** a series of volcanic spires (up to 4,800 feet), an extreme mountaineering challenge.

Contact **Izembek National Wildlife Refuge,** PO Box 127, Cold Bay, AK 99571; (907) 532-2445.

SUGGESTED READING

Alaska Geographic. Quarterly issues: *The Alaska Peninsula* (1994) includes a section on the Aniakchak Caldera; *Islands of Seals: The Pribilofs* (1982) explores the Pribilofs' cultural and natural history.

Garfield, Brian. *The Thousand Mile War.* New York: Mc-Graw-Hill, 1979. The story of World War II in Alaska and the Aleutian Islands.

Hubbard, Father Bernard. *Mush, You Malemutes* (1932) and *Cradle of the Storms* (1935). An adventuring priest and one of Aniakchak's earliest explorers wrote about his expeditions all over Alaska.

Morgan, Murray. *Islands of the Smokey Sea: The Story of Alaska's Aleutian Chain.* Fairbanks, Alaska: Alaskan Prospectors Publishing, 1981. (Formerly *Bridge to Russia,* published in 1947 by E. P. Dutton & Company, Inc.)

National Geographic Society. *Alaska's Magnificent Parklands.* 1984.

Torrey, Barbara Boyle. *Slaves of the Harvest.* TDX Corporation, 1983. Gives a history of the Aleut people of the Pribilofs.

Index

B

The Backdoor Cafe, 26
Bagel Factory, 106
Baja Taco, 137
Bald Eagle Music
  Festival, 55
The Baranof, 46
Baranof Wilderness
  Lodge, 27
Barrow, 240
Bartlett Cove, 47
Bathtub Race, 262
Bayview Restaurant, 24
Becharof Lake, 302
Becharof National
  Wildlife Refuge, 301
Bed & Breakfast on the
  Park, 110
Bed & Breakfast
  Reservation Service,
  226
Bentley's Porter House
  Bed and Breakfast, 282
Bering Land Bridge
  National Preserve, 264
Bering Sea Ice Golf
  Classic, 262
Beryl's, 177
Best of All Bed and
  Breakfast, 132
Best Western Hotel
  Seward, 150
Bethel, 280
Betty's Igloo, 263
Big Delta State
  Historical Park, 78
Bison Range, 80
Blue Mountain Lodge,
  302

The Boardwalk Hotel,
  167
Bombay House, 96
Brooks Lodge, 276
Brooks Range, 245-253
Broom Hus, 33
Brower's Cafe, 243
Buckwheat Ski Classic,
  60
Bun on the Run, 222
Buskin River Inn, 177
The Buzz, 165

C

Cafe Cups, 159
Cafe of the Lyon Family,
  111
Camai Dance Festival,
  282
Camp Denali, 201
Camp Kushtaka, 154
Campo Bello, 103
Cannery Bunkhouse,
  138
Captain Bartlet Inn, 226
Captain Cook State
  Recreation Area, 151,
  154
Captain's Quarters Bed
  and Breakfast, 13
Carl's Bayview Inn, 297
Casa De La Bellezza,
  132
Center for Alaskan
  Coastal Studies, 163
Central, 229
Chalet Center Cafe, 198
Channel Bowl Cafe, 44
The Channel Club, 25

The Chart Room, 296
Chartroom Grill, 176
Chatanika Days, 222
Chatanika Gold Camp,
  229
Chatanika Lodge, 229
Château de Cape Nome,
  263
Chena Hot Springs
  Road, 227
Chena River State
  Recreation Area, 227
Chenik Camp, 272
Chicken, 71
Chief Shakes House, 28
Childs Glacier, 135
Chilkat Dancers and
  Salmon Bake, 52
Chiniak, 174
Chitina, 85
Chugach National
  Forest, 122
Chugach State Park, 99,
  114
Chugach State Park
  Headquarters, 115
Church of the Holy
  Ascension, 294
Cinder River Lodge, 302
Circle, 229
Circle Hot Springs, 229,
  230
Circle Hot Springs
  Road, 230
**Circular Route, the,
  80**
Cleft of the Rock Bed
  and Breakfast, 70

Whittier, 122
Whole Earth Grocery &
Deli, 224
Wilder House B&B, 270
Winter Solstice, 117, 237
Wiseman, 244
Wonder Lake, 192, 196
Wood-Tikchik State
Park, 277
World Eskimo Indian
Olympics, 221

World Extreme Skiing
Championships, 131
World War II, 292, 294
Worthington Glacier
State Recreation Area,
128
Wrangell, 28
Wrangell Museum, 29
Wrangell-St. Elias
National Park and
Preserve, 83, 84, 128

Y
Yes Bay Lodges, 14
Yukon Delta National
Wildlife Refuge, 279
Yukon Quest
International Sled Dog
Race, 222
Yukon River, 229, 279

Alaska Best Places

REPORT FORM

Based on my personal experience, I wish to nominate the following restaurant or place of lodging as a "Best Place"; or confirm/correct/disagree with the review.

_____

_____

_____

_____

_____

Please include address and telephone number of establishment, if convenient.

REPORT:

Please describe food, service, character, style, comfort, value, date of visit, and other aspects of your visit; continue on other side if necessary.

_____

_____

_____

_____

_____

_____

_____

I am not concerned, directly or indirectly, with the management or ownership of this establishment.

Signed _____

Name (please print) _____

Address _____

_____

_____

Phone Number _____

Date _____

Send to: *Alaska Best Places*
615 Second Avenue, Suite 260
Seattle, WA 98104

Alaska Best Places

REPORT FORM

Based on my personal experience, I wish to nominate the following restaurant or place of lodging as a "Best Place"; or confirm/correct/disagree with the review.

_____

_____

_____

_____

_____

Please include address and telephone number of establishment, if convenient.

REPORT:

Please describe food, service, character, style, comfort, value, date of visit, and other aspects of your visit; continue on other side if necessary.

_____

_____

_____

_____

_____

_____

_____

I am not concerned, directly or indirectly, with the management or ownership of this establishment.

Signed _____

Name (please print) _____

Address _____

_____

Phone Number _____

Date _____

Send to: *Alaska Best Places*
615 Second Avenue, Suite 260
Seattle, WA 98104

We Stand by Our Reviews

Sasquatch Books is proud of *Alaska Best Places*. Our editors and contributors go to great lengths and expense to ensure that all of the reviews are as accurate, up-to-date, and as honest as possible. If we have disappointed you, please accept our apologies. However, if recommendations in *Alaska Best Places* have seriously misled you, Sasquatch Books would like to refund your purchase price. To receive your refund:

1) Tell us where you purchased your book and return the book receipt and the book to: Satisfaction Guaranteed, Sasquatch Books, 615 Second Avenue, Suite 260, Seattle, WA 98104.

2) Enclose the original receipt from the establishment in question, including date of visit.

3) Write a full explanation of your stay or meal and how *Alaska Best Places* misled you.

4) Include your name, address, and phone number.

Refund is valid only while this first edition of *Alaska Best Places* is in print. If the ownership of the establishment has changed since publication, Sasquatch Books cannot be held responsible. Please allow six to eight weeks for processing.

Did you enjoy this book?

Sasquatch Books publishes high-quality books and guides related to Alaska, the Pacific Northwest, and California. Our books are available at bookstores and other retail outlets throughout the region. Here is a partial list of our current titles:

ALASKA AND THE NORTHWEST

Alaska Passages
20 Voices from Above the 54th Parallel
Edited by Susan Fox Rogers

Way Out Here
Modern Life in Ice-Age Alaska
Richard Leo

West Coast Workboats
An Illustrated Guide from Bristol Bay
to San Diego
*Archie Satterfield with Illustrations
by Walt Crowley*

Native Peoples of the Northwest
A Traveler's Guide to Land, Art,
and Culture
Jan Halliday and Gail Chehak

Gone Whaling
A Search for Orcas in Northwest Waters
Douglas Hand

The Encyclopedia of Country Living
An Old-Fashioned Recipe Book
Carla Emery

GUIDEBOOKS

Northwest Best Places
Restaurants, Lodgings, and Touring in
Oregon, Washington, and British Columbia
Edited by Stephanie Irving

Northern California Best Places
Restaurants, Lodgings, and Touring
Edited by Rebecca Poole Forée

Seattle Best Places
Restaurants, Lodgings, Shopping, Nightlife,
Arts, Sights, and Outings
Edited by Nancy Leson

Vancouver Best Places
Restaurants, Lodgings, Shopping, Nightlife,
Arts, Sights, and Outings
Edited by Kasey Wilson

Portland Best Places
Restaurants, Lodgings, Shopping, Nightlife,
Arts, Sights, and Outings
Edited by Kim Carlson

CHILDREN'S

O Is for Orca
A Pacific Northwest Alphabet Book
*Andrea Helman with Photographs by Art
Wolfe*

1, 2, 3 Moose
A Pacific Northwest Counting Book
*Andrea Helman with Photographs by Art
Wolfe*

FIELD GUIDES

Field Guide to the Bald Eagle
Field Guide to the Geoduck
Field Guide to the Gray Whale
Field Guide to the Grizzly Bear
Field Guide to the Humpback Whale
Field Guide to the Orca
Field Guide to the Pacific Salmon
Field Guide to the Sasquatch
Field Guide to the Slug

For a complete catalog of Sasquatch Books titles, or to inquire about ordering our books, please contact us at the address below.

SASQUATCH BOOKS

615 Second Avenue, Suite 260, Seattle, Washington 98104
(206)467-4300 or (800)775-0817 Fax (206)467-4301